MW01092747

Lawyers in Your Living Room!

Law on Television

Michael Asimow, Editor

AMERICAN BAR ASSOCIATION
Defending Liberty
Pursuing Justice

Cover design by ABA Publishing.

The materials contained herein represent the opinions and views of the authors and/or the editors, and should not be construed to be the views or opinions of the law firms or companies with whom such persons are in partnership with, associated with, or employed by, nor of the American Bar Association or the Section of Administrative Law and Regulatory Practice, unless adopted pursuant to the bylaws of the Association.

Nothing contained in this book is to be considered as the rendering of legal advice, either generally or in connection with any specific issue or case; nor do these materials purport to explain or interpret any specific bond or policy, or any provisions thereof, issued by any particular franchise company, or to render franchise or other professional advice. Readers are responsible for obtaining advice from their own lawyers or other professionals. This book and any forms and agreements herein are intended for educational and informational purposes only.

© 2009 American Bar Association. All rights reserved.

No part of this publication may be reproduced, stored in a retrieval system, or transmitted in any form or by any means, electronic, mechanical, photocopying, recording, or otherwise, without the prior written permission of the publisher. For permission, contact the ABA Copyrights & Contracts Department at copyright@abanet.org or via fax at 312-988-6030.

Printed in the United States of America

13 12 11 10 09   5 4 3 2 1

Library of Congress Cataloging-in-Publication Data

Lawyers in your living room! law on television / edited by Michael Asimow.—1st ed.
   p. cm.
 Includes index.
 ISBN 978-1-60442-328-0
 1. Justice, Administration of, on television. 2. Lawyers on television. 3. Legal television programs—History and criticism. I. Asimow, Michael.

PN1992.8.J87L39 2009
791.45'6554—dc22

2009008058

Discounts are available for books ordered in bulk. Special consideration is given to state bars, CLE programs, and other bar-related organizations. Inquire at Book Publishing, ABA Publishing, American Bar Association, 321 North Clark Street, Chicago, Illinois 60654-7598.

www.ababooks.org

CONTENTS

FOREWORD

SAM WATERSTON

Jack McCoy. When people have asked about the ways my career as an actor became associated with Lincoln—theatre, TV, documentaries, readings, speeches, and performances at Ford's Theatre, the White House, and around the country—I'd say, "If you're going to get stuck in a role, you could do worse than be typecast as Abraham Lincoln." That also goes for Jack McCoy.

There are many interesting things about this guy, but maybe the most amazing is that he's been around so long, and that he's been allowed to change over time, to weary, to darken, to get older, to change jobs.

This last is a big deal in a show like *Law & Order*. In a show as plot-driven as ours, what a character's job is very much influences who the character is. The attributes of the job inevitably become the attributes of the character. Dick Wolf wasn't the first to say so, but he regularly reminds us about the old show-business maxim that "action is character." In our show particularly—all narrative all the time—you are what you eat.

McCoy as the ADA was the man who confronted the villains in court, the man who got the criminals to "face the music," who ultimately put the bad guys on the spot where they couldn't lie their way out, and who, in his summations, told us how to think about it. On *Law & Order*, the ADA was the matador. He also made you want to throw a shoe at him, because he had an uncompromising way of looking at things and used the mighty powers of his office to advance it—in circumstances that were not all black and white. The action required of him week after week neatly fit in with his nature, which we agreed from the beginning was that of a "merry attack dog," eager to confront, eager to win, happy in his work, unworried about politics, happy to stick his neck out, and usually not too sensitive about other opinions until you rubbed his nose in them. Adam Schiff was the careful master, and so were the characters that succeeded him. But Jack McCoy was always straining away at the end of the leash. "Lemme at 'em. . . . Lemme at 'em" was his permanent mantra. His innate sense of moral outrage and his built-in eagerness to win suited his job. The job fed his nature. His nature fit his job.

Then he got promoted. Very much to their credit and my delight, Dick Wolf, Rene Balcer, and the rest of the writers—the people who weekly call this fiction that is Jack McCoy into being—took his whole character with them when they moved him into the head office. And suddenly, here was a character who wasn't designed for the job. Without anybody lifting a finger, life in the DA's office was made more complex. We had had new DAs before, but this was the first one with a whole history behind him that everyone knew, and a nature that didn't, necessarily, naturally fit the job.

It's no slur to Fred Thompson or to Diane Wiest, who have no peers anywhere, to say that Steven Hill defined the job and the role of the DA on *Law & Order*, just about as indelibly as did the real-life DA who was his character's inspiration—Robert Morgenthau (whose 33-year run as the actual DA of Manhattan makes our 18 years on the air seem like a flash in the pan).

I have read a rough version of the essay on *Law & Order* that appears in this book. The phrase the essay applies to Schiff, "moral realism," exactly describes him, and he embodies the political and social instincts required of a law enforcement agent who is also an elected official. My favorite show is one about the death penalty, in which, while his wife is in a coma, sick unto dying, Adam Schiff, always an opponent of the death penalty, must, for legal and political reasons, let an execution go forward "on his watch." The show ends with a silent scene of Schiff at his wife's bedside, after she has been removed from life support, as he waits for her to die. Steven's face wore all these circumstances, and without saying a word, and apparently doing nothing (as was his wont), he made the scene real and heartbreaking, the indigestible best that could be done in an intolerable circumstance.

So, how was a "merry attack dog" going to learn and do the job of a moral realist? How was a character who had worn his scorn for politics like a medal going to handle a job where the good that he can do cannot be entirely separate from politics? How was this going to be done in the firmly established voice of the show, where the narrative is king, and the case at hand is king of the narrative? The answers being written give Jack, the old warhorse, a new lease on life.

What has made this show so durable? It was a good idea to start with. The fact that it was an idea born of necessity is a great advertisement for necessity. One-hour drama wasn't doing well when *Law & Order* was first proposed, and I understand the show was sold on the basis that you could split it in two and make two half hours if you wanted. Additionally, there has been a lot of work by a lot of talented people over the years who were determined to keep the standard up. How to get justice right, using stories out of the news, has its own intrinsic, perennial, attraction. And the show, TV though it is, has been pretty careful about sticking to law—even though the speed at which we get from crime to resolution is the envy of every criminal lawyer. But my personal theory is that it endures because it describes life at work the way we all know it to be, and not just in law offices. In this sense, it's a cousin of *MASH*, where, like on *Law & Order*, whatever else is going on, the doctors are there for the duration, there's always another chopper landing with a painful crisis to handle, and the basic personal question is, "Are you in shape to work?" *Law & Order* takes that to the limit. This hard-bitten, hard-driving way of working is very New York, and feels real, I think, to plenty of non-lawyers, even in places where co-workers are more inquisitive about what people did over the weekend than any of us at *Law & Order* ever are. The job's the thing. People know this world.

I was glad to learn from the essay that my character was based in part on RFK. It was the first I'd heard of it, but it makes sense. And, second to Lincoln, if there were another American political figure I could be associated with in the public mind, I sure wouldn't mind it being Robert

Kennedy. He was a great inspirational leader, like A. Lincoln, and—what's nice for an actor—he was quite a lot better looking.

But we have to regularly remind ourselves and our audiences that we're just a bunch of fakers. The cases we bring to trial and resolution, in the 40 or so minutes between commercials, would take up a month of Sundays in real life. The tidiness with which TV heroes get to have the last word, just when the plot needs it most, has nothing at all to do with reality. In reality, conclusions are muddy, there are no final curtains, and life just goes on. We tell stories. I think the long popularity of *Law & Order* is also, in part, due to our need to have the confusion of current events, particularly about what's fair and what's just, made into stories. We need to have the issues and questions inside those events put on display, so we can get our minds around them, or just get to know them.

So we do a good thing.

But the real-life legal profession, and the law itself, at their best, are heroic in ways we can't touch, daring to attempt the impossible by setting out to navigate, in a fair and orderly way, all the cross-currents, eddies, and turbulence—all the mess—that's real life. We do a pretend version of that. We're just fooling around. *Real* lawyers, amid the crazy quilt of politics, principle, and precedent, the *real* practice of law, do the tough stuff. But fooling around beside the field, watching from close up how the pros play the game and imitating their moves, is fun.

FOREWORD

JAMES WOODS

Playing a hard-driven, unscrupulous defense attorney-turned-prosecutor in *Shark* was a real eye-opener for me as an actor and, more importantly, as a citizen. Not only were many members of our writing staff attorneys themselves, but our technical advisers included Robert Shapiro and Ira Reiner. Ricki Kleiman, a judge in real life, was a frequent cast member as well.

The basic conceit of our show was that, in general, defense attorneys are unscrupulous dogs who make huge fortunes defending the absolutely guilty with impunity, while prosecutors are stern and humorless guardians of the justice system, hamstrung by their own ethics and the regulatory impediments of the system. My character, Sebastian Stark, was a clever creation thrown into that ethical cesspool: an arrogant, brilliant, unprincipled superstar defense attorney who loses a woman client to an abusive batterer husband whom Stark's prowess in the courtroom had recently saved from certain conviction. In an impulsive moment of atonement, he takes on the job of prosecutor in a high-profile crime unit of the city of Los Angeles.

What I found most fascinating was the paradigm for victory concocted by this legal fish- (sorry, can't resist it—shark) out-of-water character. From the writing staff, I anticipated brilliant courtroom maneuvers and wasn't disappointed. My character's greatest victories, however, emanated from backroom chicanery and clever twists, not only of plot, but ethics as well. The first season culminated way outside the moral boundaries with an extraordinary premise: Sebastian Stark, frustrated in his inability to convict a heinous serial killer, literally frames him for murder.

The cleverness with which the character engaged the enemy made the show a hit, especially when contrasted with his devotion to his difficult teenage daughter, whom he was raising alone. I personally was fascinated most by the constant walk along the razor's edge of legal ethics. Every episode was a tarnished morality tale, often with a surprisingly frustrating lack of emotional closure. Bad guys often win, and at times the best one can do is make a deal. When the good guys win, it is often at the expense of one's hubris, sanity, and once in a great while, one's very soul.

I liked that our show and others peppering the current entertainment landscape reflect the slippery and sloppy moral malaise of contemporary times. As outraged as everyone seems to be these days over hot-button social issues, we would be hard-pressed to say that any consensus exists about the fundamental right or wrong of any particular cultural issue. There was a time not so long ago when Sebastian Stark would indeed have been a shark. Nowadays he is more probably a very big fish in a school of casually lethal legal piranha.

When I was a child, my aunt was the secretary to the Public Defender in the State of Rhode Island for roughly three decades. Rhode Island was generally known as the charming New England state that was a hotbed of low-level but nonetheless lethal organized crime. Often jokingly referred to as "the parking lot of the New England Mafia," Rhode Island has had a history of colorful characters, culminating in the outrageous but lovable Vincent "Buddy" Cianci, who actually pleaded no contest to a felony assault charge in between mayoral stints, and later did federal prison time for conspiracy.

Organized crime guys often used the Public Defender's office as a front in their criminal trials, claiming that they were just poor laborers who had been wrongly accused. If, their argument often went, they were these "Mafia big shots," how did they happen to be here in court with the lowly Public Defender as their only sad champion? In the background, of course, pulling the legal strings and most probably greasing a few outstretched palms, were the state's high-powered and highly paid top criminal defense lawyers.

Shark made me appreciate the eternal adage, "The more things change, the more they stay the same." If Sebastian had defended Joey "Bag of Donuts," the guy most surely wouldn't have spent the rest of his days walking the yard at the Rhode Island Adult Correctional Institution. If Sebastian had prosecuted him, however, old Joey would have probably been hanged in the courtyard at midnight. Oh, and a little note about my aunt. As an elderly retiree she was once mugged and hurt by some street thugs in what was commonly known as a Mafia neighborhood, a classic no-no that only a crack-addicted trio of street criminals would be stupid enough to violate. She had always been cordial to the defendants who came through her office and, as a matter of policy, had never passed judgment. She even made cookies for the most ruthless Syndicate hitmen. Suffice it to say the street thugs were found and never had to endure the rigors of the Rhode Island legal system. Conventional wisdom at that time had it that they experienced a simpler, more Biblical rendition of justice. Sebastian would no doubt have been proud.

PREFACE

Popular Culture Matters

MICHAEL ASIMOW

Lawyers in your living room! Eeek! Most people would rather find vampires with chainsaws rather than lawyers in their living rooms. But the fact is that the lawyers have always been there, and they always will be. Lawyers have been a fixture on television since the 1960s and lawyer shows (fictional, docudrama, and reality-based) continue to proliferate today.

This book contains seven somewhat arbitrarily divided Parts that cover numerous aspects of legal television: domestic and foreign, civil and criminal. It contains essays about many dramatic lawyer shows of the past and present. It contains chapters on TV shows not primarily devoted to law but in which lawyers played important roles, such as *The West Wing*. It includes a set of articles about the law-on-TV genre, including discussions about writing and furnishing technical advice for TV. It covers the *Judge Judy* phenomenon. All in all, the essays in this book convey a sense of the richness and vigor of legal television, past and present, foreign and domestic.

You'll be reading about dozens of television lawyers and judges. Most of the chapters will tell you about the *character* of the lawyers who've been hanging out in your living room. What kind of human beings are they? Heroic role models—or miserable, dysfunctional, greedy sleazebags? What kind of lawyers are they? Ethical, competent, and dedicated—or unethical, conniving, and incompetent? Or somewhere in between? We hope you'll be inspired to buy (or borrow) DVDs of old television shows so you can revisit the shows you once enjoyed, that you missed the first time around, or that disappeared long before your time. But we'd also like to educate you about the medium and the importance of popular cultural representations of lawyers. And I would like to make a few remarks on the subject of media effects.

Why should we care about pop culture—meaning, for present purposes, entertainment media (including but not limited to film and television) that is produced for profit and intended for mass consumption? Most of us enjoy pop culture and consume quite a lot of it, but we usually regard it as fluff—trivial entertainment that is quickly forgotten. Indeed, much of it is trash by any reasonably objective measure. Yet, in my opinion and that of my coauthors, pop culture is important and well worth studying. Why is this?

First, popular culture reflects what people actually believe (or at least what the makers of pop culture believe that people believe). Of course, the mirror is always distorted, given the biases of filmmakers and their need to entertain and turn a profit. Still, pop culture products often furnish tantalizing clues about public attitudes and beliefs. Looked at in this way, popular culture can teach us a lot about the public's opinion of lawyers and justice. If, for example, most current film and television shows depict lawyers as unethical and greedy scoundrels, those representations reflect the stereotypes that people carry around with them. Very few movies and television shows concern dysfunctional grandmothers, rabbis, or algebra teachers, but a great many of them show dysfunctional lawyers—which, unfortunately, is exactly the way most people view lawyers these days. If people expect their justice system to deliver the truth, rather than merely adversarial combat between lawyers, we will see many movies and TV shows cast from the familiar (and trite) mold of *Perry Mason* and *Matlock* in which crafty lawyers overcome the odds to acquit the innocent. We will also see many others, like *Law & Order* and *Shark*, in which tenacious prosecutors convict the guilty.[1] If people wish they could denounce others as irresponsible creeps, they will enjoy watching

Judge Judy do it for them. People like to consume media that echoes and reinforces their preferences and preconceptions.

Second, pop culture serves as a powerful teacher, instructing millions of its consumers about what lawyers do and how legal institutions function. Media *always* influences and affects those that consume it, just as they are influenced by personal experiences or by the news, commercials, or political advertisements. As a thought experiment, ask yourself what it was like to fight in Vietnam or in World War II. Undoubtedly you have a lot of information on that subject, but where did it come from? For most people, such information could have been derived only from pop culture treatments of those wars. Similarly, do you know anything about the lives of cowboys or detectives? Undoubtedly, you do—and that information (or misinformation) probably came exclusively from pop culture narratives. How is it that in France when people are arrested they demand their *Miranda* warnings—even though this concept is unknown to French law? Or that French people, even lawyers, frequently address judges as "your honor," when this is completely inappropriate?[2] They could only have picked up this misinformation from American television shows.

My barber told me recently that he was part of a jury panel that was being questioned by the lawyers. A defense lawyer asked a juror whether one police officer would lie to protect another officer. "Of course," the juror replied, "I've seen it on television many times." Elayne Rapping, in her introduction, reports that a student said that he didn't need to read newspapers. "I watch *Law & Order* every week and since their stories are drawn from the headlines, that's how I keep up with current events." Perhaps many readers could recount similar anecdotes—or even recognize themselves in these little stories.

What is the mechanism that allows us to internalize information from media? The best documented approach is called "cultivation theory," which was developed by researchers in the fields of social and cognitive psychology.[3] Cultivation theorists treat pop culture media as the common storyteller of our age. Television is consumed in massive amounts by nearly all members of the general public. It transmits a consistent set of images and messages about social reality into nearly every home.

Numerous studies indicate that people's opinions are influenced by long-repeated, consistent themes in fictitious pop culture. If you ask them whether they will get mugged if they go to New York, people who watch a lot of television are more likely to say "yes" than those who watch little or none. People who watch a lot of TV believe in a meaner world—more crime, more drugs, more prostitutes—than people who don't watch much TV.[4] Heavy watchers of *Judge Judy* have entirely different beliefs about the appropriate role of a trial judge than those who don't watch the show.[5] Heavy watchers of TV crime dramas are more favorably disposed toward capital punishment than light watchers. Many believe that a *"CSI* effect" predisposes jurors to acquit unless the prosecutor presents forensic evidence.[6] Studies indicate that jurors are heavily influenced by news media coverage of trials.[7] Other studies indicate that media exposure to information about particular crimes (such as rape) influences the way potential jurors assess evidence.[8]

The cultivation effect works because people soak up the "information" conveyed by pop culture media without being critical about its source. We maintain "files" or "schemas" in our brain on every conceivable subject and constantly add materials to the files from our personal experiences, conversations with others, and what we read and see in the news and entertainment media. According to cultivation theory, when we respond to a question like "do you trust lawyers," we access material in the "lawyers" file in order to give a quick answer. Whether we access a particular bit of information in the file depends on how recently it was filed, how many similar items are lodged in the file, and the vividness of the experience that put it there. Most importantly, we don't "source discount" very well. This means that we store and retrieve data that we have extracted from popular culture in the file, failing to recall that it was a fictitious story that provided the material.[9] We are also more heavily influenced by stories about subjects with which we have little or no personal experience and that seem to be "realistic."[10]

Another approach to media effects is sometimes referred to as "viewer response" or "reception" theory.[11] The viewer response approach contends that viewers are not passive sponges who soak up whatever pop culture comes their way. Instead, media is subject to interpretation and consumers construct their own personal interpretations—make their own meanings—from the materials in a film or TV show. The emphasis in viewer response theories is what the viewer does to the text, not the other way around. Such interpretations may be the same as the ones intended (or "encoded") by the persons who wrote and directed the film or television show, but they may also be quite different (or "opposed"), particularly in the case of minority or other nonmainstream viewer communities. In her chapter in this book, Cynthia Cohen provides an example of viewer response theory in action. Contrary to what one might expect, her studies show that people who watch the rather dysfunctional lawyers on *Ally McBeal* and *Boston Legal* have *more* confidence in their own lawyers, because they seem so unlike the characters on television.

The two approaches to media effects (the more passive cultivation theory and the more active viewer response theory) are not inconsistent with each other. Each describes different media consumers, and most of us probably fall into each of the groups at different times. Whether one prefers the cultivation or viewer response frame for analyzing media effects, the bottom line is that pop culture images are exceptionally powerful. In this book, Barbara Villez, Anja Louis, and Stefan Machura discuss the educational function of lawyer shows in France, Spain, and Germany. In Spain, for example, the show *Anillos de oro* helped Spanish viewers understand and appreciate the new divorce law in the post-Franco transition period; in France, the show *Avocats et Associés* taught viewers that French law and legal procedure are very different from the American versions that people had absorbed from TV.

In so many ways, what people learn about law and lawyers from pop culture seeps right back into law and legal practice. Jurors apply this knowledge in evaluating cases. Prosecutors believe that jurors will not convict without forensic evidence, because they have learned it is essential from the many *CSI*-type shows.[12] Legislators will draw information and opinions from media in deciding what laws to pass. Clients have learned from pop culture what to expect from their lawyers. Litigants in small claims court learn from *Judge Judy* that the judge will ask the questions and present their case for them. Lawyers have learned that their case must be backed up by a good story—preferably one familiar from pop culture. And they must use plenty of visual aids and keep their closing arguments punchy and concise. It is said that a group of young lawyers started a firm and held a meeting each morning to discuss their cases. Of course, it was a total waste of time, but they had learned it from *L.A. Law*. And we can only hope that young lawyers won't learn their ethics from watching Sebastian Shark or the many other corner-cutting lawyers Carrie Menkel-Meadow describes in her essay.

It has been a pleasure and a privilege to have brought together the authors of the essays in this book.[13] I would like to express my gratitude for the dedicated work of all of those volunteer–authors who produced their chapters under unreasonable time pressure and restrictive word limits, yet met the highest standards of scholarship. I also would like to thank Justin Smith, my research assistant, who helped greatly in the editing process and in assembling the photographs. Justin was so enthusiastic about the project that he wrote the chapter on *JAG*. I would like to thank my wife, Merrie Asimow, who, in addition to engaging in countless spirited discussions on the subject and enduring many hours of watching legal shows on television, was able to untangle numerous computer problems. Tal Grietzer was also a huge help when it came to word processing. Keith Rowley suggested the title and did yeoman editing work far above and beyond the call of duty. All of us who have worked on this book hope that it will entertain and inform the legions of fans of law on television around the world.

So, esteemed reader, browse through this book and read about your favorite legal television shows. Get acquainted or reacquainted with the golden oldies, such as *Perry Mason, The Defenders, Matlock,* and *L.A. Law.* Enjoy the pleasures of more recent but nearly forgotten shows like *Picket Fences, girls club,* or *Murder One.* Spend time with all the lawyer friends that you've made while watching the shows of the present or recent past like *Law & Order, Boston Legal, The Practice, Damages, Ally McBeal, JAG, Judging Amy,* or *Shark.* Cringe at the antics of *Judge Judy* and her many clones, as well as the different versions in Germany and Brazil. Chuckle at the lawyer spoofs on *The Simpsons, Green Acres,* and *Seinfeld.* Get to know the lawyer series in the U.K., France, and Spain, like *Rumpole of the Bailey, Avocats et Associés, Anillos de oro,* and the many other foreign shows discussed in the chapters on *Matlock* and *Judge John Deed.* But don't stop thinking about tomorrow, and don't forget about the potent media effects of lawyer narratives from film or television.

Endnotes

1. We might even see numerous movies and television shows in which lawyers sell out clients they know to be guilty in order to protect the public from vicious criminals or evil corporations. *See* Michael Asimow & Richard Weisberg,

When the Lawyer Knows the Client is Guilty: Client Confessions in Legal Ethics, Popular Culture, and Literature, 18 So. CAL. INTERDISC. L.J. __ (2009).

2. See Barbara Villez's chapter "French Television Lawyers in *Avocats et Associés.*"

3. George Gerbner is generally credited with pioneering cultivation theory. *See generally* George Gerbner, et al., *Growing Up With Television: Cultivation Processes,* in MEDIA EFFECTS: ADVANCES IN THEORY AND RESEARCH 43 (Jennings Bryant & Dolf Zillman eds., 2d ed. 2002). *See also* Michael Morgan & James Shanahan, *Two Decades of Cultivation Research: An Appraisal and Meta-Analysis,* 20 COMM. Y.B. 1 (1997).

4. Gerbner, *supra* note 3, at 52–53.

5. Kimberlianne Podlas, *Please Adjust Your Signal: How Television's Syndicated Courtrooms Bias Our Juror Citizenry,* 39 AMER. BUS. L.J. 1 (2001).

6. *See* Tom R. Tyler, *Viewing CSI and the Threshold of Guilt: Managing Truth and Justice in Reality and Fiction,* 115 YALE L.J. 1050, 1056–63 (2006) (indicating that anecdotal accounts of a *CSI* effect are plausible in light of existing juror research). Tyler points out that an offsetting *CSI* effect may work in the opposite direction: based on watching *CSI,* jurors may overestimate the probative value of the prosecution's scientific evidence. *Id.* at 1063–76. On the other hand, an empirical study of 1,027 people who had been called for jury duty failed to substantiate the *CSI* effect, although it did indicate that *CSI* watchers had higher expectations than others that the prosecution would present forensic evidence in various types of cases. The authors conclude that a "tech effect" exists, according to which many jurors will acquit defendants in cases involving circumstantial evidence and no forensic evidence. However, the "tech effect" was not limited to *CSI* watchers and seems to be based on broader cultural influences than just one type of television show. Donald E. Shelton, Young S. Kim, & Gregg Barak, *A Study of Juror Expectations and Demands Concerning Scientific Evidence: Does the "CSI Effect" Exist?* 9 VAND. J. ENT. & TECH. L. 331 (2006).

7. Tyler, *supra* note 6, at 1057–63.

8. *Id.* at 1057–60.

9. *See* L.J. Shrum, *Media Consumption and Perceptions of Social Reality: Effects and Underlying Processes,* in Bryant & Zillman, *supra* note 3, at 69–91.

10. *See* Michael A. Shapiro & T. Makana Chock, *Media Dependency and Perceived Reality of Fiction and News,* 48 J. OF BROADCASTING AND ELECTRONIC MEDIA 675 (2004).

11. For accessible treatments, see LAWRENCE GROSSBERG, ELLEN WARTELLA, & D. CHARLES WHITNEY, MEDIAMAKING: MASS MEDIA IN A POPULAR CULTURE 235–57 (1998); Alan M. Rubin, *The Uses-and-Gratification Perspective of Media Effects,* in Bryant & Zillman, *supra* note 4 at 525–48.

12. *See* Tyler, *supra* note 6.

13. I would also like to acknowledge an earlier book about law on television, *Prime Time Law*, edited by Paul Joseph and Robert Jarvis and published by Carolina Academic Press in 1998. Paul Joseph, tragically, has passed away, but Bob Jarvis wrote the chapter in this book on *Seinfeld*. We have tried to build on the foundations that Paul and Bob laid 10 years ago. Finally, I would like to thank Kim Knight for suggesting this project and the ABA Press, particularly Sarah Orwig and Rick Paszkiet, for wholeheartedly supporting it.

INTRODUCTION

The History of Law on Television

ELAYNE RAPPING

My interest in TV series about lawyers and the law came about in a perhaps unusual way. I am not a lawyer myself; in fact, I don't even play one on television. And most of my work regarding television has been about very different kinds of programming than law shows— things usually considered "junk," such as soap operas, talk shows, and TV movies. That's because I have always had an interest in the kinds of things educated viewers usually dismiss, but which the less educated, especially women, find enthralling. "Do you really watch that junk?" I am often asked. (I am happy to say that this occurs less these days, because pop culture has become a major academic field.) To which I usually say, "It's a dirty job, but someone's got to do it."

So why my sudden interest in legal series? Simple, really: my son became a lawyer. And not just the kind that mothers proudly brag about for working at white-shoe firms and pulling in the big bucks. No, my son chose to become perhaps the most publicly reviled of lawyers, a criminal defense attorney. And, at least early in his career, what made matters worse was that Jon chose to become a public defender. Even my progressive friends would ask me if Jon ever felt "guilty" about defending "those people." At the same time, others gave me sorrowful looks of pity. "Poor kid, couldn't do any better than that." In fact, in Jon's office at the Washington, D.C. Public Defender Service, the staff attorneys actually wore buttons saying "Don't tell my mother I'm a public defender. She thinks I play piano in a whorehouse." But Jon neither felt guilty, nor did he lack for "better" offers. This was the work he wanted to do; that he believed was important. And so did I.

And so my interest in legal series began with a question: why are defense attorneys portrayed so negatively, as sleazy, corrupt, or incompetent? And it is this question, or issue really, that I want to discuss in this introduction to a book about the portrayals of lawyers, not just today, but over time. But before giving an overview of how, since the earliest days of TV, the portrayal of lawyers has experienced a variety of mutations—most, interestingly and importantly, running parallel to the climate of the times in which particular shows were produced—let's go back to the roots of television itself, and its role in negotiating the most central issues and problems facing society, both personal and public.

Ward Cleaver, Perry Mason, Walter Cronkite, and Westinghouse Come to Dinner

The importance of television in post–World War II America cannot be overstated. This was a time of enormous social change, as the economy shifted from heavy industry to reliance on consumer goods and services. In the wake of this economic transformation, the lives of Americans changed drastically. It had once been a country of small towns where generations stayed indefinitely, as boys followed their fathers' paths in running family farms and businesses, and girls, like their mothers, married the boys next door, helped with family businesses, and, of course, made their own clothes and grew and cooked their own food. Think *Little House on the Prairie*. All this disappeared with the rise of industrialization and the new emphasis on mass-produced commodities bought in stores.

More and more young people left the family homesteads for jobs in the new urban corporate world. As this trend continued, the nation became more and more fragmented. The stability of old traditions gave way, people moved from city to city and job to job, the divorce rate rose, and family values were further eroded by things like juvenile delinquency.

In such a world, television—which had been ready to go as early as the 1930s—suddenly became important enough for the government to provide licenses for the new medium to use precious airwaves. Why? Because the fragmentation of society left us devoid of a common sense of community and values, so it seemed important—and it was—for there to be a medium through which the government could send messages from the center to the periphery. These messages, in both fiction and news, were all the same. They taught us how to live in this brave new world and attempted to create a new sense of shared values and traditions, much like the ones that were disappearing. These values might give us the feeling that, despite indications to the contrary, we did indeed live in a common world with a shared sense of national belonging.

Thus, television became the primary form of socialization and education in a floundering world. Today, as the Internet further fragments ideas and social groups and it becomes more difficult to feel part of a national entity, I would argue that television's role is more important than ever. When major events occur, it is still the networks (and especially 24-hour cable networks) to which most Americans turn for the latest news. During the 2008 electoral campaigns, for example, ratings for CNN and MSNBC rose sky-high.

But when television first became a national necessity, in the late 1940s and 1950s, it was family values that most concerned government and corporations. After all, this was a medium that sat, literally, in our "living" rooms, holding us captive to what used to be three more or less identical channels, each offering the same lessons in what to buy and how to raise our families, in ways that reinforced the values under threat. *Father Knows Best* and *Leave it to Beaver* are the most obvious examples of this. However, more pressing public issues soon began to appear as guests in our living room.

Why It Is Important to Study Fictional Series on Television

It seems important to address the issue of why it is worth studying fictional series at all, since many of us believe that fictional shows are somehow not as "serious" or influential as nonfiction programming. We seem to think that only "true" events really matter, while fictional series are mere fluff. I want to strenuously argue against this view because it bears on the question that many picking up a book like this might ask: why read a book about fictional lawyers? For the truth is—as I've discovered in my classrooms as well as casual conversations with friends and colleagues—that fictional programming actually has a much greater influence than the news on how people view the legal system. That's because people watch more entertainment series than news, and they take these series much more seriously than one might realize.

A priceless example of this occurred when a friend of mine who was teaching a class on social theory asked her students what, if any, newspapers they read. One young man eagerly raised his hand and said, "I don't read the paper but I watch *Law & Order* every week and since their stories are drawn from the headlines, that's how I keep up with current events." We'll get back to this show later, but the point I want to make here is that, as my friend's story illustrates, people do indeed get most of their ideas about how lawyers behave and how the system, and even society itself, works from fictional series. Consequently, a book like this one is more important than its subject may seem.

The Arrival of Lawyers on the Small Screen

Having made that point, let's return to the main topic: the rise of lawyer series and the various phases they have taken. To be sure, lawyer programs were slow to be produced and gain popularity. While the first legal series were social issue discussion shows covering various public concerns, by the early to mid-1950s more and more legal series began to hit the airwaves and became quite popular. The first law series, begun way back in 1948, was called *On Trial* and lasted four seasons. This version merely discussed legal issues. But when it was revived in 1956, it became an anthology series of actual courtroom dramas. This revival wasn't politically biased, but it was a landmark in initiating courtroom drama as a winning idea. For courtrooms are, of course, arenas of powerful drama, conflict, and suspense.

By 1957, a series called *The Court of Last Resort* had appeared.[1] It was based on an actual organization of criminal law experts whose purpose was to aid defendants whom they believed had been unjustly convicted. Soon thereafter, the most outstandingly courageous series of all time, *The Defenders*,[2] appeared. It ran from 1961 to 1965, a period of obvious political turmoil, as conservative values of all kinds were being questioned, including the authority of the government itself. Among the many controversial issues the father–son law team tackled were abortion, the draft, and even the blacklist.

And so began a run of popular new law series. What is most interesting in this historical overview is the dramatic difference between the earlier series and those that emerged, after a long hiatus, in the 1990s. Reviewing the series that ran from the late 1950s through the 1970s, for example, it is quite remarkable to see how progressive they were and how much they tended to portray idealistic defense attorneys giving up lucrative careers to serve the indigent and the underdog.

I am primarily talking about popular series like *Perry Mason*, which ran from 1957 to 1966.[3] While this series was often laughably unrealistic, it presented the defense attorney in a positive light while portraying the prosecutor as a bumbling fool. It was fun to watch the hapless prosecutor getting trounced every week by the star. But what made the series so unrealistic was that every defendant was innocent. The lawyer operated more as an investigator than an attorney, always finding the true culprit, who at the last minute confessed from the witness stand or the back benches that, yes, he was the real killer.

Nonetheless, this series did portray defense attorneys as heroes and prosecutors and police as fools, no small thing when we look, as we will later, at the series that have emerged since the early 1990s. Following *The Defenders* and *Perry Mason* were numerous little-known or -remembered series that were far more serious about social issues and much more interesting than the more famous *Perry Mason*. Perhaps most notable was *Owen Marshall: Counselor at Law* (1971–74), whose title character followed in the noble footsteps of *The Defenders* by defending the indigent and underdogs while dealing with important issues.

Then came *Petrocelli* (1974–76), which featured a Harvard-educated lawyer who moved his family into a trailer and gave up vast opportunities for financial wealth to pursue a calling: to defend the poor and seemingly hopeless. Lesser-known, minor series during this period followed the same format as *Petrocelli*. One particularly outstanding series, *Storefront Lawyers*, ran only from 1970–71, perhaps because it was too progressive even for those days. It was about three lawyers, one of whom was a woman, who operated a nonprofit Legal Aid office. Indeed, from 1961 to 1976 a surprising number of series featured similarly socially conscious defense attorneys. *The Trials of O'Brien* (1965–66) was the least political, dealing largely with the personal life of its main character. On the other hand, *The Law and Mr. Jones* (1960–62) featured a compassionate fighter for social justice who was fond of quoting Oliver Wendell Holmes. By the late 1960s, law series were even more progressive. *The Lawyers* (1969–72) featured three lawyers committed to unpopular causes, *Judd for the Defense* (1967–72) showcased a lawyer who defended a variety of radical groups, including anti-war protesters, and *The Young Lawyers* set up offices in poor neighborhoods to defend the indigent.

The Subtle Shift

For several years after the liberal 1960s and early 1970s, lawyers seemed to disappear as stars of TV series. But by the 1980s, lawyers gradually began to reappear. The first show of this era was the highly popular *L.A. Law*, which was about a firm of high-rent lawyers who were more concerned with domestic and financial cases than social issues. Nevertheless, the lawyers of McKenzie Brackman, particularly Michael Kuzak, tried a lot of criminal cases. The show treated the criminal defense function fairly and reasonably. In the character of Grace Van Owen, it also featured a quite sympathetic prosecutor. *L.A. Law* was a transitional lawyer show that led directly to the present era of idealization of prosecutors.

After *L.A. Law*, a lot of equally successful series featured issues of law (especially criminal justice), but switched gears dramatically in that they starred police officers rather than lawyers. These "quality" series included *Hill Street Blues*, *NYPD Blue*, *Cagney and Lacey*, and *Homicide: Life on the Streets*. I think of these as the "Cops with a Heart of Gold" series because they began an intriguing new, and in some ways contradictory, trend.

Unlike the hopeless cops on *Perry Mason*, now it was the police who were the bleeding-heart liberals. The producers of these series, now older but still veterans of the more liberal decades preceding the Reagan/Bush years, were still true believers, and the series were all decidedly liberal and notably "politically correct." It was the cop heroes, not the lawyers, who wept for the underprivileged when an innocent person was wrongly convicted. And it was they—*Cagney and Lacey* was especially interesting here—that presented women, for the first time, as openly feminist. Why these liberal, feminist shows needed to have their heroines be cops rather than, say, social workers, is obvious. Violence sells. And whether the heroes are cops or lawyers, dramas involving serious crimes are also easier to sell. In 1963 a truly unusual series called *East Side/West Side* did indeed feature George C. Scott as a social worker who tackled some serious social issues. The series, not surprisingly, lasted a single season. No guns, no dead bodies, no ratings.

The Return of the Lawyer as Hero

And then, starting in 1991—which also saw the rise of *Court TV*—came the most significant shift: the return of lawyers as heroes. But in these new series, prosecutors rather than defense attorneys were usually cast in the heroic roles. When significant cultural changes occur, there are always overlaps between old values and those they replace, so there were a few exceptions to the idealization of prosecutors. *The Trials of Rosie O'Neill*, for example, featured a public defender from a wealthy family and placed considerable emphasis on her personal "trials." Repeatedly, she and her therapist struggled with her conflicts with a family that had nothing but contempt for the work she was doing. Another very progressive series, *Sweet Justice*, featured two women attorneys, one black and one white, fighting for social justice in a Southern community. And another, *The Client*, about another liberal female defense attorney, was based on John Grisham's novel of the same name. All three of these progressive series ran in the 1990s, but it is often hard to remember them because they came and went so quickly. Perhaps the most successful of these shows was *The Practice* (1997–2004), involving a group of bottom-feeding criminal defense lawyers who often suffered great angst at having to represent their detestable clients.[4]

Law & Order,[5] on the other hand, began in 1990 and at this writing is still going strong, as are its two spin-offs, *Law & Order: Special Victims Unit* and *Law & Order: Criminal Intent.* By tracing the shifts from and returns to a variety of ideological positions, we can see clearly how law TV has tended to move more or less consistently with the tides of change in dominant social values and in people's thinking about law and lawyers. These changes, often subtle but important, have influenced the portrayal of prosecutors. *Law & Order* actually followed a format invented in 1963 with a series called *Arrest and Trial,* in which the first half hour featured two police officers whose job it was to solve a crime and arrest the person alleged to have committed it. In the second half, the ADA and his second in command tried the case in court.

When *Law & Order* began, the detectives were played by Chris Noth (now back as a detective on the spin-off *Criminal Intent*) and George Dzunda, while the head ADA was played by Michael Moriarty. His sidekick was played by a black actor, Richard Brooks. This version, which lasted about four years, was probably the least ideologically complex, as each team played straightforward versions of apolitical professionals; by which I mean that there was little questioning of the rightness or wrongness of whatever legal issues arose: they simply followed the rules. Although the two cops often engaged in political debates about social issues, they did their jobs with equal commitment.

In 1994 however, a far more politically concerned set of teams took over. The Brooks character became more race conscious and left to become a defense attorney. The new legal team was headed by Jack McCoy, a man with a liberal background, and his cochair Claire Kincaid, an outspoken feminist. This turn made the series far more interesting but also, inevitably, given the conservatism of the times, more contradictory as well. The new cops (particularly Lennie Briscoe, played by the great actor Jerry Orbach) were hard-boiled types straight out of *film noir,* and their attitudes ranged from cynicism about the world in general to a strong commitment to family values. But even here, Rey Curtis, a family-values guy, was seen to slip up and cheat on his wife.

McCoy and Kincaid grappled with issues of ethics and the political aspects of their cases. In the end they always worked to convict the accused. Time after time, the team's liberal values would fall prey to hard-line prosecution. The conflicts were resolved when the defendant proved more deserving of conviction than he or she had seemed at first.

However, once the death penalty was reinstated in New York, the show took a decidedly conservative turn. McCoy stayed on but became more disgusted with the "psychobabble" of liberalism and began speaking more and more about criminals being "evil" and needing to purge them completely from the community, not simply through imprisonment but by death itself. Indeed, the producers literally killed off Kincaid at this point, replacing her with a series of attractive women prosecutors who were more and more conservative and who were convinced that guilt was obvious in every case, as was McCoy.

At this point, the series was losing viewers, not so much for political reasons but because the formula seemed to be getting stale. And then, in the 2007–08 season which, as I write, has just ended, it picked up new energy and become more interesting. McCoy, now the DA, has returned to his liberal roots, while the chief ADA, Mike Cutter, is more inclined to be tough on crime and is more flexible on ethical issues. Similarly, *Shark*, another show that glorified prosecutors and demeaned defense lawyers, found a devoted audience in its two seasons.[6] Prosecutor Sebastian Stark, played with great skill by James Woods, consistently acted as though the ends justified the unethical means and never hesitated to twist the truth to get a conviction. Whether television producers will continue to find demographic gold in trashing criminal defense lawyers may depend on how the political winds blow. Only time will tell, not only about prosecutor shows like *Law & Order* and *Shark*, but about the future of law TV and its protagonists.

Endnotes

1. For treatment of all television series past and present, see ALEX MCNEIL, TOTAL TELEVISION (4th ed. 1996).

2. See David Ginsburg's chapter "*The Defenders:* TV Lawyers and Controversy in the New Frontier. "

3. See Francis Nevins's chapter "*Perry Mason.*"

4. See Jeffrey Thomas's chapter "*The Practice:* Debunking Television Myths and Stereotypes."

5. See Shannon Mader's chapter "*Law & Order.*"

6. See Nancy Rapoport's chapter "Swimming with *Shark.*"

PART I

Dramatic Lawyer Series—The Genre

This book is about law on television, including fictional dramatic shows about lawyers. Dozens of these shows are discussed in Parts II through V. (Of course, as Elayne Rapping points out in her introduction, there have been many more of these shows than can be analyzed in this book, because of space limitations). These dramatic shows involve lawyers who work in both the criminal and civil justice systems. They practice in the United States and in foreign countries. This array of fictitious dramatic television shows about law and lawyers should be considered a genre.

A *genre* in film or television consists of pop culture products (that is, films or television shows) that have many narrative elements in common and share stock characters, plots, and conventions (such as costumes or locations). Familiar examples are doctor shows, westerns, cop shows, and soap operas. TV producers rely on genre to predict what shows might be marketable, while audiences recognize and feel comfortable with new shows that fit within a familiar genre.

Dramatic lawyer shows involve conflicts between the state and the defendant in criminal cases or between opposing private parties in civil cases. These conflicts are fought out in adversarial courtroom trials conducted by opposing lawyers. The trials are set in elaborate courtrooms and are presided over by gowned judges who serve as neutral arbiters. Typically the trial process serves to drive the narrative, often exposing various secrets, and it culminates in a decision, usually a jury verdict, that resolves the conflict.

Genres are always changing to satisfy contemporary tastes. The dramatic legal genre has been radically transformed over the 50-plus years that it has been in service. Most obviously, nobody would remake *Perry Mason* or *Matlock* today. Their painfully formulaic plots and flat, boring characters would hold little appeal for contemporary audiences. When it premiered in 1986, *L.A. Law* transformed the genre by making lawyer characters into multidimensional human beings with personal lives and by siting law practice within a profit-making law firm. It turned out that millions of people enjoyed the legal soap opera format of *L.A. Law,* and its commercial success spawned the incredible variety of dramatic law shows of the last twenty years. Undoubtedly, the genre will continue to mutate in future decades, just as it has in the recent past.

Just consider some of the genre-busting TV lawyer shows that followed *L.A. Law. Ally McBeal* was much more about the dysfunctional personalities and confused love lives of its lawyer characters than about the irreverent cases handled by their law firm. Clever visual effects and music allowed us to experience Ally's thoughts and fantasies, such as the famous dancing baby. On *The Practice,* a bottom-feeding law firm scratched for business, often pushing the ethical envelope, while the lawyers experienced generally miserable personal lives. Guilty clients sometimes got off and innocent ones sometimes got convicted. Today, the lawyers on *Boston Legal* and *Shark* get away with flouting every ethical rule in the book, and many of them are not very nice people. Even on the more traditional *Law & Order*, lawyers are beginning to display more attitude and to cut a few ethical corners.

Part I contains four essays that cut across the dramatic legal television genre. Jill Goldsmith gave up her career as a Chicago public defender to become a successful L.A. television writer. She tells us how the writing process works and how she comes up with stories. Another way lawyers get into the TV world is by serving as technical advisers. Chuck Rosenberg has advised on more than 300 scripts, trying (against the odds) to make the stories just a little more accurate. He warns us not to expect anything remotely resembling verisimilitude in lawyer shows.

Cynthia Cohen is a jury consultant who studies media closely, because jurors are very much affected by the news and by fictional television shows. Jurors' preferences can often be revealed by considering the TV shows that they like to watch. Some of Cynthia's findings about the effects of television on jurors will surprise you.

Finally, Carrie Menkel-Meadow looks at the ethics of the lawyers in dramatic series over time. She identifies bushels of gross ethical violations in contemporary shows, because ethical conflicts make for gripping stories in which moral values collide with expediency and client service. Usually, the lawyers conclude that the ends justify the means and the rules of ethics take another hit. At least, Carrie points out, we can be thankful that real people haven't been hurt by the gross lawyer misconduct we watch on TV. Let's hope that future lawyers don't learn their ethics from watching law on television.

CHAPTER 1

Writing for Television: From Courtroom to Writer's Room

JILL GOLDSMITH

Like many people, growing up, I wasn't even aware that someone was actually writing the television I watched. The shows just magically appeared. I'm not sure if I thought the actors on the programs were spontaneously speaking the words, or if there was some invisible force, some deity of entertainment, conjuring the stories for my viewing pleasure. I raced home after school to watch shows like *Gilligan's Island*, anxious to find out what plan Gilligan and the Skipper had come up with to really get them off the island this time. I wondered who the Professor found more attractive, the smart, sensible girl-next-door Mary Ann, or the sexy, glamorous Ginger. And I tuned in to *The Brady Bunch* to see if Jan Brady would ever find her self-esteem, despite being the middle child.

So while I didn't know there were actual human beings writing these shows, I did sense that television was a powerful medium. Otherwise, why would my viewing time be limited by my parents? Clearly, television had the power to alter the fabric of my being in ways I could only imagine. It was so powerful, so potent, that I could only be exposed to it in limited doses, like radiation or chocolate.

Because it didn't occur to me that anyone actually wrote for television, it didn't occur to me that it was a career option. Law became a way to use skills like writing, critical thought, and even creativity. And somehow I always knew I wanted to be a Public Defender. The first image I remember seeing of a Public Defender on television, and of a female lawyer as well, was Joyce Davenport, on *Hill Street Blues*. On the show, she was romantically involved with the police captain. As testament to the power of suggestion on television, years later when I was a Public Defender in Chicago, I had a new client in the lockup who refused to talk to me because I reminded him of Joyce Davenport, and he thought I must be involved with the police, just like her. I tried to explain she was a fictional character, to no avail. Finally, another client of mine, whose trial I had won and who was waiting to be released, put in a good word for me and managed to convince the guy that I was there to help him.

From Law to Writing

The career path of law is like a ladder with well-defined rungs. There are clear steps, from taking the LSAT, to going to law school, to passing the bar exam. The path to writing for Hollywood has no orderly steps. It feels more like Sea World, a venue where everything's a little murky, like being underwater. The first step that was necessary for me to make the transition from law to writing was, in fact, the most important. It involved changing the way I perceived the world and my path through it. As someone who was trained in a profession as analytical as law, I had to reach a point where I was willing to take the leap of faith necessary to pursue a path full of mystery and uncertainty.

Seven years as a Public Defender, over four hundred trials, and countless cases had stretched the limits of my conscious mind. The stakes were high, including loss of liberty, and even life, because Illinois is a death penalty state. There were so many judgment calls to be made, so many unknowable decisions that would so greatly affect the lives of people. I found myself listening to my intuition in a way I never had before. And I became aware of how seeming coincidence and synchronicity were having an impact on my cases. Out of the blue, I would find something relevant to one of my cases, a witness would turn up, I would suddenly think of something. My cases were acting as a kind of laboratory to raise my awareness about how interactive the world is. It felt like a process of co-creation, where I would do my part, but help would always seem to come.

And then the synchronicities began showing up around my writing. I have always written, for as long as I can remember, from short stories to plays, even creation myths. During an internship with U.S. Senator Paul Simon, I wrote position papers for the Senator, reviewing issues that came before the Senate Judiciary Committee. As an attorney in Chicago, I found opportunities to write wherever I could. I took writing classes at the University of Chicago. I studied improv in the Conservatory of the Second City, to have a creative outlet. I joined the Bar Association Grid-iron Revue, writing legal parody. And working up a trial, with the opening statement, closing argument, direct and cross-examination questions, with all the possible twists and turns, was a major writing job in itself.

But never, in all that time, did I consider writing full-time for a living. I recently read about an informal poll in which almost ninety percent of people surveyed in Los Angeles said they were working on a screenplay. But living in the Midwest at that time, immersed in Law World, I wasn't aware of screenplays. I figured one day I would retire to a cabin in the woods where I'd write prose, fiction, maybe a novel.

Then one day, a script was submitted to the Cook County Public Defender's Office to be reviewed for legal accuracy. That led to me reading anything and everything that had to do with screenplays. As I read script after script, it was like I discovered that I spoke a language I never even knew existed. I understood how the stories were pulled through the acts, how the scenes fit together, how the characters were voiced. It was such an immediate and contemporary form of storytelling. I also knew that without even realizing it, I had amassed a mountain of story material over my years as a Public Defender. As one friend put it, I didn't need to come up with stories, I needed to get rid of them. But I was still in Chicago trying cases, with little time or energy to actually write.

I had a deep sense that it was time to shift into the next phase of my life and focus on writing, but I had no idea how to make that transition. My discontent was reflected back to me by a State's Attorney in my courtroom one day, while we were waiting for a case to be called. He asked why I didn't just put everyone out of their misery and write a screenplay already. Apparently, I had been talking about it between the cases, burdening the court staff with my career dilemma. I told him that it felt like trying to bail out the ocean with a teaspoon. It felt like a distant dream I had no way to access. I said that if only I had some sign that it was real, I'd feel much more motivated to move forward.

Later that afternoon, I was given that sign. I was on my way home when a client popped into my mind. I couldn't get his case out of my thoughts, so I turned my car around and went to pay him a jail visit. When I arrived, I saw a crew filming in the parking lot, which was quite an unusual occurrence. I remember thinking it was strange that I had just been talking about wanting to write a script, and here I was, walking onto some sort of film set. I'd never seen production before, so I walked over to a couple of guys on the crew to ask if I could watch. It turns out they were filming the movie *Primal Fear*, and I was talking to the director and executive producer. When they found out I was a Public Defender, they asked me questions about my job, then offered me a seat, where I was a guest for the rest of the day's shoot. They talked to me about the script, about the process of making the movie, about the lighting in a shot. And they brought Richard Gere, who was starring in the film, over to where I was sitting and introduced me.

There were plenty of other synchronicities that unfolded before I eventually left the Public Defender's Office, but none of them can top that story. The people I met that day were not involved in how I wound up writing for television, but that day holds tremendous significance for me, because I asked for a sign, and was given something so much bigger than I ever could have anticipated. It was the catalyst I needed to really listen to my internal sense that it was time to leave.

When I submitted my resignation, everyone thought it was crazy. They couldn't believe I would leave without the guarantee of another job. The law focuses on reasonableness, from "beyond a reasonable doubt" to the "reasonable man" standard. And what I was doing seemed anything but reasonable. When I told them I was taking my pension, which was enough to float me for a year, they made dire predictions. Somehow, I had broken from the institutional thinking that safety comes from clinging to what you have, rather than taking a risk. And somehow, despite my years in law, I became aware of an even greater law. I had reached a point where I knew that the only safety was in following where my heart was leading me.

Finding the First Opportunity

I arrived in Los Angeles feeling exhilarated, only to feel like I had slammed into a brick wall. I had no idea how to break into the industry. The currency in television writing is known as the spec script, which is essentially a sample script of a particular show, written to demonstrate your writing ability. The goal is to find representation, and ultimately to find a staff position on a show. I tried to take a meeting here and there, join a writing group, everything I could think of. But nothing was really happening.

And, unexpectedly, I was going through an identity crisis. I was used to getting up in the morning, going to court, being professionally recognized in a certain way, handling enormous responsibility. Now I was waking up, putting on sweats, and going to Starbucks with all the other aspiring writers. I came to realize how much we identify with what we do in the world, rather than who we are. It was a whole new way of learning to relate to myself, of stripping away layers of the outer identity. I was challenged to believe in something that was not visible to the rest of the world, to hold a vision even when nothing seemed to be coming together.

Six months into what had seemed like such a good idea back in Chicago, I was beginning to question my decision. And that's putting it mildly. I only had a few more months before I was broke, I had no prospects, and I was at a low point. One Saturday night I had reached my limit and decided that on Monday, I would call the California Bar and see about going back to the practice of law. Then I decided that I needed chocolate. I knew of one chocolate shop nearby, and decided to go there. I wanted the highest cocoa content possible to help elevate my mood, not some cheap grocery store candy bar.

When I arrived at the chocolate shop, there was a long line. A man walked in at the same time as me, and motioned for me to go ahead of him. I thanked him, saying I was so depressed, if I could get chocolate ten seconds sooner, I'd be happy. He asked why I was depressed, and ordinarily I would never have shared details about my life with a stranger, but for some reason, it all came pouring out. I told him about being a Public Defender back in Chicago, about giving up everything to come out to L.A. to write. He asked what I had written, and I told him I'd written nothing professionally, because I didn't know how to get my foot in the door. He then handed me his business card and introduced himself. It was David Milch, the writer and executive producer who created the Emmy-winning series *NYPD Blue* with Steven Bochco. And he was generous enough to offer to read a script. I subsequently wrote a spec script for *NYPD Blue*, and got a meeting, at which I expected to get notes. Instead, he told me he wanted to buy the script, and it became an episode of *NYPD Blue*. That seemingly chance meeting, or cosmic choreography, as I like to call it, led to jobs writing for shows including *The Practice*, *Ally McBeal*, *Law & Order*, and *Boston Legal*.

So that's how my first break came. It was simply a matter of giving up everything, moving across the country, reaching the end of my rope, and seeking the medicinal comforts of chocolate. Of course, it was necessary to be prepared when the opportunity came, but there was a lot of unforeseen help as well. As Scottish expeditionist W. H. Murray said, in a quote often attributed to Goethe, "The moment one definitely commits oneself, then providence moves too. All sorts of things occur to help one that would never otherwise have occurred. A whole stream of events issues from the decision, raising in one's favor all manner of unforeseen incidents and meetings and material assistance, which no man could have dreamed would have come his way." I believe that principle applies to everyone, in whatever they endeavor to accomplish. And now that I had navigated the transition into writing for television, the focus shifted to story.

Writing the Legal Drama

There are various ways the writing process can be structured on a show, from a writer's room, where a group of writers contributes to fleshing out a story, to a more independent arrangement where ideas are pitched directly to the showrunner by the writer. Once a story is approved, the writer goes off to write the script, which is a fast process, sometimes completed within the span of a week or two. In my experience, this is actually helpful because the adrenaline needed to write so quickly energizes the script.

At the heart of this process is always story. And law shows are a versatile container for many types of stories. First, there are stories that are directly about the practice of law, that comment on the system and its flaws, ironies, or inequities. I think part of the appeal is that we love to see behind the curtain of a cloistered world. We want to see what really goes on in a hospital, an evidence lab, a courthouse. And since the justice system is fundamental to our democracy, as citizens we want an understanding of how our system works, or how it fails us. Many people perceive the practice of law to be an exclusive fraternity with its own language and rules. To make this accessible through story helps to demystify the process.

Another type of story uses the law as an analytical tool to examine both sides of social issues, rather than using the law as an end in itself. In this context, the framework of a trial serves to highlight the different perspectives, to examine the pros and cons, to shine a light on the truths of a particular issue of the day. Then there are stories that feature the law's impact on a character, where the case serves to further a character arc, influencing the character's growth in some way. Sometimes all of these dynamics are present in the same story, to varying degrees.

Against this backdrop, lies the appeal of a good mystery and its resolution. A legal drama can provide closure and certainty to doubts never assuaged in the real world. In the alternative, it can also reflect an ambiguous outcome in a morally complex world. In fact, the way lawyers, themselves, have been portrayed in legal dramas over time has shifted from the heroic Perry Mason to a much more complex, often flawed protagonist. In many ways, this mirrors our society's shift in consciousness as it evolved from the idealized *Father Knows Best* paradigm to a willingness to peel back the layers and look at much thornier truths.

Finding Stories

Television chews up so much material, turning out shows week after week. Finding stories involves a combination of pulling from personal experience, reading newspapers, books, and journals, talking with former law colleagues, and just generally keeping receptors open. Sometimes an idea will come from a dream, or from activities like sitting in traffic, when the conscious mind is relaxed enough to allow inspiration to filter through. And sometimes stories find you. Once you know what stories will work for a given show, you see stories everywhere. You're always trying them on for size, to see if they will hold, if there are enough twists and turns, if there's something at the heart of the story worth exploring.

Sometimes a unique set of facts can spark a story. The first script I wrote for *NYPD Blue* involved putting a spin on a case from my Public Defender days, then deconstructing it to fit into the cop universe. In the episode, a law-abiding man is forced to kill in self-defense, but becomes worried the police might not see it that way. Under the heading of Bad Ideas, he decides to dismember the body to dispose of it. He doesn't want to make a mess, so he puts the body into his bathtub and runs the water, then uses an electric saw, not considering the ramifications of mixing water and electricity. When the detectives arrive, they find one partially dismembered body in the tub, and another man passed out from an electrical shock on the floor. The man's daughter has hidden the saw to try to protect her father, and the detectives have to piece the story together. Because it's a cop show rather than a legal drama, the story plays out in the interrogation room instead of a courtroom.

There are times when a moment from real life, a fragment of a trial, or a memorable client has inspired a story. Once I had a drug case where the defendant came to court so high that he passed out during the trial. I had to pry my legal pad out from under him, and during closing arguments, he started snoring. Even with all of that, he was found not guilty, a victim of overcharging by the State. Rather than the drug dealer they were trying to portray him as, he was an addict in need of help. So the darkly comical elements of the story were grounded in a deeper truth, and that became a case that defense attorney Ellenor Frutt handled on *The Practice*.

Some stories originate with an intention to show the way a case or client can impact the attorney. In another episode of *The Practice*, I wrote a script about a shaken-baby trial. While there were twists and turns in the case, the story is really about denial. Helen Gamble, the prosecutor, suggests the defendant is in denial about what she did, and has blocked out the truth. Bobby Donnell, who represents the accused, so believes in her, that he can't hear it. Ultimately it's his own denial and disillusionment that he is left with.

Sometimes the desire to explore an interesting question can lead to a story. I wrote a script for *Law & Order* that looked at the validity of psychic experience. The case involved a psychic who was charged with a murder because he knew so much about the crime. I also wrote a script for the show examining whether racism could be considered a mental illness. There are experts who believe hatred based on skin color can be considered a delusional disorder, and I wanted to examine that in a legal context. In another script I did for *Law & Order*, a defense attorney was charged with killing his wife and framing a client. The idea originated at a dinner party, where some defense attorney friends were debating whether they knew the system well enough to commit the perfect murder, and I thought I'd explore that.

Social and political issues often provide fertile ground for stories. I thought the Falun Gong movement in China would make a good backdrop for a script, and it became an episode I wrote for *Law & Order*. Members of the movement claim it's a spiritual practice that is persecuted by the Chinese government, while the government claims the movement is a dangerous cult. I set the issue in the context of a case where a Chinese dignitary is found murdered in New York, raising international and diplomatic legal issues.

More recently, in a script for *Boston Legal*, I wrote a story about a woman suing the Catholic Archdiocese for not allowing women to be ordained as priests. There are a growing number of priests ordaining women in secret, all of whom risk excommunication, so I thought it was an issue worth exploring. The plaintiff challenges the Church for benefiting from tax-exempt status while discriminating against women. The trial examines how Church doctrine, which in the past supported slavery and the Inquisition, has changed and evolved over time.

On the lighter side, I wrote a cleavage suffocation story for *Ally McBeal*, which was based on a case that was actually even less censor friendly. In fact, unusual human behavior in the context of intimate relationships provides a wealth of material. For *Boston Legal*, I did a story based on a lawsuit for theft of sperm, where a woman impregnated herself in an unorthodox manner, as well as a story about a spray containing oxytocin, known as the "love hormone," which can provoke desire.

Sometimes there are stories that dovetail nicely with the issues of a particular character. This was the case with another story I wrote for *Boston Legal* about cloned cows. While looking at the health risks to humans and cows posed by such a practice, as well the FDA's track record of approving things later found harmful, the story line had the added benefit of mining Denny Crane's history of mad cow disease.

Of course, the examples I've just cited, along with all stories you see on a legal drama, are what I would call a "high points" version. They're not meant to be an exhaustive depiction of reality. Just imagine an episode involving countless hours of document production. Perhaps you'd rather not. Exact reality does not always make for scintillating television, so what emerges is a heightened version of reality. The goal is to be accurate yet not all-inclusive, to find the truth in a story in the most efficient, entertaining way. As Alfred Hitchcock once said, "Movies are life, with the boring parts cut out."

Conclusion

The medium of television often takes a hit for helping to make our society a cultural wasteland, but ultimately, television is only a tool for communication, to be used for the good or the bad. Historically, storytellers would gather around the communal campfire, wrapping truths in the forms of stories and myths. Television, with its presence in so many homes, serves as the communal campfire of our time. And as a staple of the medium, legal dramas, at their best, have the capacity to examine human experience, to raise the consciousness around social injustice, and most of all, to just tell a good story.

As for my own story, what I wish I'd known back when I was practicing law, mired in cases, was how nothing in our human experience is lost. Everything I experienced was a necessary precursor to my life now as a writer. In the end, all the roads of our lives merge to form a superhighway, where everything makes sense, where all that we have learned along the way finds a place.

CHAPTER 2

27 Years as a Television Legal Adviser and Counting . . .

CHARLES B. ROSENBERG

In the fall of 1982, I was teaching full time as a visitor from practice at the UCLA School of Law. One day, as I was sitting in my office, the phone rang. I picked it up. The caller announced herself as the executive producer of *Paper Chase*, which had mutated from a movie (where it had done well at the box office), to a prime-time series on the CBS television network (where it had not done very well), to a PBS series (where it had still not done very well), and then, finally, to Showtime (where it was doing OK).

The producer, Lynn Roth, then told me that the show's legal technical script adviser was moving to another city and they needed a new one. I had been recommended by a mutual friend.

"Why me?" I asked.

"Well," she said, "you're a law professor, you went to Harvard, Kingsfield is a law professor, and our show, although we never actually mention the law school by name, is set at Harvard."

"Oh, so I'm being hired for local color."

"Yes."

"I've never read a TV script," I said. "What would I have to do?"

"Mostly we just want you to read the scripts and comment on their legal accuracy. Sometimes we will want to ask you broader questions.

For example, each show has an emotional theme, and we try to find a legal case for a Kingsfield classroom scene that matches the theme. Our current theme is *commitment*, but we haven't been able to come up with a case to match the theme."

"You could," I suggested, "use the gratuitous promise cases."

"What are those?"

"Say someone nurses you back to health from a serious illness, without expecting anything in return—just does it out of the goodness of his or her heart. When you get up off your sickbed, healed, you gratuitously say, 'Hey, I'm so grateful I'll pay you $1,000!' Then you don't. Then your gratuitous caregiver sues you for the money. The legal question is, was your statement a binding promise? Was it a *commitment*?"

"It's perfect," she said. "You're hired."

I had a lot of fun with *Paper Chase*. Most of the writers weren't lawyers, and I occasionally even got to write a few lines here and there (don't tell the Writers Guild). Most memorable was the day a script arrived with a bracketed line that said, "[Kingsfield wipes the floor with two students; Chuck to fill in]." I did my best.

Since that day, as the credited technical legal consultant not only to *Paper Chase*, but also to *L.A. Law, The Practice,* and now *Boston Legal*, I've read over 300 scripts for prime-time TV legal dramas and discussed them with dozens of television writers and producers.[1] I've also had the pleasure of addressing many groups of lawyers, judges, and law students around the country who were interested in learning how "legal TV" is made. I have noted from the questions and comments that there is among some a strong desire to see more verisimilitude in legal dramas— more reflection of what lawyers really do and how trials really work. This essay explains why I don't think legal dramas on television are ever likely to become truer to life than they already are.

Criminal Trials: The Perfect Dramatic Form for TV

All drama, at least in Western culture, is about conflict and resolution, often followed by dénouement, the little tag scene after the resolution that wraps up the emotional loose ends for the audience. Court cases, especially criminal cases, fit that cultural space perfectly. They bring the protagonists head to head in a conflict-enhancing small space—a courtroom—and resolve the conflict in the form of a jury or judge verdict. If dénouement is needed—if we feel, emotionally, that the person who lost should have won—the hallway right outside the courtroom is always available. The loser can shoot the winner. Therefore, the fictional form (drama), whether in TV, movies, novels, or plays, fits the real-life function (criminal courts) perfectly.

Another advantage to courtroom drama is that writers don't need to waste time explaining courtrooms and how they work to an American audience. The courtroom drama and its forms, whether real or fictional (who sits where; what the roles of lawyers, judge, and jury are; what a verdict is), are well-grounded in Anglo-American life, having buried their roots in the cultural soil long before the first TV screen flickered to life or the first piece of celluloid ran through a movie projector.[2] Even small children generally get it.

Criminal trial stories predominate because they're easier to tell than civil trial stories. In part, that's because the rules, procedures, and language are better understood by the public—indictments instead of complaints; guilty or innocent in place of liable or not liable; jails and fines in lieu of judgments and injunctions. Mostly, though, it's because, as writers would say, the stakes in a criminal case are higher. A conflict whose resolution may result in deprivation of liberty, or, better yet, death by execution,[3] is of much greater emotional interest to audiences than, say, whether someone is going to recover $100,000 for breaking an arm because he or she slipped on a banana peel.

Indeed, when civil cases do become the subject of legal dramas, they often involve matters with emotionally high stakes similar to those in criminal trials: Should the comatose patient's life support be turned off? Should a minor be permitted to have an abortion against the wishes of her parents? Should the government be permitted to torture someone to prevent a postulated prospective harm to thousands?

Constraints of the Genre and the TV Medium

However perfect for drama the basic courtroom form might be, writers who want to write a one-hour legally themed TV drama are not free to create whatever they want. Neither audience expectations (usually referred to as "genre expectations") nor the practical constraints of the medium give writers free will.

There is an old saying among writers, attributed to everyone from Dostoyevsky to the novelist John Gardner to various movie directors,[4] that there are only two stories in the world: (1) a man (or "person," if you'd prefer it to be gender neutral) goes on an adventure, and (2) a stranger comes to town. The two are, of course, the same story with different directional arrows.

Whether that old saw is true or not, I've become persuaded that there really are only two stories told in criminal trial dramas, at least on TV: (1) an innocent person is at risk of being convicted, or (2) a guilty person might get away with it. Those are the stories audiences have come to expect. If you credit genre theory (i.e., the idea that audiences are uncomfortable with new dramatic storytelling forms), those are the stories they demand. A writer who dares to tell a different type of one-hour legal story on TV risks the show-killing sound of thousands of remotes clicking.[5]

Indeed, the long-term success of *Perry Mason,* which started out as a series of novels,[6] can be attributed in part to the fact that the show managed to introduce and resolve both of the classic story lines at once. The innocent person represented by Perry Mason (who appeared at first to be guilty based on the facts, but whom we knew emotionally must be innocent because Perry was the defense lawyer), is saved from the gallows at the last moment, while the truly guilty person is nailed right there in the courtroom, either by confessing on the witness stand or by bursting through the courtroom doors and confessing.[7]

Another constraint for the writer of a one-hour TV legal drama is the amount of time available to tell the story. An hour is not a lot of time,[8] and, due to ads, it's not really even an hour. Not to mention that the time available has been shrinking. Today's hour-long dramatic shows clock between 42 and 45 minutes of actual dramatic airtime. Perry Mason had 48 to 50 minutes. In today's time-pressured setting, 25 seconds of talk use up 1 percent of the total dramatic airtime. The result is a dearth of time for procedural verisimilitude, particularly in shows that spend a lot of that precious time telling personal stories to develop their characters.

To demonstrate the impact of this, take out a watch with a second hand, read each of the following two versions of a courtroom event out loud, and time each version.

Version 1

QUESTION TO WITNESS: What happened next?

WITNESS BOB: Fred told me Jane really hated Jack.

OPPOSING LAWYER: Objection, hearsay! Ask that the answer be struck.

JUDGE: Sustained. The answer will be struck from the record, and the
jury is instructed to disregard the answer.

Version 2

QUESTION TO WITNESS: What happened next?

WITNESS BOB: Fred told me Jane really hated Jack.

OPPOSING LAWYER: Objection!

JUDGE: Sustained.

Another constraint for writers is that dramatic television is a visual medium. That may seem rather obvious. After all, people *watch* TV shows. The problem is that audiences would find watching what lawyers mostly do in real life—read, write, talk on the phone, answer e-mail and, sometimes, meet with people—visually boring (even snoring) to watch. Even when lawyers go off to court to argue a motion (which is how a large portion of a litigation lawyer's time is spent), they usually just *stand* at a podium or table. Lawyers are the ultimate talking heads. Writers see that as a giant problem to be overcome. They have several solutions.

One solution is just to *X* out a lot of lawyer life by ridding the law office of most of what lawyers do in a real law office: legal research, document review, and phone calls, among other things. A second solution is to liven up the law office by emphasizing movement and sound: people stomping out of rooms, getting in each other's faces, slamming doors, touching each other, or constantly poking fun at one another.

Still another solution is to spend as little time as possible in the law office and turn instead to the potentially more dynamic setting of a courtroom. Indeed, when writers first think about trials, they imagine protagonists meeting head to head, witnesses suffering through withering cross-examination, passionate and moving jury arguments, and suspenseful verdicts.

Unfortunately, *potentially more dynamic* is the operative phrase. When writers attend a real trial (which many do to get the feel of the thing), they observe that lawyers in real courtrooms, even if they are among the few capable of withering a witness, don't really move around a lot. They're often chained to a podium or table while doing their questioning, are forbidden to walk into the well of the court, must usually ask permission to approach a witness, and certainly cannot walk up to the jury box during closing argument and point at individual jurors.

That lack of movement will not do. In a writer's universe, motion is *the* antidote to visual boredom. So, in dramatic television, lawyers must be left free to roam about the courtroom, lean over the witness, or sit on the rail of the jury box. Were it otherwise, even trial lawyers would appear on TV to be just . . . talking heads.[9]

Writers must also take account of the main goal of drama, which is not to stimulate the intellect directly, but to do so by first manipulating emotions. Put another way, the path to the intellect in drama is through feeling. An audience must be compelled, not only to take an interest in the plot, but also to have some feeling for each character, whether through antipathy, sympathy, or empathy. The audience members must imagine themselves into the situation.

As a probe of this theory, one might pose this hypothetical to a writer: "If, after an audience has watched a dramatic TV show you have written, you are able to choose its reaction, would you prefer the average person who watched to say, 'Hey that was interesting, let's discuss it,' or would you prefer that everyone sob?" Most good writers would answer, "Well, I'd like them to do both." But were you to say, as a professor might in a law school classroom, "It's my hypo, pick one or the other," I think most writers would pick "sob."

The consequence of this likely answer is that writers don't find topics that are intellectually interesting to lawyers, intellectuals, and policy wonks to be well suited to drawing intense emotion from a TV audience, at least not in 42 minutes. Thus, intellectual issues usually get short shrift in one-hour storytelling. At the very least, they are eviscerated. The Constitution is a perfect example. Many constitutional issues are endlessly fascinating, not just to lawyers, but to laypeople, too. But can you think of a way to turn a Commerce Clause issue into an emotionally charged drama? Can an audience be made to fret about whether California can tax wine from Georgia?

Murder works so much better.[10]

Choices Writers Must Make

The creator of a one-hour dramatic legal TV series—someone who wants to get a television pilot made and on the air—must choose between creating a show that is character-driven and creating one that is plot-driven.

In TV terms, a character-driven drama focuses as much time and energy delving into the personalities of its characters as it does on developing a detailed legal plot. A plot-driven show, by contrast, reverses the time focus and time allotment. That is because, to tell their stories, plot-driven dramas don't necessarily need "big" characters with what writers call changing "arcs" to their lives—loves lost, diseases endured, promotions denied. So plot-driven dramas can dispense with such things in order to lavish more time on the plot.[11]

Law & Order is an example of a TV drama that is primarily plot-driven. *The Defenders*, beloved by many for its social daring,[12] was also largely plot-driven. If you're old enough to have watched it (it went off the air in 1965), do you remember very much about the father and son lawyer team who were the main characters, beyond their earnestness and good lawyering? Do you even remember the names of those characters?[13]

Boston Legal is, by contrast, primarily character-driven. With all due respect to the other excellent actors in the show, if Denny Crane (William Shatner) and Alan Shore (James Spader) were to disappear from *Boston Legal*, the show would disappear with them.[14] By contrast, if all of the characters in *Law & Order* were killed in a tragic bus accident (fictionally only, of course), I really believe that the show could hire an entirely new slate of actors, move them onto the set and into the plots, continue right along, and keep most of its audience. What are most interesting about that show are its plots.[15]

The choice to create a character-driven TV drama versus a plot-driven one has consequences for audiences. One flows from an earlier-discussed issue: the dearth of dramatic airtime in today's "one-hour" television drama. If the average one-hour drama is now only 42 minutes, then a character-driven show will have even less time than a plot-driven show to tell the legal part of its story. Do the numbers: if a character-driven TV show spends half its time on character development, it has only 21 minutes to tell the entire legal story. A plot-driven legal TV drama, by devoting less time to character development, might have 35 minutes for the legal story. A 140-minute, legally themed feature film, even if character-driven, has perhaps 70 minutes to develop its legal story.

You'd think that one solution for a character-driven legal show (or any show) that wanted to tell more subtle, detailed legal stories would be to carry the legal stories over from one week to the next. In fact, that does not usually work very well. The core audience of a TV series might watch or record all of the episodes in a season, but a large chunk of the audience will only watch some of the shows, and not always sequentially. For most people, tuning in to the middle of a three-part legal story, not having seen the first two parts, leads to their changing the channel.[16] *Murder One* (aired 1995–97) is an example of a critically acclaimed show that tried to tell a year-long legal story, but failed to achieve high ratings for its efforts.[17]

Character development, by contrast, does not have to be viewed consistently from week to week to maintain viewer interest. For example, in *Boston Legal*, every episode ends with a balcony cigar-smoking scene between Denny Crane and Alan Shore. To enjoy the scene, you don't have to know what they said to each other the week before if you happened to miss it. All you have to know is that every episode has such a scene. That's because what is happening in each such scene is not the unfolding of a legal plot, but character development—two people who differ from one another in age, philosophy, and politics seen in the process of crafting a deep and abiding, if odd, friendship.

Consequences?

Many lawyers and judges worry about the negative consequences that portraying law on TV in such a shorthand and sometimes inaccurate manner might have on the public's understanding of law and its regard for lawyers and the justice system in general. I would concede that the shows must have *some* influence, but it's hard to say just how much. After all, there are multitudinous influences on people's perception of law and lawyers besides fictional TV.

Personal contact with the legal system is one of them. For example, in 2007, in California alone, there were approximately 173,000 felons in prison,[18] and it seems logical to assume that each such imprisonment generated contact with lawyers for many people, from victims and witnesses to prisoners and their families.[19] Another influence is the long-running campaign by insurance companies to vilify plaintiffs' lawyers. A third is the public's consumption of real-world legal events, in the form of newspaper reports, televised trials, and on-air legal commentary.[20] A fourth is the heavily politicized—on both sides—discussion of Supreme Court and other appellate decisions.

TV writers do not live on Mars. They live in the real world.[21] They read the same newspapers (including the *National Enquirer*) and magazines as everyone else. They watch the same live broadcasts of real trials. They watch the same local news crime reports. They access the same quirky legal stories making the rounds on the Internet. They even read the same reports of true lawyer and judge malfeasance, which are, unfortunately, not all that rare.

As a result of the fact that TV writers live in the world, I used to think the question at issue very much resembled the chicken-and-egg conundrum: are legal TV shows the chicken or the egg? In recent years, however, I have come to think that the best one can say is that the entire thing has become an inseparable chicken scramble.

Final Thoughts

Much lawyer criticism of legal TV shows focuses on the way in which the shows distort trial procedure, including the application of the rules of evidence and the marginalization of legal ethics. Some of that criticism is valid. The shows do distort and marginalize. The question for me, though, is how much of the distortion involves things that are truly important to the administration of justice.

Lawyers are, of course, proceduralists. They're trained to be. They sometimes regard procedure, as currently practiced, as if it were holy writ, frozen in time. They tend to treat its misdepiction as sacrilege. Yet procedure has varied tremendously over time and, even today, varies tremendously among states, among different courthouses within a state, and even from courtroom to courtroom within the same courthouse. One might also observe that some judges use the rules of procedure and the rules of evidence to move a trial in the direction they think it ought to go, just as judges in fictional TV shows sometimes do.

What legal TV shows do not generally distort, however, are the constitutional fundamentals of the justice system. Defendants in criminal trials on dramatic television are not required to testify (although they often choose to do so for dramatic effect). They are given the right to confront their accusers. They get a jury trial if they demand one, and the government is required to prove their guilt to that jury beyond a reasonable doubt. If a defendant is acquitted by a jury, it's over. They walk free. To me, those are the important things, and they are protected, even glorified, by the writers of one-hour legal dramas.

Endnotes

1. I'm often asked if I've ever wanted to write a script myself. Although I've written a novel (as yet unpublished), my answer is "No." In some quarters in Los Angeles, this is considered a character defect.

2. Consider, for example, the intense public and journalistic interest in the trial of Mary Surrat, who was accused of housing and helping the conspirators who assassinated Abraham Lincoln on April 14, 1865. Surrat was tried before a special military commission and executed in public on July 7, 1865, less than three months after the assassination. ROBERT A. FERGUSON, THE TRIAL IN AMERICAN LIFE 153–89 (2007).

3. The writers of *Boston Legal*, which is set in Massachusetts (a state with no death penalty), have sometimes sent their lawyers to other states in search of a death penalty case. The firm conveniently has offices in multiple cities.

4. As far as I can find, it's one of the few truisms of drama not attributed to Aristotle.

5. There are from time to time, of course, a number of shows that feature civil trials (or feature them on occasion), but they are the exception and, as noted earlier, tend to focus on high-stakes civil matters that aren't just about money.

6. The first was called *The Case of the Velvet Claws* and was published in 1933. The novels were then turned into a successful radio series, into long-running TV series (twice), and, at various points, into a number of TV movies. See Francis M. Nevins's chapter "*Perry Mason.*"

7. Indeed, the "*Perry Mason* ending" has become so entrenched in our culture that Woody Allen, in his movie *Bananas* (1971), was able to parody it by having the defendant badger a witness to confess even though the defendant was gagged during his cross of the witness. Not to mention that a man burst through the doors of the courtroom and confessed to a crime, only to find that he was in the wrong trial.

8. Movies and plays are traditionally much longer than one hour. The total hours of a TV series in a single season, of course, run to much more than that— 15 to 16 hours of drama in a 22-episode season. However, procedural accuracy has to be shown in the moment, not episodically.

9. The failure of a relatively recent TV show set in the U.S. Supreme Court might be attributed, in part, to the writers' failure to find an effective way to animate anyone in that setting. On the other hand, when people did become animated in the solemnity of the Supreme Court courtroom (including questions from the audience!), it was too ludicrous even for TV. By contrast, *The West Wing*, based in part on boring policy-wonk chatter, was enlivened by constant motion—characters walking, sometimes hustling urgently, as they talked, moving about on Air Force One, getting up as the President entered the room, going to campaign rallies, etc.

10. Documentaries, docudramas, and biopics, if well done, tend to do a better job than one-hour dramatic television shows of making intellectual legal issues interesting, at least to a select audience. See Norman Rosenberg's chapter "*Gideon's Trumpet*: The 'Very Best.'"

11. One test of whether a drama of any kind is character-driven or plot-driven is whether, years later, you can remember the plot over the characters. *Superman*, for example, is character-driven. Superman, Clark Kent, Lois Lane, Jor-el, Perry White—everyone who ever read the comics or watched the TV show or the movies remembers them. Who on Earth (or even Krypton) remembers the plots?

12. Social daring on TV doesn't age well, though. It's time sensitive. On a number of occasions, I have showed an episode of *The Defenders* called "Old Lady Ironsides" (first aired on December 21, 1963) to my Law and Popular Culture course at Loyola Law School in Los Angeles. It involves the fairly intellectual (but also emotional) issue of whether a girl can be expelled from high school because she is pregnant. Many students find it boring, although they do love the old commercials. (I know, I know; maybe I should stop showing it.)

13. The lawyers were named Lawrence Preston, played by E.G. Marshall, and Kenneth Preston, played by Robert Reed. Reed is probably better known for his role as Mike Brady in *The Brady Bunch*. See David R. Ginsburg's chapter "*The Defenders:* TV Lawyers and Controversy in the New Frontier."

14. See Corinne Brinkerhoff's chapter "Reality Bites: *Boston Legal*'s Creative License with the Law."

15. I do not mean to suggest that the characters in *Law & Order* are not interesting or would not be missed, were such a tragic accident to befall them. It is simply that they are not as fleshed out as their counterparts in more character-driven shows. However, in recent years, as *Law & Order* has begun to see its ratings fall, it has tended to put somewhat more emphasis on character development. See Shannon Mader's chapter "*Law & Order*."

16. TV shows try to overcome that problem by showing, at the start, a retrospective called "Previously on. . ." It tries to catch the audience up on what happened in the last one or two episodes. Of course, doing so simply takes away even more seconds of the airtime needed to tell the new legal story.

17. *See* Michael Asimow's chapter *"Murder One:* The Adversary System Meets Celebrity Justice." See also Christine A. Corcos's chapter *"Damages:* The Truth Is Out There." *Damages* also involves a serialized story and, as of this writing, has been renewed. Of course, it plays on FX and therefore does not need as large an audience as a network show.

18. *See* Executive Summary of California Department of Corrections Fall 2007 Population Projections, http://www.cdcr.ca.gov/Reports_Research/Offender_Information_Services_Branch/Projections/F07pub.pdf (last visited Jan. 15, 2009).

19. There were even more arrests. In 2006, the arrest rate in California was over 5,000 per 100,000 people, which works out to more than 1,500,000 arrests. Some, no doubt, were multiple arrests of the same person and some people were no doubt quickly released without any contact with lawyers and judges. Still, a very large number of those arrests must have generated contact with law, lawyers, and judges. *See* DIVISION OF CALIFORNIA JUSTICE INFORMATION SERVICES, CALIFORNIA DEPARTMENT OF JUSTICE, REPORT, CRIME IN CALIFORNIA, Bureau of Criminal Information and Analysis Criminal Justice Center Data Tables, Table 16, Total Arrests, 1952–2006, Number and Rate per 100,000 Population at Risk, http://ag.ca.gov/cjsc/publications/candd/cd06/dataTables.pdf (last visited Jan. 15, 2009).

20. I have written elsewhere of the odd coincidences I have found between lawyers' criticisms of fictional trials on TV and their criticisms of the very real (and very broadcast) criminal trial of O.J. Simpson. *See The Myth of Perfection*, 24 NOVA LAW REVIEW 639 (2000).

21. Well, OK, many of them live in Los Angeles. But still . . . .

CHAPTER 3

Media Effects from Television Shows—Reality or Myth?

CYNTHIA R. COHEN

"The TV shows and movies that I watched actually give me a better image of lawyers (for the people like in *Law & Order*), but also give a bad image of any lawyers defending criminals."

Mock juror
Asian-American woman in her 20s

Think Denny Crane hurts lawyers' image at trial? Think again. Series like *Boston Legal* and *Ally McBeal* improve public trust in real lawyers. Extreme characters, such as William Shatner's Denny Crane or Calista Flockhart's Ally McBeal, create a contrast effect when compared to a real lawyer. *Ally McBeal*'s character boosted competence perceptions of female lawyers in the 1990s, just as male lawyers receive a boost in perceived trust when compared to Denny Crane today.

As a jury consultant and a research psychologist who studies effects of the media, I'm always fascinated by jurors' perceptions and television influences. Jury consultants were first mentioned on television in an *L.A. Law* segment in 1987. That program stopped me in my tracks. I was proud to have started my own consulting firm. When the segment aired, I couldn't believe that the jury consultants were changing Michael Kuzak's wardrobe even before he had the case file! Oh my, I thought, if this is what the public or lawyers think of jury consultants, I'd better quit my day job and turn in my "LA Psych" vanity license plate. Fortunately, that same week I was off to my first American Bar Association Annual Meeting, where Chuck Rosenberg, the *L.A. Law* technical consultant, was scheduled to speak.[1] I could tell him about this inaccuracy.

Since that first meeting, Chuck and I worked together on real trials, on several bar association panels, and in his law school classes. Chuck introduced me to the *L.A. Law* actors, writers, and executive producers. My continued search for the truth in storytelling never faltered. The writers and the executive producer recognized my exuberance over jury consultants getting equal time. However, they saw the situation differently. If their *L.A. Law* episode stirred controversy, why produce another episode on real practices of jury consultants? They reran the wardrobe episode instead. So I decided to do what every good psychologist does—I analyzed it.

Television Law Show Ratings by Mock Jurors

Since the 1980s, I have consistently asked mock jurors what television law shows they watch as well as questions about their personal experiences that are related to the issues in the case. Then the mock jurors hear both sides of a real case. After the closing arguments, I ask about the basic issues in the case as well as who should win, and if they would award damages, how much? Over the years, I've found that viewers' preferences in television series often relate to whether they are for the plaintiff or for the defense in our mock trials.

From 1987 to 1991, the television series in my inquiry included *L.A. Law, Matlock, Night Court, People's Court,* and *Perry Mason. Night Court* and *Perry Mason* viewers, especially the female viewers, tended to favor the defense in our real trials. *Perry Mason* viewers liked the theme of responsibility and often favored the corporate defendant. *L.A. Law* viewers also slightly favored the defense. *Matlock* viewers tended to slightly favor the plaintiff. In one mock trial, the *Matlock* viewers awarded damages against a bottle manufacturer to the mother of a two-year-old injured by an exploding bottle. Those who watched *Matlock* were motivated by sympathy.

At the same time, I found that mock jurors who had a more positive attitude toward lawyers were more likely to be defense oriented. These jurors responded positively to a number of statements such as "In a society where justice is held up as the highest ideal, lawyers are always looking for technical means of bending the law to their advantage;" "Lawyers are helpful to people in our society;" and "Lawyers are good at settling arguments between two people."

The 2006 Study/Trust in Professions

From 2004 to 2006, I was on the ABA Litigation Section's Task Force on the Image of the Profession. At the ABA Annual Meeting in 2006, the task force held a program in Los Angeles entitled "I'm Not a Lawyer, but I Play One on TV." I measured the attitudes about lawyers and other professionals of 619 Los Angelenos. I also measured their experiences with television law shows and law-themed movies, along with their reaction to a case scenario based on the Vioxx litigation.[2]

Results indicated that lawyers are trusted more than building contractors, CEOs, congressional representatives, tobacco executives, and used-car salespersons. Jurors trust professors, judges, and television writers more than they trust lawyers. So what we see on a television series is often deemed credible by the public, especially if the judge makes rulings.

This data, collected during the week of March 20, 2006, was not a Nielsen rating. Individuals were simply asked which of the current television law shows they had viewed at any time. The shows included *CSI*, the most watched show, with 55 percent, followed by *Law & Order*, watched by 51 percent; *Law & Order: Special Victims Unit* (48 percent); *CSI Miami* (41 percent); *Law & Order: Criminal Intent* (40 percent); *CSI NY* (31 percent); *Boston Legal* (29 percent); *JAG* (28 percent); *NCIS* (28 percent); *Medium* (25 percent); *Conviction* (12 percent); and *InJustice* (12 percent).

Media Effects from Television Shows—Reality or Myth?
The *CSI* Effect

I was looking to see if a *CSI* effect existed. That is, do jurors believe that prosecutors cannot establish guilt beyond a reasonable doubt without presenting scientific evidence such as the jurors have seen on *CSI*? What

I found was that 88 percent of the Los Angeles mock jurors thought that DNA evidence should be analyzed in all criminal cases. The high percentage of belief in DNA evidence correlates to the *CSI* effect.

Following our ABA program, Dick Wolf, the creator of *Law & Order*, was the lunch speaker. I asked Dick Wolf what he thought of the *CSI* effect. He chuckled and said, of course, that it should be known as a *Law & Order* effect.

The *Law & Order* Effect

Wolf's argument that *Law & Order* preceded *CSI* in covering crime scene evidence is valid. Popular television shows like *Law & Order* improve lawyers' image through viewers' familiarity with the courtroom setting. Based on revisiting the 2006 study, and the fact that you can watch *Law & Order* reruns on television at any hour of the day, I see an effect on lawyers' image. Trust in lawyers increased with the number of *hours* of television watched and the number of *different* television law shows watched. The *Law & Order* effect is as follows: the more television law shows watched, the more individuals trust lawyers.

Those who do not trust lawyers simply do not watch television law shows. They do not like lawyers and they do not like television shows about lawyers. Reliance on television viewing for impressions of the profession is higher if viewers do not personally know any lawyers. Viewers then rely on the information gleaned from television shows to decide whether lawyers are trustworthy. A viewer's trust in lawyers is higher if he or she has hired a lawyer. The viewer could have hired a lawyer to write a contract or a will, or for something other than a lawsuit. The more lawyers viewers know, the better their perceptions, unless, of course, they know or had hired a bad seed.

The Denny Crane Effect

Most of us would expect that Denny Crane and his cohort Alan Shore would tarnish the profession. The results of the 2006 study were not always what you might guess they would be, as I mentioned earlier regarding Denny Crane's and Ally McBeal's characters. I'll call the contrast effect "The Denny Crane effect." The public's reaction to watching pundits discuss celebrity trials like the O.J. Simpson case is consistent with the Denny Crane effect: viewers trust neither Denny Crane nor the pundits. When viewers compare television pundits to their own familiar lawyers, they trust their own counselors more. You might hear a client say, "You aren't like that lawyer on television!" If viewers personally know a lawyer, negative characters from television law shows generally are dismissed.

My Cousin Vinny, Runaway Jury, and other law-themed movies do not produce the same contrast effect on lawyers' image as a Denny Crane character in a weekly series. While both movies and television have extreme characters, the weekly series character has a stronger influence, because character development occurs over time. Movies based on real cases, such as *Erin Brockovich* or *A Civil Action,* affect public perceptions of lawyers' image more than do fiction. Perhaps, in this era of reality television, dramatically telling a true story set in a courtroom is more powerful than telling a fictional story.

Real Quotes from Mock Jurors

Let's listen to what mock jurors have to say. Below are some quotes from mock jurors in the 2006 study, provided in response to what lawyers can do to improve their image:

- "I believe the TV *Law & Order* series has probably done a lot to help already. Some others may have had a detrimental effect." (Caucasian woman in her 60s)
- "Cut the courtroom TV shows. People believe what they see on TV; many think that is reality." (Caucasian woman in her 40s)
- "I think there should be more of the true trial shows that show the legal process from beginning to end. The show that followed the San Diego DA's office through trials was great. I also enjoy the show *Vegas Law* on Court TV." (Caucasian woman in her 20s)
- "TV shows such as *Law & Order,* I think, give lawyers a good image overall. However, to change the image of lawyers to a more positive one, I would not televise high-profile (celebrity) cases. Lawyers in these cases tend to project the negative stereotypes." (Asian-American woman in her 20s)
- "TV shows and movies do depict lawyers somewhat negatively. Maybe they should stop that." (African-American woman in her 20s)

- "Instead of just showing or talking about the shady, seedy ones on TV news or shows, they can show some honest ones who actually want to find justice." (Caucasian woman in her 20s)
- "Show programs where the attorney fights against a corrupt system against all odds and wins!" (Hispanic woman in her 30s)
- "They need some good PR; TV usually shows them as greedy or dumb." (Caucasian woman in her 60s)
- "Pop culture and the entertainment world [are] too soft on the image of lawyers. The image of lawyers needs to be portrayed more realistically and [be] less flattering, certainly not more so. Lawyers are boring and I generally hate shows dealing with the legal profession." (Caucasian male in his 40s)

Determining Verdicts in Real Trials

Television law series influence trials because jurors have acquired greater expectations—for better storytelling and graphics—about trials. Graphics displayed in opening statements better explain concepts. Today's technology makes it possible for jurors to comprehend more complex medical evidence and visually compare differences, especially in technical areas like prior art in patent cases or construction defects.

Myths like "the case is decided by jury selection" and "jurors have made up their minds by opening statement" have some truth inasmuch as the better-prepared trial team is more persuasive from the get-go. Nevertheless, if the evidence in a case seems balanced, jurors will change their minds throughout the trial. We hear in juror interviews that change happens. Some jurors gather more data than others, and do not make up their minds until they hear all the evidence. Some jurors wait until they hear other jurors in deliberations. Some cling to their early perceptions, regardless of the evidence. Experiences are a stronger determinant of verdicts than are attitudes. Individuals are products of their genetic makeup and environment. Events and cognitive processing shape their attitudes. Attitudes shift, but experience lasts forever.

Some jurors conjure "facts" that do not exist in the case. They say, "what if . . ." and draw instances from their own experience. In the hundreds of cases that we have studied, there are common obstacles. Viewpoints about insurance companies and about punishing corporations vary. Some jurors do not like insurance companies. Of course, there also are jurors who strive to keep insurance rates down. Other jurors add dollars to the damages even if the verdict form does not ask for additional compensation or punitive damages.

Although 90 percent of respondents in the 2006 Los Angeles venue study believe there are too many frivolous lawsuits, overall there is good news for the law profession. Lawyers are seen as helpful to our society by 82 percent of the public. People who believe that lawyers are helpful and who do not believe lawyer jokes trust lawyers more. Several court-related experiences, such as having been a civil juror or a plaintiff, make a difference in increasing trust in lawyers.

Current Events

Current events affect trials, and most television law shows draw from current events. Local crises, such as fires, floods, hurricanes, tornados, or school shootings, draw a community together. If a tragedy occurs, jurors bond more readily. In a case where a homeowner claims construction defects, the jurors who know devastation from fire or floods may see the case differently than those in another venue. High rates of mortgage foreclosures and high gas prices affect suburbs. The jury consultant studies how those factors impinge on the community and helps fine-tune the lawyer's presentation to be more persuasive. Local color usually is a nuance.

Many jurors watch reality television and newsmagazine shows such as *60 Minutes, Dateline,* and *20/20.* The newsmagazines generally cast a negative light on defendants. Producers looking for stories of possible misdeeds by corporations often tell just one side of the story and poison the jury pool. *Dateline* covered a story on automobile rollovers and Firestone tire defects. The next day we picked a jury in Los Angeles for a lawsuit involving a different tire manufacturer. We looked at the jury questionnaires and gleaned that a majority of the jurors had heard of the Firestone incidents. It did not make sense to eliminate all the jurors who had heard of Firestone's quandary because, in essence, we would have been left with a less-educated pool. During voir dire the defense lawyer did a remarkable job by focusing on the cause of the tire separation, the jurors' experiences with driving, and sympathy factors. Once jurors talked of their experiences with road conditions, the obstacle was overcome.

Often news stories provide incomplete coverage about a case or verdict—for example, the McDonald's coffee spill, General Motors' truck fires, claims about the harmful effects of tobacco, silicone breast implants, reactions to fen/phen, automobile rollovers, defective tires, and Vioxx. In focus groups and voir dire, the McDonald's award inevitably comes up. Jurors often mention it as a gross injustice to the legal system. To be effective in voir dire, lawyers need to know jurors' perceptions of the news coverage and television law shows. Sometimes giving the jurors additional information about the case can change attitudes. Other times, the issues are best left alone.

Perceptions of Jury Consultants: Television versus Reality

Jurors are a collection of strangers. Effective voir dire is the key to deciding which jurors to keep or strike. A jury consultant assesses jurors' experiences, attitudes, knowledge, abilities, and skills for comprehension of the case. Real jury consultants (unlike Gene Hackman's Rankin Fitch in *Runaway Jury*) don't blow up jurors' houses. Unlike the fictional juror who suspiciously got on the jury, real jurors are randomly selected from the jury commissioners' wheel. It is not possible for a juror to select a case in which to render a verdict.

Secondary to personal experience, jurors' presumed knowledge of the law factors into deliberations. Most jurors obtain their knowledge of the law from television. Jurors have heard or read something about the legal system prior to their jury service. Virtually all jurors watch television. Some jurors are addicted to depictions of trials à la *Ally McBeal, Boston Legal,* or *Judge Judy.* John Grisham's popular novels often show up on the laps of jurors waiting to be called into the courtroom. Whether or not television drama accurately shows the courtroom, these depictions become part of the jurors' knowledge base. What matters to the outcome of the trial are the perspectives that the jurors bring to the deliberations.

In the social science arena, trial consultants measure media influences through venue studies. If there is no venue change, we suggest ways to attenuate the negative influences at trial. If there has been a toxic spill, chances are the newspapers and television stations in the vicinity of the venue have covered the story and jurors have seen the coverage. Jurors may have read *A Civil Action* or seen the movie. A smart plaintiff's lawyer brings out the negative media influences if the judge allows it. Here is an example.

> PLAINTIFF'S LAWYER: Ms. Jones, have you seen the movie *A Civil Action*?
>
> JUROR: Yes.
>
> PLAINTIFF'S LAWYER: Do you remember when the families of the children who were killed weren't allowed to testify?
>
> JUROR: No, I'd forgotten about that.
>
> PLAINTIFF'S LAWYER: Do you think that it is fair that the victims or the victims' families are not always in court to speak for themselves?
>
> JUROR: Fair? They should tell their story!

The good defense lawyer must turn such responses to his or her advantage. In the example above, the defense counsel might ask, "Ms. Jones, you said earlier that you thought that the families should have been given an opportunity to tell their story. In *A Civil Action*, the trial was divided into two stages to separate the cause of the spill from any sympathy about these children who may or may not have been affected by the spill. Can you separate the cause of a toxic spill from sympathy?"

In conclusion, public perceptions of trust in lawyers are increased through watching television law shows and watching real lawyers on television. People who watch a lot of television law shows trust lawyers more than individuals who do not watch such shows. People who do not like lawyers do not watch television law shows or real lawyers on television. They rely more heavily on negative stereotypes.

Jury experts have a beneficial impact throughout the trial that goes beyond understanding television influences. Jury consultants help tailor voir dire questions, opening statements, graphics, verdict forms, and closing arguments. And yes, some jury consultants help with wardrobe, too.

Endnotes

1. See Charles N. Rosenberg's chapter "27 Years as a Television Legal Adviser and Counting."

2. http://www.verdictsuccess.com/pdf/Media_Influences_on_Public_Perceptions_of_Lawyers.pdf (last visited Jan. 15, 2009).

CHAPTER 4

Is There an Honest Lawyer in the Box? Legal Ethics on TV

CARRIE MENKEL-MEADOW

When did issues of legal ethics first appear on TV? Are you thinking of a particular TV show from the "golden age," such as *Perry Mason* or *The Defenders?* If so, you would be wrong. The lawyers on those programs were generally models of good, if unrealistic, behavior (more on that below).

Legal ethics first became an issue on TV during the congressional hearings following the Watergate break-in of 1972.[1] John Dean, then counsel to President Nixon, appeared before an investigative committee and brought with him a now-mostly-forgotten list of key players in the White House. Some of the names had stars; others did not. To the surprise of the committee members, Dean said that the starred names were involved in the cover-up of illegal activities. A great many of them were lawyers. They included Dean, President Nixon himself, Attorney General John Mitchell, some other very important government officials, and a few lower-level campaign operatives, such as Donald Segretti.[2]

When the dust cleared from the hearings and prosecutions (whose results included incarceration for some and disbarment for others, including President Nixon), the American Bar

Association responded to the growing public dissatisfaction with lawyers by imposing a mandatory legal ethics requirement for all law students.[3] Thus began the "big bang" of study, disciplinary enforcement, and TV viewing of legal ethics.

I was among those who graduated just before this requirement was imposed in the mid-1970s, but like many who had gone to law school to seek justice, I had been marked by reading about and watching the legal ethics of fictional lawyers, like the canonical Atticus Finch of *To Kill a Mockingbird*,[4] who took on an unpopular client and became a hero of the civil rights movement generation. Harper Lee and Gregory Peck probably sent thousands of young people—aspiring Atticus Finches—to law school to seek justice and right legal wrongs.[5]

The power of media to dramatize and educate was not lost on me or on the new generation of TV writers about lawyers. The films and television programs that came after Watergate marked a great change in the depiction of legal ethics on both the small and large screen. Many of us who write about law and popular culture have tried to understand and explain why the depictions of lawyers changed from "good" to "evil."[6] Why did popular-culture images change from legal heroism to legal cynicism? Does TV reflect an accurate depiction of increasingly unscrupulous lawyers in the real world, or is reality better than fiction? Does TV influence public opinion about law and lawyers, or the behavior of real lawyers?

Popular-culture depictions of lawyers' ethical failings may have resonated to an audience hearing about Charles Keating and the Lincoln Savings and Loan scandal, as well as Watergate (all before more recent scandals like Enron and MCI cast accountants and corporate executives in similarly sinister lights). Or, as I was once advised when serving as an ethics adviser to a TV program, "We can't do it ethically—that has no drama to it." In the earlier years of lawyer television programming, writers were writers; now a good number, if not the majority, are former lawyers who draw on what they have seen or imagined in their actual practice. The two most famous of these are David E. Kelley, writer and/or creator of *Picket Fences, L.A. Law, Ally McBeal, The Practice,* and *Boston Legal,* and Bill Fordes, a former New York assistant district attorney who is a writer and producer for *Law & Order.*

Legal Ethics in Film and Television

I began teaching legal ethics just before *L.A. Law* came on the air.[7] That show was a treasure trove of teaching hypotheticals about legal ethics. I used to write my own scripts and role-plays for use in class, which were, like *Law & Order*, "ripped from the headlines." I was thankful when *L.A. Law* came on the air, because I could defer to the professional TV writers for at least some material to spark student interest in dry analysis of the Model Rules of Professional Conduct.

I spent years spotting ethical issues in the movies,[8] including my all-time favorite example, Paul Newman's Frank Galvin in *The Verdict*, who turned down a settlement offer without consulting his client. However, I quickly saw that TV could plumb the fullness of a character's *character* and develop it over time. It could also treat ethical issues in much greater depth, both at the macro level (Whom should I represent? What kind of lawyer/person do I want do be?) and at the micro level (What should I do in this instance?).

Like the Dickensian novel issued in installments, a TV series allows action to take place over an extended period of time (a season of at least 13 weeks and several which lasted many years). This allows the writers to develop the characters and to allow viewers to speculate about what will happen next. Characters can grow and change, like Helen Gamble did as the lead prosecutor on *The Practice*.[9] Gamble morphed from a no-holds-barred prosecutor into one who chastised her junior colleagues for ethical misadventures, such as when the overly ambitious Richard Bay "overcoached" a witness and produced perjurious testimony.

Other commentators have suggested that, because TV shows last longer and require ongoing advertising, the characters must be more "likable" than those in the movies to bring viewers back.[10] I would argue they do not need to be likable (especially if they play within an ensemble—think Arnie Becker), just interesting. Character change itself is an important organizing principle for many TV shows (think of those great soaps *Dallas* and *Dynasty*). An ethical dilemma (whether to turn over an incriminating piece of evidence, whether to discredit a truthful witness, whether to sleep with the judge or juror or opposing counsel) forces the characters to make hard choices and makes professionals seem more like regular human beings.

Bill Fordes suggests that the best thing a TV script can do with a small repertory cast, such as that of *Law & Order*, is to develop as many opinions about what to do as there are actors in the program. *Law & Order* scripts frequently include arguments about ethical issues between Jack McCoy, his various female second chairs, and the District Attorney.[11] Indeed, the depiction of ethical issues in lawyer shows is a good way for the viewer to confront larger personal, as well as professional, issues: When is it appropriate to lie or dissemble? When do the ends justify the means? What does personal–professional loyalty require of us? How far would we go to seek justice? What would we do for others that we would not do for ourselves? How should we treat others we interact with in life?

Ethical Issues on TV Lawyer Shows

Lawyers on TV often take ethical shortcuts, either to help solve the problems of their clients or to achieve social or individual justice. The stories juxtapose formal ethical or procedural rules against more foundational notions of justice. Verdicts announce the "just" result, even if they are secured by tainted evidence or inappropriate cross-examination or closing arguments. One commentator has labeled this ability to manipulate the rules to achieve greater justice "moral pluck,"[12] and there is more moral pluck demonstrated on recent TV programs than on their formalistic predecessors.

Indeed, many practicing lawyers believe that the pithy (and often inappropriate) closing arguments depicted on *L.A. Law* and *Law & Order* (vouching for clients, casting aspersions on other parties, directly addressing jurors and witnesses) have changed the expectations of jurors about how such arguments should be conducted. Indeed, many prosecutors believe that television is responsible for the "*CSI* effect," according to which jurors believe that the prosecutors cannot prove a case beyond a reasonable doubt without introducing forensic evidence.

Ethical issues in TV law programs have included:

- Use of deception, misleading conduct, and outright lies
- Too much zeal, or its cousins, too little zeal and/or incompetence
- Conflicts of interest

- Failure to communicate appropriately with clients by failing to inform them of settlement offers or failing to allow them to make fundamental choices, such as whether they should testify
- Coaching of witnesses[13] (which is prohibited in virtually every other legal system but our own)
- Coercing statements, confessions, or actions from clients or opposite parties, lawyers, and witnesses
- Sexual misconduct, a perennial favorite on TV, involving the unlikely pairings of lawyers and judges (*The Practice*'s Jimmy Berluti and Judge Roberta Kittleson), clients and lawyers (*L.A. Law*'s Arnie Becker and his divorce clients), and lawyers on opposite sides of the same case (Helen and Bobby on *The Practice*)
- Use of perjured testimony
- Giving questionable or wrongful advice to a client
- Falsely suggesting alternative guilty parties or theories (the infamous "Plan B" of *The Practice*)
- Stealing, moving, or making up evidence
- Pressuring clients to accept pleas or civil settlements for a variety of bad reasons
- Manipulating fees
- Betraying trust

Ethical issues on TV are played to illustrate both big-picture issues, like the nature of justice and to whom lawyers owe their duties (the client, the truth, or the rest of society), and the everyday issues that lawyers face, such as whether to call or cross-examine a witness, whether to produce a document in discovery, whether to mislead an unsuspecting witness or object of investigation, what language to put in a transactional document, or what to counsel a client to do.

Both *L.A. Law* and *The Practice* used lawyer disciplinary hearings to dramatize ethical issues (often putting them inside the substantive case instead of in a separate State Bar hearing where they belong). Ally McBeal was subject to a disciplinary hearing in Massachusetts because of her emotional outbursts and erratic behavior. An episode of *Eli Stone* included a full-blown disciplinary proceeding before the California State Bar, challenging the title character's capacity to practice law, given his singing in court. Eli has an inoperable brain aneurysm, which eventually allows him to make an Americans with Disabilities Act discrimination claim to keep his license. The hearing raises interesting issues of what a competent lawyer should be able to do and what should happen to lawyers (and doctors) who lie and deceive. Because of his aneurysm, young Eli Stone has begun to care about his clients, and not just about winning cases, satirizing the assumption that in the civil law world of the big firm, anybody who is "well" would think only about making money.

Moral Issues of Criminal Defense in the "Golden Age" and in Contemporary Drama

In TV's "golden age," *Perry Mason* and *The Defenders*[14] did the right things, exposed the truth, put the state to its proof in criminal matters, got the innocent acquitted, and pointed a finger at the guilty party. In *The Practice,* the technique of developing doubt so that a jury would not convict, by suggesting that someone other than the firm's client actually committed the crime, was referred to as "Plan B." Over the years of its use, Plan B became more and more sinister, and it is safe to say that Plan B has probably made it into the common vocabulary of lawyers and viewers. In reality, some forms of Plan B are used in courtrooms every day, and their use may be quite legitimate if the doubt is real.

More importantly, *The Practice* has been one of the few modern TV programs to actually present discussions about the purpose and function of criminal defense work. An especially memorable example was the tearful and eloquent explanation by Eugene Young (actor Steve Harris) to his son that he defends sometimes guilty (and black) criminal defendants to ensure the system stays fair and to challenge its continuing racism.[15] Jack McCoy's search for truth and fair convictions on *Law & Order* depicts an upstanding prosecutor who usually counsels both his seniors and juniors on how to do things the correct way.

Only beginning in the 2008–2009 season, in which Jack is promoted to District Attorney, are we allowed to see his more human (and political) side. The real world of politics enters into the search for justice, as in an episode that thinly disguises the facts of New York Governor Elliot Spitzer's fall from grace. In the episode, the governor successfully blackmails and outmaneuvers our hero. The departure from McCoy's usual moralistic character is all the more dramatic because he has to bend to his new and more politicized role. Similarly, the less scrupulous

Sebastian Stark, a Los Angeles prosecutor on *Shark*,[16] will stop at almost nothing to "get his man." He bends virtually every ethical rule in the book. Moreover, his particular form of macho mentoring is used to indoctrinate the young and ambitious lawyers who work for him and who seek to climb legal hierarchies of fame and power, if not money.

These programs demonstrate not just ethical decision making, but also ethical learning, as mentors shape the professional development of younger professionals. (This is also a common theme on TV's medical programs). Occasionally a younger lawyer manages to challenge the suggested course of action of the senior (as when, on *The Practice*, Jimmy and Rebecca challenge Bobby and Lindsay both on choices of clients and tactics and strategies employed in particular cases). On *Boston Legal*[17] we see disagreements about strategies, tactics, ethics, and politics in the testy relationships between Denny Crane, a political conservative who likes to take on controversial cases, Shirley Schmidt, who has re-joined the firm she founded in order to "fix it," and the younger and ethics-defying Alan Shore.

Criminal vs. Civil Law Shows

Criminal law shows are especially good at dealing with major issues of ethics and justice, such as assessing whether worthy ends can justify unworthy means. How far can the prosecutor go to convict someone known to be guilty? Can he or she use untruthful witnesses, threaten codefendants, talk to represented parties, hide exculpatory evidence? What tactics can a defense lawyer use to win his or her case? Ellenor Frutt in *The Practice* altered evidence in several cases, using means including washing bloody and incriminating clothes and encouraging a client to drink more after an accident to frustrate a breathalyzer test. Her partners in the Bobby Donnell firm often argued blatantly false facts (and unethically "vouched" for their own clients) in closing arguments.

In shows that concentrate on civil cases, the fundamental issue is ethical decision making versus serving clients and making money. *L.A. Law* dramatized cases involving divorce, personal injury, environmental issues, discrimination, and ordinary business disputes, along with a few entertainment cases (a nod to the firm's filmic home). The firm's patriarch, Leland McKenzie, led firm meetings in the opening moments of the show, enforcing discipline and good judgment from above. The writers of *L.A. Law* were able to deploy its large and talented cast of characters to dramatize disputes about litigating versus settling, how much to "prepare" their clients' testimony, and what to do about secreting witnesses and documentary evidence. Arnie Becker's extreme zealousness and unethical behavior in divorce cases (not to mention his sexual promiscuity) were offset by explicit discussions between Ann Kelsey and her husband Stuart Markowitz about the appropriateness of taking particularly controversial cases and what tactics were appropriate. Both *The Practice* and *Boston Legal* have featured law firm discussions and disagreements about whether to take particular matters for the fees they might earn.

Must a Good Lawyer Be a Good Person?

In their own ways, all of the TV shows depicting lawyers ask the never-fully-resolved question: must a good lawyer also be a good person? The shows vary dramatically in how much they present the personal lives of their characters. *Ally McBeal* is located at one end of the continuum; it mostly dealt with sexual and social relationships but presented very little law.[18] *Law & Order* holds down the other end; after almost 20 years on the air, we know very little about the lawyers' private lives. *Eli Stone* is now explicitly asking these questions, but *L.A. Law, The Practice,* and *Boston Legal* (all David Kelley shows) probably have done the best job of demonstrating variations on its themes.

Personal conflicts of interest abound on television. The episodes often focus on narratives in which lawyers who are lovers, marriage partners, close friends, parents and children, in-laws, former marital partners, and former professional law partners appear on opposite sides of the same case. In the real world, of course, issues relating to conflict of interest are more likely to arise from prior legal relationships (such as lawyers who switch firms and find themselves on opposite sides of cases). TV shows, however, like to "juice" up the conflicts issues by concentrating on sexual, familial, and social relationships between lawyers on opposite sides of the same matter.

Many stories dwell on the way in which lawyers treat their family members, colleagues, and assistants at work. Secretary Rebecca Washington goes to law school and graduates to become a member of the firm in *The Practice*, but not before she has raised numerous questions about how the lawyers in the firm treat her, each other, and their clients. Often the "lay" assistant is the conscience of the practice, reminding the professional that there is a higher, perhaps more important, justice. Eli Stone's assistant often has been used to provide personal, moral, and ethical commentary.

The increasing number of women lawyers on these programs in the last two decades has also dramatized issues of parenting and the tensions of work–family balance. Who is humanly responsible for whom—clients, employees, colleagues, bosses, and juniors, as well as loved ones, family members, and opposing lawyers and their clients—is a relatively new and broader development in the depiction of the lawyer's moral universe.

The TV series is also an appropriate forum for demonstrating the camaraderie and colleagueship of group practice. While movies typically explore the developmental and moral challenges faced by individuals, a television series shows us the interplay of many people sharing decisions of, caring for, and mentoring each other in the workplace. *Trial by Jury* (a short-lived spin-off of *Law & Order*) was especially strong in demonstrating the group life of young prosecutors learning and living together. A TV series framed around a repertory cast can explore the context and situations in which moral and ethical decisions are made, often providing a multigenerational perspective on difficult professional dilemmas.

Most poignantly, TV shows demonstrate how partners at work shape and help each other, often caring for and "redeeming"[19] their colleagues and friends who make mistakes. On *The Practice*, Bobby and Lindsay helped each other through many professional and personal setbacks. Also on that program, Jimmy Berluti, who came from a less prestigious background than his colleagues, was nurtured and trained, and Rebecca Washington moved from secretary to lawyer with a social conscience, who returned the training by teaching her senior colleagues about social justice.

Conclusion

Many law professors have learned to teach legal ethics through TV shows.[20] Whole courses and curricula have been based on *L.A. Law*, *The Practice*, and now *Boston Legal*. These programs demonstrate that life is complicated, legal ethics are complex, and "doing the right thing" is not always so clear. We are able and privileged to watch actors make choices that do not hurt real people and to think about what we might do in similar situations. For all the humor, overdone drama, and occasional lack of realism, legal ethics on TV is enlightening, instructive, redemptive, and certainly more interesting than reading formalistic and disembodied ethics rules. In my view, perhaps the most instructive way to think about difficult ethical dilemmas is to watch them dramatized on television and ask what you would have done if you had been in the same spot. [21]

Endnotes

1. The hearings were conducted and transmitted live (in the days before C-SPAN) in 1974. Several congressional committees explored various issues related to the break-in, ultimately including the impeachment of President Nixon. Nixon resigned before formal proceedings to impeach him were begun. *See, e.g.*, JOHN DEAN III, BLIND AMBITION (1976).

2. Segretti was disciplined by the California State Bar for his "fraternity pranks" during the campaign. Segretti v. State Bar, 15 Cal. 3d 878 (1976). Mr. Segretti may have been one of the first disciplined lawyers to be ordered to take a legal ethics course as a sanction for misbehavior.

3. ABA Standards for Approval of Law Schools, Standard 302 (a) (5), 2005–2006, *available at* http://www.abanet.org/legaled/standards/2005-2006 standardsbook.pdf.

4. HARPER LEE, TO KILL A MOCKINGBIRD (1960). Gregory Peck starred in the classic movie version (1962).

5. *See, e.g,.* MILNER BALL, THE WORD AND THE LAW (1995).

6. *See, e.g.*, Michael Asimow, *Bad Lawyers in the Movies*, 24 NOVA L. REV. 533 (2000).

7. See Phil Meyer's chapter "Revisiting *L.A. Law.*"

8. By my count the movie with the most ethical violations or dilemmas is *Class Action* (1991). As a bonus question on an exam, I asked a group of my legal ethics students to count the number of ethical quandaries in that film; we came up with over 30, including conflicts of interest (father and daughter on opposite sides of the same case, document destruction and deception, witness tampering, consultations with represented parties, etc.).

9. See Jeffrey Thomas's chapter "*The Practice:* Debunking Television Myths and Stereotypes."

10. Naomi Mezey & Mark C. Niles, *Screening the Law: Ideology and Law in American Popular Culture*, 28 COLUM. J. L. & ARTS 91 (2005).

11. See Shannon Mader's chapter *"Law & Order."*

12. William Simon, *Moral Pluck: Legal Ethics in Popular Culture,* 101 COLUM. L. REV. 421 (2001).

13. The classic depiction of witness coaching is the movie *Anatomy of a Murder* (1959).

14. See Francis Nevins's chapter *"Perry Mason"* and David Ginsburg's chapter *"The Defenders:* TV Lawyers and Controversy in the New Frontier."

15. *The Practice,* "Cross-Fire" (March 4, 1999) and *The Practice,* "Target Practice" (March 7, 1999).

16. See Nancy Rapoport's chapter "Swimming with *Shark."*

17. See Corinne Brinkerhoff's chapter "Reality Bites: *Boston Legal's* Creative License with the Law."

18. See Cassandra Sharp's chapter *"Ally McBeal*—Life and Love in the Law."

19. *See* Paul Bergman, *The Movie Lawyers' Guide to Redemptive Legal Practice,* 48 UCLA L. REV. 1393 (2001).

20. Steven H. Goldberg, *Bringing The Practice to the Classroom: An Answer to the Professionalism Problem,* 50 J. LEGAL EDUC. 414 (2000).

21. *See* Carrie Menkel-Meadow, *Telling Stories in School: Using Case Studies and Stories to Teach Legal Ethics,* 69 FORDHAM L. REV. 787 (2000).

PART II

Foundations of Law on Television

The history of the law-on-television genre begins with two pioneering shows of the late 1950s and mid 1960s—*Perry Mason* and *The Defenders*—that ran back-to-back on CBS and laid the foundation for all that came later.

Perry Mason is a true icon of American popular culture. He was a stolid, asexual drone who lacked any private life and seemed unconcerned about making a living. His clients were *always* innocent, and he *always* relied on brilliant detective work and inspired cross-examination (usually in a preliminary hearing) to nail the guilty party. The police and prosecutor *always* had the wrong murderer. Such hopelessly formulaic narrative structure and predictable characters could not survive in present-day television. Yet *Perry Mason* (whether in his print, radio, television, or movie phases) proved to be tremendously profitable, and he, along with his Southern-fried clone *Matlock*, have been highly successful in syndication. You can catch Perry and Ben just about every day on cable in major markets.

The Defenders could not have been more different from *Perry Mason*. At one level, however, the two shows were similar. Like Perry Mason's office, the father-and-son firm of Lawrence and Kenneth Preston seemed indifferent to fees, and, like Perry himself, the lawyers appeared to lack any semblance of a private life. However, *The Defenders* was about *issues.* Every episode tackled a new, cutting-edge social issue, always from a liberal point of view. What could lawyers do to help a client who found himself on the anti-Communist blacklist? (Very little, it turned out.) *The Defenders* demonstrated that a show based on thorny social issues can draw decent audiences, if it is packaged within a law-on-television format that involves familiar and likeable characters and some adversarial conflict between lawyers. Today's lawyer television shows (including *Law & Order, JAG,* and *Boston Legal*) often focus on sensitive and controversial social issues, wrapped up in a lawyer story. *The Defenders* showed them the way. The show is fondly remembered by those greybeards who watched it back in the 1960s, but, sad to say, it is unavailable today either in DVD form or syndication. Let's hope that changes soon!

In 1980, the classic docudrama *Gideon's Trumpet* was presented by the *Hallmark Hall of Fame.* Like *The Defenders, Gideon's Trumpet* showed that people will watch a television program about major legal and social issues (in this case, whether every criminal defendant has a right to have a lawyer provided by the state). *Gideon's Trumpet* set a standard for legal docudrama that has seldom been matched.

Finally, *L.A. Law* broke the genre wide open in 1986. Lawyers suddenly became real human beings with personal lives. Law was a business, practiced in a firm, and it had to earn a profit. The office was a place for romance as well as for work. Some lawyers at Mackenzie Brackman were admirable human beings; others were anything but. Some of the lawyers were women and some were ethnic minorities. All were multidimensional. Lawyers worked on a variety of interesting civil and criminal cases and clients weren't always so nice. It turned out that millions of people enjoyed the legal–soap-opera format of *L.A. Law,* and its commercial success spawned the incredible variety of dramatic law shows that have appeared over the last 20 years.

CHAPTER 5

Perry Mason

FRANCIS M. NEVINS

Erle Stanley Gardner

Gardner's Bio

The creator of the best-known lawyer character of all time had a background remarkably free of legal ties. Erle Stanley Gardner was born on July 17, 1889, in the small town of Malden, Massachusetts, to a mother whose ancestors came over on the Mayflower and a civil-engineer father who was descended from a long line of sea captains. This boy, whose earliest years coincided with the heyday of social Darwinism, was a born combatant with a boundless zest for competition and an unstoppable drive to succeed. In 1899, while in fourth grade, he wrote a school essay on the Greek myth of Atalanta, whose theme is that whoever loses the race dies. Later that year, his family moved west, settling in 1902 in a prosperous California mining town. He spent his early teens traveling with his father through remote stretches of California, Oregon, and the Klondike, and developed a zest for outdoor living that was to become a hallmark of his fiction.

In school, Gardner was a maverick and a troublemaker. He earned pocket money by boxing in unlicensed matches, and his interest in law seems to have grown out of hunting for

Perry Mason

Created by:
- Erle Stanley Gardner

Aired:
- September 21, 1957–May 22, 1966, CBS

Cast:
- Raymond Burr (Perry Mason)
- Barbara Hale (Della Street)
- William Talman (Hamilton Burger)
- Ray Collins (Lt. Arthur Tragg)
- William Hopper (Paul Drake)

Awards:
- Raymond Burr, Emmy for Outstanding Performance by an Actor in a Series (1961)
- Raymond Burr, Emmy for Best Actor in a Leading Role in a Dramatic Series (1959)
- Barbara Hale, Emmy for Best Supporting Actress in a Dramatic Series (1959)
- Most Popular Overseas Drama, Logie Awards (1959)

loopholes in the California statutes that made prizefighting illegal. After completing high school in 1909, Gardner was admitted to Valparaiso University in Indiana, but was soon expelled for slugging a professor. He went back to California, apprenticed himself to one established lawyer after another, and in 1911 passed the state bar. Over the next 20 years he discovered that litigation was a form of combat at which he could excel, and his courtroom tactics, usually employed on behalf of the Chinese community in Oxnard, earned him a reputation as one of the state's most flamboyant trial lawyers. Everything in his bag of tricks and courtroom fireworks he eventually handed over to his fictional alter ego, Perry Mason.

Pulp Fiction

Long before turning to courtroom novels, Gardner had become known as one of the most ingenious and prolific purveyors of shorter fiction for the so-called pulp magazines that made up most Americans' entertainment in the years before radio and TV. *Black Mask, Top-Notch, Argosy, West, Clues, Air Adventure, Detective Fiction Weekly, Three Star, Prize Detective, Detective Action Stories, Gangland Stories, Western Trails, Gang World, Dime Detective*—the entire list of magazines in which Gardner published would fill most of this page. "For a period of several years," he said, "I pounded out stories on the typewriter at the rate of a novelette every third day, and at the same time practiced law, much of it trying cases in front of juries, which I can testify is a very exhausting occupation." His nightly writing stint usually lasted from ten at night until around two in the morning. "I would sleep about three hours a night, then I would take a shower, shave, pull up my typewriter, and write until it came time to go to the office. It's a wonder that I didn't kill myself with overwork. If I finished one story at twelve-thirty at night, I couldn't go to bed without starting another." Eventually he switched to a primitive dictating machine and set himself a quota of 100,000 words a month.

Writing so much so fast, Gardner often lost track of various elements in his plots. He claimed that the breakneck pace of his tales made it next to impossible for readers to catch the flubs: "After all, on a trotting horse who is going to see the difference? The main thing is to keep the horse trotting and the pace fast and furious." He wrote a surprising number of westerns and science fiction tales, but most of his pulp stories were contemporary crime thrillers with "good bad man" protagonists in the vein of silent western film star William S. Hart. Legal elements sometimes appear in his stories, but not to an overwhelming extent. What almost all Gardner protagonists have in common is that they are scam artists.

The *Perry Mason* Novels—Hired Gun

In 1931, during the pit of the Depression, Gardner made over $20,000 from pulp writing on top of his income as a lawyer, but this success almost killed him. Hoping to free himself for the nomadic life he wanted, he decided to cut back his torrent of wordage for the pulps and start writing, or rather dictating, novels for hardcover publication. The result was Perry Mason, who debuted in *The Case of the Velvet Claws* (1933) and eventually made his creator one of the wealthiest and most widely read authors in the world.

Gardner never claimed that he wrote with literary skill or grace. His characterizations and descriptions tend to be perfunctory, and are often reduced to a handful of lines recycled in book after book. Indeed, virtually every word not within quotation marks could be left out of any Perry Mason novel and little would be lost. For what vivifies these novels is the sheer readability, the breakneck pacing, the convoluted plotting, the fireworks displays of courtroom tactics based largely on Gardner's own law practice, and the dialogue, that inimitable Gardner dialogue, whose every line, whether spoken in or out of court, is a jab in a complex form of oral combat.

The earliest Perry Mason novels are set in the dog-eat-dog milieu of a free enterprise system in the depths of its worst depression, and Gardner, born scrapper that he was, revels in it. The Mason of these books is a tiger in the social Darwinian jungle—totally self-reliant, asking no favors, despising the weaklings who want society to care for them, and willing to take any risk for a client, no matter how unfairly the client plays the game with him. On the first page of *Velvet Claws* we are told of Mason, "He gave the impression of being a thinker and a fighter, a man who could work with infinite patience to jockey an adversary into just the right position and then finish him with one terrific punch." A few pages later comes this telling exchange between Mason and the beautiful but treacherous woman who has consulted him:

MASON: People come to me because they need me. They come to me
          because they want to hire me for what I can do.

WOMAN: Just what is it that you do, Mr. Mason?

MASON: I fight!

Again and again in these early novels, Mason says of himself, "I am a paid gladiator." If Gardner had wanted to show off his erudition, he might have had his character call himself the servant of the "bad man" Holmes had evoked in *The Path of the Law*, who cares only for the requirements of the law rather than morality. If he had wanted to link back to his western stories, he might have had his hero describe himself as a hired gun. In her first incarnation, Mason's secretary Della Street was cut from the same cloth. In the words of Gardner's publisher Thayer Hobson, Della was "a gal who would poison her mother, eat unslaked lime, and twist a baby's wrist for the man she cared for."

Later in *Velvet Claws*, Mason outlines his creed to private detective Paul Drake: "I'm a lawyer. I'm only presenting the defendant's side. If the District Attorney would be fair, then I could be fair. I use everything I can in order to get an acquittal. My clients aren't blameless. Many of them are crooks. Probably a lot of them are guilty. That's not for me to determine. That's for the jury to determine." One of the unpleasant aspects of the earliest Gardner novels is that Mason thinks nothing of using as his tools the "little people" whose financial desperation forces them to accept almost any risk in return for a little money. In *Velvet Claws* he also loosens the tongue of a hostile witness by pretending to frame him for a murder, and manipulates estate funds to prevent a murderer who is not his client from financing his defense. In *The Case of the Howling Dog* (1934), he twists evidence to get an acquittal for a client he knows to be guilty so that she can never be tried again. "I'm not a judge and I'm not a jury," he reminds Della Street. "I'm a lawyer, a partisan whose solemn duty it is to present the case of the defendant in its strongest light." An ambivalent Della tells him, "You are a cross between a saint and a devil." "All men are," he replies.

"I don't ask a man if he's guilty or innocent," Mason tells newly elected district attorney Hamilton Burger in *The Case of the Counterfeit Eye* (1935). "Guilty or innocent, he's entitled to his day in court, *but if*

I should find one of my clients was really guilty of murder and wasn't legally or morally justified, I'd make that client plead guilty. If a person is morally justified in killing, I'll save that person from the legal penalty if it's possible to do so." Clearly Mason is referring to what he did for his guilty client in *Howling Dog*. But in a letter to his publishers, Gardner expressed bitter resentment that he had been compelled for commercial reasons to water down his Darwinian notion of law practice. For the original, unsanitized Perry Mason, "my client right or wrong" is the prime, and indeed the only, directive.

How did that character mutate into the radically different Mason of the TV series? The process accelerated around 1937, when the *Saturday Evening Post* began offering big bucks for the right to serialize Gardner's novels before their hardcover appearance. But in return Gardner had to tone down Perry Mason to satisfy the magazine's requirements. He did so in a way that was nothing short of brilliant. He effectively promised his readers that Mason's clients would always be innocent, so that the reader could enjoy the way Mason skated on the thin edge of the law without suffering any moral qualms about the causes he served. This was Gardner's personal "contract with America," which he kept until the day he died.

In *The Case of the Perjured Parrot* (1939), Gardner denounced precisely the kind of lawyer he had originally wanted to portray as a hero. Mason, reading his mail, says to Della, "Oh, Lord, here's another one. A man, who's swindled a bunch of people into buying worthless stock, wants me to prove that he was within the letter of the law. I never take a case unless I'm convinced my client was incapable of committing the crime charged." In the Mason novels dating from the late 1930s to the late 1950s, not only are the clients always innocent, but the ruthlessness is muted, "love interest" plays a stronger role, and Mason becomes increasingly more stodgy, eventually refusing even to drive above the speed limit. Nevertheless, the oral combat remains breathlessly exciting, the pace frantic, and the plots twisty as ever.

In the 1950s, Gardner was still allowing millions of readers to delight in Mason's lawyerly hocus-pocus without moral twinges, while creating ingenious variations on his standard themes. *The Case of the Hesitant Hostess* (1953) begins in mid-trial and is built almost entirely around Mason's desperate attempts to demolish the chief witness against the derelict defendant. In *The Case of the Terrified Typist* (1956), Gardner turns handsprings to keep to his contract despite a jury verdict against Mason's client and in the teeth of the fact that this defendant is both guilty and morally unjustified. This was the Mason of the print media at the time he first came to television.

Perry Mason on Television

Perry Mason began its long prime-time run on CBS in the fall of 1957. Paisano Productions, the company that produced the series, was named after Gardner's Rancho del Paisano in Temecula, California, which in turn had been named for El Paisano, one of the dozens of characters Gardner had created for the pulps. Gardner not only owned a controlling interest in the company but also put in long hours closely supervising the scripts and even picked the actor who would embody his hero. Overweight Raymond Burr (1917–1993) had specialized for years in playing hulking *film noir* menaces. Having portrayed the sadistic district attorney in George Stevens's *A Place in the Sun* (1951), Burr was asked to audition for the part of Hamilton Burger in the *Mason* series but insisted on trying out for the title role too. Gardner watched the test, jumped up, and cried: "That's Perry Mason!" Burr reportedly lost between 80 and 100 pounds between that day and the filming of the pilot.

There is no better index of how far Gardner's view of lawyering had changed since the early 1930s than the memoranda he dictated in his capacity as adviser to the TV series. "[O]ne of the first things to do is to start with some character who is to become Perry Mason's client and to make the audience like that character. Therefore when I see these scripts come in [where, although Gardner doesn't put it this way, the client is a Holmesian 'bad man'] I feel that we are selling our character down the river. I want to vomit at the idea of the great Perry Mason with his sense of justice, his basic faith in human nature, descending so low as to be hired to represent a person of that caliber. [I]t is a basic rule of the Perry Mason stories that the audience must want the character to be represented by Perry Mason to come out on top."

Music, Writing, and Acting on *Perry Mason*

Offering the early segments of the series on video several years ago, Columbia House advertised that they were shot in the *film noir* style—

an absurd claim that is almost justified, considering that much of the background music for the first *Perry Mason* episodes was composed by Bernard Herrmann (1911–1975), who was soon to score Alfred Hitchcock's masterpieces *Vertigo* and *Psycho,* and had already written the music for earlier *noirs* like *On Dangerous Ground* and that spiritual godfather of *film noir, Citizen Kane.* Whether in the form of original scores for specific episodes or of "suites" written for the CBS Music Library and later "tracked" into episodes by editors, his music also graced the first seasons of other classic CBS TV series like *Have Gun Will Travel, Rawhide,* and *The Twilight Zone.* Much of the remaining

Courtesy of Photofest.

PERRY MASON
Mason (Raymond Burr) contemplates another devastating cross-examination that will cause the witness to confess to murder.

music for the early *Mason* episodes was composed by René Garriguenc (1908–1998), whose sound, when he wanted it to be, was so much like Herrmann's that even experts are sometimes fooled. The first several minutes of "The Case of the Restless Redhead" (September 21, 1957), the earliest broadcast *Mason* episode, are especially rich in Herrmann/ Garriguenc themes, as are several sequences in "The Case of the Nervous Accomplice" (October 5, 1957).

My favorite example of the music's contribution comes at the climax of "The Case of the Sulky Girl" (October 19, 1957) when, while cross-examining the crucial witness against his innocent client, Mason hands him a set of flash cards and asks him to read from them. A chord sounds. The witness reads, "The quick brown fox jumps over the lazy dog." Mason takes a few steps back. Another chord sounds. "The early bird catches the worm." Mason, stepping further back, says "Louder, please, Mr. Graves." (Chord.) "A bird in the hand is worth two in the bush." Mason steps even further back. (Chord.) "In a democracy all men are created equal." Mason shouts,*"What was that? I can't hear you, Mr.*

Graves!" He repeats the line. (Chord.) Graves turns to the next card. "As the twig is bent, so grows the tree." Mason responds, *"Louder, please!"* (Chord.) "A stitch in time saves nine." Mason, now at the courtroom door, shouts, *"The next card!"* The witness starts to read, then stops. Music (perhaps Garriguenc's) thunders on the soundtrack. *"Go on, Mr. Graves!"* Mason shouts. "Crinston, I want Graves to go with you." "Read it again, Mr. Graves. LOUDER, MR. GRAVES! GO ON!" "CRINSTON, I WANT GRAVES TO GO WITH YOU!" That is all Mason needs to break down the witness and expose the plot to frame his client. Thanks in part to the music, but also to director Christian Nyby and scriptwriter Harold Swanton, it is the most dramatic climax in any *Mason* episode, and nothing like the dénouement in Gardner's novel of the same name.

According to their credits, all but three of the first season's 39 episodes were based on Gardner's fiction. But it would be more accurate to describe most of them as transporting parts of Gardner's plots and some of his characters into new and simpler stories that lacked the breakneck pace, dynamism, scams, and aggressive dialogue of the originals. Though less complex in their plotting than Gardner's novels, the *Mason* scripts were far more involuted and difficult to devise than those of any other TV series of the time, yet also so formulaic that the survival of the series for nine full seasons in prime time (271 60-minute films) is all but a miracle. Lawyers among the viewership tended to laugh at the oversimplified trials, the courtroom Q&A that in the name of storytelling efficiency violated the most basic rules of evidence, and the weekly parade of murderers blurting out confessions from witness box or spectator's seat, but they recognized that the series in general and Raymond Burr in particular were performing a superb public relations job for the American legal system. As Burr became an ever more frequent speaker at Bar Association functions, defense lawyers in real criminal trials often found it necessary to say in effect to juries: "This is not *Perry Mason*. I do not have to identify someone else as the real criminal or make somebody confess on the stand. In order to be entitled to an acquittal, all I have to do is to raise in your minds a reasonable doubt."

One element in the prodigious success of the series was the superb ensemble playing of the regulars—not only Burr but Barbara Hale (1922–) as Della Street, William Talman (1915–1968) as District Attorney Hamilton Burger, and Ray Collins (1887–1965) as Lieutenant Tragg. The actors and crew worked long hours to shoot each episode in six days.

"I average four or five hours of sleep a night," Burr told *TV Guide*. "It's not enough, but I'm an ox. Actually my stand-in does my sleeping for me." Perhaps it was sleep deprivation that accounted for the sometimes manic atmosphere on the set. One typical moment, captured in print by a *TV Guide* reporter, took place on the last day of shooting "The Case of the Purple Woman" (November 22, 1958). In the scene where Mason is interviewing his client (Bethel Leslie), the dialogue is meant to go as follows:

> BURR: In the first place, you are not responsible for the torts of your husband.
>
> LESLIE: Torts?
>
> BURR: Wrongful acts for which civil action can be brought.

Director Gerd Oswald called for a dress rehearsal and Burr spoke the first line quoted above. Then:

> LESLIE: Torts?
>
> BURR (deadpan):   Strawberry torts.
>
> HALE: He's off. It's going to be a long day, kids.

Late in the afternoon, Burr started drinking Hale's iced coffee when she wasn't looking. Then he tied himself up with the cameraman's measuring tape and stood there looking like a half-wrapped mummy. "We've reached the silly stage," said Hale. But by 8:40 PM the episode was finished. "We've got the greatest crew in the business," Burr said. "Without them we'd be nowhere."

By all accounts the four series regulars went out of their way to make each other look good. "When one of us is off," William Talman told *TV Guide*, "there's always another to take up the slack." Ray Collins, in his seventies the oldest of the regular cast, seemed to disagree. "[W]e all try to protect ourselves. If Willie Talman can get better lighting than I can, well, I assure you I'll try to change that." Then he paused. "And yet there is an affection and respect that makes it all tolerable," he added, and marveled at Burr, who appeared in almost every scene and was always letter-perfect in his lines but still "devote[d] himself to making it better for other people." "We just happen to like each other," Talman said. That affection is apparent on the screen, and helped keep the series high in the ratings.

Perry Mason's Fadeout

During the program's nine-year run Gardner somehow found time to dictate new Perry Mason novels, but he soon came to think of them as fodder for the TV series, and they began showing the marks of the medium's infantile restrictions. The courtroom tiger of the earlier novels, who had evolved into the kinder and gentler lawyer of the middle period, now mutated into a close cousin of the character Raymond Burr was portraying every week on the TV series, a ponderous functionary mindful of the law's niceties. Plot holes left unplugged, ludicrous motivations, mush-witted reasoning, characters who knew things they could not possibly have known, solutions that don't begin to explain who did what to whom, and daisy chains of multiple coincidences are all found abundantly in late Mason novels. Even the courtroom sequences are often as wretchedly constructed as their TV-series counterparts. In *The Case of the Daring Divorcée* (1964), Hamilton Burger introduces totally irrelevant evidence just so certain story elements can be furthered, and in *The Case of the Worried Waitress* (1966) he forgets to present evidence that a crime was even committed.

The TV series ended its long run with "The Case of the Final Fadeout" (May 22, 1966), with Gardner himself playing the judge. By then, the Supreme Court under Earl Warren had almost completely undermined what had always been the premise of the Mason novels: that defendants menaced by the underhanded tactics of police and prosecutors needed a pyrotechnician like Mason in their corner. Once the Court had ruled that convictions obtained by such tactics were unconstitutional and must be reversed, Mason lost his *raison d'être*. The new wave of Court decisions roughly coincided with Gardner's discovery that he had cancer. He responded to both threats in the same way: by carrying on as if nothing had happened. No changes in the American legal system or within his slowly dying body could keep him from doing what he wanted with his own life or the life of the universe he had created. When Mason in *The Case of the Velvet Claws* said, "I fight!" he was speaking for Gardner too. What he had written in *The Case of the Lucky Loser* (1957) about the bedridden tycoon Addison Balfour, Gardner lived in his own flesh. "Despite the sentence of death which had been pronounced upon him, he continued to be the same old irascible, unpredictable fighter. Disease had ravaged his body, but the belligerency of the man's mind remained unimpaired." Gardner kept fighting till the end, which came on March 11, 1970.

After his death an attempt was made to reconfigure his best-known character as younger and hipper, but *The New Perry Mason* (CBS, 1973–74) died after 15 episodes. An older and portlier Raymond Burr returned as Mason in a cycle of two-hour TV movies (NBC, 1986–93) that were more successful, but slow and feeble vis-à-vis the original series or Gardner's novels. The character who served for decades as "America's lawyer" in books and on TV may not be viable in the 21st century, but he will never be forgotten.

CHAPTER 6

The Defenders: TV Lawyers and Controversy in the New Frontier

DAVID R. GINSBURG

I wish to emphasize that law is the subject of our programs; not crime, not mystery, not the courtroom for its own sake. We were never interested in producing a "who-done-it" which simply happened to be resolved each week in a flashy courtroom battle of wits.

Reginald Rose
Television Quarterly
Fall 1964

On Saturday evening, September 16, 1961, a definitive boundary in the depiction of lawyering on television was crossed. The 125th episode of *Perry Mason* had just been broadcast, and a new program endeavoring to portray counsel, clients, and the conflicts with which they dealt—all in a fundamentally different way—had commenced its extraordinary and still-acclaimed run. A noble fanfare accompanied the majestic leftward sweep of the camera looking down over Foley Square in New York City, from the United States Courthouse to the New York County Supreme Court Building, and bold main titles introduced American television

The Defenders

Aired:
- September 16, 1961–
  May 13, 1965, CBS

Cast:
- E. G. Marshall
  (Lawrence Preston)
- Robert Reed
  (Kenneth Preston)

Awards:
- Emmy for Outstanding Program Achievement in the Field of Drama (1962, 1963, 1964)
- Emmy for Outstanding Continued Performance by a Lead Actor in a Series (1962, 1963)
- Emmy for Outstanding Single Performance by an Actor in a Leading Role (1964)
- Emmy for Outstanding Writing Achievement in Drama (1962, 1963)
- Emmy for Outstanding Writing Achievement in Drama–Original (1964)
- Emmy for Outstanding Individual Achievements in Entertainment–Writers (1965)
- Emmy for Outstanding Directorial Achievement in Drama (1962, 1963)
- Emmy for Outstanding Individual Achievements in Entertainment–Directors (1965)
- Golden Globe Award for Best TV Show–Drama (1963)

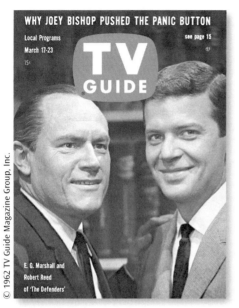

© 1962 TV Guide Magazine Group, Inc.

WHY JOEY BISHOP PUSHED THE PANIC BUTTON
Local Programs   see page 15
March 17-23
15¢
TV GUIDE

E. G. Marshall and
Robert Reed
of 'The Defenders'

THE DEFENDERS
Lawrence (E.G. Marshall) and Kenneth
Preston (Robert Reed) as socially and ethically conscious father-and-son litigators at
the height of their first of four seasons

audiences to *The Defenders*. This
was a show designed to be something innovative: serious but
entertaining television; episodic
drama delivered with conviction
and resolve; a bridge between
the just-past "golden age" of live
anthology and the future of filmed
series. At its birth, the audience
was weaned from the expectation
of a weekly, routine murder case:
The inaugural episode explored
the principled defense of a physician charged with euthanizing a
baby born with Down syndrome,[1]
and those who watched it (I was
among them) sensed that something compelling had arrived in
the hour between *Perry Mason*
and *Gunsmoke*.

Studio One: "The Defender"

The originating writer, creative producer, and principal
characters derived from a two-part February 1957 live
production of CBS's *Studio One* entitled "The Defender,"
starring Ralph Bellamy as lawyer Walter Preston and William Shatner as
his son and associate, Kenneth. (A young Steve McQueen played their
client, who was accused of felony murder.) It was written by Reginald
Rose (the son and grandson of lawyers), produced by Herbert Brodkin,
and directed by Robert Mulligan. Embedded within it were elements that
would later inhabit its descendant series, as well as several others that
would be changed. The essence of the lawyers remained recognizably the
same. The father was highly experienced and guided by a strong code of
ethical obligation, tempered by a sound familiarity with the pragmatics
of law practice. The son, by contrast, was a neophyte, freshly schooled in
the law but guided more by instinct and passion.

In "The Defender," Walter is willing to mount a competent, professional defense in the interest of due process, but no more, because he

is only reluctantly serving as appointed counsel for a defendant whom he believes to be guilty. Conversely, Kenneth is convinced of the client's innocence, and is determined to prove it by a courtroom "trick" rejected as unacceptable theatrics by his father. Hinted at but undisclosed until the final scene, the younger lawyer arranges the deft swap of a close lookalike for the defendant, successfully casting reasonable doubt on an eyewitness identification of him. The defense prevails, but both father and son come away from the trial with an unhappy blend of victory and unease. Displeased with some adverse reaction to the teleplay, producer Brodkin offered an ironic comment to *The New York Times*: "The fact that it got blasted is going to make it difficult to do something along the same line in the future."[2] On that score, he was to be proven spectacularly wrong.

Resurrection: *The Defenders*

On May 9, 1961, Federal Communications Commission Chair Newton Minow gave his debut address to the National Association of Broadcasters, in which he included this remark, one that still reverberates both in the television industry and in American culture:

> I invite each of you to sit down in front of your television set when your station goes on the air and stay there, for a day, without a book, without a magazine, without a newspaper, without a profit and loss sheet or a rating book to distract you. Keep your eyes glued to that set until the station signs off. I can assure you that what you will observe is a vast wasteland.[3]

Some observers have linked Minow's speech—which also included comments about FCC licensure that TV executives took as threats of censorship—directly to the development of *The Defenders* as a "quality" series at CBS.[4] While it is true that Minow's overall agenda was instrumental in incentivizing dramas that examined controversial subjects in American society, the chronology does not permit a causal connection between his speech and the new show. Months before, in October 1960, CBS had announced that the series, based on its *Studio One* antecedent, would be filmed in New York City, with Brodkin producing and Reginald Rose writing several episodes. The characters had been recast: E. G. Marshall as the father (now renamed "Lawrence," or "Larry" to friends) and Robert Reed as his son Kenneth (usually called just "Ken").[5] By March 1961, five episodes had already been filmed and *The Defenders'* fall debut on CBS had been announced.[6]

Just before the start of the 1961–62 television season, the producers and CBS shared their ambitions for *The Defenders*.[7] The show would feature outstanding veteran performers as guest stars, who, over the course of the four broadcast years, imparted the feel of a repertory troupe. (Individual episodes also included early appearances by Robert Redford, Dustin Hoffman, Robert Duvall, Gene Hackman, Dennis Hopper, and James Earl Jones.) Contrary to the general trend of filming in Los Angeles, which began with the decline of live television, actual New York locations allowed the city to serve as a "character," informing the show's realistic urban aesthetic (much as it has done on *Law & Order*). Not only did the show employ a consultant (who was Reginald Rose's personal lawyer) to vet questions about legal content and technical verisimilitude, but the scripts bore this uncustomary, cautionary legend:

NOTE TO DIRECTOR

NO CHANGES OF ANY KIND ARE TO BE MADE IN PORTIONS OF THE SCRIPT WHICH INVOLVE LEGALITIES, WITHOUT FIRST CONSULTING BOB MARKELL, REGINALD ROSE OR DAVID SHAW. THIS IS EXTREMELY IMPORTANT.

IF NONE OF THESE PEOPLE CAN BE REACHED, CONTACT OUR LEGAL CONSULTANT, JEROME LEITNER, AT MA 4-6[XXXX].[8]

Rose drew a bright-line contrast between *The Defenders* and television's lawyer predecessors: The earlier shows were not about law. Rather, they were "entertaining mystery" programs, with "the same elements to be found in any western or detective series."[9]

The Defenders shattered a genre's formula.

A refreshing approach to the weekly shows will be the twist that Preston & Preston does not win every case it tries. When they lose a case and a possible client, a moral will be pointed out, each will learn something about human nature and gain deeper insight into his fellow man. . . . Mr. Brodkin said that the purpose was to have a "realistic portrayal of the legal profession at work, dealing with real people involved with everyday-type problems. There will be none of the unconvincing would-be detective work by lawyers and none of the last-minute witness nonsense."[10]

The famed criminal practitioner Edward Bennett Williams noted in a thoughtful essay that, when the Prestons lose, the episode is "attacking legislation or a decision that can be overruled only by courts higher than the one" in which they practice,[11] thereby presenting a defeat as a moral victory. Rose's formula was a methodically constructed drama featuring a meaningful and engaging ethical or legal conflict, which was resolved in what was often an ambiguous climax.

> Characterization, too, bears the Rose brand of moral paradox: The character who commits an action deemed evil by law and/or public opinion usually turns out to be a "good guy" with noble motives; while the character who commits an action normally thought good turns out to be a "bad guy" with wicked motives.[12]

A cohort of outstanding writers and directors, many of whom had previous experience working in live television, were engaged and worked under Rose's constant oversight.

Television shows have both personal and literary genealogies, and *The Defenders* has another crucial link in the helix of its DNA. Rose had crafted a 1954 *Studio One* teleplay, "Twelve Angry Men," about the deliberations of a jury on a murder case and the power of a single juror to persuade 11 colleagues, who were otherwise ready to condemn the defendant, to scrutinize the evidence diligently and to entertain the notion that reasonable doubt might exist. Three years later—the same year that "The Defender" aired on *Studio One*—Rose wrote and, with its star, Henry Fonda, produced the classic feature-film remake of the same title, directed by Sidney Lumet. The superb cast of that film is revelatory: Juror Number 4 was played by E. G. Marshall, and the actors portraying seven other jurors would return more than once to *The Defenders* as part of its stable of players.

Preston v. Preston

Rose designed the dramatic core of *The Defenders* to feature two parallel sets of opponents. The first set, comprising each case's attorneys—the Prestons against the prosecution or a civil litigator—is common to virtually all dramas dealing with lawyers. But the fresh insight Rose brought to essaying the practice of law was seen in the second set: the father and son partners, with their dynamic clashes.

> It is important to recognize that the two central characters of *The Defenders* are adversaries. They are bound together in professional as well as fraternal regard and affection for each other. But because they are different in age, experience and their view of the world, their interplay can spark far more thinking and dispute than the blunt prosecution-versus-defense situation can generate.[13]

In *Studio One*'s "The Defender," the father barely conceals his contempt for the brash inexperience of the son, while the son is locked into an obligatory apprenticeship in the long shadow of his father. Their emotional distance borders on the tragic. This relationship was redrawn for the series, and was executed by actors well-suited to the demands of the new archetypes. Lawrence Preston as inhabited by E. G. Marshall has a persona quite different from that of Ralph Bellamy's character. Where Bellamy is brusque and imperious, Marshall is patient and acts as a mentor. Where Bellamy's attire is tweedy, Marshall's is elegant, and he usually appears in a courtly three-piece suit. William Shatner's and Robert Reed's interpretations of the son are closer, but Reed's face conveys more empathy and sensitivity and less guile. Lawrence is a seasoned, decent, scholarly counselor whose professional objective is "to use what is in the law for the benefit of the people he represents."[14] Where another might be baldly cynical, he simply manifests a mature comprehension of human nature: "The dominant character trait he has acquired over the years is the capacity to compromise when necessary with dignity."[15] Ken, imbued with youth, intelligence, commitment, and idealism, "does not understand, or want to admit, that there can be such a thing as compromise, in law or in life."[16]

A scene in one of the series' most honored episodes, "Blacklist,"[17] addresses the father-and-son issue squarely. Lawrence proposes a strategy to get a client off the movie industry's blacklist via a ritual of "rehabilitation" and the engagement of a well-connected public relations firm. Ken instead angrily urges that they make a direct legal attack on the list itself, but the father responds that this approach is not their task; they were retained only to represent their client's best interests (impliedly even to the point of mere expediency):

LAWRENCE: I don't want you to do that again in front of a client.

KEN: What about you? Rapping my knuckles in front of him. Sometimes it isn't easy to be in partnership with your father.

LAWRENCE: It has nothing to do with the fact that I'm your father. I don't expect my junior law partner to start an emotional argument like that, jumping in on an issue before we've had a chance to study it.

KEN: What do we have to study? It's rotten on the face of it.[18]

E. G. Marshall's own midseries observations, given from the point of view of an experienced performer, showed that life and art intersected:

> When I first began working with Bob Reed, for example, I was apprehensive because he was young—and an unknown quantity to me. He was a little awkward at the outset and I worried about him. As a father—and as an actor. In one sense, the fictional, he was a young law-school graduate coming into practice with me, and so this made me nervous. And in the real sense, he was a raw actor who might trip over furniture. And then I became more comfortable with him in *both* senses—as an actor, and as a character. There was a true development in a father-son relationship.[19]

Rose's perspective was that the basic themes of the series are found, and the key to the episodic stories should be sought, "in the relationship of these two men, because they symbolize, in a way, the contradictory forces in mankind."[20] The father exemplifies a "political man" conducting the art of the possible, while the son is diametrically opposed to the father, passionately seeking the ideal, and "able to resist the kind of compromise that his father knows must be effected if any progress is to be made."[21]

A corollary of the show's emphasis on the dramatic center of the two men is that women as fully realized romantic counterbalances were marginalized (though as clients they were clearly present as the dramatic engine of many episodes). The father's wife was referred to in "The Defender," but by early in the series she had apparently died. In the first season, Ken had a girlfriend, a social worker named Joan. Her character is accused of throwing a brick at a city official during a protest against the demolition of a city playground so that an expressway can be built through lower Manhattan. One evening, Ken drives Joan to the playground site. Their scene offers witty repartee, and her knowing forwardness imparts a *frisson* of sexual undercurrent.

JOAN: There's the park, only I don't know why you wanted to see it tonight.

KEN: Well, I thought it might inspire us.

JOAN: To do what?

KEN: Well, plan your defense.

JOAN: Legal—or otherwise?

KEN: I wouldn't worry. This car was designed by a Puritan elder. It's impossible to make a pass in a bucket seat.

JOAN: Have you considered trading it in? [22]

Although Ken was seen in the company of other women sporadically over the series, neither lawyer was shown as having a significant other. On *The Defenders*, the law was evidently a jealous mistress.

Lawyering as the Liberal Drama of Controversy

Even if Chairman Minow's speech was not the proximate cause of CBS's decision to commission *The Defenders*, his description of contemporary television is illustrative of what immediately preceded its arrival.

You will see a procession of game shows, formula comedies about totally unbelievable families, blood and thunder, mayhem, violence, sadism, murder, western bad men, western good men, private eyes, gangsters, more violence, and cartoons. [23]

Rose and Brodkin—with the support of CBS and at least the acquiescence of the sponsors—sought to revolutionize the above perception with a lawyer show that was open to jurisprudence other than murder cases. They asserted the unabashed perspective of the liberalism that was flourishing afresh in the New Frontier under the Kennedy administration. The series set for itself and its presumed audience an ethos of progressiveness, of equality compelled by constitutional law, and of the protection of individual rights against the prosecutorial state, all in a creative atmosphere unafraid of controversy. The soul of *The Defenders* was

its nuanced ethical conscience. Conceived during the civil rights movement, it was also among the very first dramatic shows to present African-
American actors in significant roles (including Ossie Davis in a recurring
role as a tough prosecutor). This was even more notable because the
show's characters were often cast "color-blind," as they could have also
been white.

Through the medium of one-hour fictional drama, *The Defenders*
visited terrain that, in the 1960s, pushed the envelopes of both acceptable topics and entertainment. It did so in a stream of episodes addressing subject matter that, even almost half a century on, remains current:
euthanasia, post-traumatic stress disorder, parental custody, eminent
domain, capital punishment and the execution of the innocent, sports
fixing, defense of a fascist, child molestation, abortion—and that was just
in the first season. In subsequent years, the show's writers would deliver
scripts on issues that would inspire the next two generations of their
successors as they gave voice to lawyers and clients on television: spou-
sal abuse, hate crime, the decriminalization of narcotics, rehabilitation
on death row, birth control, obscenity, teenage pregnancy, espionage,
wiretapping, and over 100 others. The cultural impact of *The Defenders* was powerfully evidenced by the reaction to its more controversial
projects. When its three mainstay sponsors and several affiliates withdrew their support from an announced episode advocating abortion
rights, and despite other substantial objections and pressure, CBS admi-
rably authorized and broadcast it anyway, to critical acclaim and a vast
audience.[24]

Brodkin noted the following, no doubt with the best of classic liberal good intentions:

> [T]he scripts will have the kind of substance not ordinarily found in
> television series. There will be such presentations as the problems
> of a mixed marriage, a mercy killing, and a case of a young woman
> involved in a hit-and-run case while intoxicated. *The series will try to
> range over the spectrum of human experience* [italics added].[25]

From today's vantage point, however, there is a telling anomaly—a missing subject that remained taboo, as Reginald Rose acknowledged in 1962.
"Sure, there are topics you can't touch," he said, but he named only one:
homosexuality.[26] (In fairness, he added: "But now I'm beginning to
wonder, considering some of the things we've done on *The Defenders*.")

By 1959, after much of the Production Code governing "good taste and community value" in feature films had been abandoned, if a "moral conflict" set forth "the proper frame of reference," a Code-approved film could present almost any subject except homosexuality.[27] The series' otherwise courageous writing-and-producing team must have felt this to be a saddening, lingering constraint. It was one that was destined to outlive the show.

Dialogue and Character

Though all filmed entertainment is the result of a complex collaboration of talents, the source of great and enduring drama is the words that bring characters to life. Alone and unadorned on the printed page, the dialogue of *The Defenders* stands as a testament to the best of television, and it still feels contemporary despite the passage of over four decades. In the canon of its teleplays, several are cited by commentators as extraordinary milestones: "Blacklist" (about actors and McCarthyism), "The Benefactor" (about abortion), "A Book for Burning" (about obscenity), and "Madman" (about legal insanity) are frequently referenced in analyses of the series because of the sheer quality of the writing, directing, and acting, in addition to the controversy their broadcast engendered. I have thus instead turned to three diverse lesser-known episodes to illustrate *The Defenders'* authority and craftsmanship.

"The Turning Point" by James Lee[28]

Ken is unrelentingly troubled by the execution of a convicted client, and, in his quixotic search for the ultimate truth, he crosses a low-level wise-guy and is framed for assault. The heart of the episode is Ken's arrest and sudden, bleak exposure to the criminal justice system, not as he has experienced it as a lawyer, but as a pretrial defendant. He vents to his father his contempt for what he encountered, and how it changed him:

> Don't assume that the law is practiced as it's preached. Don't assume that the first regard is for human dignity. Accept the reality no matter what is says in the books. You are guilty until proven innocent.

> Get yourself arrested and watch your cherished theory of the individual's place before the law evaporate in the dawn's early light over

Foley Square. I'll tell you one thing . . . I am never again, if I live to be 150, going to watch a man who's spent a night in jail, guilty or innocent, being brought into court without getting just a little bit sick to my stomach.

But *The Defenders* could be counted upon to balance the scales of dramatic justice, and, in a subsequent scene, Ken's arresting officer gives another viewpoint, in a different voice and from a different perspective.

> OFFICER TOLLER: Ninety-nine percent of the people booked in the city *are* guilty! That's why they're treated as though they were. . . You listen to me, I been fourteen years in the department. I know what I'm talking about. A police officer in this town is fighting a war! A war against the scum of the earth. Twenty-four hours a day! We start playing girl's rules and you won't be able to walk the streets.

> KEN: How do you know if it's never been tried? You might just wind up finding it was lack of respect for people's dignity [that] may be breeding the lack of respect for people's lives and property.

> OFFICER TOLLER: Okay, okay, I won't argue with you. Keep your head in the clouds. But do me a favor, will you? Wait 'til next time you're mugged. Wait until some pervert molests your child. Then come tell me the Police Department should run this city like a day camp. You won't. You'll bring petitions to get the cops to carry sub-machine guns. You'll write the Mayor to put through a law to bring back flogging. You'll want us to break heads of people who don't have their shoes shined.

"Judgment Eve" by Reginald Rose[29]

The ethical philosophy of the Preston law firm comes alive in this troubling episode in which the client is a mob racketeer accused of murder. Structured largely as two-actor duets, the action moves backward and forward in time via intricate intercuts among pairs of jurors: the lawyers discussing and presenting the case, the defendant sparring with his jailer, and the judge ruminating to his wife. Ken bluntly asks his father, "Do you think he's guilty?" Lawrence's reply reveals the philosophical essence of his lifework, both as a criminal lawyer and as a guardian of the justice system: "I don't know and I don't care. We did our jobs. We protected his civil liberties, and that's more important than anything." Just as the jury is about to exonerate him, the client whispers tauntingly to Lawrence that, indeed, he is guilty. Having absorbed that knowledge, Lawrence approaches the prosecutor and offers him in defeat both solace and a hint at the truth as Preston now knows it. "Once in a great while a guilty man goes free. We can afford that a lot better than we can afford to have an innocent man convicted."

"Claire Cheval Died in Boston" by Ernest Kinoy[30]

This rare comedic episode takes a canny look at entertainment law. Lawrence represents a real estate mogul who foreclosed on a theater and decided to take over and produce its current play. While visiting Boston to see the show, he is drawn into acting as counsel for the producer against key talent who are breaching their agreements. Kinoy is a knowing observer of theatrical lawyers and clients alike. Lawrence comments on the lead actress's excuse for walking out of rehearsals: "I think she's coming down with a severe case of laryngitis brought on by a draft of her contract." He then notes to Ken that the "actress and the writer can't make up their minds if they love each other or hate each other's guts; probably both." Ken replies wryly: "If you had known that, you could have had it written in their contract that the parties are not responsible for an act of Freud." Later, while watching a tense rehearsal at which the understudy fills in for the still-absent female lead, Lawrence has this amusing exchange with the incognito missing star:

> DIEDRE: She's a little flat, isn't she?
>
> LAWRENCE: I understand they are going to alter the costumes appropriately.
>
> DIEDRE: I meant her performance.

Exhausted, he ultimately concludes that fashioning transactional solutions to satisfy all of the temperamental parties is vastly more tiring and difficult than litigation, and much more intrusive on his personal time.

Epilogue   In its first two seasons, *The Defenders* was the most honored series on television, sweeping victories in the key Emmy categories of Drama Program, Lead Actor, Drama Writing, and Drama Directing. It was awarded the Outstanding Drama Program Emmy in three of its four seasons. Yet in 1965, after 132 episodes, the network decided upon a major overhaul of its prime-time schedule, and the program's eventual cancellation was mourned. *The Defenders* is the direct ancestor of all modern law series, with dense, adult dialogue and an attentive, engrossing, and accessible presentation of legal substance and procedure. It is the clear link between the shows that preceded it and those that followed. *L.A. Law, Law & Order, The Practice,* and their progeny would have been unthinkable without *The Defenders.* But perhaps its worthiest legacy is that it left those who watched it with the profound sense that there is great honor, pride, and high ethical purpose in being a lawyer.

Endnotes

1. *The Defenders: The Quality of Mercy* (CBS television broadcast Sept. 16, 1961).

2. J. P. Shanley, *Producer's Problems,* N.Y. TIMES, Mar. 24, 1957, at 129.

3. http://www.americanrhetoric.com/speeches/newtonminow.htm (last visited Jan. 15, 2009).

4. *See* Steven Classen, *Lawyers Not in Love: The Defenders and Sixties TV,* TELEVISION NEW MEDIA 2007, at 148, *available at* http://tvn.sagepub.com/cgi/reprint/8/2/144 (last visited Jan. 15, 2009); MARY ANN WATSON, THE EXPANDING VISTA: AMERICAN TELEVISION IN THE KENNEDY YEARS 43 (Oxford University Press 1990).

5. Richard F. Shephard, *C.B.S.-TV Weighs 'The Defenders',* N.Y. TIMES, Oct. 27, 1960, at 75.

6. Val Adams, *Court Series Set for C.B.S. in Fall,* N.Y. TIMES, Mar. 31, 1961, at 53. The series' producing partners were Brodkin's Plautus Productions in association with Rose's Defender Productions and the CBS Television Network.

7. Alfred E. Clark, *'The Defenders' and the Law,* N.Y. TIMES, Aug. 20, 1961, at X9 [hereinafter Clark].

8. James Lee, "The Turning Point" (unpublished teleplay on file with UCLA Performing Arts Special Collections) [hereinafter Lee]; *The Defenders: The Turning Point* (CBS television broadcast Nov. 5, 1964).

9. Reginald Rose, *Law, Drama and Criticism,* TELEVISION QUARTERLY, Fall 1964, at 23 [hereinafter Rose].

10. Clark, *supra* note 7.

11. Edward Bennett Williams, *The High Cost of Television's Courtroom,* TELEVISION QUARTERLY, Fall 1964, at 12.

12. Edith Efron, *The Eternal Conflict Between Good and Evil,* in TV GUIDE: THE FIRST 25 YEARS 60 (Jay S. Harris ed., 1980).

13. Rose, *supra* note 9, at 22.

14. *Id.*

15. *Id.* at 22–23.

16. *Id.* at 23.

17. CBS television broadcast Jan. 18, 1964. Written by Ernest Kinoy, directed by Stuart Rosenberg, and guest starring Jack Klugman, "Blacklist" was awarded the episodic Emmys that year for acting and writing, and was nominated for directing and Program of the Year.

18. Ernest Kinoy, "Blacklist," in ELECTRONIC DRAMAS: TELEVISION PLAYS OF THE SIXTIES 112 (Richard Averson ed., 1971).

19. E. G. Marshall and George C. Scott, *The Creators: A Dialogue*, TELEVISION QUARTERLY, Winter 1964, at 52.

20. Rose, *supra* note 9, at 23.

21. *Id.* at 22.

22. *The Defenders: The Man with the Concrete Thumb* (CBS television broadcast Nov. 18, 1961). Writer Ernest Kinoy used this teleplay to jab at New York civic construction czar Robert Moses, who was planning to build just such an expressway at the time, against strong public opposition. For aficionados of *Defenders* trivia, this episode also yields two New York jewels: the address of the Preston & Preston law firm (1019 Columbia Building, a probable homage to CBS) and the license plate of Ken's Triumph convertible (7J1070).

23. http://www.americanrhetoric.com/speeches/newtonminow.htm (last visited Jan. 15, 2009).

24. *The Defenders: The Benefactor* (CBS television broadcast Mar. 28, 1962). Its teleplay was by Peter Stone and it was directed by Daniel Petrie. *See* Jack Gould, *Drama Used as Editorial Protest*, N.Y. TIMES, Apr. 30, 1962, at 43. The three intimidated sponsors were Kimberly-Clark, Brown & Williamson, and Lever Brothers. Speidel (the manufacturer of the famous "Twist-O-Flex®" watchband) seized the initiative and bought the episode's national advertising time, which was understood to have been offered at a substantial discount. *See The Best of Both Worlds*, TELEVISION MAGAZINE, June 1962, at 68 [hereinafter *Best*]. Speidel's decision proved to be shrewd. Though *The Defenders* averaged a respectable 25.5 million viewers weekly, "The Benefactor" drew 28 million. *Id.* at 68, 70.

25. Clark, *supra* note 7, at X9.

26. *Best*, *supra* note 24, at 70.

27. Bob Mondello, *All Things Considered: Remembering Hollywood's Hays Code, 40 Years On* (NPR radio broadcast Aug. 8, 2008), *available at* http://www.npr.org/templates/story/story.php?storyId=93301189 (last visited Feb. 11, 2009).

28. CBS television broadcast Nov. 5, 1964. *See also* Lee, *supra* note 8.

29. CBS television broadcast Apr. 20, 1963.

30. CBS television broadcast Jan. 4, 1964.

CHAPTER 7

Gideon's Trumpet: The "Very Best"

NORMAN ROSENBERG

April 30, 1980, marked a milestone in the relationship among law, lawyers, and television. The *Hallmark Hall of Fame*, one of TV's most prestigious anthology series, unveiled another of its prime-time features, *Gideon's Trumpet*. The CBS offering built on a 1964 book by journalist Anthony Lewis and dramatized events surrounding the U.S. Supreme Court's 1963 decision in *Gideon v. Wainwright*.[1] It showed the struggle of an obscure prisoner in a Florida penitentiary, Clarence Earl Gideon (portrayed by Henry Fonda), to overturn his 1961 conviction for robbing a pool hall.

A close-up of Fonda begins this docudrama. As Gideon, Fonda admits to a checkered past and having always been a rebellious "individualist." *Gideon's Trumpet* then flashes back to how Gideon, for the fifth time in his life, landed in prison. Proclaiming his innocence, Gideon initially fights alone. Lacking money to hire a lawyer, Gideon insists that Florida give him one. He needs a lawyer, Gideon claims, if he is to have a fair trial—a proposition that virtually any TV show of Gideon's time seemingly confirmed. Following Supreme Court rather than television precedent, the judge denies Gideon's request. Forced to represent himself, Gideon

Gideon's Trumpet

Aired:
- April 30, 1980 on CBS, *Hallmark Hall of Fame*

Cast:
- Henry Fonda (Clarence Earl Gideon)
- José Ferrer (Abe Fortas)
- John Houseman (narrator and Chief Justice Earl Warren)
- Lane Smith (Fred Turner)

Awards:
- Robert E. Collins, DGA nomination for Outstanding Directorial Achievement in Specials/Movies for TV (1981)
- John Houseman and David W. Rintels, Emmy nomination for Outstanding Drama or Comedy Special (1981)
- Henry Fonda, Emmy nomination for Outstanding Lead Actor in a Limited Series or a Special (1980)
- David W. Rintels, Emmy nomination for Outstanding Writer in a Limited Series or a Special (1980) Peabody Award (1981)

Courtesy of Photofest.

GIDEON'S TRUMPET
Clarence Earl Gideon (Henry Fonda), an indigent Florida prisoner, initially relied on hand-drafted petitions and the U.S. mail when appealing to the U.S. Supreme Court.

performs ineptly and ends up, once again, behind bars.

While incarcerated, Gideon haunts the prison's library, working with a few rudimentary legal texts and an eighth-grade education to draft an appeal. In a handwritten document he reiterates his contention that Florida violated his constitutional rights and asks the U.S. Supreme Court to review his conviction. Although the deck seems stacked against Gideon, the nation's highest court accepts his petition for certiorari.

Once Gideon's case reaches the Supreme Court, powerful lawyer-allies enter the picture, converting his personal crusade into a much broader one. *Gideon's Trumpet* speculates on how closed-chamber deliberations among the Justices of the Warren Court might have produced a decision to accept Gideon's petition. Then, it shows the high-powered Washington lawyer Abe Fortas, portrayed by José Ferrer, assuming control of the appeal. Several sequences vividly contrast the vast legal resources at Fortas's command to the meager ones that had been available to Gideon. During a longer sequence, based on actual transcripts, *Gideon's Trumpet* restages the lawyers' oral arguments before the Supreme Court. Here, it shows Fortas easily outmaneuvering Florida's overmatched advocate. When Fortas later calls his client to tell him of the Court's decision, few viewers are likely surprised to learn that Gideon has won his case, by a margin of nine to zero.

Gideon's Trumpet constantly informs, perhaps over-informs, viewers that Gideon's personal victory will herald a "landmark" constitutional ruling. In deciding for Gideon, the Court requires that every state must provide a lawyer to any defendant charged with a serious crime. The Justices thus overrule *Betts v. Brady* (1942),[2] which had required states to appoint lawyers for indigent defendants only in "special circumstances." Even if the *Betts* decision were not "wrong the day it was decided," as

Fortas had argued to the Court, "time" clearly demonstrated the need for rejecting it now, as he also had insisted.

Gideon's Trumpet ends with Clarence Earl Gideon himself becoming an early beneficiary of the new rule. Although the decision had prompted Florida officials to free thousands of other prisoners who had lacked legal representation when convicted, they did not let Gideon go in peace. Offered assistance by two lawyers from the American Civil Liberties Union (ACLU), Gideon insists on a local lawyer, Fred Turner (Lane Smith). After Gideon makes a last, ill-informed, and futile argument on his own behalf, claiming that the Fifth Amendment's guarantee against double jeopardy prevents Florida from retrying him, he allows Turner to conduct a professional defense. A lengthy retrial sequence ensues, during which Smith seems intent on channeling Gregory Peck's performance as Atticus Finch in *To Kill a Mockingbird* (1962). It underscores how a trained professional can dismantle, far more easily than any amateur, a prosecution based almost entirely on eyewitness testimony. The jurors return a verdict of not guilty, and Gideon goes free.

Gideon's Trumpet concludes with a 1963 commentary by Robert Kennedy on the historical significance of the *Gideon* decision.

> If an obscure Florida convict named Clarence Earl Gideon had not sat down in his prison cell . . . to write a letter to the Supreme Court . . . the vast machinery of American law would have gone on functioning undisturbed. But Gideon did write that letter, the Court did look into his case . . . and the whole course of American legal history has been changed.

Using a "voice of God" narrative style, John Houseman intones these words as Fonda's Gideon walks away from the camera. This TV version of *Gideon's Trumpet* follows the Anthony Lewis book in ignoring Clarence Earl Gideon's troubled post-*Gideon* life, including his 1972 death and the need for the ACLU to place, in 1984, a marker on his previously unadorned grave.

Gideon's roundabout journey through the U.S. legal system parallels *Gideon's Trumpet*'s circuitous route to television. Producing a successful television show has never been a simple task. Even executives with programming skills roughly comparable to the legal ones of Abe Fortas and Fred Turner cannot always convert a promising concept into a successful TV show. Even if, as a law professor has recently claimed, the Gideon story immediately looked like the kind "that makes Hollywood producers drool," neither Tinseltown nor the TV networks rushed to dramatize Lewis's phenomenally successful 1964 book.

Similarly, Henry Fonda took a meandering path toward *Gideon's Trumpet*. His first foray into TV, a Western series entitled *The Deputy* (1959–61), plodded through three low-rated seasons. His next TV project fared even worse. *The Smith Family* (1971–72), in which Fonda played a police detective, lasted a single season. Although far more obscure TV entries have leapt from archival oblivion to DVD memorials, *The Deputy* and *The Smith Family* remain safely hidden from easy viewing. Subsequently, though, Fonda achieved success on the small screen, especially in productions that nostalgically emphasized his own advancing age. *The Oldest Living Graduate* (1980), for instance, offered a double dose of nostalgia by harkening back to TV's early days and by airing as a live production. Television also provided the medium for Fonda's final acting appearance in *Summer Solstice* (1981) and for his most famous TV role, that of Clarence Earl Gideon.

The fate of subsequent TV productions focused on the Supreme Court further underscores the special nature of Fonda's work in *Gideon's Trumpet*. The first full-scale dramatization of the U.S. Supreme Court at work, it hardly blazed a trail for others to follow. Most TV critics, for instance, quickly dismissed a highly publicized 1991 miniseries about *Brown v. Board of Education*[3]—entitled *Separate but Equal* and co-starring Sidney Poitier and Burt Lancaster—and only a few noticed *Against Her Will: The Carrie Buck Story* (1994), a dramatization of *Buck v. Bell* (1927).[4] Moreover, two highly promoted TV series, with major stars portraying members of fictive Supreme Courts, quickly disappeared. *First Monday* (2002) staggered through an apparently unlucky 13 episodes, while *The Court* (2002) recessed after a mere 3 sessions in prime time.

The gift of hindsight suggests several factors that, in retrospect, helped *Gideon's Trumpet* attain "Hall of Fame" status. First, the production benefited from its identification with the enduring mystique of "quality television." In addition, *Gideon's Trumpet* embraced the powerful media model of *12 Angry Men*, a legal drama closely identified with the same star who played Gideon. Finally, *Gideon's Trumpet* tapped into a treasure trove of reassuring pop culture image clusters commonly used to suggest how the American legal system, at its very best, should operate.

Gideon's Trumpet and the Mystique of Quality Television

Even before director Richard Collins had shot a single scene, *Gideon's Trumpet* could claim the label of "quality television." Once TV sets began replacing motion picture screens as the primary places for viewing daily life, past and present, critics and chroniclers began debating the cultural gravitas of what appeared on television. As hopes that TV might devote itself to cultural uplift quickly faded, television's critics made the search for any sign of quality programming a special obsession. Invariably dismissing the vast bulk of TV fare—the successful series from which the TV networks reaped their profits—cultural sleuths focused on more specialized offerings, such as those presented on the *Hallmark Hall of Fame*.

Debuting in 1951, the *Hallmark Hall of Fame* joined a relatively short list of similar corporate-enabled efforts. Companies such as Alcoa and General Electric proudly placed their own brand on anthology-style programming in which the offerings, generally high-minded dramas, stood on their own rather than flowing from episode to episode as did series such as *Perry Mason*. Anthologies seemed aimed at those viewers and critics who disdained almost everything else that appeared on television. The type of programs sponsored by Hallmark, in the view of their admirers, stood out from other, lesser monuments across that vast wasteland called "network television."

Early television's other anthology series have disappeared, but the *Hallmark Hall of Fame* endures. Several times each season, it reappears on network TV with new examples of what the company's publicists, and most critics, judge to be quality programming. From this perspective, the *Hallmark Hall of Fame* continues to offer TV viewers what Hallmark also promises to provide consumers of its lucrative lines of greeting cards: only "the very best." The *Hall of Fame*'s initial entry, broadcast live on Christmas night in 1951, was *Amahl and the Night Visitors*, the first opera written specifically for television. In 1955, the company began presenting 90- to 120-minute works adapted for television from the stage. *Yankee from Olympus* (1965), a play about the career of U.S. Supreme Court Justice Oliver Wendell Holmes, Jr., represented the *Hall of Fame*'s initial Court-related offering. Individual specials such as *Yankee from Olympus* never gained a mass audience, but the *Hall of Fame* allowed Hallmark to continue celebrating a commitment to quality over quantity. Initially, the series featured live productions, the format favored by TV's critics during the 1950s. And, not surprisingly, the *Hall of Fame*'s intermittent offerings appeared alongside important holidays, just when TV viewers might expect to see Hallmark greeting cards in their future.

Almost immediately, Hallmark won over those who tracked "the very best." By one 2008 count, the *Hall of Fame* could claim nearly 80 Emmys, 11 Peabody Awards, and 9 Golden Globes. This anthology series also attracted a number of performers rarely seen on the small screen. The chance to reprise their roles in the Broadway version of *Yankee from Olympus*, for example, enticed the celebrated stage duo of Alfred Lunt and Lynn Fontanne to appear on television. Similarly, *Gideon's Trumpet* showcased Fonda. *Yankee from Olympus* won an Emmy for Best Dramatic Show of the 1964–65 season, while *Gideon's Trumpet* received a Peabody Award and three Emmy nominations in 1980. In sum, long before *Gideon's Trumpet* ever aired, the Hallmark label suggested a production that would continue a tradition of providing "the very best" in TV programming.

Two Media Models: *12 Angry Men* and Henry Fonda

Gideon's Trumpet also looked back to the 1950s in seeking the model for a successful legal drama. The 1950s, in perhaps the still-dominant historical frame, remains TV's Golden Age, an era distinguished by productions such as *Ahmal and the Night Visitors* and, arguably the most celebrated legal drama in any medium, *12 Angry Men*. Written for TV, *12 Angry Men* debuted as a 1954 entry in CBS's live anthology series, *Studio One*. Immediately called a preeminent example of quality television, it won three Emmys, including one for its writer, Reginald Rose. Another Emmy went to the versatile Robert Cummings, who played the role later identified, as the result of a 1957 Hollywood adaptation, with Henry Fonda.

TV's *12 Angry Men* quickly faded from view. Although the networks recognized that live dramas generated considerable cultural capital, these difficult-to-recycle offerings provided short-lived revenue streams. TV executives managed to preserve many of these productions by filming them off the live feeds playing on in-studio video monitors, using a process known as "kinescoping." Even so, the permanent archiving of kinescopes remained a haphazard proposition. The earliest *Hall of Fame* productions, under the direct control of Hallmark, fared far better than other live dramas of the 1950s. The company insisted on preserving kinescopes of all of its early productions and subsequently donated them to UCLA for archiving.

Television's initial *12 Angry Men*, in contrast, appeared to have disappeared, allowing the 1957 Fonda film version to dominate the popular legal image bank. The entire *12 Angry Men* enterprise, which ultimately included stage versions and a 1997 TV remake, became thoroughly identified with Fonda. It even seemed as if he, rather than Bob Cummings, had appeared in the live TV version. Finally, in 2003, *The History Channel* accidentally discovered a grainy kinescope, now preserved at the Museum of Television and Radio, of the original *Studio One* production.

Every rendition of *12 Angry Men*, with or without Henry Fonda, offers the same story line. Charged with determining the fate of a youth, seemingly of Puerto Rican background in the productions of the 1950s, accused of fatally stabbing his father, 11 of 12 jurors seem either eager or willing to rush to judgment with a verdict of guilty. Only Juror Number 8 holds out, waging an initially lonely struggle against odds that seem as long as those Gideon will later face. *12 Angry Men* departs from the dominant *Perry Mason* formula by never establishing the innocence of its defendant character. The dissenting juror even claims to be uncertain about whether or not the boy actually stabbed his father. But the solemn duty of any jury, he repeatedly insists, involves remaining open to the possibility that the evidence, when critically dissected, might show "reasonable doubt" about a defendant's guilt. One by one, the 11 other jurors come to admit such a possibility, and finally find the defendant not guilty.

The image of Henry Fonda instructing his fellow jurors on legal–constitutional principles remains a staple of popular legal culture. Over time, *12 Angry Men*'s fictive representation of jury-room deliberations has come to seem so compelling that legal observers sometimes hold it up as a model for real jurors. Moreover, several studies suggest that some actual jurors do tailor their behavior to that of Fonda's character. And pop culture products, including such diverse offerings as *Jury Duty* (1995), *My Cousin Vinny* (1992), and a celebrated episode of *The Simpsons* entitled "The Boy Who Knew Too Much" (1992), either implicitly or explicitly reference image clusters from the Fonda version of *12 Angry Men*.

12 Angry Men and *Gideon's Trumpet* frame the trial system as capable of providing justice in criminal cases through adherence to transparent and rational procedures that seek to ensure fairness rather than to reach an unequivocally "correct" result in every single instance. They suggest that a search for absolute certainty is less important than a heroic commitment, as undertaken by Juror Number 8 and by Gideon and his lawyers, to rational deliberation and procedural safeguards. Both *12 Angry Men* and *Gideon's Trumpet*, viewed in this framework, celebrate lawyers and jurors who insist on scrutinizing the evidentiary case against all criminal defendants. As in *12 Angry Men*, the final judgment in Gideon's cause is not made by some "eye of God" narrator, but by anonymous jurors who find an obviously fallible Gideon not guilty rather than innocent.

The writer–producer of *Gideon's Trumpet*, David Rintels, claims the Fonda movie as his inspirational touchstone. Initially writing for TV at the urging of *12 Angry Men*'s Reginald Rose, Rintels subsequently became part of several law-related projects. Before working with Fonda on *Gideon's Trumpet*, Rintels scripted *Clarence Darrow* (1974), a one-person stage play (and later a made-for-TV special) in which Fonda portrayed the celebrated defense lawyer from Chicago. The *Darrow* production featured direction by the multitalented John Houseman, who had worked in virtually every form of media. Shortly before undertaking *Darrow*, the 70-something Houseman had belatedly made his first (credited) screen appearance, capturing an Academy Award for his performance as Harvard Law School's favorite fictive professor, Charles Kingsfield, in *The Paper Chase* (1973).

Gideon's Trumpet and Nostalgia

Much of the nostalgia-drenched imagery in *Gideon's Trumpet* comes from the veteran performers who worked with Henry Fonda. Absent from movies and TV for more than 25 years, Fay Wray, once the obsession of King Kong in the 1933 movie (and the mother-in-law of David Rintels), returned for what would be her final role, portraying Gideon's landlord. Other familiar film and TV figures (familiar, at least, to older and more savvy viewers), including Sam Jaffe, Dean Jagger, and Ford Rainey, made brief but evocative appearances as members of the Warren Court. José

Ferrer, as Abe Fortas, drew on his assured performance as the no-nonsense defense lawyer Barney Greenwald in *The Caine Mutiny* (1954). And Houseman, also *Gideon*'s executive producer, played Chief Justice Earl Warren in ways that can recall his earlier turn as Professor Kingsfield.

Gideon's Trumpet provided another curtain call for Henry Fonda. Beginning in the late 1930s, Fonda's iconic image invariably signaled a character with an almost religious devotion to the pursuit of justice. Fonda had attained star status by playing a heroic and resourceful defense lawyer—Abraham Lincoln, no less—in John Ford's *Young Mr. Lincoln* (1939). Later, he battled injustice as the wrongly labeled outlaw-hero Frank James in *Jesse James* (1939) and *The Return of Frank James* (1940), and as a heroic Wyatt Earp in *My Darling Clementine* (1946). As the shy college professor Tommy Turner, Fonda fights for First Amendment liberties in *The Male Animal* (1942) every bit as tenaciously as he argues for a fair trial in *12 Angry Men* and *Gideon's Trumpet*. With a quiet desperation, Fonda's Manny Balestrero, falsely arrested on suspicion of robbery, looks for justice in Alfred Hitchcock's *The Wrong Man* (1956). Even when Fonda fails to achieve a clear-cut victory, as when playing Tom Joad in *The Grapes of Wrath* (1939) or Gil Carter in *The Oxbow Incident* (1943), he nonetheless represents the ideal of justice struggling to become the reality.

In *Gideon's Trumpet*, Fonda once again becomes this iconic "Henry Fonda character." Beginning with the opening sequence, in which Fonda stares directly into the camera as in *12 Angry Men* and *The Grapes of Wrath*, he personally challenges viewers to consider the price of allowing an injustice to stand, a right to go without a remedy. In every subsequent sequence in which Fonda reappears, his performance dominates the legal imagery. Most obviously, *Gideon's Trumpet* shows other prisoners, particularly an illiterate African-American inmate, thoroughly engaged by Gideon's struggle to get the U.S. Supreme Court to review his and, by extension, their convictions. Some might doubt the ability of the real Gideon to play such a symbolic role, but there seems little reason to question Fonda's capacity to do so. His portrayal of the 53-year-old Gideon turns more on his character's being worn down by struggling against injustice than on his being enfeebled by advancing age.

Fonda's long career in legally themed productions, then, seems crucial to underscoring the popular legal-constitutional notes that *Gideon's*

Trumpet sounds. It almost seems as if Tom Joad has returned for one final legal battle, but without the energy required to fight effectively, let alone to prevail. At the same time, though, the iconic image that Fonda brings to *Gideon's Trumpet* makes him an ideal embodiment of a crucial aspect of the legal logic that frames this TV production: People such as Gideon can perform heroically by calling out for justice, even if it will ultimately require armies, commanded by lawyers such as Abe Fortas, to actually deliver the goods. *Gideon's Trumpet*, of course, employs image clusters from the world of cinema and television rather than the language of the law to depict this legal-constitutional logic in action. It thus works with the special kind of visual imagery that some students of law and film have come to call "legal reelism."

Take, for instance, how *Gideon's Trumpet* uses all the resources of a highly visual medium to portray the claims made in Abe Fortas's brief in the *Gideon* case. In this document Fortas had insisted that only an "experienced lawyer" could possibly marshal "all of the factual and legal considerations" that make up a criminal defense. The frequency with which defendants negotiated guilty pleas suggested "that those who are arrested, particularly the penniless and persons who are members of minority groups"—a claim that *Gideon's Trumpet* emphasizes through Gideon's fatherly relationship to the African-American prisoner—"are more likely hopelessly to resign themselves to fate than aggressively to *act like the defense counsel portrayed on television*" (emphasis added). Without a lawyer in the picture, in other words, real-life trials simply cannot look as good or as fair as the fictive ones people can easily find in the realm of "reel life," especially on TV. *Gideon's Trumpet*, in short, provides moving pictures of what Fortas could only render through the print medium.

Gideon's Trumpet and the "Passage of Time"

Seen through today's often ironic lens, *Gideon's Trumpet* almost begs for critical re-viewing. It shows Fortas, for example, urging the Court to reject the vision of justice that had informed *Betts*. "The passage of time," he pointedly tells the Justices, should impel all of us to reconsider how we see images from the past. How might this injunction apply to a re-viewing of *Gideon's Trumpet* today?

From a technological perspective, *Gideon's Trumpet* no longer sounds or looks as it did in 1980. Although the march of time has been kinder to *Gideon's Trumpet* than to the 1954 kinescope of *12 Angry Men*, there is no remastered version currently available, "Due to the age of this program," warns the distributor of the 2007 DVD version of *Gideon's Trumpet*, viewers may "notice occasional flaws in image and audio . . . that were beyond our ability to correct from original materials."

The passage of time has also yielded historical scholarship that may remove a bit of the luster from the substance of *Gideon's Trumpet* and the "landmark" decision it celebrates. Archival materials available neither to Anthony Lewis nor to David Rintels suggest a Supreme Court fully informed, even before Fortas's brief and oral argument, about right-to-counsel jurisprudence. Records kept by several of the Justices reveal cases, involving crimes far more gruesome than Gideon's, in which a majority of the Court was inclined to discard *Betts*. A complicated convergence of forces, one historian of the Warren Court has explained, delayed formal rulings in these cases until after the Court had dealt with the hardly ferocious Gideon. Gideon himself "could have argued *Gideon* and won 9–0," this historian has quipped.[5]

Moreover, the passage of time has thrown into sharper relief the spirit of "liberal legalism" behind the *Gideon* decision. Encased within a historical time zone when the Warren Court remained relatively popular and still in session, and this liberal legalism dominated the profession, *Gideon's Trumpet* hardly acknowledges post-*Gideon* developments. Framed as an uplifting tale from the past, it only hints at the epochal criminal procedure cases, such as *Miranda v. Arizona*,[6] to come. This carefully circumscribed historical frame also allows *Gideon's Trumpet* to avoid any mention of the subsequent rise of Abe Fortas to the Supreme Court (and his fall from it). A similarly time-bound approach to "legal reelism" allows this 1980 program to ignore the changing popular legal culture. The kind of image clusters featured in movies such as *Dirty Harry* (1973) and *Death Wish* (1974), works of "legal reelism" that challenged the Warren Court's vision of criminal procedure, never appear in *Gideon's Trumpet*. A 2008 YouTube posting, entitled "Gideon's Trumpet of Blood," for instance, satirically notes this absence.

Despite the passage of time, TV and legal observers generally see *Gideon's Trumpet* as still among "the very best" in television drama. Release of the 2007 DVD edition, for example, prompted new testimonials to its canonical status. *DVD Talk* hailed it as a legal drama "of the finest kind" and "a triumph of televised storytelling." Recent law review essays on the Supreme Court's *Gideon* decision acknowledge *Gideon's Trumpet* as having now become part of the broader story of this case. Moreover, nearly every commentary, in whatever field, singles out Fonda's portrayal of Gideon for special praise. Perhaps most importantly, the legal-constitutional image clusters featuring Henry Fonda seem less affected by the passage of time than do other aspects of *Gideon's Trumpet*, such as individual shots that last far longer than today's norm. In the world of legal imagery, the Supreme Court decision in *Gideon* and the Fonda TV show about that ruling often meld together. Internet searches for "Clarence Earl Gideon" and *"Gideon v. Wainwright"* will turn up images of both the real Gideon and of Henry Fonda portraying him in *Gideon's Trumpet*.

In sum, as in so many other areas of contemporary legal culture, legal realism and "legal reelism" constantly intersect and intertwine. These convergences can help viewer-jurors to render their own verdicts on what still counts as "the very best" in both public law and in popular legal entertainment on television.

Endnotes

1. 372 U.S. 335 (1963).
2. 316 U.S. 455 (1942).
3. 347 U.S. 483 (1954).
4. 274 U.S. 200 (1927).
5. LUCAS A. POWE, JR., THE WARREN COURT AND AMERICAN POLITICS 379–86; quote at 385 (2000).
6. 384 U.S. 436 (1966).

CHAPTER 8

Revisiting *L.A. Law*

PHILIP N. MEYER

The Back Story

Years ago, I was a big fan of *L.A. Law*. In 1986, the same year the ubiquitous legal drama began its run, I had recently left the practice of law in a midsized firm in Connecticut and, after obtaining a midlife and midcareer LL.M., began teaching in the Lawyering Program at New York University School of Law. Coincidentally, this was the inaugural year of the Lawyering Program, a program that combined teaching "real-world" clinical skills with legal writing and research assignments, all based upon a sequence of complex simulations developed from actual case files. The problems in the simulations were factually complex, as were the ethical and moral dilemmas. It was like I was back in practice, playing the role of a senior partner. I supervised the work of 40 neophyte associates in my own first-year law firm.

I remember heading home by train with endless stacks of papers to grade and a big duffel bag filled with videotapes of client interviews or motion arguments to view on my VCR. I quickly learned that law school teaching—at least this type of clinical and legal writing teaching—was not an easy and relaxed job with time for reflection and scholarship. Neither was

L.A. Law

Aired:
- September 15, 1986–May 19, 1994, NBC

Cast:
- Corbin Bernsen (Arnie Becker)
- Jill Eikenberry (Ann Kelsey)
- Alan Rachins (Douglas Brackman, Jr.)
- Michael Tucker (Stuart Markowitz)
- Richard Dysart (Leland McKenzie)
- Harry Hamlin (Michael Kuzak)

Awards:
- Emmy for Outstanding Drama Series (1987, 1989, 1990, 1991)
- Emmy for Outstanding Writing in a Drama Series (1987, 1990, 1991)
- Jimmy Smits, Emmy for Outstanding Actor in a Drama Series (1990)
- Larry Drake, Emmy for Outstanding Actor in a Drama Series (1988, 1989)
- Richard Dysart, Emmy for Outstanding Supporting Actor in a Drama Series (1992)
- Emmy for Outstanding Editing for a Series—Single Camera Production (1988)
- People's Choice Award for Favorite TV Dramatic Series (1987, 1988, 1989, 1990, 1991, 1992, 1993)

it a respite from the grind of serving as a litigation associate in a prosperous suburban law firm on Connecticut's "Gold Coast," where I had struggled for an elusive partnership during the Reagan economic boom years of guiltless greed and conspicuous consumption.

I had often struggled with aspects of practice. I especially recall one troubling case. My client's wife had left him after she entered a relationship with another man. My client had received sole custody of his young child in a divorce settlement agreement negotiated by the powerful senior partner in my law firm. Although I recall that the wife had not been represented by counsel in the divorce, she obtained counsel for a subsequent effort to secure joint custody. Her young lawyer was a friend of mine from the local bar association. This friend called and informed me as a "professional courtesy" that she was seeking to secure joint custody and was about to serve my client with a capias order to compel his appearance at a hearing. I knew that my client still hated his wife for her betrayal and was planning to move to Florida soon. When I hung up the phone with the young lawyer, I talked to the partner who had negotiated the divorce settlement. He told me that the courtesy phone call from the ex-wife's lawyer was "boneheaded" and that I had no choice but to call my client immediately and tell him that he would be served if he returned to his home. I did as instructed. I reached my client and informed him of what was about to happen. As best I can recall, I did not directly suggest or advise him to leave town with his daughter.

Apparently, the man never returned home after receiving my phone call. He left for Florida with the child immediately, before the service of the capias could be completed. There were no uniform interstate laws in force at that time that would give Connecticut courts jurisdiction after he moved to Florida, provided that the capias had not been personally served. And I knew that his ex-wife, a secretary and visual artist, did not have the financial resources to pursue custody litigation in Florida. Initially, I feared that there would be ethical repercussions because of my call tipping off the client. There were none, but the young lawyer who represented the ex-wife never spoke to me again. The episode stayed with me, and the story, like many other practice experiences, troubled me. I realized that I may have been complicit in the husband's abduction of his daughter. At the very least, I had prevented the little girl from establishing a relationship with her mother and had personally betrayed a friend. Many of my decisions in practice had been like that—unreflective and reactive. My quick actions often set in motion unanticipated forces and chain reactions that had consequences far beyond my control.

My work week ended on Thursday evening, and after I returned home that night, I watched television. My favorite show was *L.A. Law*. I guilt-lessly indulged in my weekly fix of popular-cultural depictions of legal practice and lawyering, and the show's highly romantic and dramatic reimaginings of the private practice of law that I had recently left behind.

L.A. Law was not just my own personal refuge. It provided an equally compelling and addictive fantasy for many NYU students who were hooked on the program for a different reason. For some, *L.A. Law* had significantly influenced their decision to enter a life in the law. The program seemed to embody a professional dream couched in the milieu of economic self-absorption and professional narcissism that prevailed at the end of the 1980s, and best captured by Gordon Gekko's cry, "Greed is good," in Oliver Stone's *Wall Street*. *L.A. Law* offered a vision of a profession where young lawyers participate in the high-stakes litigation of complex and compelling social issues. The lawyers lived luxuriously. Their personal lives were full of romance and drama, and they were driven by their pursuit of power and privilege as well as celebrity.

L.A. Law touched all these bases simultaneously. It served the function that afternoon soap operas had long provided to a different audience: escape to a world of drama and romance that unfolded between commercial breaks. It offered an inviting dreamscape during a curiously self-absorbed and economically self-indulgent time.

Writing this essay provides me with an opportunity to revisit Steven Bochco's *L.A. Law* over 20 years later. My purpose, initially, was to explore what made the program so compelling, what gave it its popular-cultural stickiness. I wondered whether *L.A. Law* would still hold the same traction for me now that it did then. Unfortunately, at the time of this writing, the episodes of the various seasons had yet to be released on DVD. Therefore, I bought the original 1986 pilot (97 minutes) on videotape and watched it on a borrowed VCR. The styles, dress, settings, and scenes have changed and aged, but the dialogue generally remains spot-on.

What now strikes me is the narrative structure of the program, which alternates between two primary genres: a linear plot-driven melodrama

Courtesy of Photofest.

L.A. LAW

For 8 seasons, the firm of McKenzie (Richard Dysart, front row left) Brackman (Alan Rachins, 2d row right) served up legal comedy and melodrama. It's the ancestor of current legal drama.

and a character-based black comedy. These storylines are cleverly matched and balanced against one another in a multiplot format. In this essay, I provide brief summaries of two illustrative subplots from the pilot episode. Then, comparing and contrasting these subplots, I observe why the black comedy has aged well and the characters remain interesting. I also explain why the melodrama has not aged as well. While this subplot, too, is clever and engaging, it is also more predictable than the black comedy, and the characters are obvious and less compelling.

The Pilot Episode—Summarizing Two Illustrative Subplots

Arnie's Ethical Dilemma—A Black Comedy

When Arnie Becker, the divorce specialist at McKenzie, Brackman, Chaney & Kuzak, finally arrives at his office—in a Porsche 911 with vanity plates—after a flirtation with an attractive woman during an L.A. freeway traffic jam, there is a peculiar smell in the air. Suddenly, a gun-wielding maniac appears in Arnie's office. He is the ex-husband of one of Arnie's clients, who was ruined financially in his divorce. The man pulls the trigger, but the gun is a starter pistol and, metaphorically, only fires blanks. Coincidentally, the source of the smell is detected: Norman Chaney, the tax partner, has died of a heart attack at his desk sometime during the weekend. "If he's dead, I've got dibs on his office," Arnie announces.

Arnie meets a new potential client, Lydia Graham. Lydia is concluding a divorce based upon irreconcilable differences with her husband, with whom she has amicably worked out the terms of the dissolution.

Nevertheless, she has come to Arnie for a second opinion. Lydia explains that what she desires most is to preserve a relationship with her former husband for the sake of her two children. Arnie is certain that Lydia's husband is having an affair. Without Lydia's permission, he hires a private investigator who obtains compromising pictures of Lydia's husband and his new paramour. Arnie predicts that Lydia will emerge from his lunch meeting with her prepared to extract economic revenge, after retaining Arnie to represent her. Arnie can then bill the lunch meeting to the new client. Of course, matters work out precisely as Arnie anticipates. After viewing the pictures, Lydia realizes that her marriage is a sham and that her husband is both a cheat and a liar.

At the settlement conference, Lydia's fury escalates as Arnie reveals the explicit and compromising pictures of the husband with his new girlfriend. Then Arnie reveals additional evidence: Lydia's husband is a crook who has been skimming cash to finance his peccadilloes. Lydia explodes with righteous and vengeful anger at the revelations. Arnie uses the new evidence to extort a much better settlement for Lydia. After the meeting, Arnie is pleased, but Lydia is still furious. "I've lost my life; my children lost a family. And there's no amount of money that can compensate for that," she says. Arnie explains that Lydia may hate him now, but in several weeks she will be recommending him to her girlfriends, and in several months she will be inviting him home for dinner.

Michael Kuzak's Ethical Dilemma—A Melodrama

Michael Kuzak, the handsome ace litigator, must defend Justin Pregerson, an evil and unrepentant rapist. Pregerson is also the son of one of the firm's most important and lucrative clients. Pregerson, along with two other men, is acccused of raping a woman. He claims that the woman enticed him and that she enjoyed the experience. Expressing no remorse, he even tells Kuzak that the victim had it coming. At Pregerson's preliminary hearing, Adrianne Moore, the articulate and attractive African-American rape victim, tells a poignant story of her abduction and rape and of being thrown into a dumpster by the three men. On cross, one of the other defense lawyers suggests that Moore invited the attack and that she was high on marijuana (a drug that Moore was taking legally to counteract her chemotherapy treatments for leukemia). The cross-examination degenerates and Moore explodes in anger and frustration.

Moore says that her only recourse will be to get a gun and kill the men who raped her, since she is going to die soon anyway. The judge holds her in contempt and sends her to a holding cell.

Meanwhile, Kuzak is arrested for unpaid parking tickets and sent to a cell adjacent to Moore's. Kuzak tells Moore he is "deeply sorry" for her treatment in court. "Very big of you. I could tell you were deeply outraged," she answers him. Kuzak speaks of his role as a lawyer and the rights of the defendant to representation. Moore responds, "What about my rights? I was raped and beaten and thrown into a dumpster."

Back in court, Moore recants her testimony and feigns memory loss based on the drugs she is taking for cancer treatment. The charges against Pregerson and his codefendants are dropped. Later, in the parking garage, Pregerson robs Kuzak at gunpoint. Kuzak reveals to the police that Pregerson is carrying a concealed weapon without a permit. Pregerson is arrested for parole violation, for possession of drugs, and for resisting arrest.

Kuzak continues to represent Pregerson, who offers to plead guilty to assaulting Moore and will testify against his codefendants if the other charges are dropped. The three rapists are each sentenced to 18 months for assault. Leland McKenzie, the kindly senior partner, expresses discomfort at Kuzak's questionable ethics in betraying Pregerson. McKenzie observes that Pregerson will not survive 18 months in Vacaville prison without getting raped, so there will be some sort of justice. In the coda, Adrianne Moore comes to the firm's office late at night and confesses to Kuzak that she is afraid to die. Kuzak and Moore embrace tenderly.

Observations

Melodrama

In *L.A. Law*, the narrative structure pairs darkly comedic and ironic subplots against traditional stories of heroic lawyers fighting villains. For example, in the melodramatic[1] sub-plot, Kuzak battles against his client. He must choose between loyalty and his professional obligation to his client on one hand, and his feelings for Adrianne Moore and desire to achieve a more poetic and satisfying justice on the other. But the dramatic potential of this situation is left unfulfilled, because the material is transformed into a standard television melodrama with a predictable and obvious outcome. My dissatisfaction is not based upon a critique of the "realism" of the narrative. It is, instead, an aesthetic reaction to a plot that does not fulfill the dramatic potential that the material suggests. That is, the narrative panders to the audience's most obvious expectations and does so while somehow suggesting to viewers that something more significant is going on. As interesting as the dramatic situation is, it is used as fodder for a standard linear television melodrama.

In terms of characterization, Pregerson is a completely flat caricature—a drug-addicted rapist who wants to escape responsibility for his actions by blaming the victim. There are no explanations for his actions other than his own narcissism, racism, and viciousness. He is privileged and unrepentant. In sum, he is a stock villain, a real scumbag. He is a person who must be punished for his crime so television justice will be served and the viewer will receive satisfaction. Likewise, Adrianne Moore is the stock victim. Her character is depicted as completely sympathetic; she is gentle, thoughtful, and articulate. Further, she is African American and, apparently, a person with limited financial resources. Finally, she is a victim not only of rape but also of leukemia.

Although Kuzak speaks to Moore about the importance of his role as a defense lawyer, he has no real choice but to rescue Adrianne Moore and sell out his client. He must act in accord with a standard television melodramatic template. Viewer satisfaction lies in rooting for the victim and against Pregerson. The story is about how Kuzak will cleverly provide justice for Moore, and how the evil Pregerson will receive his comeuppance. This melodramatic subplot, I think, satisfies the viewer's expectations too easily.

Likewise, the plotting now seems somewhat obvious. Of course, there are the coincidences that are apparent in all television stories. Kuzak conveniently ends up in the holding cell next to Moore, and Pregerson conveniently robs Kuzak at gunpoint, which gives Kuzak an opening to betray him. However, I am not referring merely to narrative coincidences. There is something more deeply wrong in the narrative structure, several turns in the plot that are troubling because they are too fortuitous and obvious. For example, after Pregerson robs Kuzak and Kuzak turns him in for a gun violation, Kuzak continues to represent Pregerson and negotiate his plea bargain. The plea bargain achieves perfect balance and symmetry by providing rough justice for Kuzak's client while vindicating Moore. As Leland McKenzie observes, although the 18-month sentence seems relatively light, Pregerson will unlikely serve out his term without getting raped himself. This is television's version of poetic justice easily achieved, providing viewer satisfaction before the cutaway to the final set of commercials.

The melodramatic hero Michael Kuzak is not particularly interesting or compelling. There are no reverberations within his character or even self-reflections based upon the choices he has made. He is a stock television hero: superficially handsome, with excellent credentials and a somewhat supercilious manner. For example, Kuzak engages in little internal struggle before he turns Pregerson over to the police. His actions play out exactly as he intends them, so Kuzak suffers no personal or professional consequences from his decision to violate the rules of professional conduct to achieve justice for Moore.

Kuzak's character is in accord with that of the stock melodramatic hero. In television melodrama, psychological self-doubt is short-lived. Good characters have good outcomes, and the plot resolutions affirm audience expectations. By the end of the story, Kuzak's unethical conduct has even received the professional blessing of the paternal senior partner Leland McKenzie. In the predictable coda, Kuzak and Moore tenderly embrace, thus providing an "up" ending and an easy affirmation for the viewer.

This stock plot is developed within the framework of a "professional" soap opera. The dialogue is cutting and edgy. The actors playing the heroic characters are extremely attractive, and there is plenty of additional "eye candy." But the subplots confirm, rather than challenge, the expectations of the audience within the framework of a standard television melodrama. The familiar afternoon soap-opera forms are blended with the simple linear plotting of old-school lawyer hero programs and repackaged with snappy dialogue typical of mid-1980s TV.

Black Comedy

For me, the strongest subplots in the *L.A. Law* pilot are the black-comedic character-based critiques of private law practice in the greedy 1980s, and the most compelling characterizations are of the money-obsessed, manipulative, selfish, and self-absorbed lawyers who inhabit this landscape. These darker comedic stories can be told because they are balanced against the aforementioned traditional plot-driven melo-dramas, with heroic lawyers and easy-to-identify villains. The lawyer characters emphasized in the black comedy subplots (such as Arnie Becker) are more interesting and edgy than the stereotypical protago-nists in the more melodramatic plot-lines, who are highly predictable both in their actions and in their psychological construction.

There is an intriguing complexity to Arnie's character, and a certain self-effacing quality that compels the viewer's attention. Likewise, Arnie's relationships with his clients are more nuanced and sophisticated than those between the heroic lawyers and their clients.

In many ways, Arnie Becker is the antithesis of a hero, although in later seasons he gradually evolves into a more sympathetic charac-ter. In the pilot episode, Arnie is depicted as cynical, manipulative, and shrewd. For example, he guiltlessly undermines his client Lydia's desire for an amicable divorce when, without Lydia's permission, he hires a detective to confirm his suspicion that her husband is having an affair. He maneuvers to land her as a client. He even arranges to meet her at a fancy restaurant so that he can be spared an uncomfortable moment when he presents her with the evidence of her husband's philandering. Arnie vicariously enjoys enabling Lydia's fury. He manipulates her into a destructive and explosive confrontation with her husband at the settle-ment meeting by exposing her husband as a philanderer and a crook. The public humiliation pushes the passive Lydia into an altercation with her husband and provides a curious type of client empowerment. Arnie then maximizes Lydia's economic leverage, extorting a settlement after threatening to expose the husband's illegal business practices. Unlike Kuzak, Arnie creates the story rather than merely reacting to events. There is even an intimation that Arnie is steering the attractive divorcée-to-be toward a sexual relationship with him.

Yes, Arnie is guilty of unethical practices: he violates his client's inter-ests and also commits extortion. Yet, somehow, Arnie remains a compel-ling character, and the audience is intrigued, not repelled, by his actions. Unlike other lawyers in the comic subplots (like the two-dimensional Brackman), Arnie is not pompous or stuffy. He is extremely intelligent, honest, and self-effacing. He is also cunning and shrewdly effective in maximizing what he determines to be his client's interests. Although Arnie's professional conduct is unethical, he is not completely venal or so self-absorbed as to be clueless. I believe that Arnie is what many view-ers think of as a "good" (effective) litigation lawyer—and just the divorce lawyer they would want if they sought revenge upon a deceitful spouse. Viewers are intrigued by Arnie Becker because his actions confirm popu-lar notions about unethical divorce lawyers. The audience understands and appreciates Arnie's decisions and the calculated risks he takes. It also recognizes him as an example of a clear professional archetype, once labeled by an NYU student from the West Coast as "the high-end model of a California land shark."

Just as Arnie's psychology is more complex than Kuzak's, so are his relationships with other characters, especially with his clients. For exam-ple, the comedic design of the plot affords Arnie latitude to develop a nuanced relationship with Lydia. In addition to providing legal repre-sentation, Arnie teaches Lydia dark and important lessons about domes-tic life in Los Angeles. Arnie also shows Lydia that she is a stronger and more resilient person than she realizes. The viewer recognizes that Arnie's technically unethical professional conduct empowers and liber-ates Lydia. In Hollywood script-writing terminology, the through-line of Lydia's character arcs from a passive and fearful character into a more independent, better-informed woman who is capable of standing up to her husband, and, in turn, to Arnie Becker. In addition to securing an economically advantageous divorce, Arnie facilitates Lydia's personal transformation.

The coda captures the complexity of Arnie's relationship with Lydia. Lydia tells Arnie how much she detests what he has done and how Arnie's actions have destroyed her relationship with her husband and left her children without a father. The viewer perceives that, despite the strength of her admonitions, Lydia has benefited from Arnie's represen-tation both psychologically and economically. Lydia, at the start of her story, probably would not have been able to confront Arnie *or* her hus-band. Thus, she is richer and wiser than she would have been had he not represented her. Further, the viewer understands the subtext of the final scene and is left to agree with Arnie's comment to the extremely attractive, soon-to-be-single Lydia as he accurately predicts the future: Lydia may hate Arnie and be unhappy now, but in a few weeks, she will be recommending Arnie to her friends, and in a short while, she will be inviting Arnie home to dinner (presumably to deepen their personal relationship).

The television viewer is intrigued by Arnie because Arnie never quite crosses over the line into unlikability. This is because Arnie acts within the professional context of domestic litigation practice, which, in turn, is set within a corrupt, decadent, and money-driven society. Here, working inside the framework of a dark comedic subplot, Arnie Becker is the perfect lawyer for the job.

Conclusion   In this essay, I revisited excerpts from the pilot episode of *L.A. Law*. Like an old popular song, the program still has a strong emotional resonance for me and recalls a different time. I am also struck now by the complex narrative structure of the program, and especially how it pieces together two discrete types of stories. There is a conventional television "heroic" melodrama and also a darker character-based comedy. Of the two types of stories, the black comedy has aged remarkably well, and the character of Arnie Becker remains especially compelling.

Endnote

1. Melodrama provides viewers with easy confirmation of the belief that evil is easily identified. We root for the hero, who takes action to defeat the bad guys, as if on our behalf, and we cheer when the bad guy is defeated and the evil is eradicated. *See* HERMAN NORTHROP FRYE, ANATOMY OF CRITICISM: FOUR ESSAYS 40 (Princeton University Press, paperback ed., 1971); MICHAEL ROEMER, TELLING STORIES: POSTMODERNISM AND THE INVALIDATION OF TRADITIONAL NARRATIVE 280–82 (1995).

PART III

The American Criminal Justice System

You just can't beat the criminal justice system for inspiring great lawyer stories. The cases are usually whodunits, so we enjoy the pleasure of the traditional detective story along with courtroom drama. Often the story presents interesting moral and ethical issues of whether a person should be considered responsible for a homicide—and how defense lawyers can live with themselves.

We're not just talking about money, as in civil cases. At stake is 20-to-life in a cell shared with Bubba—or sometimes the death penalty. There is conflict aplenty—not only between prosecutors and defense lawyers, but also between the lawyers and the judge, the lawyers and the cops or other witnesses, and the defense lawyers and their clients. We do not waste a lot of time in the law office; criminal cases either get plea bargained or go to trial. Since there isn't much pretrial discovery, the trial is bound to bring out surprising information about the crime, the defendant, and the witnesses. Cross-examination skill is at a premium. And there's always suspense—the jury gets to decide whether the defendant walks out the door to freedom or into prison. Above all, crimes and criminals are just so damn interesting!

Perry Mason, discussed in Part II of this book, proved that a show based on criminal trials could reliably attract viewers, and so Perry has been followed by legions of television prosecutors and defense lawyers. This part is organized by the premiere dates of the series discussed, oldest first. It includes shows that were concerned primarily with criminal cases, even though the lawyers occasionally took civil cases, as on *The Practice.*

Part III opens with an essay by three skeptical British writers about *Matlock*, which premiered just eight days after *L.A. Law* did, back in 1986. While *L.A. Law* looked to the future, and is the common ancestor for almost all post-1986 legal television dramas, *Matlock* looked to the past. Ben Matlock was a clone of Perry Mason, and the show involved the same tired plot contrivances dressed up in Southern drag. Yet, surprisingly, the show had a highly successful nine-year run and is fondly remembered by millions. Our British commentators are mystified by its success.

Law & Order began its astounding run in 1990. Who would have guessed that it would be so successful, since the show seems to violate every rule about how to attract an audience? It has no sex, no violence, and very little information or plot development regarding the personal lives of its characters. There is considerable turnover among the actors from season to season. More important, the stories are quite intricate. If you get up to go to the bathroom or answer the phone, you're toast. You'll never catch up to the plot twists that occurred while you stepped away. Every episode comes down to the same basic theme: dedicated cops catch the crooks and dedicated prosecutors put them away. It's about law enforcement personnel doing their jobs well. However, the stories, as they say, are "ripped from the headlines," and in this respect *Law & Order* can trace its ancestry to *The Defenders*, with its focus on the interface between law and hot-button social issues. *Law & Order* exalts police and prosecutors and paints a pretty nasty picture of defense lawyers, but that theme seems to resonate with many viewers.

Murder One, which had a two-year run beginning in 1995, was quite different from all the other criminal law shows because it serialized a single celebrity murder case over an entire 23-episode first season. Having many episodes to tell a single story enabled the show to delve much more deeply into character, plot, and criminal procedure than is possible in a single one-hour episode. In particular, the series showed the devastating effect that high-stakes litigation can have on the personal lives of the lawyers. The first season was a gripping whodunit: who raped and killed 15-year-old Jessica Costello? It's set in a sleazy world of celebrities, involves a truly unforgettable defense lawyer named Teddy Hoffman, and roars to a stunning climax.

JAG, which also premiered in 1995, involved military justice and enjoyed 10 years of network success. The show was unabashedly pro-military and enjoyed legions of loyal viewers who tuned in each week for the newest legal depiction of current military and political events. It frequently raised important issues involving the military, such as "don't ask, don't tell," harassment during training, and casualties caused by friendly fire. The two lead characters, Harmon Rabb and Sarah MacKenzie, often opposed each other in court-martial proceedings, and had an unresolved personal relationship as well. This show always delivered crisp plotting and interesting trials, giving viewers a peek into the unfamiliar life of military lawyers.

The premiere of *The Practice* in 1997 was a landmark event in the development of criminal law on television. This show had an excellent seven-year run. It completely deglamorized the practice of criminal law. Bobby Donnell's firm of bottom-feeders took the cases nobody else wanted and cut a lot of corners in the process. Frequently, the show explored fascinating moral and ethical issues. The lawyers, who mostly had troubled personal lives, sometimes questioned the way they made their living. Their job was to defend vicious and depraved criminals, but that is what criminal lawyers do, and they did it well.

Finally, *Shark* had an unfortunately brief two-year run from 2006–2008. With James Woods in the title role as Sebastian "The Shark" Stark, the show looked at criminal law from the prosecution side. However, Stark and his assistants treated their job very differently from the straight-arrow prosecutors on *Law & Order*. Ethics went straight out the window in an all-out attempt to win and put the bad guys away. As Stark liked to tell his staff, in post-modern style, "Truth is relative. Pick one that works." The shows were always entertaining, but often a bit over the top.

Another criminal law show, Steven Bochco's *Raising the Bar*, premiered in 2008, too late to be included in this book. It concerns the highly adversarial combat between a small group of prosecutors and public defenders who work against each other every day in the same courtrooms—and spend plenty of time in each other's beds. *Raising the Bar* treats public defenders with respect and even some admiration, a welcome antidote to the trashing of defense lawyers in *Law & Order* and *Shark*.

CHAPTER 9

Matlock—America's Greatest Lawyer? A Transatlantic Perspective

STEVE GREENFIELD, GUY OSBORN, AND PETER ROBSON

Matlock is an almost entirely unknown series to people in Britain, and the eponymous hero is remembered very vaguely as a slimmer, rather more handsome successor to private eye Frank Cannon. We are interested in writing about *Matlock* from a British perspective because he seems to us, curiously, to exemplify American cultural hegemony at both its strongest and weakest. We are aware that *Matlock* contains many cultural references that will pass over the heads of the British audience, but that will have been appreciated by an American audience. We hope that our restricted understanding of the nuances in this portrayal of an American Southern lawyer will not limit our remarks too much. Indeed, *L.A. Law* has been on British TV screens for the past 20 years almost continuously, and its characters and situations have been appreciated and understood on this side of the Atlantic. Despite our suggestion that Ben Matlock is, for British audiences, largely forgotten or misremembered, we in Britain may be about to take him to our hearts at the end of

Matlock

Aired:
- September 23, 1986– May 7, 1995, NBC/ABC

Cast:
- Andy Griffith (Benjamin Matlock)
- Nancy Stafford (Michelle Thomas)
- Kene Holliday (Tyler Hudson)
- Clarence Gilyard Jr. (Conrad McMasters)
- Linda Purl (Charlene Matlock)

Awards:
- Emmy for Outstanding Individual Achievement in Music Composition for a Series (1992)
- Emmy Nomination for Outstanding Achievement in Music Composition for a Series (1987, 1990, 1991)
- Julie Sommars, Golden Globe Nomination for Best Performance by an Actress in a Supporting Role in a Series (1990)
- BMI TV Music Award (1988, 1989, 1990, 1991)

Courtesy of Photofest.

MATLOCK
Ben (Andy Griffith) prepares for some homespun courtroom
wizardry so his client can be freed at the last second.

the first decade of the 21st century in a way undreamt of when he first
came to the small screen. Perhaps he even has the potential to overtake
L.A. Law in the public imagination. To explain why this might happen,
we need to provide a little bit of context on 'screen lawyers.

**Film and
TV Lawyers**

There are over 700 films in the Tarlton Law Library film
collection at the University of Texas School of Law that
feature lawyers in a major or secondary role. Unlike
the private eye and police film subgenres, however, there are no repeat
players, only bravura performers. We meet Frank Galvin once and leave
him alone in his hotel bedroom in *The Verdict* (1982). We may wonder
how his life progresses in his fight against corruption, alcoholism, and

Charlotte Rampling, but we can only speculate. Martin Vail transforms himself from a publicity-seeking egomaniac to a caring fighter for the underdog in *Primal Fear* (1996). How will he respond to disappointment at the discovery of human frailty? Will Amanda Bonner really enter the upcoming political race against Adam, as we suspect, or will she transmogrify into some kind of desperate housewife from Betty Friedan's *The Feminine Mystique*, recognizing the incompatibility of uxorial and professional life? Will she indeed become no more than *Adam's Rib* (1949)? Nobody knows, but we carry with us an image of them, whole and complete, based on their 90 to 120 minutes in our company.

Television lawyers are a very different beast. They remain with us for at least six hours, and in a significant number of cases, for several years. We know how they develop as professional and private individuals because we live with them over a period of time. Professional success, personal failure, and the way they respond to the vagaries of life bring us into a much closer relationship with them. Or so you would think.

As teachers of courses on law and popular culture, we continue, however, to be surprised that only scholars make a distinction between film and TV lawyers. Members of the public seem to make no such distinction. When we have spoken with, and issued questionnaires to, our students about fictional screen lawyers, they make no differentiation between those on film and those on television. Despite the fact that Atticus Finch's career as a lawyer lasted for only two hours in *To Kill a Mockingbird* (1962), he is talked of in the same breath as Perry Mason, whose screen time amounts to some 286 hours. There is, however, a much less vibrant and extensive scholarship around TV lawyers than there is around their film counterparts. Our bibliography in *Film and the Law* (2009) lists over 500 articles on film lawyers, while there are fewer than a tenth of that number of articles on small-screen lawyers.[1] In the English language there are some 13 books and collections on film and law, and only two on TV and law. If, as we have found, the coverage is different and yet the impact seems to be the same, we are left to consider the reasons. Our most obvious response, but one to which few would admit, is the cultural hierarchy. Film, while it may be below theatre and literature, is certainly placed above television. However, consideration even of low-grade fodder for the masses can help us in our quest for clues as to how popular culture buttresses social institutions. For us, this is the focus, and importance, of law and popular culture.

One reason why this collection is particularly interesting is that it offers opportunities for some arcane and potentially significant TV lawyers to be rescued from the memories of scholars and replayed to a new audience. Step forward, Atlanta lawyer Ben Matlock. Where have you been, and what have you been doing?

TV Lawyers 'Round the World	Ben has been circulating the world, successfully spreading the popularity of the adversarial system. The dramatic possibilities of courtroom drama were recognized in film long before the advent of TV. Here was a

cheap and easy way to meet the demand of the public for something that seemed to touch their lives. A single indoor set and a bunch of actors were all that was necessary. The success of "whodunits" in popular literature offered a source of ready-made scripts. When TV came into existence as a mass medium in the late 1940s and early 1950s, courtroom conflict was a type of drama that could be shot using the limited technology available. Just like the apprehension phase in the cop show, the jury deliberation provided a neat, self-contained segment that could be packaged into the 60-minute slots favored in the early years of TV. It was in this way, of course, that Reginald Rose first brought *12 Angry Men* to the public's attention in 1954 on CBS's *Studio One*.

The spread of the popularity of indigenous TV lawyers into other parts of the world in the past 50 years has been impressive. Canada has reflected the lives and loves of a bunch of young Torontonians in *The Associates* (2000), while Australia and New Zealand have produced law shows featuring a range of urban and rural settings. Most recently, *The Circuit* (2007) told the story of a young city-educated Aboriginal lawyer going for a sabbatical in the Northwest Outback and encountering conflicts that arise from the imposition of the legal system on his own people. Spain has produced half a dozen series, from *Anillos de oro* (*Wedding Rings*, about a pair of divorce lawyers)[2] to *Al Filo de la Ley* (*On the Edge of Law*, a Spanish *L.A. Law*), since the fall of Franco in 1975. These provide the setting for an account of the stresses of adjusting to democracy after 40 years of dictatorship. Viewers in France have enjoyed more than a decade of the law firm series *Avocats et Associés* (*The Law Firm*).[3] This, like the Spanish series, manages to create the drama of the adversarial system within the culture's truth-seeking, paper-based inquisitorial system.

Most recently come *Lawyers,* from South Korea, and *Common Lawyers,* from Japan, each of which is centered on teams of young lawyers fighting for justice.

What unites all these examples of the struggle for proper treatment in the courtroom are their settings, which are crafted to approximate the dramatic Anglo-American model. Because these series have become available for us to view on DVD, we can now judge to what extent the issues that are featured in other cultures resemble our own. It is certainly fascinating to watch every weekday afternoon current German television programs like *Das Jugendgericht* and *Das Familiengericht* and observe how these appear to be adversarial, yet take place within an inquisitorial framework. And therein lies the issue of cultural dominance.[4]

The Anglo-American Hegemony

Television executives report that while they can fill their time slots easily with imported material, the public actually prefers home-produced material. This explains the appearance of the series we mentioned above, as well as the slew of other material we discuss in our forthcoming book *TV Lawyers Today.* For a range of reasons, home-produced product is not always an option, so there is a need to rely on foreign series. Two countries have produced significantly more TV lawyer drama series than the rest. In the United States there have been over 100 series featuring lawyers, and 30 British lawyer series have been broadcast in the past 50 years. Thus, there is a considerable body of examples of Anglo-American, adversarial screen lawyers to enjoy and explore.

In Britain we are in an interesting situation. We have experienced the cultural inflow of the vast American output of TV law programs. What we saw depended on the purchasing decisions of the television companies. From 1955 and 1967, with only two channels running between lunchtime and 11 PM, Britain had the opportunity to watch *Perry Mason* and *The Defenders* on the noncommercial channel.[5] These were followed by *Petrocelli* in the 1970s. As such, people in Britain felt they knew pretty much what lawyers did: they supplemented the inadequate forces of law and order in solving crime. This came as no surprise to us, because we were familiar with the work of Sherlock Holmes, Miss Marple, and Hercule Poirot, both in fiction and on the small screen.

This was all part of the modern cultural flow from West to East. From *I Love Lucy* and *I Married Joan* through *Happy Days* and *The Waltons* to *Dallas, Dynasty,* and *Knots Landing,* British viewers have learned about American culture directly. We are familiar with American life because we have seen it in its fullness, from the South of *The Beverly Hillbillies* and *The Dukes of Hazzard* to the Florida of *Miami Vice* and the New York of *NYPD Blue* and *Friends*. People in London know more about Boston from *Cheers* than they know about Wales or Belfast. It is little wonder that with the advent of cheaper airfares the United States has become the number-one holiday destination for people from Britain. We are going abroad to somewhere that we already know pretty damned well.

When there have been exports from Britain to the United States, as with *Till Death Us Do Part* (aka *All in the Family*) and *The Office,* they have generally been reformatted to translate culturally. Those that were not reformatted (like *Absolutely Fabulous*) have not been ratings successes. Visual comedies like *Benny Hill* and *Mr. Bean* have fared better. This, then, is the context in which we find someone like Ben Matlock reaching our shores in the late 1980s. How have he and his blue-and-white seer-sucker suit fared in the damp, miserable climate of Britain?

The Lifespan of TV Lawyers

He is a forgotten man. Why? There are two principal reasons. First, there is the question of cultural impact. Although scholars might like to think that cultural figures persist from generation to generation, this does not appear to be borne out by our work. The icons of today are the forgotten people of the next generation. Over the past few years, we have explored the nature and extent of our students' knowledge of a range of cultural figures. From Atticus Finch to Ally McBeal, from Sir Wilfrid Robarts to Theodore Gulliver, we have inquired as to who sits in the students' mental in-box. Who do they think of when asked about lawyers in film or TV? For the vast majority, this knowledge is limited to those currently on screen. A significant number lack even this knowledge. The same goes for the general public, as far as we can judge.

The fond idea that we all carry around with us a store of heroic images of lawyers culled from popular culture is less than accurate. A few film buffs do. Some TV fans may. Most do not. Similar work carried out with practicing lawyers suggests that individuals retain knowledge only of the lawyers of their formative years. As adults, they consciously avoid watching the versions of lawyers presented on screen. Doctors find their professional lives trivialized on screen; lawyers in Britain complain to us of the same problem. The stresses of days spent wrestling with the complexities and frustrations of modern legal practice perhaps are not best relieved by watching shiny-suited smoothies or eager young whipper-snappers challenging and storming the bastions of power and privilege with awesome ease. Comparing the TV documentary series *Boston Law* (2001) with the fictional *Boston Legal* (2004) is a salutary lesson for the ordinary viewer. For the average working person, it is a reminder of the disjunction between what we can achieve in life and what we dream of.

One of our early ideas, when we started looking at lawyers in popular culture, was to draw a distinction between those who were clearly role models and those who performed a comedic function, or who were technically lawyers but spent all their time in detective work. Again, from our interviews and discussions with students, it is clear that they make no distinction between "proper" models and slight, comedic figures. It is always dangerous to assume that audiences will regard as irrelevant some show that we regard as pure fluff. Similarly, the notion of differentiation between crime solvers and courtroom protagonists does not appear to be in any sense embedded. So the unlikely nature of Ben Matlock's setup, with individual clients paying huge fees to be exonerated through his team's investigative work, should not provide an obstacle to his rise to the status of Perry Mason or Horace Rumpole.[6]

L.A. *Law* and *Matlock* in Britain

Ben Matlock has run into competition in his quest for global success, and this has somewhat stunted his achievements. Within a fortnight in autumn 1986, two long-running shows commenced their lives on American television. One, *L.A. Law,* has gone on to influence the way we see law and lawyers represented,[7] but is, in a sense, forgotten in America. The other, *Matlock,* achieved a long run with its simple story lines and recognizable characters. It lives on in DVD form, although the publicity says, "America's Greatest Lawyer. Case Closed." We are fascinated to note this apparent paradox and explore some of the reasons for it.

L.A. Law was imported into Britain soon after it started its first U.S. run. Perhaps recognizing its likely wide appeal after the success of Steven Bochco's previous show, *Hill Street Blues*, it was scheduled in prime time, although British television had become a 24-hour-a-day phenomenon. It achieved significant audience figures and ran from 1986 through to 1994, with 171 episodes in eight seasons. Even before terrestrial TV channels in Britain expanded, and cable and online channels exploded, this was a major achievement. So great was the perceived impact of the show that it was used as a catchline to attract students to British universities. In *10 Reasons to Study Law* this was listed as number four: "You've seen *L.A. Law* and fancy this could be you." It was to potential students in the 1980s what *Ally McBeal* (1997) became in the 1990s.[8]

Matlock, by contrast, exemplifies late night/afternoon fodder. As TV hours expanded and the competition between channels intensified, material was purchased to fill the space. In came an old American detective series. It starred someone with unlikely, insincere American silver hair in the style of *Dynasty's* John Forsyth. No one in Britain had heard of Andy Griffith or knew of Sheriff Andy Taylor. The tiny British audiences who watched during the only season when it was shown would soon discover that this was not a follow-up to *Cannon,* but rather a fresh version of *Petrocelli* without the house-building in the desert. It went largely unnoticed and, after one season, it disappeared from the post-midnight schedule. With its predictable storylines and hammy acting, its passing went unmourned. It came as something of a shock to us to read in Gail Richmond's 1998 article on *Matlock* in *Prime Time Law*[9] that Griffith actually went on to film a further eight seasons until 1995 and was an American institution.

It seems to us, though, that the different fates of *L.A. Law* and *Matlock* in Britain sum up the relative importance of the programs. One seems groundbreaking and truly engaging. The other is a reworking of a tried and tested format with stock stories. *L.A. Law* emphasized that lawyers were driven by factors other than the pursuit of truth and justice. It also illustrated that ambition and rivalry played a major part in the trajectory of their careers. Moral issues are discussed and played out both within the courtroom and in the office of the firm of Mackenzie Brackman. These issues range from the abuse of dwarfs and the reproductive rights of those with learning difficulties to the progress of women, ethnic minorities, and gays in the legal profession. Through the voice of Douglas Brackman, these debates are placed in the context of the need for the firm to operate in a commercial context. The barriers to the progress of ethnic minority, female, and GLB lawyers are all charted in a way that had never been done in any previous lawyer show.

Matlock seems to offer a marked contrast, although it recognizes that we have reached the 1980s. Unlike *Perry Mason*, *The Defenders*, and *Petrocelli*, there is a black face, in the form of Tyler Hudson—and not just as domestic help but as a reluctant private investigator. There is a female presence by way of the occasional female judge as well as a feisty young woman lawyer, Charlene Matlock. Her role is not simply to be supportive but to act as Matlock's associate. Her symbolism is, however, somewhat limited since she is Matlock's daughter. The programs involve Matlock as a defense lawyer for a variety of people accused of murder.

All 22 cases in the first series, aired in the United States between September 1986 and May 1987, involve Matlock defending someone on a murder charge. The potential victims of miscarriages of justice vary from a nurse ("The Nurse," Feb. 3, 1987) and a hostess on a TV show ("The Chef," Jan. 6, 1987), to a sex therapist ("The Therapist," Mar. 3, 1987), a police officer ("The Cop," Nov. 18, 1986), and even, as if one could credit the prosecution's foolhardiness, a law professor—albeit one who wore a bow tie ("The Professor," Dec. 2, 1986). The one slight variation is the episode in which Matlock himself is accused of jury tampering during his defense of a union organizer accused of murdering a politician ("The People v. Matlock," Mar. 24, 1987). The rich and famous somehow know about Matlock, and clients fall over themselves to be defended by this "überlawyer." In the Fulton County courthouse, Ben is invincible, and not a single client is ever convicted.

What is so fascinating about the contrast between *Matlock* and *L.A. Law* are the different eras their formats represent. *Matlock's* style is from the 1950s. It is *Perry Mason* in color. It has a simple setup. We see a murder and someone implicated. This person is then arrested and Ben Matlock is called in. With his investigator and his daughter lending a hand, along with his homespun charm, the true murderer is unveiled. When shown in Britain, the assumption was that this was a program from a far-distant era. Part of this came from the way in which the technical process of American programs used to translate into rather garish colors on British TV sets. It felt like the 1970s, much as *L.A. Law* felt like the 1990s.

Matlock on its own home turf was a tribute to its market. It was renewed repeatedly and lasted for nine seasons between 1986 and 1995. It is comfort TV. Just like the less well-dressed detective, *Columbo* (1971), *Matlock*'s setup is familiar and is repeated in every episode. In *Columbo*, we actually know who did the crime; the pleasure, week in and week out, is seeing Peter Falk stumble his way to the truth as if by accident. Yet it still fascinates. A good parallel is "rom-coms," where we know that Sandra Bullock and Hugh Grant (in *Two Weeks Notice* [2002]), Pierce Brosnan and Julianne Moore (in *Laws of Attraction* [2004]), or whomever might be the leads will end up together after initial repulsion, attraction, misunderstanding, and resolution. We still watch.

At a sociopolitical level, Ben Matlock inhabits a world in which some people are driven by personal greed or jealousy to commit murder. Just when it looks as though they are going to escape, our plucky hero brings them to justice. The legal process makes it safe. We will not end up on death row due to a pile of circumstantial evidence. It is all much less unsettling than the world of nuanced motives and ethical dilemmas that is inhabited by Michael Kuzak, Grace Van Owen, Victor Sifuentes, and their coworkers in *L.A. Law*.

Conclusion

Strangely, for reasons of commerce rather than any question of serious impact or social value, the world of *Matlock* is available to modern-day viewers in a way in which *L.A. Law* is not. The latter, having set the benchmark, has been overtaken by new developments in both style and focus. Having discovered the world of multiple-partner practice as an alternative to the problems of the falsely accused, Steven Bochco and others have gone on to expand the TV lawyer genre. We have seen the coming together of the apprehension and adjudication phases of the justice system in the prosaic *Law & Order* (1990). In the shift to Bobby Donnell's office in Boston in *The Practice* (1997),[10] we move away from the problems of the largely affluent clients of Mackenzie Brackman. We have seen postmodern twists and spoofs on the genre in *Ally McBeal* and *Boston Legal*.[11]

One can only wish for DVDs of *L.A. Law* to come to the market—and wonder whether we really will see the rest of *Matlock*. For us in Britain, with only the DVD of Series One, we are left where we came in. We have a reminder of a largely forgotten one-year wonder. Short of emigrating, we may never know whether our lack of conviction that he is, indeed, America's Greatest Lawyer can be properly assessed. Given the cost of producing DVDs and the profit margins, we suspect that we may be in a position to give a more rounded judgment sometime in the not-too-distant future. Descriptions of subsequent series do not, however, bode well for change of mind. So far, we are not totally convinced. We might just go as far as one of his clients, the rock star Angel, who summed Ben up after he successfully defended her on a charge of murdering a rock promoter: "You know, for a lawyer, you're OK" ("The Angel," Nov. 25, 1986). Maybe it's just a cultural divide thang.

Endnotes

1. STEVE GREENFIELD, GUY OSBORN, AND PETER ROBSON, FILM AND THE LAW (Hart Publishing, Oxford, 2009).

2. See Anja Louis's chapter "Divorce in Your Living Room: TV Lawyers in Spain's Transition to Democracy."

3. See Barbara Villez's chapter "French Television Lawyers in *Avocats et Associés*."

4. See Stefan Machura's chapter "German Judge Shows: Migrating from the Courtroom to the TV Studio."

5. See Francis M. Nevins's chapter "*Perry Mason*" and David Ginsburg's chapter "*The Defenders*: TV Lawyers and Controversy in the New Frontier."

6. See Paul Bergman's chapter "Rumpole and the Bowl of Comfort Food."

7. See Phil Meyer's chapter "Revisiting *L.A. Law.*"

8. See Cassandra Sharp's chapter "*Ally McBeal*—Life and Love in the Law."

9. Gail Levin Richmond, "Matlock," in *Prime Time Law* (Robert M. Jarvis & Paul R. Joseph, eds.) (Carolina Acad. Press 1998).

10. See Shannon Mader's chapter "*Law & Order*" and Jeffrey Thomas's chapter "*The Practice*: Debunking Television Myths and Stereotypes."

11. See Corinne Brinkerhoff's chapter "Reality Bites: *Boston Legal*'s Creative License with the Law" and Cassandra Sharp's chapter "*Ally McBeal*—Life and Love in the Law."

CHAPTER 10

Law & Order

SHANNON MADER

Before it became indelibly associated with the most successful legal drama and second longest-running prime-time drama in television history, the phrase "Law and Order" was better known as a campaign slogan—one that Republican presidential nominees from Richard Nixon to George H.W. Bush used with considerable political success.[1]

To its liberal critics, the slogan "law and order" was a racist code word. As early as 1968, liberals were decrying Richard Nixon's pledge to restore "law and order" as carrying an "undertone of racism" and an attempt to "get the support of the white backlash people around the country."[2] By the late 1980s, however, liberals had begun to recognize that dismissing voters' desire for "law and order" was not a recipe for electoral success. Indeed, in a 1989 piece on the mayoral race between David Dinkins and Rudy Giuliani, the *New York Times* noted the changing political climate, one that would eventually culminate with the election of Bill Clinton as a self-described tough-on-crime New Democrat:

> Not long ago, law and order was one critical test that divided liberals from conservatives. Today, with crime the top issue on voters' minds, there is no candidate who

Law & Order

Aired:
- September 13, 1990–present, NBC

Cast:
- Steven Hill (Adam Schiff)
- Michael Moriarty (Ben Stone)
- Richard Brooks (Paul Robinette)
- Jill Hennessy (Claire Kincaid)
- Sam Waterston (Jack McCoy)
- Carey Lowell (Jamie Ross)
- Angie Harmon (Abbie Carmichael)
- Diane Wiest (Nora Lewin)
- Elisabeth Röhm (Serena Southerlyn)
- Fred Dalton Thompson (Arthur Branch)
- Annie Parisse (Alexandra Borgia)
- Alana de la Garza (Connie Rubirosa)
- Linus Roache (Michael Cutter)

Awards:
- Emmy for Outstanding Drama Series (1997)
- Emmy for Outstanding Cinematography for a Series (1997, 1998)
- Sam Waterston, SAG Award for Outstanding Performance by a Male Actor in a Drama Series (1999)
- Jerry Orbach, SAG Award for Outstanding Performance by a Male Actor in a Drama Series (2005)
- Golden Globe nomination for Best TV Series—Drama (1992, 1994, 1998, 1999)

117

will not promise to get tough with criminals. Mr. Dinkins has called for both more police and more social programs, for both enforcement and treatment in the war against drugs.[3]

It was in the midst of this changing political climate that *Law & Order* was conceived and born. (The pilot was filmed in 1988, and the first episode aired on September 13, 1990.)[4] Understanding this political climate is critical to understanding the politics and characters of *Law & Order*.

As the introduction to this volume indicates, the politics of *Law & Order* are often dismissed as, if not conservative, at least center-right.[5] But with a recurring cast of villains that includes anti-abortion protesters ("Life Choice," "Progeny"); greedy executives (pick an episode); conservative politicians ("Virtue," "Pride"); and right-wing militiamen ("Nullification," "Open Season"); not to mention such one-off villains as the sexist military man who believes his naval career has been ruined by feminism ("Conduct Unbecoming"), many conservatives would disagree. And as Dick Wolf told the *New York Times* in 1992, "You'd have a hard time finding anybody who associated with this show who would identify himself as a conservative Republican."[6] Of course, this was before Michael Moriarty's political odyssey and before Fred Dalton Thompson joined the cast, but the reality is that until Assistant District Attorney (ADA) Abbie Carmichael, District Attorney (DA) Arthur Branch, and, to a lesser extent, ADA Alexandra Borgia joined *Law & Order*'s cast of characters, the show's prosecutors were all liberals of various stripes, with the short-lived DA Nora Lewin as the most stereotypically liberal of the group.

It is the thesis of this essay that *Law & Order*'s portrayal of a group of largely liberal prosecutors and its use of the politically charged phrase "law and order" in its title were not coincidental, but rather a deliberate attempt to reconfigure the politics of the crime drama and craft a new role model or image for liberals, one that would allow liberals to recapture the "law and order" mantle.

Fortuitously for the show, a politician emerged on the national scene who shared this agenda. But despite the fact that the politics of the show closely approximated those of Bill Clinton, it was Robert F. Kennedy, not Clinton (who in 1990 was still the governor of Arkansas), who appears to have been the show's inspiration for its two principal characters, Executive Assistant District Attorney (EADA) Ben Stone (Michael Moriarty) and EADA Jack McCoy (Sam Waterston).

Courtesy of Photofest.

LAW & ORDER
Ben Stone (Michael Moriarty), Clare Kincaid (Jill Hennessy),
and Adam Schiff (Steven Hill—seated) plan prosecutorial
strategy in another tricky case.

The figure of Robert F. Kennedy—who, after all, was a lawyer
(indeed, the nation's highest-ranking lawyer for three years), and who
initially came to public attention through his relentless pursuit of Jimmy
Hoffa—looms large in *Law & Order*, if not always as conspicuously as in
the series pilot, wherein a large RFK poster is prominently displayed in
Stone's office.[7]

In attempting to synthesize the cop show and the legal drama, *Law
& Order* was also attempting a political synthesis of sorts—a melding of
the generally conservative politics of the cop show with the more liberal
politics of the legal drama. The model for this synthesis appears to have
been RFK, who (at least in liberal legend) transcended, if only for a few
months, the political polarization of the 1960s by magically winning the
support of both working-class whites and inner-city blacks with a tough-
guy liberalism that fused liberal compassion with conservative rhetoric
about law and order and personal responsibility.[8]

**Ben Stone,
Jack McCoy, and
Adam Schiff**

In the characters of Ben Stone and Jack McCoy—both, significantly, Irish Catholics—*Law & Order* attempted to recreate the RFK myth by creating characters who practiced, albeit on a much smaller and more human scale, the tough-guy liberalism that RFK preached. But the series changed dramatically between its first season (when Ben Stone first appeared) and the fifth season (when Jack McCoy first appeared), and those differences in tone, style, and substance explain in large part the differences between the two characters.

Ben Stone: The Force of Moral Conviction
and Reasoned Argument

In at least the first two seasons of *Law & Order*, New York City frequently plays the role of 1960s America in a microcosm—a city constantly on the edge, with racial and ethnic tensions threatening to boil over at any time. Although superficially resembling then-contemporary New York City under the tumultuous tenure of David Dinkins, the New York City of the early seasons is actually drawn from the cop shows and movies of the 1970s and early 1980s (*The French Connection, Serpico, Fort Apache the Bronx, Kojak, Prince of the City*), as well as the social-realist television shows and movies of the 1960s and 1970s (*Dog Day Afternoon, The Pawnbroker*).[9]

The character of Ben Stone—whose soft-spoken manner is so jarring to viewers accustomed to the fiery Jack McCoy—serves in part as a foil to this hothouse atmosphere with its often histrionic acting, hectic courtroom scenes, and frequently over-the-top plots. Many plots are loosely based on tabloid fodder like the Bernard Goetz incident ("Subterranean Homebody Blues"), the Tawana Brawley case ("Out of the Half-Light"), the Edmund Perry shooting ("Poison Ivy"), and the Robert Mapplethorpe controversy ("Prisoner of Love").

In style and temperament, Stone appears at first blush to bear a closer resemblance to such coolly intellectual liberals as Eugene McCarthy or Adlai Stevenson than to RFK. With his seemingly unemotional courtroom demeanor (Stone almost never raises his voice at defendants or witnesses, except when preparing his own witnesses to testify—see, for instance, his prep of a rape victim in "The Violence of Summer") and detached rhetorical style (in his openings and closings, he frequently looks away from the jury, whether up, down, or to the side—indeed, he even occasionally turns his back to the jury), Stone hardly approximates the passionate oratory we typically associate with RFK.[10] But that is because he appears to have been patterned on a very specific RFK—the RFK who informed a largely black audience in Indianapolis, Indiana, that Martin Luther King, Jr., had been shot. The calming voice of reason in a city gone mad, Ben Stone's role is that of a seemingly neutral moral arbiter who, through dispassionate argument and analysis, convinces a jury to render the legally (and morally) correct verdict.[11] But unlike his successor, Jack McCoy, Stone wants the jury to reach the correct verdict in the same way he reached it—by coolly analyzing the evidence and rendering the correct judgment based on that evidence. This is a deliberative process that has the effect of both calming the city's passions and sating its thirst for justice. In this respect at least, Stone's self-appointed role seems to be the same as that which fate foisted upon RFK on that dark night in Indianapolis.

More so than McCoy, Stone also captures the brooding, introspective aspect of RFK. A man of deep moral convictions, Stone frequently grapples with the morality of his own conduct. In "Point of View," the defendant, a woman accused of murder, claims self-defense based on her reasonable fear that she was about to be raped. Dr. Olivet interviews the defendant, and finds her fear of imminent rape credible. Stone decides not to call Dr. Olivet, but a summary of her opinion ends up in the hands of the defense, so the defense calls her. Recognizing that Dr. Olivet will make an effective witness for the defense, DA Adam Schiff (Steven Hill) suggests that Stone question Dr. Olivet about her own recent rape in order to raise doubts about the objectivity of her analysis. Stone, however, is reluctant to sandbag Dr. Olivet and tells Schiff that he would like to warn her. "She is a colleague," he tells Schiff. "She deserves our consideration." Schiff scoffs at Stone's chivalry, noting that any such consideration would be construed an attempt to influence a witness. "If you want to play nursemaid," Schiff concludes, "do it after the trial." Stone's cross-examination of Dr. Olivet is effective, and her objectivity is seemingly punctured. Subsequently, the woman's claim of self-defense is exposed as a fraud. At the end of the episode, Stone approaches Dr. Olivet and apologizes. The apology is sincere, but Stone does not look at Dr. Olivet when he makes it. Instead, he gazes downward, a glance suggesting not only shame or guilt but also penance. In essence, Stone is apologizing or repenting to himself.

Stone's moral self-questioning culminates with his resignation in the final episode of season four ("Old Friends"). And what causes Stone to resign is guilt—guilt for having compelled a reluctant and frightened witness to testify against a Russian mobster. After the witness (whose testimony provides the only corroboration for that of a coconspirator) changes her testimony on the stand, Stone has her arrested for felony perjury and subsequently threatens to prosecute her for conspiracy to commit murder. ADA Claire Kincaid and Schiff each try to persuade Stone to drop the charges, but Stone refuses. In the end, the witness agrees to testify, and the mobster is convicted. But the witness is later gunned down. Kincaid finds Stone sitting in his office, wallowing in guilt and nursing a drink. In a well-meaning but somewhat awkward attempt to console him, Claire Kincaid remarks, "Knowing who you are, Ben, you didn't have any choice."

In the next scene, we learn that Stone has resigned. In a brief but moving exchange with Schiff, Schiff asks Stone how he's doing. Stone replies, "I'm as clear as a bell"—a seemingly incongruous remark, given that Stone is resigning precisely because of a guilty conscience. But upon further reflection, it is apparent that there is a certain logic to the remark. By resigning, Stone is punishing himself and, thus, clearing his conscience. Moreover, the remark suggests a new level of self-awareness on Stone's part: he now recognizes that, given the type of person he is, he will always make the choice he did, and that he must therefore never be in a position to make that choice again. In short, he recognizes that he cannot be trusted to wield the power of a prosecutor—a remarkably humble insight that suggests a possible critique of the RFK model of tough-guy liberalism.

The departure of Stone also reflected an underlying shift in the style and tone of the show. With the election of Bill Clinton as president and Rudy Giuliani as mayor of New York City, a new centrist consensus on crime seemed to be emerging that rendered the first two seasons' stark racial and ethnic polarization and boiling-cauldron image of New York City less relevant. The show's third and fourth seasons had already modulated the tone, but Stone's departure confirmed it.

Jack McCoy: The Force of Moral Indignation
and Impassioned Argument

With his lanky frame and large flop of sloping hair, McCoy bears a distinct physical resemblance to RFK. But even more pronounced than the physical similarity is the similarity in their temperaments. Driven to win at nearly any cost, and possessed by a moral fervor that can strike others as arrogant and self-righteous, McCoy embodies both the moral passion and the ruthless competitiveness of RFK.

However, McCoy is a far more down-to-earth figure than RFK. The son of a long-time police officer (who, we learn in the pivotal episode "Aftershock," abused his son), McCoy is no patrician or child of privilege. Nor does he have RFK's (or Stone's) brooding, introspective quality. He is a man of action, not reflection, and is no ivory-tower or limousine liberal.

The first episode of season five ("Second Opinion") cannily and economically draws the character of Jack McCoy in a scant 25 minutes. (He does not appear until nearly 20 minutes into the episode.) Among other things, we learn that he (1) had romantic relationships with the three previous ADAs who worked under him, even marrying one of them; (2) works lying down—we see him reading documents while stretched out on his sofa; (3) changes into jeans before leaving work (and, even more shockingly, disrobes with Claire Kincaid in the room); (4) enjoys a drink with his colleagues, or at least his female colleagues, after work; and (5) rides a motorcycle (we see him leaving the office with a motorcycle helmet under his arm). In short, he is not the stuffed shirt that Ben Stone was. He is casual, sociable, and relaxed.

But we also learn in that first episode that McCoy is a relentless and determined prosecutor who will employ whatever legal theory he has to in order to prosecute the offenders—especially those who offend his moral sensibilities. The victim in "Second Opinion" is a breast cancer patient who dies of . . . well, breast cancer. But despite the fact that she died of natural causes, McCoy is determined to prosecute the victim's "doctor," a PhD whose treatment for breast cancer consists of a metabolic therapy similar to laetrile. The doctor's sin, in McCoy's eyes, is that she "sells false hope to unwitting victims." Therefore, McCoy is willing to employ whatever legal theory he has to—first fraud, then murder—in order to put her out of business and behind bars. As she often does,

Kincaid resists McCoy's black-and-white moral certitude. Having interviewed several of the practitioner's current and former patients, Kincaid develops sympathy for them and their desire, in the face of terminal cancer, to "die with dignity" rather than undergo a mutilating mastectomy and a hopeless course of chemotherapy. When McCoy protests that the doctor is "fleecing" her patients, Kincaid responds, "Maybe they want to be fleeced." But once it is revealed that the doctor did in fact mislead the victim into believing that her treatment was a cure, it is Kincaid who demands that the doctor serve the maximum sentence.

Moral indignation and moral disgust are the emotions that drive McCoy. In "Rage," for instance, McCoy tells the defendant, "You don't scare me, Mr. Greer. But you do disgust me." In "Second Opinion," when the accused doctor tells McCoy, "You make it sound like I am some sort of confidence man selling swampland in Florida," McCoy replies, "Don't flatter yourself." In "Bounty," McCoy tells a defense lawyer who attempts to defend his client, an African-American journalist patterned after Jayson Blair, by claiming that he cracked under the pressure of affirmative action, "I'm not just tired of you. I'm disgusted. I'm disgusted that you would take these global travesties and bend them and twist them and turn them inside out just to get a murderer off."

Moral indignation and outrage are also the emotions that McCoy hopes will drive the jury. In contrast to the seemingly affectless Stone, McCoy marshals the full range of affect—from a frequently raised voice to frequently raised eyebrows—to instill in the jurors the moral outrage and indignation he feels.[12] This is no mere appeal to the jury's emotions, however. Rather, McCoy's courtroom dramatics are an appeal to the jury's moral sensibilities. There is a critical difference between the two. McCoy does not want the jury to base its verdict on pity for the victim. Accordingly, bloody photographs of the victim's lifeless body and testimony from bereaved relatives typically play very little role in McCoy's case in chief. Instead, McCoy wants the jury to render a judgment based on moral outrage at the defendant's conduct and character—a character revealed not only in the crime (and whatever prior bad acts McCoy manages to get in front of the jury), but also in his or her courtroom demeanor.[13] In asking the jury to render a guilty verdict, therefore, McCoy is not asking the jury to vent; he is asking it to express a deeply felt moral norm, the defendant's violation of which is an appropriate cause for moral outrage and indignation.

Liberal and Conservative Critics of Tough-Guy Liberalism

At different points in the series, McCoy is paired with female ADAs who are more liberal than he is: Claire Kincaid, Jamie Ross, and Serena Southerlyn. And in one season, McCoy's superior is a female DA who is more liberal than he: Nora Lewin. At different points in the series, McCoy is also paired with female ADAs who are more conservative than he: Abbie Carmichael and, to a lesser extent, Alexandra Borgia. Later, McCoy's superior is Arthur Branch, a male DA who is considerably more conservative than he.[14]

While each of these characters is unique and cannot be reduced to his or her political views, their collective role is to serve as critics, from opposing sides, of McCoy's tough-guy liberalism. This criticism allows the show to portray a variety of political viewpoints—none of which is portrayed as being entirely right or wrong—and to position McCoy as the centrist despite his fundamental liberalism.

While the liberal critics of McCoy's tough-guy liberalism generally do not meet happy fates (Kincaid is killed in a car accident, Ross leaves due to family issues and subsequently becomes a defense lawyer, Southerlyn is fired, and Lewin lasts a single season), it would be unfair to claim that the show is somehow dismissing or slighting their views. Not only are they portrayed as much stronger characters than such an argument suggests, but they are portrayed as stronger *because of* their views. While they constantly struggle with the dilemmas posed by their liberal ideals and duties as prosecutors, they never shirk their duties. They therefore function as more than simply counterpoints to McCoy; they function as role models as well, by demonstrating that one can be both a committed liberal and a good prosecutor.

Adam Schiff: The Voice of Moral Realism

On paper, Adam Schiff is the most clichéd of *Law & Order*'s characters—the crusty old-timer who sees the world through seasoned and somewhat cynical eyes. Purportedly modeled on Robert Morgenthau, Manhattan's legendary district attorney, Schiff also bears a certain resemblance to Frank Mankiewicz, RFK's press secretary and a lawyer himself. Indeed, the more clichéd aspects of Schiff's character seem patterned on the cantankerous newspaper and newsroom editors from countless TV shows and movies, such as Lou Grant (Ed Asner) in *The Mary Tyler Moore Show*.

But thanks in part to deft writing and Steve Hill's richly detailed perfor-mances, which never appear mannered, even though mannerisms play a memorable part, Schiff emerges as the voice of moral realism. He is a veteran prosecutor who recognizes the practical realities of criminal pros-ecution (such as plea bargaining, getting a favorable judge, appealing to the jury, and maintaining the public image of the DA's office) without falling prey to an easy cynicism about the criminal justice system. With a portrait of Oliver Wendell Holmes prominently displayed on his office wall, Schiff has clearly taken to heart Holmes's famous dictum that the "life of the law has not been logic; it has been experience."

With his practical bent, Schiff frequently butts heads with Stone and McCoy, both of whom tend to turn cases into moral or legal crusades. In "Sanctuary," for instance, the trial of an African-American defendant clearly guilty of murdering an innocent passerby during a riot ends with a hung jury. Stone wants to retry the defendant, but Schiff demurs. What follows is perhaps one of the best-written and -acted scenes in the entire series:

SCHIFF: Not gonna be a retrial.

STONE: Isaac Roberts killed an innocent man. You're gonna let him walk?

SCHIFF: If I thought we could empanel a jury that would give us a chance of convicting, I'd try the case myself. Now you'd think that 20 years in this office, you'd have a sense of reality.

STONE: Reality? The reality is that nobody's willing to draw a line in the sand. Nobody's willing to say that the Law is the Law and if you break it you will be prosecuted, win, lose or draw.

SCHIFF: Nobody except you.

STONE: It's better to light a match than to curse the darkness.

SCHIFF: Even if it lights a fuse that could blow up the city?

STONE: What do you want? Peace without justice?

SCHIFF: I'm trying to straddle a fence so that this city can heal. Can you understand that?

STONE: Yep. I understand. (pause) I understand that the cure is worse than the disease. (long pause) And that it's a solution I just can't be part of.

In this single scene, which in fewer than 20 sentences encapsulates nearly 20 years of political rhetoric on the law-and-order issue, the show crystallizes not only its political centrism—neither position is portrayed as wholly right or wrong—but also the personalities of Schiff and Stone, the pragmatic problem-solver and the principled prosecutor.

Of course, prosecutors are not the only lawyers in *Law & Order*. Indeed, the show portrays at least five categories of lawyers: (1) prosecutors, (2) defense lawyers, (3) judges, (4) lawyer-victims (such as Sarah Maslin in "Virtue"), and (5) lawyer-defendants. This last group includes Spender Talbert in "Virtue;" Paul Kopell in "House Counsel;" Joel Thayer, a judge as well as a lawyer, in "Censure;" James Smith in "Pro Se;" and Ted Schwimmer in "Bodies". A full treatment of the show's portrayal of lawyers would take these other categories of lawyers into account. At the very least, it would discuss the defense lawyers, many of whom, as recurring characters, were some of the most memorable characters on the show.

Still, by focusing on Ben Stone, Jack McCoy, and Adam Schiff, the most prominent of the prosecutor characters in the astounding 18-plus–year run of *Law & Order*, it is possible to understand Dick Wolf's vision of legitimizing law and order as an appropriate issue for liberals.

Endnotes

1. For an excellent recent history of the politics of the law-and-order issue, see MICHAEL W. FLAMM, LAW AND ORDER: STREET CRIME, CIVIL UNREST, AND THE CRISIS OF LIBERALISM IN THE 1960S (2005). For a journalistic discussion of the politics of the law-and-order issue, written at about the same time *Law & Order* first appeared and from a similar center-left perspective, see E.J. DIONNE, JR., WHY AMERICANS HATE POLITICS 77–97 (1991).

2. John Herbers, *McGovern Urges Drive on Slums; Says 'Law and Order' Pleas Have Racist Undertone*, N.Y. TIMES, Aug. 16, 1968, at 1 (quoting Senator George McGovern).

3. Celestine Bohlen, *Campaign Matters; Is 'Liberal' a Dirty Word in New York?*, N.Y. TIMES, Aug. 21, 1989.

4. Although filmed in 1988, the pilot ("Everybody's Favorite Bagman") was aired as the sixth episode of the first season.

5. See Elayne Rapping's introduction to this volume, "The History of Law on Television."

6. Bruce Weber, *Television; Dick Wolf Breaks and Enters with 'Law and Order' on NBC*, NEW YORK TIMES, Mar. 1, 1992.

7. The poster vanishes in later episodes, replaced by a framed photograph on Stone's wall. In "Sanctuary," in which Stone prosecutes an African-American

teenager for beating and killing an innocent passerby in a riot, defense lawyer Shambala Green (Lorraine Toussaint) sarcastically references the RKF picture: "Hanging a picture of Bobby on your wall just ain't gonna cut it anymore."

8. For a discussion of Kennedy's law-and-order posturing, see Flamm, note 1 at 148–50. See also RAY E. BOOMHOWER, ROBERT F. KENNEDY AND THE 1968 INDIANA PRIMARY 78–81 (2008).

9. Although not set in New York City, *Police Story* and (especially) *Hill Street Blues* were clear influences on the early seasons.

10. Stone's closing argument in "Mushrooms" is a striking example of Stone's rhetorical style. The crime—the shooting of two children, a 12-year-old and an 11-month-old—is an especially emotional one, and the closing, as written, contains incendiary language ("slaughter in our streets," "slaughter of an innocent"), but Stone's delivery is understated and deliberate, and he looks at the courtroom floor almost the entire time.

11. Frequently Stone's audience is not the jury, but opposing counsel. In "Subterranean Homeboy Blues," for instance, he convinces opposing counsel to accept a guilty plea to a misdemeanor gun charge even though Stone has just dropped the murder charge against her client, a female vigilante based on Bernard Goetz, because recently uncovered evidence would have likely resulted in jury nullification of the gun charge as well. "This isn't a question of winning or losing," he tells the defense lawyer. "It's a question of justice." Implausibly, the defense counsel accepts the plea. A similar but more credible encounter with defense counsel occurs in "Point of View."

12. Indeed, in some cases, McCoy is clearly hoping to instill in the defendant a sense of moral outrage at his or her own conduct. (See, for instance, McCoy's cross-examination of the defrocked priest in "Progeny.")

13. In this respect at least, McCoy's fiery cross-examinations serve the important function of drawing out the defendant's moral *in*sensibility—his or her utter inability to recognize or acknowledge the moral repugnance of his or her crimes.

14. In the first three seasons, Stone is paired with ADA Paul Robinette (Richard Brooks). The Stone-Robinette relationship is different not only because both characters are men and because Robinette is the show's sole African-American prosecutor, but because they are not positioned as political antagonists. Indeed, they both appear to be variations on the RFK tough-guy liberal, with Robinette embodying the more impassioned side of RFK. (This passion is on display in "Out of the Half-Light," in which Robinette excoriates an African-American politician who cynically manipulates a fabricated racial incident.)

CHAPTER 11

The Practice: Debunking Television Myths and Stereotypes

JEFFREY E. THOMAS

The Practice was a revolution in the genre of legal television. Although other modern serials had begun to explore some of the "realist" difficulties of the legal system, *The Practice* fully embraced and explored those dilemmas in a postmodernist way.[1] It turned many of the conventions of legal television on their heads. The legal system was portrayed as arbitrary and subject to manipulation by the players, and the players—lawyers, judges, and clients—were depicted as shady and scheming, in conflict with Hollywood stereotypes.

This characterization of *The Practice* should not be taken as a criticism. On the contrary, its cynicism made it interesting and unpredictable. You could never be sure of the guilt or innocence of an accused, and even if you thought you knew, that person's culpability did not govern the outcome of the narrative. To be fair to real lawyers and the actual legal system, some representations were so extreme that they approached satire. Nevertheless, many of the criticisms were justified. The legal system is not perfect. Guilty people are set free, innocent people are convicted, and lawyers sometimes

The Practice

Aired:
- March 4, 1997–
  May 16, 2004, ABC

Cast:
- Michael Badalucco
  (Jimmy Berluti)
- Camryn Manheim
  (Ellenor Frutt)
- Lisa Gay Hamilton
  (Rebecca Washington)
- Steve Harris
  (Eugene Young)
- Dylan McDermott
  (Bobby Donnell)
- Kelli Williams
  (Lindsay Dole)
- Lara Flynn Boyle
  (Helen Gamble)
- Marla Sokoloff
  (Lucy Hatcher)
- Holland Taylor
  (Judge Roberta Kittleson)
- James Spader
  (Alan Shore)

Awards:
- Emmy for Outstanding
  Drama Series (1998, 1999)
- James Spader, Emmy for
  Outstanding Lead Actor
  in a Drama Series (2004)
- Camryn Manheim, Emmy
  for Outstanding Supporting
  Actress in a Drama Series
  (1998)
- Michael Badalucco, Emmy
  for Outstanding Supporting
  Actor in a Drama Series (1999)
- Holland Taylor, Emmy for
  Outstanding Supporting
  Actress in a Drama Series
  (1999)

129

Courtesy of Photofest.

THE PRACTICE
Bobby Donnell (Dylan McDermott) and his associates and staff
are the bottom feeders of the law.

act unethically. While the legal system of *The Practice* was not very close
to reality, it was certainly closer than the sterile and flawless system portrayed in the iconic *Perry Mason* in the 1950s and 1960s.

The Practice was in many respects a reaction to, and the antithesis of,
L.A. Law,[2] which stopped airing three years prior to *The Practice*'s debut.
David E. Kelley, the creator of *The Practice*, was a major creative force
behind *L.A. Law*. He was a writer and producer of that show, for which
he won two Emmys for Outstanding Writing in a Dramatic Series. He
created *The Practice* to contrast with the glamour of *L.A. Law* by showing
the nuts and bolts of legal practice.[3] Kelley, like the show's lead character
Bobby Donnell, was a graduate of Boston University, and practiced law
for three years in Boston, where *The Practice* is set. Bobby's firm in *The
Practice* is much different than *L.A. Law*'s McKenzie, Brackman, Chaney
and Kuzak. McKenzie Brackman was a successful, primarily civil law practice with beautiful high-rise offices and affluent attorneys. Bobby's firm
struggles to make ends meet. It is behind on its rent for a gritty, urban
space in which only Bobby has a private office. The firm handles small or
difficult civil cases, but its "bread and butter" is criminal defense work.

The narratives of *The Practice* also represent the antithesis of *L.A.
Law*. Although *L.A. Law* recognized some difficult legal and social issues,

and occasionally left the viewer a little uncomfortable with the outcome, those were the exceptions to fairly traditional plot resolutions. With *The Practice*, such discomfort is often the point of the narrative. Where *L.A. Law* touches on an issue, *The Practice* delves into it and puts the dubious outcome directly in the viewer's face. These differences were also reflected by the shows' respective titles: *L.A. Law* suggests that outcomes are governed by the "law," while *The Practice* suggests an ongoing effort to try (and try again) to get the result that the client wants, regardless of the law. These general themes and their postmodern character will be explored in more detail in the following two sections. The first section will consider three illustrative narratives, and the second will examine three main characters.

The Narratives

The first narrative, involving George Vogelman, typifies the series. It was part of multiple episodes over the first three years. It starts innocently enough, then spins and turns in many directions. It also illustrates the close circle of connections among the main characters. The second narrative concerns Randall Jefferson, actual innocence, and the death penalty. It shows the arbitrariness of the legal system and suggests a role for race. It also provides an accused's unique perspective on the death penalty. The third narrative is about one of the most arrogant and provocative characters on the show, Joey Heric, who manipulates the lawyers and the legal system for his own benefit.

George Vogelman Narrative

A postmodern world is one in which the "truth" is uncertain and relative. In the modern world, society works toward absolute truths through science, competition, or consensus. These structures break down in a postmodern world, leaving varied and uncertain "truths." One of the best examples of this characteristic is the ongoing story of George Vogelman. We are first introduced to George in the third episode of the first season ("Trial & Error"), and over the course of three seasons, the writers use his narrative to play with the viewer's perceptions of his guilt or innocence.

George is introduced in a way that makes him appear sympathetic and innocent. He is first mentioned as a contact that Ellenor Frutt, one of Bobby's experienced senior associates, makes through a personal advertisement. At first they just talk on the phone. Although Ellenor is somewhat embarrassed about having met someone through the personals, she shares her enthusiasm for George, a podiatrist, with her coworkers. After a couple of weeks, they finally meet, but Ellenor—who is not very attractive herself—finds George unattractive and rejects him. Thus we initially feel sorry for George.

Some six months later, George decides to fight back. He sues Ellenor for fraud and intentional infliction of emotional distress. Although Ellenor moves to dismiss the lawsuit, the judge denies the motion and allows George limited discovery. During her deposition Ellenor says George seemed like a "loser" and that she didn't go out with him because she "didn't want to play the fat girl by the punch bowl that leaves with the nerd." Ellenor has a tear in her eye, and is sorry for having hurt George, so he drops the suit. Although George shows some backbone in bringing the suit, the fact that he drops the suit after the depositions shows that he just wanted Ellenor's attention and honesty. He does not seem vindictive and continues to have our sympathy, perhaps with a little more respect.

A year later, George comes to Ellenor and the firm with a serious legal problem ("Body Count"). He has a human head in his medical bag. He enters the firm agitated and panicky, and before he can explain the situation he passes out. He claims to be innocent, and the viewers' previous sympathy for him, combined with his demeanor, tend to make him seem innocent. Ellenor and Eugene Young undertake his defense.

Initially, there is little evidence against George. Although he admits to having been with the victim, there is no physical evidence linking him to the murder. On the other hand, while George insists that he is being "framed," there is no evidence that the victim was killed by another or that anyone would have a motive to frame him. The viewers' sense of George's innocence is eroded by the police's discovery of a pornography collection in his apartment ("The Defenders").

Faced, in "The Battlefield," with an absence of exculpatory evidence, Eugene, who has taken over as first chair because Ellenor is afraid she is too close to George, decides to use the "Plan B" defense to suggest that George was framed by the victim's brother. Although this defense is built on innuendo and a total absence of evidence, Eugene is so persuasive that we almost believe that the brother might have done it. The brother's apparent motive—to inherit all of his father's estate—is supported by the rivalry and disagreements between him and his sister. He does not have a very good alibi for the time of the murder, and to top things off, Eugene introduces evidence that the brother takes antidepressant medication. The defense works, and George is exonerated ("One of Those Days").

In one of my favorite moments on *The Practice*, after the trial is over George and Ellenor are sitting in the witness room. After verifying that he cannot be tried again for the crime, George tells Ellenor that he wants to tell her something. The camera zooms in on Ellenor's face, and we expect him to confess to the crime, but he says:

> I'm going to tell you something. We both know that I've always had some motive to tell you that I'm innocent. It allowed you to let me testify. It allowed you to—I don't know—try harder. But now, the evidence being closed, it doesn't matter what I tell you. . . I didn't do it. When you looked at me a few months ago, you said you believed in me, but you couldn't fully trust yourself to believe in what you believed. You can trust yourself, Ellenor. You've been right all along. I didn't do it.

At this point, with the protection against double jeopardy, George has little reason to maintain his innocence, so viewers want to believe him. Apparently, zealous advocacy has avoided a great injustice, and the price that was paid—in embarrassment of the victim's family—was worth it.

This sense of George's innocence, however, is eroded again. Near the end of the season (in "Happily Ever After"), some six months after George's acquittal, Lindsay Dole, one of the firm's attorneys, is stabbed by an unknown assailant wearing a nun's habit. The episode ends by showing George wandering the streets of Boston in a nun's habit, implying that he may be Lindsay's attacker. And if he is crazy enough to attack Lindsay, he also might have committed the first murder as well.

Our uneasiness bears fruit several months later in "Free Dental," when George is kicked out of his co-op because of the accusation against him and asks Ellenor to represent him in the legal proceedings. Although the defense is unsuccessful, George and Ellenor have dinner together afterwards. He makes a bad joke about having to "sever" their relationship. A couple of weeks later ("Losers Keepers"), Ellenor and her roommate, Helen Gamble, the Assistant District Attorney who so often was the firm's nemesis, are attacked in their apartment. During the attack, George is shown in a nun's outfit, confirming his responsibility for Lindsay's attack. Ellenor gets a gun and shoots George, and it appears he is dead. But he arises and tells Ellenor that he just simulated his death. He locks Ellenor in the apartment and is about to stab her when, with her characteristic tenacity, Ellenor tells George she can get him off with an insanity defense if he does not kill her. As George is about to strike, Helen, who had been rendered unconscious in the other room, shoots George in the back, putting us out of our misery of uncertainty.

Although this uncertainty about guilt or innocence obviously con- tributes to the drama of the show, it also demonstrates a postmodern sensibility about truth. The truth is elusive, uncertain, and relative. We cannot be sure of what appears to be, and with repeated narratives about the failings of the legal system, we cannot be sure that the system reaches "true" or "just" results.

Randall Jefferson Narrative

Even where the truth is less elusive, the legal system still may fail to pro- mote it, as illustrated by the narrative of Randall Jefferson. In "Spirit of America," Randall has been sentenced to death and is just 18 hours away from execution when Bobby and his firm enter the case. Jefferson's con- viction rests upon a jailhouse confession to a cellmate, who was rewarded with a sentence reduction for testifying. No weapon, motive, or forensic evidence supported the conviction. With thorough investigation, Ellenor and Eugene discover that the witness who testified against Randall had been given a polygraph exam that showed him to be borderline truthful, and that the prosecution had not disclosed this to the defense. Although this is sufficient to obtain a stay of execution from the Fifth Circuit, the Supreme Court lifts the stay just minutes before the scheduled execution and Randall is put to death.

Even though Randall's innocence seems fairly clear, the legal system is ill-equipped to protect it, thus illuminating the arbitrariness of law as well as the role race plays in criminal proceedings. Eugene notes that a black man who kills a white person is "12 times more likely to end up on death row than a white man who kills a black person." Unfortunately for Randall, he is in the former category. Interestingly, in another death penalty narrative several seasons later ("Liberty Bells"), the white defen- dant is successfully exonerated. The arbitrariness of the legal system is also reflected by the defendant's luck of the draw in receiving a sympathetic judge to review the petition. The viewer gets a further sense of arbitrariness from the weakness of the evidence against Jefferson and the recognition that a made-up jailhouse confession could be used against virtually anyone.

This arbitrariness of the legal system is contrasted with the sympathy that develops for Randall over the course of the episode. He is shown as a humble, dignified person who is loved and supported by his extended family, including his little nieces. This provides a perspective on the death penalty that is very different than the one usually shown in popular culture (such as the film *Dead Man Walking* or in other episodes of *The Practice)*, where criminal defendants are often depicted as despicable and deserving of execution. The image of a sympathetic defendant leaves the viewer with the sense that a friend or neighbor, who is in the wrong place at the wrong time, might end up in the same predicament. It also shows the shortcomings of a system that is driven by reason and law rather than emotion. The rules and procedures, even if logically fair and justified, leave us feeling emotionally dissatisfied.

Joey Heric Narrative

The brilliant, manipulative, and narcissistic Joey Heric, played by John Larroquette (who won an Emmy for his depiction), shows that lawyers—the "priests" of the legal system—are fallible. Although the modern trend has been to show lawyers as more and more human (and *The Practice* certainly follows this trend), lawyers have traditionally been depicted on television as competent professionals. Perry Mason, the iconic lawyer of 1950s television, was infallible. More recently, lawyers on shows such as *L.A. Law* and *Law & Order* appear on the whole to be in control and to do good, professional work. When television lawyers do make mistakes, it is typically due to the difficulty of the circumstances. The Joey Heric case, however, shows that a person can outsmart the system and its players, including lawyers and judges.

"The Betrayal" opens with an agitated Joey Heric listening to classical music and pacing around his living room in front of a man's dead body with a knife sticking out of its chest. Joey is waiting for Ellenor and Eugene to come to his apartment. They are surprised when they see the dead man, who was Joey's lover and a city councilman. Ellenor asks if he is dead; Joey responds acerbically, "No, he's faking it to get attention." It seems obvious that Joey has killed the man, and he implies as much, but as he is talking with his lawyers for advice, looking for an angle, it occurs to him that his other lover, Marty, may come under suspicion. Joey uses this to his advantage. Although Joey appears reluctant to give information about Marty, his lawyers "convince" him to do so.

Bobby and Ellenor persuade Joey that testifying against Marty is his only meaningful option if he is to avoid suspicion. Joey acts reluctant, but ultimately agrees to testify in exchange for immunity. Joey cleverly words his testimony so that while he implies that Marty did it, he never actually makes that accusation. As he is testifying at the preliminary hearing, Joey states that he "picked up the knife and stabbed [the victim] . . . right in the heart; he went down like a sack of bricks." The Assistant District Attorney is shocked, and says that Joey never said that before, to which he responds, "Of course not; I didn't have immunity then . . . *now I do.*" The judge rules that the immunity agreement is enforceable because Joey testified accurately to every fact as agreed. The Assistant District Attorney had never directly asked Joey if he did it. Joey quips, "And you wonder how I can strut around feeling like I'm smarter than you."

Joey's case is not the average guilty-go-free scenario. He murdered his lover, asked for his lawyers' help, and then manipulated them and the system to avoid responsibility. Although the judge and the DA suspect that Bobby and Ellenor were involved, she remarks, "I was as duped as you." This narrative reduces law and the legal system to tools for the clever and powerful. In this depiction, law is no longer the modern "ideal" of the social ordering of society, but instead is deconstructed into yet another means for getting what one wants. In Joey's case, the legal system is used to get away with murder. So not only is truth uncertain, and the system arbitrary and uncaring, but they can be actively manipulated to frustrate justice.

The Characters

Even though the narratives provide great analytical material, television shows are driven by their characters. Viewers come back to watch episode after episode because they care about the characters. Although the firm carries Bobby Donnell's name, the cast is really an ensemble with about six or eight main characters. One of the greatest contributions of *The Practice* was to shatter the stereotype of television lawyers. While this may not really be a "postmodern" development, it provided welcome variety and diversity to the genre, and gave viewers characters that were more human and more like themselves. Although all of the characters were interesting and added some new perspective to the depiction of lawyers on television, my favorite characters were Ellenor, Eugene, and Jimmy.

Ellenor Frutt

The Hollywood stereotype of a female lawyer is beautiful, thin, and sufficiently feminine to be attractive to male viewers. She can be clever and assertive, but not so much as to be threatening. Ann Kelsey, Grace Van Owen, and Abigail Perkins of *L.A. Law* represent this archetype. Similarly, although *Law & Order* was initially male dominated, the female lawyers who were Assistant District Attorneys, such as Claire Kincaid, Abbie Carmichael, and Connie Rubirosa, also fit this formula. Interestingly, these female characters are nearly always subordinate to more powerful male characters. Although she was not a lawyer, depictions of women lawyers on television tend to carry the echo of Della Street, Perry Mason's faithful secretary.

Ellenor breaks the stereotype. She is a large woman and knows the pain of rejection due to physical appearance. But at the same time, she is not jaded or bitter. She still wants a relationship. When she rejects George Vogelman, she feels badly about it, and simply says that she "wanted more." Nevertheless, her demeanor is tough and assertive, and she will not back down when she believes in something, regardless of whether the person on the other side is a man or woman. Although she is not a partner in the firm, she acts as the equal of the men. For example, in the pilot, while acting as second chair to Bobby, Ellenor objects to a DA's questioning even though Bobby does not want her to. Afterwards, Bobby and Ellenor argue about it, and when Bobby threatens to fire her, Ellenor is not at all intimidated and challenges him to do it. Later, when she has trouble hailing a taxi, she yells "stop the car," and a taxi stops. As creator David E. Kelley puts it, Ellenor is a "great street fighter."[4]

Eugene Young

Eugene breaks the stereotype of the token black lawyer—the lawyer with an elite academic background who is comfortable in white society and who might be considered the beneficiary of affirmative action. The archetype of this kind of lawyer is Jonathan Rollins on *L.A. Law*, whom the firm never fully embraces as an equal. By contrast, Eugene is not a token black. He is a senior associate and a leader in the firm. He is one of the best lawyers in the office. He rarely, if ever, loses. He is so confident that he bets an Assistant District Attorney on two different occasions that he can win a case that looks like a loser. He wins both cases purely by the power of his advocacy. He is respected for his skill, not for his skin color. He is also street smart and tough. When representing a woman whose husband is stalking her in violation of a court order, Eugene confronts the man when he comes to the firm's office. He threatens retaliation if the man hurts his wife. When the man laughs at him, Eugene grabs the guy and physically restrains him ("Part I"). Eugene did not adopt an approach contrary to his nature or personality to fit in. The audience knows he is genuine.

Although Eugene's presence in the firm is based on his skill as a lawyer, not on his race, he is sensitive to issues of concern to African Americans. When Jimmy has a friend who is seeking disability benefits, claiming that he became a racist from working as a Boston cop, Eugene agrees to assist in the case ("First Degree"). Rebecca Washington, the firm's African-American secretary, does not agree with Eugene's defense, noting that Eugene was once pulled out of a car by the police and beaten because he was black. But Eugene wants to pursue the case because he views racism as a disease, and he hopes that recognition of it as a disease might encourage people to start addressing it. During the hearing, Eugene's views about racism come out. He argues that racism is an "epidemic" among the Boston police, that it is a "cancer" that should be rooted out and destroyed, and that leaving racist cops on the street is "more hateful" than giving them disability pay. He concludes that "maybe it is time you all started owning some blame [for racism]."

Jimmy Berluti

Jimmy Berluti is so different from other television lawyers that there isn't even a relevant stereotype to consider. Michael Badalucco, the actor who plays Jimmy, summarized the character well: he is "a blue-collar guy in a white-collar world."[5] Jimmy is a loser who joins the firm because Bobby feels responsible when Jimmy gets caught in a fraud scheme to help

Bobby's firm get a loan. When he joins the firm, he has never won a case. In order to help attract business, Jimmy runs a commercial in which he describes himself as a "grunt" who will help other "grunts."

While Jimmy is perhaps not a model lawyer, his earnestness and sincerity make him popular with viewers. Like so many other underdogs, we want to see him succeed. We are rewarded, because Jimmy has one success after another. He initially turns a sow's ear of a dog-bite case into a silk purse by doing careful research and holding out for a settlement beyond the client's (and the firm's) expectations. A few episodes later we see Jimmy winning his first trial for a client who was fired because he looked like a monkey. We smile with him as he exclaims, "I won!"

Jimmy represents the deconstruction of the elite lawyer stereotype. When he advertises himself as "Jimmy the grunt," a phrase the firm considers beneath its dignity, dozens of potential clients fill the office. Through Jimmy, the practice of law is shown as similar to any other small business. Jimmy could as easily be a plumber as a lawyer. This makes the practice of law more accessible to the masses, both to those who may aspire to become lawyers, and to potential clients who might perceive lawyers through a more realistic lens.

Conclusion

The Practice boldly broke new ground with both its narratives and its characters. It challenged many assumptions about law, legal practice, the legal system, and the character of lawyers. It broke old stereotypes, provided unpredictable plot lines, and challenged us to think about our assumptions and cultural values. And it was very entertaining television.

Endnotes

1. I developed a similar theme for a conference on law and popular culture hosted by UCLA in 2001. See *Legal Culture and "the practice:" A Postmodern Depiction of the Rule of Law in America*, 48 UCLA L. Rev. 1495 (2001).

2. See Phil Meyer's chapter "Revisiting *L.A. Law*."

3. See *Setting Up the Practice*, featurette on DVD released in 2007.

4. *Setting Up the Practice, supra* note 3.

5. *Setting Up the Practice, supra* note 3.

CHAPTER 12

Murder One: The Adversary System Meets Celebrity Justice

MICHAEL ASIMOW

Murder One was a groundbreaking legal drama created by Steven Bochco.[1] Each episode built upon the previous ones, and a single story—the "Goldilocks Murder Case"—consumed the entire first season. Each episode asked the questions "Who killed Jessica Costello?" and "How do skillful criminal defense lawyers represent a client in a difficult case?" Always in the background lurked some larger questions: "How does the American legal system determine the truth about what really happened?" "Can the adversary system deliver in a case of celebrity justice?" "What does high-stakes legal practice do to one's personal life?"

The serialization approach made for gripping drama. It turned television into a different kind of experience, more like reading the serialized episodes of a Charles Dickens or Arthur Conan Doyle novel than watching the customary, neatly packaged, one-hour story. Serialization permitted Bochco to tell a story in vastly greater depth than could be achieved during a one-hour television show, or even a miniseries or movie. However, the disadvantages of serialization were obvious. Viewers who missed earlier shows found it difficult to catch up, which undoubtedly limited the size of the audience.[2]

Murder One

Aired:
- September 19, 1995–May 29, 1997, ABC

Cast:
- Daniel Benzali (Theodore "Teddy" Hoffman)
- Stanley Tucci (Richard Cross)
- Barbara Bosson (Miriam Grasso)
- Michael Hayden (Chris Docknovich)
- Mary McCormack (Justine Appleton)
- J.C. MacKenzie (Arnold Spivak)
- Jason Gedrick (Neal Avedon)
- Linda Carlson (Judge Beth Bornstein)

Awards:
- People's Choice Award for Favorite New TV Dramatic Series (1996)
- American Society of Cinematographers Award for Outstanding Achievement in Cinematography in a Regular Series (1996, 1997)
- Emmy for Outstanding Individual Achievement in Art Direction for a Series (1996)
- Emmy for Outstanding Individual Achievement in Main Title Theme Music (1996)
- Pruitt Taylor Vince, Emmy for Outstanding Guest Actor in a Drama Series (1997)

© 1995 TV Guide Magazine Group, Inc.

MURDER ONE
Teddy Hoffman (Daniel Benzali) and his associates contemplate the daunting task of defending celeb Neal Avedon who's accused of murdering Jessica Costello.

(The availability of *Murder One* on DVD now makes it far easier—and more pleasurable—for fans of legal drama to experience or re-experience this outstanding series.) Moreover, the serial format limited the possibilities for successful syndication through reruns on cable.

Nevertheless, viewers who stayed with the entire 23-episode first season of *Murder One* found the experience riveting and unforgettable. *Murder One* was, and is, one of the best plotted and characterized—and most gripping—legal dramas in television history. The story builds to an almost unbearable tension by the final episode, a smashing conclusion that won't be revealed here. The series also explores every phase of the criminal justice legal process in fascinating detail. The lawyers on both sides of *Murder One* are skilled and ethical professionals and decent human beings. They fight hard but fair. Lawyers and the criminal justice system could ask for no more favorable representation.

The first season of *Murder One* takes us through every twist and turn of the prosecution of Neal Avedon for the murder of Jessica Costello. We ponder bail motions, countless hard-fought evidence rulings, arguments over cameras in the courtroom, negotiations over the jury questionnaire, skillful direct and cross-examination, closing arguments, post-trial motions, the whole shebang. Nearly two entire episodes are devoted to the cat-and-mouse game of jury selection, with each side trying to get the judge to dismiss a juror for cause to avoid wasting a peremptory challenge, or to bluff the other side into accepting the juror. Normally, of course, there is never time in legal TV or movies to explore these types of legal minutia. In fact, real-life pretrial and trial proceedings can be unbearably tedious. But they are never tedious in *Murder One*, and Bochco milks each of them for great dramatic effect.

The Murder of Jessica Costello

The "Goldilocks murder case" is about the rape and strangulation murder of 15-year-old Jessica Costello. Jessica slept with a lot of prominent men and took a lot of drugs. The story is set against a backdrop of the corrupt and hedonistic culture of the Los Angeles entertainment community, personified by the sleazy producer Gary Blondo. News reporters sleep with lawyers to get hot info, cocaine is everywhere, sex is bought and paid for, and there is nothing really wrong with bedding down with a gorgeous teenager if you don't get caught.

Who killed Jessica? There are numerous suspects. Jessica's diary is packed with the names of the famous, none of whom would care to be outed. There is also a great deal of misdirection, including several false confessions. Among the possible killers is defendant Neal Avedon, a famous actor and heartthrob of millions of teenage fans, who has serious drug and alcohol problems of his own. Neal slept with Jessica on the night she was murdered, and was known to enjoy choking his partners during sex. He had even been convicted of strangling an annoying swan at the Bel Air Hotel. Based on this circumstantial evidence and Neal's false statements to the police, the DA charges him with Jessica's murder. Later, additional evidence surfaces against Neal, including testimony that he actually confessed to his drug rehab therapist, Graham Lester, late on the night of the homicide.

The dark and mysterious Richard Cross (brilliantly played by Stanley Tucci) is a prominent philanthropist and another prime suspect. Cross has been conducting an affair with Jessica's older sister Julie, a troubled woman with plenty of her own problems. Cross owns the building in which Jessica lived, and was spotted there on the night of the murder by a security camera. In fact, Cross was the first one charged with Jessica's murder. However, the prosecutor drops the case after Cross comes up with an alibi—one that becomes increasingly shaky. Cross purports to be supportive of his friend Neal Avedon, and pays for his defense, but he keeps interfering. For example, Cross marries Julie just before she is to deliver testimony that will devastate his reputation, thus allowing her to claim marital privilege. He always seems to have some sort of hidden agenda. Why is he manipulating Hoffman's associate Justine Appleton? Why is he paying the medical expenses of the brother of a nurse who delivers key testimony against Avedon? What happened, exactly, when Hoffman's investigator (Davie Blaylock) was killed after he seemed to get too close to Cross? Hoffman loathes Cross, but cannot seem to get rid of him.

Then there is Graham Lester, the shady psychiatrist who runs the drug rehab center in Malibu where Avedon is being treated. Four of his patients come forward and testify that he had drugged and raped them, so he seems to have a taste for rape. And let's not forget the sinister and arrogant Portalegre family. Father Roberto and son Eduardo are probably heavily into the cocaine business, and Eduardo has definite date-rape issues. With so many suspects and clues aplenty, *Murder One* skillfully exploits the familiar and always pleasurable whodunit genre.

The Lawyers: Teddy Hoffman and Miriam Grasso

The first season of *Murder One* centers on the character of Teddy Hoffman, played with great authority by Daniel Benzali.[3] Hoffman is a respected Los Angeles criminal defense lawyer. He has consummate skills and is supported by highly capable investigators and loyal associates, who vie to be his second chair. If you're in trouble, you want Teddy—if you can afford him. And he costs plenty. Like all great lawyers, Hoffman has terrific judgment about people and great intuition and instincts. He is a master tactician. He can handle the press quite capably, but as Teddy sees it, the clients are the celebrities, not the lawyers. He observes the rules of legal ethics, although he sometimes stretches the envelope a bit.[4] He is respectful of his law-firm colleagues and of his adversaries.

Unlike such matinee idols as James Woods, James Spader, and Sam Waterston, or the glamour pusses on *L. A. Law* or *The Practice*, Hoffman is distinctly unglamorous and even a bit ugly (one reviewer compared him to Shrek), and he does not fool around. He is all business and is very good at his business. He does not suffer fools lightly, and is often rude or abrupt to people he dislikes or disrespects, such as Detective

Arthur Polson, the tenacious but ethical police officer assigned to the Jessica Costello investigation.

Most pop-culture lawyers are single and unlucky in love, but Hoffman seems at first to have an excellent and fulfilling personal life. His marriage to Annie Hoffman is solid and supportive, although, like most litigators, he frequently misses dinner or rushes out during intimate moments after an urgent phone call. Teddy is also very close to his daughter Lizzie. Although he is frequently gruff and dismissive in his professional life, he never acts that way at home.

The life of a trial lawyer places tremendous stress on personal relationships. Major trials are life-devouring monsters, often consuming the lawyers caught up in them on a 24/7 basis. The stakes for their clients and for themselves are frighteningly high; life in prison without possibility of parole is on the table in *Murder One*. With a major trial in the offing or in process, lawyers work insane hours and the phone never stops ringing. The clients are untruthful, overemotional, and will not do as they are told. The decisions and gambles become agonizingly difficult, and the stress levels are off the charts.

The intense stress of the Costello case cracks the Hoffman home wide open. Lizzie is briefly abducted, which turns out to be the beginning of the end for the Hoffman marriage. False rumors circulate that Hoffman is having an affair with Francesca Cross, the glamorous ex-wife of the mysterious Richard Cross. Annie detests living on the front pages of the tabloids. She loathes Avedon and all the sleaziness that surrounds the case and constantly oozes into her home. Finally she snaps, and announces that she wants a separation. Soon, she files for divorce. Teddy's precious family disintegrates before his eyes, right in the middle of the biggest case of his life. We eavesdrop on excruciating sessions with a family counselor and brutal financial negotiations between the spouses and their lawyers. As the first season finally ends, it's possible that Teddy and Annie might reconcile, but it is much too soon to tell.[5]

Indeed, Hoffman's marriage is not the only casualty of the Costello case. By the time it is over, most of the characters are dead or their lives, reputations, and careers are shattered. A monster case like this one takes no prisoners.

In the Costello case, Hoffman is up against a skilled and committed prosecutor, Miriam Grasso. Grasso is an ethical professional who often clashes with her ethically challenged boss, the despicable District Attorney Roger Garfield. The personal relationship between Grasso and Hoffman is friendly and respectful, but in the courtroom it is intensely adversarial. Grasso understands that a prosecutor must serve as a minister of justice as well as an agent of law enforcement. In one of the many satellite (or "B") cases handled by Hoffman's firm during the early episodes of *Murder One*, the defendant had killed another man in a bar fight 15 years before, probably in self-defense. He fled California and lived an exemplary life, but when he returns to Los Angeles many years later he is nabbed and put on trial for murder. The lawyers from Hoffman's firm argue to Grasso that the case should be dismissed in the interests of justice. Overruling the decision of her subordinate, Grasso agrees to drop the case.

The Avedon case consumes Grasso's entire life, just as it does Hoffman's. In the middle of the trial, Grasso's husband (a securities lawyer) drops dead. He knew he was having ominous heart problems, but felt he had to complete a merger before he could find time to get to the doctor. Grasso barely misses a beat, although she and Hoffman exchange tearful hugs in the courthouse's underground garage. It is the biggest trial of her life, too. She can grieve later.

The Adversary System Meets Celebrity Justice

The subtext of *Murder One* is the adversary system of criminal justice. The heart of the adversary system is the clash of opposing lawyers, each zealously representing a client. Lawyers do not believe that their responsibility is to help find the truth about past events. Often, it is in the interest of one or both lawyers to obscure the truth. Under the adversary system, it is their ethical responsibility to do so—as long as they play by the rules.

Rather than seeing themselves as truth-revealers, lawyers understand that their job is to represent the client zealously and work the process for all it is worth. In the adversary system, the lawyers—not the judge—make the tactical decisions, such as whether to go to trial or plea bargain and how to present their case. A neutral arbiter (either the jury or the judge) makes the ultimate decision without receiving any informational inputs other than those the lawyers choose to provide. The judge is a relatively passive figure. If the lawyers are incompetent, it's not the job of the judge to bail them out. If one side has vastly more resources than the other, the judge is not supposed to equalize things. The premise of the adversary system is that all-out conflict between the lawyers, channeled by a complex and detailed set of procedural rules, is most likely to reveal the truth about past events and assure a just outcome. This, in other words, is "procedural justice."

In contrast, the inquisitorial system used in most civil law countries is intended to reveal the truth, not to encourage lawyerly games.[6] Each of these countries has its own version of the inquisitorial system, but the common premise is that truth is most likely to be revealed by an investigation supervised and conducted by judges. There are many fewer rules restricting the investigation or excluding evidence than are present under the adversary system. Lawyers often advise defendants to provide testimony, whereas adversarial defendants are told not to cooperate with the police and seldom testify at the trial. Both prosecutors and defense lawyers are expected to participate in the search for truth, and not to use the process to score adversarial points or to obscure the truth. At the trial, the judge, not the lawyers, runs the show. Trials are designed to determine not only whether the defendant should be convicted, but also to generate reliable information on the basis of which to determine the appropriate penalty. The inquisitorial system, in other words, pursues "substantive" rather than "procedural" justice.

Readers of this essay no doubt will differ about the relative merits of the adversary and inquisitorial systems of criminal justice, but Americans are irrevocably (and perhaps constitutionally) committed to the adversary system. If that system is ever to work as an instrument to deliver justice and truth, the lawyers must be well-matched in terms of skill, experience, and resources. These preconditions are often not met in practice, because one side usually has more experienced lawyers, and there is a large disparity in litigation resources. In addition, the judge must be competent, fearless, neutral, and wholly professional. In America, where judges are appointed for their political connections and usually subject (in the state system) to some form of electoral check, these conditions are often not met either.

However, these conditions are met in the Avedon murder trial that is dramatized in *Murder One*. Skilled and experienced lawyers engage in a mannerly but intense struggle. Each side plays by the rules. Each brings adequate financial resources to the table, enabling them to hire investigators, researchers, and jury consultants. Judge Bornstein is highly competent and controls her courtroom well, even though the camera is running. If ever there was a case in which the adversarial system should reveal the truth and provide justice, this is it. And, in the end, the adversarial system works—but only because of the incredible tenacity and brilliant intuition of Teddy Hoffman. It does not get any better for the adversarial system. However, viewers should realize that actual criminal practice seldom bears much resemblance to the epic and richly financed struggle we see in *Murder One*.

Whether the adversary system can function properly in cases of celebrity justice is a serious issue. The Neal Avedon prosecution is the ultimate celebrity case. Neal is a hugely popular actor. He gets to spin the case his way in a televised interview by a Barbara Walters-like questioner, a performance likely seen by many jurors. He is stalked by a crazy groupie who, for a while, seems like the real killer. Richard Cross is a famous philanthropist with many interests in the entertainment business and great political connections. Graham Lester is rehab doctor to the stars. The Portalegres are super-wealthy Latin Americans who may be drug dealers. Jessica and her friends sniff and sleep their way through the Hollywood community. Gary Blondo is a prominent producer whose Neal Avedon movie is about to hit the multiplexes. Television news is a constant companion in each episode, and some of the broadcasters become bit players in the narrative. Secrets are leaked to the media. A broadcaster seduces one of Hoffman's associates in hopes that he might blurt out a tidbit or two. District Attorney Roger Garfield is running for governor (with heavy financial support from Cross), so the Avedon case is critically important to his political ambitions.

Because the Costello case is conducted in the scorching spotlight of celebrity, the normal processes of adversarial trial are distorted. Cameras in the courtroom bring every sweaty detail into millions of living rooms. The jurors know all about the case, and have absorbed the lawyers' competing spins, long before they are selected for the panel. Two jurors are having an affair—and a news helicopter captures their backyard antics, requiring them to be kicked off the jury. The Costello case becomes the newest monster celebrity prosecution and trial, alongside that of O.J.

Simpson, whose criminal trial ended on October 3, 1995, just a couple of weeks after *Murder One* premiered, as well as Charles Manson, Michael Jackson, Kobe Bryant, Robert Blake, the Menendez brothers, Scott Peterson, and numerous others of the past and present (and undoubtedly the future). Because of the media circus that accompanies celebrity justice, it is hard to have much confidence in the adversary system's pristine assumption that the jurors will decide the case based solely on the inputs provided at the trial.

Conclusion   This essay will not reveal the true killer or the intricate plotting that closes out the first season of *Murder One*. I wouldn't dream of spoiling your pleasure. Rent the DVDs, settle back, warm up the microwave popcorn, and immerse yourself in the suspenseful Avedon trial. You might hesitate to invite lawyers into your living room, but make an exception for *Murder One*.

Endnotes

1. For an in-depth analysis of *Murder One*, which discloses much more about the plot of the series than does this essay, see Jeffrey E. Thomas, *Murder One*, in PRIME TIME LAW (Robert Jarvis & Paul Joseph eds., 1998). Steven Bochco qualifies as one of the pioneers of law on television. In addition to *Murder One*, Bochco created, produced, and wrote *L.A. Law, Hill Street Blues, NYPD Blue,* and *Raising the Bar,* among others.

2. *Murder One* also had to contend with murderous competition from *E.R.* in its first season and *Seinfeld* in its second season.

3. During the second (and last) season of *Murder One*, Benzali was replaced by Anthony LaPaglia, who played Jimmie Wyler, the new leader of the firm. Wyler left the DA's office and went over to the defense side after Roger Garfield spitefully failed to promote him. At least to me, LaPaglia was better looking but did not come within light-years of Benzali's convincing and commanding presence. During the second season, each story extended for multiple, overlapping episodes rather than the entire season. The second season of *Murder One* lasted for 16 episodes, after which the show was dropped by ABC because of low ratings. This essay discusses only the 23 episodes of *Murder One* that comprised the first season.

4. At his most desperate in episode 23, however, Hoffman nearly falls off the ethical wagon.

5. During the second season, the show's excuse for dumping Benzali is that he has taken a leave from law practice and is spending time with Annie trying to repair their marriage.

6. Several chapters in this book furnish insights on the inquisitorial system. See Stefan Machura's chapter "German Judge Shows: Migrating from the Courtroom to the TV Studio"; Barbara Villez's chapter "French Television Lawyers in *Avocats et Associés*"; Vicente Riccio's chapter "Between the Lawyer and the Judge: Ratinho and the Virtual Delivery of Justice in Brazilian Reality Television"; and Anja Louis's chapter "Divorce in Your Living Room: TV Lawyers in Spain's Transition to Democracy."

CHAPTER 13

JAG: Maintaining the Front Lines of Justice

JUSTIN T. SMITH

When thinking of military lawyers in pop culture, most people remember Tom Cruise demanding the truth from Jack Nicholson in *A Few Good Men*. While there have been numerous big-screen depictions of military lawyers, *JAG* was the only major small-screen series that focused on the personal and professional lives of modern military lawyers. *JAG* (the abbreviation for Judge Advocate General—the U.S. Armed Forces' judicial arm) ran for a remarkable 10 seasons and was filled with the usual courtroom drama of clever lawyers eliciting shocking confessions on the witness stand. It also featured interesting side stories, most notably the ongoing love interest between Navy Commander Harmon Rabb, Jr. ("Harm") and Marine Lieutenant Colonel Sarah MacKenzie ("Mac"). However, what set *JAG* apart from the other lawyer shows discussed in this book was its depiction of the unique role of military lawyers, use of reality-based plots, ability to discuss controversial topics, and portrayal of the love-hate relationship between the Navy and Marine Corps, which was echoed by Harm and Mac's relationship. These unique features made *JAG* both highly entertaining and informative about the military legal system.

JAG

Aired:
- September 23, 1995– April 29, 2005, CBS

Cast:
- David James Elliott (Commander Harmon "Harm" Rabb)
- Catherine Bell (Lieutenant Colonel Sarah "Mac" MacKenzie)
- Patrick Labyorteaux (Lieutenant Bud Roberts)
- John M. Jackson (Admiral A.J. Chegwidden)

Awards:
- ASCAP Award for Top TV Series (2000, 2003, 2004)
- David James Elliott, TV Guide Award for Favorite Actor in a Drama (2000)
- Emmy for Outstanding Individual Achievement in Editing (1996)
- Emmy for Outstanding Costuming for a Series (1997, 1999)

JAG-of-All-Trades

JAG lawyers are the quintessential all-purpose lawyers, but the *JAG* characters focused almost exclusively on criminal prosecution and defense. (Apparently, shows based on writing contracts and wills are not ratings boosters.) Although the focus was on military litigation, there were also many crossover topics that could apply to civilian lawyers. For example, in "Rendezvous," Mac found her judgment clouded and had difficulty defending her client because he reminded her of her abusive father, whom she resented. Conversely, the role of the zealous advocate was displayed in "Ambush," in which Harm defended a Marine who violated the rules of engagement and caused six of his fellow soldiers to be killed in an ambush. When asked by Congresswomen Bobbi Latham, "Don't you see the bigger picture?" Harm stoically replied, "I defended my client, the only picture I'm allowed to see."

The unique nature of the military judicial system depicted in *JAG* resulted in some unusual situations that other legal shows cannot duplicate. JAG lawyers can be assigned to be a prosecutor one day and a defense lawyer the next. This often led to tensions in the office, such as when Harm and Mac would oppose each other one day and work as co-counsel the next or when Lieutenant Bud Roberts, the constant sidekick to Harm and Mac, was forced to choose a side to assist. (Bud once remarked that seeing Harm and Mac go at it in the courtroom was like "watching your parents fight.") An additional wrinkle in the series occurred when the JAG lawyers occasionally served as judges. In one such episode, "Ready or Not," Harm was defending in front of Judge Mac, who proved to be more critical of

Courtesy of Photofest.

JAG
Justice is safe with Bud (Patrick Labyorteaux), Harm (David James Elliott), Mac (Catherine Bell), and Adm. Chegwidden (John M. Jackson) on the case.

her colleague than a standard judge. This prompted a frustrated Harm to complain, "With any other judge, I'd have won this case days ago."

The pro-military and pro-American nature of *JAG* was evident when Harm and Mac were prosecuting a high-publicity case against Admiral Chegwidden ("The Good of the Service"). This case involved a Marine who disobeyed orders during a rescue mission that provoked a firefight in which some Haitian villagers were killed. The Marine's controversial actions led to a politically charged trial at which the "powers that be" desired a quick conviction. However, Harm, conflicted by the thought of prosecuting a person for actions that he himself felt were the right thing to do, had other plans, and asked a witness if she blamed the defendant for what happened. The witness responded with an emotional rant blaming all Americans for standing by and letting killings go on, but said she did not understand why the defendant was being punished for trying to improve the situation. The result was a not-guilty verdict for the defendant. Chegwidden remarked to Mac after the case that Harm made a "first-year law student mistake: never ask a question without first knowing the answer," to which Mac replied, "I think he knew the answer, Sir." In addition to reminiscing about first-year law school life, this passage is also indicative of the pro-military perspective that *JAG* often portrayed. Unlike some law shows and films in which negative stereotypes of civilian lawyers are emphasized to attract a larger audience, or military lawyers are depicted as politically motivated, *JAG* played to a different audience—one that wanted to see the American military and its lawyers portrayed as just and fair.

Reality-Based Plots

JAG frequently alluded to real-world events and policies in its story lines. Although many of these situations, such as the Iraqi no-fly zone of the late 1990s ("Scimitar"), the Irish Republican Army ("Trinity"), and the conflict in Bosnia ("Defensive Action"), were used merely as background for *JAG's* plots and had no real relation to the story line, some of the plots of *JAG* were indeed based on reality. In "Clipped Wings" (March 5, 1998), a Navy pilot clipped a ski helicopter in Italy, killing six civilians. This episode was remarkably similar to a February 1998 incident in which an American pilot hit an Italian cable car, killing 20 civilians.[1] Another allusion to reality was "Life or Death," in which Mac had to defend a Marine who had killed three other Marines. Five years earlier, a soldier at Fort Bragg had opened fire on a group of soldiers, killing one and injuring 18 others. Like Mac's defendant, he claimed that his fellow soldiers had harassed him and that he had been denied adequate mental health treatment before the shooting.[2] "Friendly Fire" revolved around the defense of an American pilot who accidentally killed British troops when he bombed their location. A year before its broadcast, an American pilot had bombed a group of Canadian soldiers in Afghanistan, killing four of them.[3]

Another torn-from-the-headlines episode was "Iron Coffin." This episode featured references to a then-current event as well as a tragedy from a few months earlier. In this episode, a Russian submarine exploded underwater and the Russians claimed that the United States was responsible. This episode was similar to the *Kursk* submarine disaster of August 12, 2000, when a Russian submarine suffered an explosion onboard and sank, killing all 118 crew members.[4] Unlike the spiced-up *JAG* version, there was no question of American misconduct in the real tragedy. "Iron Coffin" also included a reference to the USS *Greeneville* sinking a Japanese fishing boat. This occurred on February 9, 2001 (only 11 days before the episode aired), and was a major embarrassment for the U.S. Navy, because the *Greeneville*'s captain had ordered the surfacing maneuver to impress civilian guests on the submarine, two of whom were at the controls when the accident happened.[5] The captain of the *Greeneville* was able to avoid being court-martialed but was forced to retire from the Navy.

Although *JAG* used these events as plots, at other times reality imitated *JAG*. An unfortunate foreshadowing of reality occurred in "Code of Conduct," in which Harm defended a Navy SEAL accused of disobeying orders by returning to a hostile area in Afghanistan to retrieve a wounded comrade, which resulted in the death of another officer. Two months after the episode aired, a SEAL team was conducting a mountaintop surveillance mission in Afghanistan when its helicopter was hit by groundfire. When one of the SEALs fell out, an Army Ranger unit was dispatched on a courageous but ill-fated rescue mission that, sadly, resulted in the death of seven Rangers.[6]

Despite its desire to engage relevant topics, in one episode *JAG* made clear that it was not depicting real events. "Head to Toe" featured a female naval pilot stationed in Saudi Arabia who refused to wear traditional Saudi dress or behave like a Saudi woman. This plotline was considered so controversial that a disclaimer, "The following story is fictional and does not depict any actual person or event," appeared at the beginning of the program. In actuality, the story was similar to that of Air Force Lieutenant Colonel Martha McSally, who objected to regulations requiring that she wear an *abaya* and not drive while stationed in Saudi Arabia.[7]

In keeping with its generally pro-military theme, *JAG* sometimes commemorated forgotten events from America's past. In "Port Chicago," Commander Sturgis Turner investigated the injustice that African-American sailors suffered following the 1944 explosion at Port Chicago, California, that killed 320 men, two-thirds of whom were African American.[8] When the sailors were ordered back to work a few weeks later, 250 of them refused and demanded that safety changes be made. Two hundred of the sailors eventually returned to work, but 50 of them refused and were court-martialed and convicted of mutiny.[9] A poignant moment in the episode came when Chief McBride, a surviving sailor who was petitioning to have his conviction reversed, stated, "When the Navy looked at us, they didn't see fighting men. They saw the color of our skin and they saw cheap, expendable labor."

Another episode, "Each of Us Angels," paid tribute to the Navy nurses of World War II. Through a role-playing flashback device, the *JAG* actors played different characters aboard the USS *Goodwill* during the battle of Iwo Jima. The courageous and critical role played by Navy nurses was dramatized when the ship was hit by a kamikaze and a nurse ran to the ward to help evacuate patients, but was killed by falling equipment before she could save others.

Controversial Topics

The "don't ask, don't tell" policy is one of the most controversial issues concerning the U.S. military. *JAG* focused on the policy on three occasions. In "Heroes," a SEAL member was killed by friendly fire during an engagement. It is later revealed that the SEAL was gay, had AIDS, and felt that the only honorable way to die was in combat rather than tell his father the truth. This was a powerful display of the pressure and shame that many gay men and lesbians feel about "coming out" to those who might not be accepting of their lifestyle. In "People v. Gunny," two members of the JAG office were involved in a fight outside a gay bar and one, Petty Officer Tiner, was presumed to be gay. Ultimately, Tiner revealed that he was not gay: "No. No one asked me. I just wanted to see how it felt. Suddenly everything took on a double meaning, some people bent over backward not to be offensive, others pulled away like I was contagious." The third such episode, "Offensive Action," featured a female officer who was accused of sexually harassing a male subordinate. She revealed to Harm, who was defending her, that she was a lesbian but wanted to remain in the Navy. Harm was able to prove her innocence without revealing her secret, but when Mac asked Harm how he was so certain his client was innocent, he simply replied, "Don't ask."

Since *JAG* aimed to reflect real events and issues, the 9/11 terrorist attack and the subsequent wars in Afghanistan and Iraq predictably became a major focal point in subsequent plots. When the show came back for its seventh season on September 25, 2001, it dated the first few episodes to show that their action occurred before 9/11 (most likely because they were already produced by then and to provide some time to smooth the previous season's plot with current events). In the seventh season's ninth episode ("Dog Robber"), Gunnery Sergeant Victor Galindez, who had served as an assistant in the JAG office, was reassigned to assist in the Afghan War. A powerfully moving exchange occurred between Admiral Chegwidden and Galindez when Chegwidden told him that he only had one regret—"I'm not going with you." When Chegwidden told Galindez to be safe, Galindez captured the patriotism present in America at the time by resolutely stating, "Not until we're all safe, sir."

JAG did not ignore the more negative aspects of the war. In the episode "In Country," Bud, who had been deployed to the USS *Seahawk*, was supervising the detainment of suspected terrorists. Keeping a lawyerly level head, Bud told his partner, who had asked whether or not they were supposed to interrogate the suspects, that they were there only to make sure that protocol was observed and the prisoners were protected. When Bud's partner joked that they should just "beat the crap out of them," Bud remained true to his lawyerly duties and explained, "We'll be too busy preventing everyone else from doing that." In the following episode, the tumultuous seventh season ended quite literally with a bang. In "Enemy Below," Bud was investigating a claim in Afghanistan when his leg was blown off as he stepped on a landmine. Bud's rehab from this traumatic injury, which showed the extreme difficulties faced by wounded soldiers and their families, was a recurring storyline throughout the show's final three seasons.

Navy v. Marine Corps

One of the most interesting dynamics of *JAG* was the interplay between the Navy and the Marine Corps. Since the Marine Corps is a component of the Department of the Navy, the two branches' lawyers work together, albeit not always harmoniously. In *JAG*, most of the main characters (Harm, Chegwidden, Bud, Tiner) belonged to the Navy, but there were also a fair number of Marines (Mac, Gunny, and General Cresswell). This institutional rivalry was sometimes portrayed as causing problems, such as in "Surface Warfare," where it made investigating a case difficult, but the rivalry was often dealt with humorously. In "Baby It's Cold Outside," Harm was defending a Marine officer in civilian court when he was accused of protecting his own. Harm told the opposing counsel, "I'm in the Navy, he was a Marine." When the civilian lawyer snidely responded, "It's all the same," Harm, with a smirk, warned him, "I wouldn't tell that to a Marine." In "Force Recon," after Harm was thanked by a Marine captain for saving the lives of some of his men, Harm reminded him, "Well, Captain, they teach you a few things in the Navy, too."

Another dichotomy within the Navy—between pilots and those on the ground or on ships—was captured through Harm's career. Harm became a lawyer because he was diagnosed with night blindness and was forced to retire as a fighter pilot. Nevertheless, even as a lawyer, Harm managed countless times to get back in the cockpit and fly for various (usually outlandish) reasons. The separation between Harm and his sailor counterparts was perfectly displayed in "Cabin Pressure," in which Harm and a sailor found themselves stuck in a ship's rapidly flooding room:

HARM: Is there anything in here we could use for leverage?

SAILOR: I don't know. Maybe this isn't such a bad way for a Navy man to go.

HARM: Well, it's a hell of a way for an aviator to go, now think!

Harm and Mac

Echoing the tension between the Navy and Marine Corps was the complicated personal relationship between Harm and Mac. Their relationship mirrored many of the problems that private lawyers encounter when they form romantic relationships with other lawyers, especially within their law firms, but it had a few twists peculiar to the military. Catherine Bell debuted as Sarah MacKenzie in the first episode of the second season ("We the People"). However, it wasn't until season three that Harm and Mac's relationship began to heat up. The most crucial moment in *JAG* occurred at the end of the fourth season in the episode "Yeah Baby."

HARM: You ok?

MAC: Every time I think I've put the pieces of my life together, someone comes along and jumbles them back up. Humph. Everyone who has ever meant anything to me is leaving my life.

HARM: It will be OK, Mac. You'll get to see Chloe [a girl Mac had "adopted" as a "little sister"] again. One day you'll have kids of your own.

MAC: Yeah, not at this rate. My biological clock is going off and I keep hitting the snooze button.

HARM: Tell you what. Five years from this moment, if neither of us is in a relationship we'll have some kids.

MAC: You and me, have a baby together?

HARM: Hmm, with your looks and my brains he'll be perfect.

MAC: And what if she has your looks and my brains?

HARM: That could work, too. So, what do you say? Deal?

MAC: Don't make a promise you can't keep.

HARM: I haven't yet.

(They shake hands on the five-year deal).

Although often left unspoken, this agreement always caused a lingering tension between Harm and Mac as they worked together and dated other people while trying to deny their own chemistry. In the season six finale, "Lifeline," Admiral Chegwidden threw an engagement party for Mac and Mic Brumby (an Australian lawyer on loan to the JAG office), during which Mac had a deep conversation with Harm. They reminisced about their ups and downs and ended up kissing. Season seven began with "Adrift II," in which Mac's indecision about getting married drove

Mic back to Australia.[10] When Mac told Harm that Mic "just can't get past this thing with us," Harm, despite the amnesia he was suffering in this episode, succinctly replied, "Maybe that's because we can't get past it." Two episodes later ("Measure of Men"), Mac was aboard a Navy ship conducting an investigation when Harm arrived to oppose her on the case. However, Harm made it clear that this was not the only reason why he was there when he told Mac, "We didn't finish talking yet." Mac, epitomizing the writers' desire to string this storyline along indefinitely, replied, "What makes you think we ever will?"

Harm and Mac continued their emotional back and forth until Mac finally let the cat out of the bag in "Capital Crime" to her colleague, Commander Sturgis Turner:

STURGIS: There seems to be a certain tension with you two.

MAC: Some.

STURGIS: A lot.

MAC: Look—you're missing the point, Sturgis.

STURGIS: Come on, Mac.

MAC: I've never slept with him.

STURGIS: Is that the problem?

MAC: There is no problem.

STURGIS: Then why don't you just get over it and move on?

(Mac gets up out of her chair and moves to the door and closes it.)

MAC: It wouldn't work.

STURGIS: Why?

MAC: Because I'm in love with him. *(long pause)* Did I say that? *(Mac sighs. Another long pause while Mac moves to a chair beside Sturgis and sits down.)* You have to keep that to yourself.

STURGIS: Okay.

MAC: I mean it, Sturgis.

STURGIS: So do I.

This admission did nothing to stop Harm and Mac's feistiness with each other. In "The Promised Land," a frustrated Harm tells Mac, "You've got to stop finishing my sentences." Mac, never willing to play second fiddle to Harm, finishes the discussion by telling Harm, "Stop starting mine."

In the series' final episode, "Fair Winds and Following Seas," Harm and Mac were forced into confronting their feelings for each other and their future together. They are informed that they are being reassigned to London and San Diego, respectively.

MAC: Let's talk about you and me.

HARM: Neither one of us. . .

MAC: Wants to be the first to say goodbye. Yeah, I know the song, we've been singing it for years.

HARM: Mac, I don't think that I will ever feel about anyone else the way that I feel about you.

MAC: That's very flattering. One piece of advice—don't share that with your wife, whoever that might be, she might not understand.

HARM: Do you understand?

MAC: (sarcastically) Why we can't make it work? Why we let fate decide our futures? No. I don't.

HARM: Let me ask you a personal question. Of all the men in your life, what was it about them that attracted you?

MAC: Well, they wanted me, and they let me know it.

HARM: I wanted you. You knew that.

MAC: Harm, no woman wants to be a mind reader, and with you there's always complications—another woman, work, searching for your father.

HARM: That's all past.

MAC: Is it?

HARM: Mac, we have 12 hours.

MAC: We've had nine years.

HARM: I guess maybe I just needed a deadline.

MAC: Well, you got one, sailor. (They kiss.)

MAC: What are you proposing—and that's not a Freudian slip.

HARM: I'm proposing. Let's get married.

MAC: In London?

HARM: Yeah, London works for me.

MAC: San Diego works for me.

HARM:	This has always been the 500-pound gorilla in the room.
MAC:	If we get married, one of us has to give up their Navy careers.
HARM:	Well, we could wait until I retire.
MAC:	Yeah, what's another decade or so, huh?
HARM:	I love you, Mac. But I don't want to give up my Navy career and you don't want to give up the Marine Corps.
MAC:	So we're right back where we started.
HARM:	Do you believe in fate?
MAC:	Well, it put us together, sort of.
HARM:	Fate could keep us together forever.

The episode concluded with Harm and Mac flipping a coin to determine which one would give up his or her military career. The show ended with the coin in midair, leaving viewers to construct their own ending. While disappointing for the audience, by leaving the future of Harm and Mac literally suspended, this ending reinforced their equality as lawyers as well as the importance to each of them of their careers in the Navy and the Marine Corps.

Conclusion

After 227 episodes over 10 seasons, *JAG* departed the airwaves. Its legacy is much different than that of most shows that focus on lawyers. Although it had plenty of courtroom drama, *JAG* was more concerned with telling relevant stories by rewriting real events, taking on controversial topics, and portraying the specialized military legal system. These stories were always engaging, a result achieved by humorous dialogue, well-plotted narratives, and the ever-present romantic tension between Harm and Mac. By combining relevance and entertainment, *JAG* was able to be both informative and a joy to watch.

Endnotes

1. *See US promises cable car deaths inquiry* (BBC News broadcast Feb. 4, 1998), *available at* http://news.bbc.co.uk/1/hi/world/53097.stm.

2. *See* United States v. Kreutzer, 59 M.J. 773 (CAAF 2004) and 61 M.J. 293 (CAAF 2005), *available at* http://www.armfor.uscourts.gov/opinions/2005Term/04-5006.htm.

3. *See* MIKE FRISCOLANTI, FRIENDLY FIRE: THE UNTOLD STORY OF THE U.S. BOMBING THAT KILLED FOUR CANADIAN SOLDIERS IN AFGHANISTAN (2005).

4. *See* Pulli.com, *The Kursk Submarine Disaster,* http://www.pulli.com/kursk/ (last visited July 15, 2008) for a detailed overview of the history of the Kursk submarine disaster.

5. *Guests, failure of display cited at start of Greeneville inquiry,* JAPAN TIMES, Mar. 7, 2001, *available at* http://search.japantimes.co.jp/cgi-bin/nn20010307a1.html.

6. *See* MALCOLM MACPHERSON, ROBERTS' RIDGE: A STORY OF COURAGE AND SACRIFICE ON TAKUR GHAR MOUNTAIN, AFGHANISTAN (2005); *see also* OPERATION ANACONDA: THE BATTLE OF ROBERTS' RIDGE (Pacific Coast Video 2004).

7. For an article about the future of women in combat, see Martha McSally, *Women in Combat: Is the Current Policy Obsolete?,* 14 DUKE J. GENDER L. & POL'Y 1011 (2007).

8. For more information on the Port Chicago disaster, see Naval Historical Center, *Port Chicago Naval Magazine Explosion* (June 1, 2005), *available at* http://www.history.navy.mil/faqs/faq80-1.htm.

9. Future Supreme Court Justice Thurgood Marshall won clemency for these 50 sailors but was unable to get their convictions overturned.

10. The actor who played Australian Royal Navy lawyer Mic Brumby, Trevor Goddard, was found dead in his home on June 7, 2003, of an apparent drug overdose. At the funeral, Goddard's father revealed that Goddard had been born and raised in England and made up his Australian accent and backstory to break into the acting business. At the end of episode 183 ("Life or Death"), a montage of Goddard is featured in which the JAG cast sings the Australian folk song "Waltzing Matilda."

CHAPTER 14

Swimming with *Shark*

NANCY B. RAPOPORT

I am mourning the cancellation of CBS's show, *Shark,* for many reasons: I love the name of the show;[1] I love watching James Woods act;[2] I found the writing compelling; and I teach law students about legal ethics. Why is that last reason important? Because Sebastian Stark (James Woods's character) provides me with more ethical missteps than I could ever use in a single semester. What makes *Shark* even better is that Sebastian Stark isn't one-sidedly bad. He's a "reformed" criminal defense attorney trying to do the right thing. Unfortunately, his reformation has not improved his ethics. He is way over on the wrong side of the ethical line. (Part of the reason that Stark is so ethically challenged, of course, is that a show featuring ethical lawyers probably wouldn't draw large audiences.[3]) Fortunately for those of us who love watching TV shows about lawyers—even about ethically challenged lawyers—*Shark* drew large enough audiences to justify two seasons. I just wish that it had been renewed for a third season.

Early on,[4] we learn why Stark is working for the District Attorney's Office. Stark was an extremely successful criminal defense lawyer— one of the best—and in the case that opens the pilot, he gets a celebrity acquitted of attempted

Shark

Aired:
- September 21, 2006– May 20, 2008, CBS

Cast:
- James Woods (Sebastian Stark)
- Danielle Panabaker (Julie Stark)
- Jeri Ryan (Jessica Devlin)
- Sophia Brown (Raina Troy)
- Sarah Carter (Madeleine Poe)
- Sam Page (Casey Woodland)

Awards:
- Emmy nomination for Outstanding Art Direction for a Single Camera Series (2007)
- James Woods, Satellite Award nomination for Best Actor in a Series Drama (2007)

Courtesy of Photofest.

SHARK
Sebastian Shark (James Woods) instructs his associates in the finer points of ignoring legal ethics.

murder charges on the grounds that the celebrity meant to beat his wife up, but not to kill her. Later, when the celebrity does kill her, Stark retreats from his criminal defense practice and has a month-long crisis of conscience. During this hiatus from practice, the Los Angeles mayor approaches Stark and asks him to head a new high-profile crimes unit in the District Attorney's Office. Stark agrees, and he becomes a Deputy DA.

Joining Stark's new team is a collection of junior attorneys. Of all of the lawyers on Stark's team, only one has volunteered to work in his unit; the rest of the lawyers are on their way out the door for various reasons, and working for Stark is a last-ditch effort to save their jobs.

In the pilot episode, Stark makes it clear to his staff that he plays by three simple rules.

> My cutthroat manifesto. These rules guide every decision I make on every single case. Rule number one: Trial is war; second place is death. Rule number two: Truth is relative. Pick one that works. Rule number three: In a jury trial, there are only 12 opinions that matter, and, Miss Troy, yours most decidedly is not one of them.

To me, the point of *Shark* (aside from the sheer enjoyment of watching Woods) is watching how the junior attorneys who work for Stark slowly but surely change their ethics to conform more closely to his dubious sense of right and wrong. In fact, they have very little choice: if they do not reorient their ethics to fit into his "ends justify the means" ethos, they will be out on the street, looking for new jobs.

And there's the rub. Presumably, these new attorneys know the basic ethics rules. Don't lie to the court. Don't break the law. Don't abuse third parties. But those rules often conflict with Stark's manifesto for winning cases, and the members of Stark's team almost immediately start breaking those rules, rationalizing their decisions as they go.

The pilot episode highlights the clash between the ethics rules and Stark's rules. Stark fires Billie Willis, one of his junior attorneys, because she fails to prepare him for some surprises at trial. But the divide between the two of them was clear even at the beginning of the episode. When Stark is doling out assignments to prepare for trial, another member of Stark's team, Casey Woodland, finds himself without an assignment.

> WOODLAND: [eagerly] What about me?
>
> STARK: Oh, yeah. I want you to go down to Jensen's and get a double order of cheese fries.
>
> WOODLAND: [laughs] You're joking, right?
>
> STARK: Did I chuckle? You're gonna bring the fries to Jurors' Bailiff Ray Sabado. Ray's in charge of the jurors on this case. Two things he loves more than life itself: He loves yakking with the jurors and he loves to eat. That bag of fries is gonna buy us more insight than 10 jury consultants, okay?
>
> WILLIS: Uh, that's prosecutorial misconduct.
>
> STARK: [acting scared] Well, we'll just have to be brave on this one. [normal voice] We have to prove that Terrence Rourke was a victim of murder. We need to make that jury hear his voice.[5]

See how Stark begins the process of manipulating his subordinates' ethical sensibilities? He simply implies that they are all cheating for a good cause. And his protégés learn quickly.

It is possible, of course, that the reason that Stark cheats is that he knows, from personal experience, that some defense lawyers cheat. He knows that *he* cheated. Perhaps, from his perspective, he is just leveling the playing field. But from watching his character evolve over two seasons, I got the sense that he moved from wanting to win just for winning's sake to wanting to win in order to put dangerous people behind bars. Unfortunately, though, he never changed his own ethics rules as part of that evolution. He never evolved to understand that "the good guys" *do* need to play by the rules.

Here is another example of how quickly Stark's team supplants legal ethics with Stark's own ethics rules. In an early episode, two of Stark's team members, Madeleine Poe and Casey Woodland, fudge their way into obtaining a search warrant, although the evidence obtained in that search later gets suppressed:

POE: According to the M.E., the slug they took out of Rodriguez "appears to be nine millimeter."

WOODLAND: Ransom has a 9-millimeter handgun registered in his name. [They enter the High Profile Crimes Unit office.]

POE: The report's vague. We need a conclusive finding to have a shot at a warrant.

WOODLAND: Partner's statement puts Ransom at the scene.

POE: Judge Pearlman is a Fourth Amendment freak. We have no gun. She won't grant our search warrant petition unless the bullet's a solid match. [sits at her desk]

WOODLAND: [sits at his desk] Ballistics'll confirm the caliber of the slug in a few days.

POE: We don't have a few days. We need to get into Ransom's condo now.

WOODLAND: It's not like we can misstate the M.E.'s report.

POE: [deadpan] Of course not. That would be unethical. Unless . . . it was a simple oversight made under time pressure.

WOODLAND: [smiles] Forget it.

POE: Fortune favors the bold.

WOODLAND: And what's that supposed to mean?

POE: Sometimes you got to have some balls.

WOODLAND: [chuckles] Well, I've never had any complaints.

POE: So I hear. [They look at each other.]

WOODLAND: [agreeable shrug] So, it was an oversight.

POE: [smiles] Happens all the time.[6]

After the court excludes evidence from the faulty search, the DA (Jessica Devlin) orders Stark to reprimand Poe and Woodland. Instead, he play-acts their reprimand in the DA's presence:

DEVLIN:	Well, you dodged a bullet.
STARK:	That wasn't even a BB, everything's under control.
DEVLIN:	I want Poe and Woodland reprimanded.
STARK:	I'm . . . gonna read them the riot act.
CUT TO:	[Courthouse hallway. Day. The team stands quietly. Stark strides up to them.]
STARK:	[loudly] Listen up! Everybody stop talking and listen to me! [Jessica stands at a distance, watching the "riot act reading" unfold.]
STARK:	[quietly] Everybody nod your heads, pretend I just kicked your puppy, okay. You understand me, [loudly to Casey] right, GQ? [The kids bow their heads, looks of shame on their faces. Jessica seems to like how Stark is handling this.]
STARK:	Thank you. [quietly] Good, we're in great shape. All we have to do is break down Ransom's alibi and we are home free, all right. [to Casey] GQ, I want you to go over to the girl-friend's house, I want you to use that million-dollar smile, and I want you to knock her off her story. [loudly] Do you understand me? Say yes!
WOODLAND:	Yes.
STARK:	Thank you! [stabs his finger towards Madeleine and Martin] You and you! [quietly] Talk to Ransom's Venice neighbors and see what they know. [loudly] Got it? [He starts to leave.]
WOODLAND:	So you're not mad about the petition thing?
STARK:	[stops, looks at Jessica, loudly] Almost forgot! Consider this a lesson! The next time that you cheat, [quietly] don't get caught. [yells] Got it?! [He looks at Jessica, a world-weary look on his face. Jessica seems mollified.][7]

But Stark is far from one-dimensional. He lives by a moral code, although not the one governed by normal rules of legal ethics. He obviously loves his daughter, even though his workaholic nature means that he ignored her for most of her first 16 years. I love the fact that Stark is clearly a perfectionist about his work—and I wish that more lawyers emulated his work ethic.[8] As Stark explains, "I never make an argument in open court before it has been PERFECTED in this room."[9] Moreover, Stark does not suffer fools, firing one of his junior attorneys after this exchange:

STARK: [restrained] You missed [the evidence about] rehab?

WILLIS: [defensive] It was a voluntary commitment. If I'd had more time. . .

STARK: [gesturing angrily] Anita had one day on this case and she came up with it. What were you thinking?

WILLIS: I'm sorry. I did the best I could.

STARK: You know what, it's not your fault, it's my fault. In between writing three briefs, putting together my witness list, formulating my direct, I should have found time to do your job, too.

WOODLAND: [knight in shining armor] Look, she apologized. . .

STARK: [mad] Do you mind?

WILLIS: I don't need you to defend me.

STARK: There is no defense for mediocrity.

WILLIS: [pissed] I've been up for 32 hours. I interviewed his friends, his family, his teachers.

STARK: You want a merit badge? In jury trials, you don't get a second chance. Your incompetence has put us in a major hole.

WILLIS: [quietly, on the verge of tears] If I'm such a major screw-up. . .

STARK: Mm-hmm.

WILLIS: . . . why don't you fire me?

STARK: That's the first helpful suggestion you've had. Good luck with the rest of your career.[10]

Most of all, I love the fact that Stark really, truly wants to do the right thing: put the bad guys behind bars. (Let's leave aside the question of how someone can do the right thing when he does it 100 percent the wrong way. I am writing about a fictional character here.) He has become a true believer in the DA's mission, so much so that when his boss loses the election, he asks her to consider coming to work for him:

STARK: You really think you're gonna be happy wining and dining clients and falsifying your billable hours?

DEVLIN: Didn't hurt your bottom line.

STARK: It cost me plenty. There's no free lunch, Jess. [beat] You know, I could always use another good prosecutor.

[She looks at him apprehensively.]

DEVLIN: [laughs] You're offering me a job?

STARK: [laughs as well] Ironic, huh? But I've said it before. You're a natural-born trial attorney. You belong on the front lines putting away the bad guys.

[They stop walking and face each other.]

DEVLIN: You want me to give up a million bucks a year and house seats to the Philharmonic to make 80 grand working in a crappy office for a control freak who is eventually gonna wind up disbarred?

STARK: [smiles] That is the glass half-empty version. [seriously] Here's the thing. You can sell out, Jess. God knows I did. And for a while, everything will be okay. But then one day, you're gonna wake up and you're gonna realize you're the bad guy.

[Jessica seems to agree, yet shakes her head.]

DEVLIN: It would never work. We'd kill each other.

STARK: But you've gotta admit, we make a hell of a team.[11]

Later, we learn just how serious Stark was about switching from defense lawyer to Deputy District Attorney. When one of his earlier ethics violations catches up with him, the California State Bar disbars him, and Stark goes to Las Vegas to drown his sorrows. While he licks his wounds there, one of his former clients pressures him into returning to defense work. Stark soon discovers that he no longer has the stomach for that work. After a few more creative plot twists, Stark's willingness to frame his own client puts him back in the good graces of the California Bar, and he gets his license back. (As I watched this episode, I wondered if my criminal defense counsel friends viewed *Shark* with the same gritted-teeth resignation with which I used to view *Ally McBeal*.)

Shark is one of my guilty pleasures. I love the characters but hate their constant rationalizing. I especially hate the extent to which Stark forces his team to loosen their grip on the rules of legal ethics. When I see Stark give his team orders, I see every defendant in a corporate scandal over the past decade. ("He told me to 'make the numbers,' so I just made them up.")[12] Smart people, even very smart people, are capable of tricking themselves into doing very stupid things. Just because Stark himself manages to get out of his various ethics mishaps does not mean that his young team members will be able to avoid their own disciplinary hearings down the road.

And Stark's ethics missteps are not just a little over the line. They're outrageous. In the season one finale, Stark has spent weeks brooding over the fact that he failed to convict Wayne Callison, a serial murderer who represented himself. Stark is now determined not to let Callison get away again. Was it the fact that Stark let a guilty person get away or the fact that he was beaten by someone without a law degree? While Callison embarks on a book tour (*The Hunted Man: How I Beat the Toughest Prosecutor in America*), Stark prepares to prosecute him for a recently discovered murder that appears to have the same M.O. as Callison's prior murders. Not only does Stark want his team to "manufacture" probable cause in order to get a search warrant, but he instructs them to suppress what might very well be exculpatory evidence.[13] Suppressing exculpatory evidence is not just "bad"; it is, quite literally, one of the worst things that a prosecutor can do.

But wait! In the immortal words of TV pitchman Ron Popeil, there's more.[14] Not only does Stark actually destroy that exculpatory evidence by burning it, but late in the episode, Stark gets Callison alone and (spoiler alert!)[15] confesses to him that the murder for which Callison has just been convicted wasn't even a murder at all. (This confession, of course, comes as no surprise to Callison, who knows full well that he didn't commit the murder.) Stark explains to Callison that Stark found a suicide victim, talked to the victim's mother about using the body as a way to convict a serial killer, persuaded a young medical examiner (who owed his job to Stark) to cut up the body to make it look like Callison's M.O., and then got the medical examiner to opine that Callison had probably committed the murder. Stark then simultaneously exhibits his knowledge of, and contempt for, the rules of legal ethics.

CALLISON: [shaking his head in disbelief] And they say I'm crazy.

STARK: Trust me, you are crazy.

CALLISON: Well, I will be sure to bring all this up on appeal.

STARK: Go for it. But I've got another big one for you. Loose ends, Wayne. There's not a single scrap of paper. Not one e-mail to confirm what I just told you. Hannah Morton's remains have been cremated. None of my lawyers knows a thing, and the people who do aren't saying a word.

When a real lawyer becomes a member of any state's bar, he or she swears to uphold the law. But in TV land, Stark commits the ultimate lawyer taboos: he destroys evidence, fakes a murder, and lies to the court in order to put a serial killer in prison. And that's just in season one. Fast forwarding to the series finale at the end of season two, we find that Stark's decision to frame Callison has come back to haunt him. Callison escapes from prison, kidnaps Stark's daughter Julie, and demands that Stark present his best argument for why Callison should return Julie to Stark unharmed. During Stark's argument, Callison forces Stark to admit to Julie that he faked a murder in order to put Callison in prison.

The irony of Callison's demand ("prove to me that you deserve to get your daughter back") is that Stark, who has been an absentee father for most of Julie's life, has managed to avoid imprinting his daughter with his own lack of ethical boundaries. Stark has, however, imprinted two seasons of relatively new lawyers with the understanding that violating the ethics rules is perfectly fine as long as a higher purpose—putting the criminals away—is served. These lawyers will become the next generation of district attorneys, law firm partners, and legislators. Thanks to Stark, they have learned that they can safely substitute their own views of right and wrong for those that the legal system has put in place. They, in turn, will send forth their own trainees, also imprinted with Stark's "ends justify the means" mentality, and so on, and so on, until some brave lawyer decides that ethics must trump expediency.

In a way, Stark teaches his legal team in much the same way that the fictional Harvard law professor, Charles Kingsfield, teaches his impressionable first-year contracts students in the movie *Paper Chase*. ("You come in here with a skull full of mush and you leave thinking like a lawyer.")[16] Kingsfield teaches his students to love competition—to thrive under extreme pressure—as a way of winning Kingsfield's (temporary) approval. But the way that Kingsfield teaches his students to think like a lawyer robs them of their individuality and their compassion. They leave law school thinking in terms of rules and exceptions, not in terms of right and wrong.[17]

This whole idea of imprinting impressionable lawyers is not just fiction. In one of my favorite studies, Professor (and now Dean) Larry Hellman asked students who were enrolled in one of his professional responsibility courses to keep track of ethics violations that they spotted as they worked for lawyers during that semester.[18] As these law students were busily learning the standard ethics rules in his class—don't lie, don't steal, don't cheat, don't fake knowledge—they were also watching real lawyers violate each and every one of those rules. The students in his course reported instances of neglect, incompetence, conflicts of interest, and other equally nightmarish real-life ethics abuses.[19] Which do you think made the more powerful impression on the students—the law professor (who wasn't making a living by practicing law) talking about the "thou shalt nots," or the lawyers (with the fancy cars and houses) telling the students that the real world was very different from how things work in the ivory tower of academia?

Shark makes for mighty entertaining viewing, but the lesson is clear: when it comes to teaching right from wrong, it's what people do, not what they say, that counts.

Endnotes

1. Who wouldn't love the name of a lawyer show called *Shark?* It's obviously a play on the traditional joke about a lawyer who's been in a shipwreck and has to swim to shore in shark-infested waters, but who arrives on land untouched because the sharks line up on either side of him to guide him safely to land. Why? Professional courtesy.

2. I am not alone in thinking that James Woods is an extraordinarily good actor. After all, he has been nominated twice for an Academy Award, nominated six times for an Emmy (with two wins), and nominated eight times for the Golden Globes (with one win). For the full list of his awards, see http://www.imdb.com/name/nm0000249/awards.

3. *See* Terry Carter, *Why Are TV Lawyers Ethically Challenged? That's Hollywood, Writers Say*, http://abajournal.com/news/why_are_tv_lawyers_ethically_challenged_thats_hollywood_writers_say/ (Feb. 9, 2008) ("[Bill Fordes, a *Law & Order* writer], points out that if you want, you can watch honest lawyers on Court TV, which gets only about 600,000 viewers at most and thus nowhere near the dollars for 30- and 60-second commercials flowing to *L&O.*").

4. Spike Lee directed the pilot (2006).

5. http://www.twiztv.com/scripts/shark/season1/shark-101.htm.

6. http://www.twiztv.com/scripts/shark/season1/shark-102.htm.

7. *Id.*

8. When he was a rich defense lawyer, Stark built a replica courtroom inside his house so that he could rehearse his arguments and prepare his examinations of witnesses at home. And it's not just any old courtroom replica. Stark has floor panels taken from the U.S. Supreme Court building (I don't want to know how he managed to get them), Clarence Darrow's former chair, and Judge Lance Ito's desk lamp.

9. http://www.twiztv.com/scripts/shark/season1/shark-101.htm.

10. http://www.twiztv.com/scripts/shark/season1/shark-101.htm.

11. http://www.twiztv.com/scripts/shark/season1/shark-122.htm.

12. The push to "make the numbers" by making the numbers up is what happened at Enron, WorldCom, Tyco, etc. I have just read Cynthia Cooper's book describing her experience uncovering the fraud at WorldCom, and it is fascinating. CYNTHIA COOPER, EXTRAORDINARY CIRCUMSTANCES: THE JOURNEY OF A CORPORATE WHISTLEBLOWER (2008).

13. The failure to disclose potentially exculpatory evidence to the defense is commonly called a *Brady* violation. "[T]he term *"Brady* violation" is sometimes used to refer to any breach of the broad obligation to disclose exculpatory evidence—that is, to any suppression of so-called *"Brady* material"—although, strictly speaking, there is never a real *"Brady* violation" unless the nondisclosure was so serious that there is a reasonable probability that the suppressed evidence would have produced a different verdict." Strickler v. Greene, 527 U.S. 263, 281 (1999) (footnote omitted).

14. *See, e.g.,* http://www.npr.org/programs/morning/features/2002/june/ronco/ ("But wait! There's more!").

15. I've always wanted to say that.

16. http://www.imdb.com/title/tt0070509/quotes.

17. For an intriguing take on the "bleaching out" of lawyers, see David B. Wilkins, *Identities and Roles: Race, Recognition, and Professional Responsibility,* 57 MD. L. REV. 1502 (1998).

18. Lawrence K. Hellman, *The Effects of Law Office Work on the Formation of Law Students' Professional Values: Observation, Explanation, Optimization,* 4 GEO. J. LEGAL ETHICS 537 (1991).

19. *Id.* at 601–05.

PART IV

Criminal Justice— British Shows

The magic of televised courtroom drama has spread around the world. Of course, American television shows have a global audience, so foreign viewers often know more about the American criminal justice system than about their own. However, there is now a great deal of home-grown production. We consider French and Spanish shows involving civil justice in Part V and the German and Brazilian versions of *Judge Judy* in Part VI. This part considers four British criminal law shows, only one of which is widely known in the United States.

British criminal procedure is adversarial, like that in the United States, so it makes for riveting drama. In fact, with the lawyers at the Old Bailey resplendent in their robes and wigs, and their clipped English accents, sometimes it is even better. Britain loves its lawyer shows, and there have been many of them. By far the best-known and best-loved of the British criminal law shows is *Rumpole of the Bailey*, based on the famous Rumpole books by John Mortimer. The Rumpole books and television shows are gentle satires of the British criminal justice system—and of the stuffed shirts who serve as judges and barristers. Horace Rumpole is a curmudgeonly old barrister who regards himself as a criminal law hack. Rumpole loves ruffling the feathers of the judges at the Old Bailey as well as the other lawyers in his rather stodgy chambers. Nobody can push Rumpole around—except for his wife Hilda, who always has her way. *Rumpole* fan Paul Bergman's chapter even includes an original script that Paul has written for us.

The other British series discussed in this part are harder-edged than *Rumpole*, and they are of very high quality. *Blind Justice*, which ran for only five long episodes in the 1980s, concerned a politically committed group of barristers. Its blistering scripts explored official corruption, abuse of the Official Secrets Act, racial issues, antiterrorism laws, and numerous other hot-button issues, many of which remain relevant today. Unfortunately, no DVDs of *Blind Justice* are available in the United States, but the scripts have been novelized and published by Penguin Books (*Blind Justice*, 1988).

Kavanagh, QC ran from 1995 to 2001 and involved a British barrister who specialized in criminal law. It often included very well-written and -acted courtroom episodes as well as Kavanagh's personal and professional struggles. Often the emphasis in the *Kavanagh* episodes is on the class differences that persist in English society and in its legal system. Fortunately, DVDs of the *Kavanagh* series are available in the United States. Ysaiah Ross has written our chapters on both *Blind Justice* and *Kavanagh, QC*.

Since 2000, at least seven new lawyer shows have appeared on British television. Our British commentators (Greenfield, Osborn, and Robson) recap them for us, but they focus primarily on a pathbreaking show called *Judge John Deed*. It is no easy matter to make a television show about a judge, given that judges play a relatively passive role in the justice system. But there is nothing passive about John Deed. He grabs every politically controversial case he can get his hands on. He is at war with the government, which spies on him and exercises behind-the-scenes influence to keep him away from those very cases. The show has taken on a range of controversial issues such as police abuse, racism, domestic violence, and corporate misdeeds. It is a worthy successor to *Blind Justice* and *Kavanagh, QC* and, reaching farther back, to *The Defenders*. It explores Deed's personal life as well, and, suffice it to say, he's no saint. At present, *Judge John Deed* is unavailable in the United States, either on DVD or on BBC America, but surely a high-quality television series that is so controversial will eventually make its way to these shores.

CHAPTER 15

Rumpole and the Bowl of Comfort Food

PAUL BERGMAN

Rumpole of the Bailey

Aired:
- April 3, 1978–
  December 3, 1992, BBC

Cast:
- Leo McKern
  (Horace Rumpole)
- Jonathan Coy
  (Henry)
- Julian Curry
  (Claude Erskine-Brown)
- Marion Mathie
  (Hilda Rumpole)
- Patricia Hodge
  (Phyllida Erskine-Brown)

Awards:
- Nominated for the Emmy
  for Outstanding Miniseries
  (1988)
- Nominated for the Emmy
  for Outstanding Limited
  Series (1981)

Introduction

Rumpole of the Bailey was a delightful British television series based on the life and courtroom exploits of John Mortimer's curmudgeonly barrister, Horace Rumpole. Rumpole was a zealous if eccentric criminal defense lawyer. He was equally skilled in the arts of cross-examining police officers and plucking appropriate quotes from the *Oxford Book of English Verse*.

The series consisted of 44 episodes that initially aired during seven seasons between 1978 and 1992. The titles of nearly all of the episodes began with *"Rumpole and. . . ."* Thus, the title of this short essay captures a quality that makes the shows so enjoyable to watch. The stories' gentle satires of British traditions and justice make viewers feel as relaxed as Rumpole usually was as he sat in Pommeroy's Wine Bar after a hard day in the Old Bailey, drinking a glass of the cheap house wine that he affectionately called "Chateau Thames Embankment" or "Chateau Fleet Street."

Courtesy of Photofest.

RUMPOLE OF THE BAILEY
Rumpole (Leo McKern) smirks after again besting chamber-mate and favorite patsy Claude Erskine-Brown (Julian Curry).

A Chambers Meeting

Chambers Meetings were a regular feature of the *Rumpole* shows. Rumpole and the other barristers who had chambers in 3 Equity Court were often called to meetings by Guthrie Featherstone, who was the head of Chambers until he went on the bench (often to preside over cases that Rumpole tried). Sam Ballard, who succeeded Featherstone as head, was a comically pompous religious zealot who often used the meetings to complain that Rumpole's low-life clients were sullying the Chambers' good name and to announce silly Chambers rules targeting Rumpole's annoying personal habits. Ballard was almost never able to enforce his rules because Rumpole inevitably set Ballard up to violate them first. Rumpole often referred to Ballard as Soapy Sam because of the latter's unctuous fawning when in the presence of an aristocrat, a judge, or a QC. Barristers who become QCs ("Queen's Counsel") have reached the top of their profession. They wear silk gowns to court and so are said to have "taken silk." Rumpole would never wear a silk gown and has no pretensions to become a QC.

Because he was repeatedly passed over for promotions to head of chambers, judgeships, and various other honors that were announced at Chambers Meetings, Rumpole was a disappointment to his long-suffering wife Hilda. Under his breath, Rumpole regularly referred to Hilda as She Who Must Be Obeyed. Hilda had a sharp tongue and she was little impressed with Rumpole's rhetorical flourishes. Her father had been the first head of 3 Equity Court, a fact that annoyed Rumpole because Hilda's father "knew nothing about bloodstains and fingerprints." When Rumpole would come home after having lost in court, Hilda was happy because "at least you're quieter, Rumpole." When he'd admit to having gone wine-tasting before coming home, she'd curtly reply, "Don't you always?"

Given its prominence in the series, a mock Chambers Meeting seems a useful medium for exploring Rumpole's character, his courtroom strategies, and the judges and other barristers whose idiosyncrasies were never-ending sources of conflict and amusement for him. The "transcript" that follows is based primarily on the following episodes of *Rumpole of the Bailey,* all of which were written by John Mortimer: "Rumpole and the Genuine Article" (1983); "Rumpole and the Old Boy Net" (1983); "Rumpole and the Sporting Life" (1983); "Rumpole and the Blind Tasting" (1987); "Rumpole's Last Case" (1987); "Rumpole and the Judge's Elbow" (1987); "Rumpole and the Old, Old Story" (1987); and "Rumpole and Portia" (1988).

> BALLARD: Well, Rumpole, I see that Hilda has finally had the good sense to throw you out of the house. But we can't have you sleeping in chambers, fouling the air with your cheap cheroots. This chambers is joining the clean air brigade, and anyone using chambers as a hotel will have to give up the leasehold.
>
> RUMPOLE: No smoking in chambers? That's against the rights of man as set forth in Magna Carta. Are you familiar with that document, Ballard?
>
> BALLARD: Henry, our chambers clerk, warned me against you, Rumpole. He said that you had a sense of humor.
>
> RUMPOLE: Only a mild one, Ballard. Nothing fatal. You've managed to keep free of it, have you?
>
> BALLARD: You should try to put more religion in your life, Rumpole. Don't you read the barristers' church newspaper?
>
> RUMPOLE: Only for the racing tips. Anyway, Ballard, as usual you are quite behind the times. Two of our esteemed members of chambers, Claude Erskine-Brown and his wife Phyllida, a QC who is my beloved Portia, have had the pleasure of my company these last few days. They and their little darlings Tristan and Isolde are so amused by the stories of my old cases at the bar.
>
> BALLARD: Erskine-Brown, can this be true?

CLAUDE ERSKINE-BROWN: For the moment, Ballard, setting aside the amusement. But this morning at breakfast, my dear little Isolde told Rumpole that according to her teacher, smoking will soon be illegal. Isolde told Rumpole that he will be sent to prison. With his usual bad taste, Rumpole told her that it was terrible what nonsense she was being taught in school.

PHYLLIDA ERSKINE-BROWN: I've been to see Hilda, to say how terrible it is that she has to live alone. I'm sorry to say that she seemed quite happy because now the flat is always clean and she can listen to the programs she likes. When I pointed out to Hilda that Rumpole lives there too, she said, "Does he? I haven't seen him living here lately."

BALLARD: Well Rumpole, at least I'm delighted that you've taken on a new pupil, Liz Probert. Her father is a canon in the church, and her presence should give this chambers the much-needed respectability that the thieves and murderers you always represent have cost it.

RUMPOLE: (Thinking to himself: Poor Ballard, you should have checked further into the family of Canon Probert. Ms. Liz's father is the radical labor leader known as Red Ron.) Ms. Probert is indeed an outstanding pupil, Ballard. She sought me out for a pupilage after watching my brilliant performance at the Old Bailey. The Bill (police officers) never get tired of giving me a chance to earn a living by representing members of the Timson family. On this occasion they had arrested Mr. Timson after finding allegedly stolen silver pieces stuffed into bags of frozen peas in his freezer. As I pointed out during cross-examination of the arresting officer, where is a single owner who has identified a piece of silver as his? Might Timson not have hit upon an excellent way to protect his valuables from thieves? Isn't an Englishman's freezer his castle? As usual, the judge took the side of the prosecution. When I told the jurors about the steps that members of my family had taken to protect art items they valued, old Judge Graves tried to put the kiss of death on the presumption of innocence by telling the jurors to "disregard anything Rumpole told you about the strange people in his family."

Shortly after Timson was quite properly found not guilty, the cops arrested him again. This time they claimed that he had bought cases of expensive wine that he knew had been stolen from a fancy wine shop. They hadn't been stolen, but I'm getting ahead of the story. Timson's solicitor came to my chambers asking if I knew about the recent House of Lords opinion on the law that applies when a crime that one attempts to commit is impossible. Of course I didn't know about it. As I had just told Ms. Liz, after a lifetime at the bar I have very little interest in the law. Give me a bloodstain or two and a bit of disputed hair, and you can keep your House of Lords opinions. Having nevertheless assured the solicitor that I was quite familiar with the case, I was lucky that Ms. Liz rescued me by putting the case right in front of me. When the solicitor had the poor taste to ask me what the case said, I put him off by saying that a written opinion would be much more helpful to him and promised to send him one. Thankfully, he finally left and Ms. Liz said that she would write the opinion because she was still interested in the law.

As for the cases of stolen wine, at trial I asked Timson, "Where did you get them? The judge may be curious." Timson said he'd bought them in a pub, but he couldn't remember the name of the person he'd bought them from. My cross-examination of the wine merchant was brilliant. I asked, "The wine was insured, was it not? When your assistant told you about the theft, your immediate response was, 'Oh well, it was insured,' correct? And when you owned a business called Banbury Fine Arts, you made a big insurance claim after a theft of artwork, right?" I was bluffing on this last one, but luckily he said yes, and added that it was only sound business practice to insure one's merchandise. Of course, Judge Graves again tried to make the case for the prosecution, immediately backing up the wine merchant. "You have to maintain insurance because of the rising tide of lawlessness that threatens to engulf us all. You should know that better than anyone, Rumpole."

I whispered down to Timson's solicitor, seated in front of me, "The judge is suffering from a bad case of premature adjudication." The judge, who suddenly developed very acute hearing, asked me to repeat what I had said. I responded aloud, "I mentioned only that there will be a full explanation, Your Lordship."

I asked the judge for permission to pour three glasses of the wine for His Lordship, my expert witness, and myself. The judge at first refused, declaring "this is a court of law, not a wine bar, Rumpole." But when I threatened to go immediately to the Court of Appeal, he relented at once. One taste and it was clear that the wine was for stealing, not for selling. Satisfied that the wine merchant was out to defraud the insurance company, and that Timson had paid a fair price for the wine, the jury did justice and set him free.

CLAUDE ERSKINE-BROWN: See here, Ballard. If there's nothing we can do about Rumpole, what about Uncle Tom? He's been in chambers here longer than any of us, but no one can remember the last time he had a brief. All he does all day is stand in the Clerk's Office and practice his putting. I've applied for silk, but the disreputable lot who are Rumpole's clients and Uncle Tom's foolishness are ruining my chances of becoming a QC. Just think of how that would sound, Rumpole—"Lord Erskine-Brown."

RUMPOLE: It sounds very promising, Erskine-Brown, if one is opposing you down at the Old Bailey.

PHYLLIDA ERSKINE-BROWN: Claude, you're such a silly prig. You know Sy Stratton, the American actor who invited me to go back to the coast with him after I got him off with a slap on the wrist when he was caught with drugs at the airport? I have to admit I was tempted to accept. I need a bit of fun; Claude just sits around all night listening to classical music. Anyway, when Sy came to chambers to urge me one last time to go with him, he saw Uncle Tom with his putter and praised our chambers for upholding British traditions. Sy promised to send us lots of business.

BALLARD: Nonetheless, Erskine-Brown is quite right about Rumpole making our chambers seem so disreputable. Even Her Majesty's expert witnesses are not safe from your scorn, Rumpole.

RUMPOLE: Most of them go out of their way to earn it, Ballard. I recently defended a wife who was charged with murdering her aristocratic husband while shooting on their country estate. I knew that my client was one of those elite country snobs who thought of me as an "NPLU" (Not People Like Us), but I didn't think she was a murderess. The autopsy on her husband had been performed by a medical examiner who had never before been involved in a murder case. He failed to notice that the husband had been shot twice, a fact that demonstrated my client's innocence. I concluded my cross-examination of the M.E. by handing him the book *Gunshot Wounds in Forensic Medicine* and telling him, "I recommend it to you if you're going to be doing this work in the future. It's quite an easy read for the beginner."

BALLARD: Nonetheless, you do no good for your reputation or that of this chambers when you persist in belittling our judges. They talk about you, Rumpole. For example, Judge Twyburn quite properly scolded the prosecutor in your last case for a mistake of grammar. When the good judge later mentioned that a witness's tone of voice was of "unimportant insignificance," you immediately stood up to proclaim that the judge was tormenting the English language by using a tautology. The prosecutor may have thanked you for taking his part, Rumpole, but you did nothing to advance your place at the bar. Judge Twyburn complained to Guthrie Featherstone about your reprehensible conduct.

RUMPOLE: Ah, dear Guthrie. In my last case before the old dear, my client Brittling was charged with forgery after passing off one of his own paintings as one that had been painted by the famous artist Septimus Crag. I proved that the painting was indeed a Crag, thus no forgery had taken place. Poor Brittling had never known success as an artist, and he was willing to go to prison for forgery in exchange for the pleasure of having one of his paintings mistaken for a Crag. As I eloquently argued to the jury, "My client is not guilty of the crime. He is guilty only of the savage bitterness sometimes felt by the merely talented for men of genius."

Afterwards Guthrie brought me back into chambers to congratulate me. He told me that he had known all along that Brittling was innocent because years on the bench had given him an infallible ability to know when witnesses were telling the truth. I then alarmed Guthrie by telling him that I had committed the indiscretion of informing the Lord Chancellor's office that Guthrie thought that he deserved a promotion. Poor Guthrie panicked. "Are you really telling me the truth, Horace?" I smiled at him. "Oh can't you tell, Guthrie? I thought you had the infallible judicial eye."

PHYLLIDA ERSKINE-BROWN: You can be so exasperating, Rumpole. Take that recent terrorism case of yours in which I was the judge. Because you were staying with Claude and me, you knew how upset I was that Claude was determined to send Tristan away to school. I had argued with him to no avail that children need to be raised by their parents. Your client in the terrorism case was a single dad, a dealer in antiques who decided to earn extra money by not asking too many questions about a shipment that turned out to consist of dangerous weapons. Your argument that Special Branch had planted the weapons didn't fool a single juror, Rumpole. Nor was I deterred from sending your client to prison by your argument that I would be separating the dad from the innocent young boy who so desperately needed him.

RUMPOLE: Portia, you were the judge and you did the right thing. At least, unlike most of our judges, you accept the presumption of innocence, the golden thread that runs though British justice. Sit on the bench if you like, Portia, but I'm glad that I don't have to punish people. I can enjoy the luxury of defending.

PHYLLIDA ERSKINE-BROWN: That's a luxury you nearly lost when Judge Bullingham was going to hold you in contempt, Rumpole. We were representing two members of the Timson family who were on trial for shooting a guard while attempting to rob a bank. You represented one

Timson and I represented the other one. When I convinced my Timson to pin the shooting on your Timson, you asked Bullingham to give your Timson a separate trial. The Old Bull responded, "So that you can maximize your fees, Rumpole?" "No, Your Lordship," you replied, "so that justice can be done." Of course I objected and the Old Bull denied your request.

You were a bit impertinent there, Rumpole, but it was your opening speech to the jury that really got to the Old Bull. You planned to retire on the winnings from the bet you had placed with the Timsons' jailer on a four-horse parlay. Thinking you were safe because this was your last case, you told the jury that according to the Old Bull, everyone charged with a crime is guilty and defending barristers are only interested in collecting fees from Legal Aid. You even had to add that the fees are barely enough to enable you to live like a clerk-typist. The Old Bull was livid, but before you could say any more, the prosecutor dropped the shooting charges. Consequently, we ended the trial at once by pleading both Timsons guilty to burglary.

The Old Bull was sweet on me and as soon as the trial was over he invited me into his chambers and offered me chocolates. I told Bullingham that it was a shame your speech had been interrupted, because you were about to tell the jury what a marvelous judge he is. When Bullingham said, "Rumpole's speech didn't start out that way," I explained that your plan was to first talk about the popular prejudice against judges, and then set the jury straight by talking about his reputation for mercy and wisdom. Bullingham decided not to cite you for contempt, but I had to eat a lot of chocolates because of you. A good thing for you it was, because the Timsons' jailer ran off with your horse-race winnings and you couldn't retire after all.

CLAUDE ERSKINE-BROWN: Why can't you defend respectable people, Rumpole? In the bank robbery case that Phyllida just spoke of, your defense was that the Timsons were thieves, not bank robbers, and that charging them with robbing a bank was like the two ends of a pantomime horse getting together to play Hamlet. And your name was all over the newspapers as the lawyer defending that disgusting man who was convicted of operating a chain of massage parlors that turned out to be brothels. You bring nothing but disrepute to these chambers.

RUMPOLE: Since when is it disreputable to provide a client with a defense, Erskine-Brown? Guthrie Featherstone presided over that case as well. The newspapers sensationalized it because so many illustrious people had patronized my client's establishments and had been foolish enough to pay by credit card. I found out from Guthrie's clerk that he had recently visited a massage parlor for treatment of an elbow that he hurt while playing tennis. Guthrie had paid by credit card, and it was obvious to me that he was terrified that he would be caught up in the scandal. When Guthrie realized that I was defending, he invited me to lunch and tried to incline me into softening my defense by claiming that he was going to put my name forward for a part-time judgeship.

When the case came to court, Guthrie immediately tried to recuse himself. Why, I asked him, surely you don't know the defendant personally? Guthrie said that of course he didn't, and that he couldn't preside because he and I had discussed the case at lunch. However, both the prosecutor and I assured Guthrie that neither of us had any doubts about his absolute fairness, so poor Guthrie was stuck.

It wasn't a happy time for Guthrie. I cross-examined a police officer and congratulated him on his willingness to carry out a public duty by having sexual intercourse. Guthrie interrupted my questioning, asking the officer to agree that "quite respectable men may go to massage parlors for injuries." And when the officer said that, from the outside, the location appeared to be a perfectly respectable health center, Guthrie made sure to repeat that testimony for the benefit of the jury.

Guthrie then recessed the case and called us into chambers. "Look, how long is this case going to last?" he asked the prosecutor. "You're not going to bother with a lot of records and credit card slips, right?" My learned friend the prosecutor was puzzled by Guthrie's comment that the case was dragging on, because the trial was only in its second day. Nevertheless, Guthrie was happy when the prosecutor agreed that he did not need to offer documents into evidence. But I kept Guthrie squirming by reserving the right to offer credit card records into evidence if I thought it necessary.

Guthrie was as miserable at home as he was in court. She Who Must Be Obeyed, my lovely Hilda, told me that Guthrie's wife, Marigold, had confided in her that Guthrie kept asking Marigold if she would stick by him, through thick and thin. Marigold didn't know what he was talking about, but told Guthrie that no, she would not. Hilda agreed, and said that she would not stick by me through thick and thin either.

The courtroom atmosphere suddenly changed after Guthrie got his credit card statement and realized that the massage parlor he'd patronized was not one that was owned by my client. Guthrie now had a free hand to trample all over the defense. For instance, after my client testified that he had no idea that sex acts were taking place, Guthrie asked him, "You expect the jury to believe that you knew nothing of what was going on? Don't you know that innocent people could be trapped?"

Even the prosecutor was surprised by Guthrie's sudden change of tone. All I could do was hold my index finger high in the air. When Guthrie asked me what I was doing, I said, "The wind seems to have suddenly changed direction, My Lord." It was the end of my client's freedom and also my part-time judgeship. I had once again disappointed She Who Must Be Obeyed.

BALLARD: That's enough of your stories, Rumpole. I declare this meeting adjourned.

Concluding Reflections

Rumpole of the Bailey is charming because it makes no pretense to realism when depicting the life of a criminal defense lawyer or the trial process. Granted, virtually every *Rumpole* episode depicts Rumpole as a clever and effective (if not always successful) courtroom advocate. Yet, unlike most courtroom shows, *Rumpole* episodes rarely focus on the "moment of truth" when the jury announces its verdict. Indeed, frequently the verdict is revealed only when a character mentions it in passing some time after a trial has concluded. In this way, John Mortimer's fictional hero and his cases serve primarily as a means of poking gentle fun at English traditions and justice.

The characteristics of Rumpole's clients also contribute to the show's appeal. Most of them are good people who may have gone mildly astray by committing low-level crimes like buying stolen merchandise and running brothels. Even clients charged with more serious crimes never seem dangerous or scary.

Moreover, while Rumpole's oratory commands the courtroom and viewers' admiration, his victories often result from obvious weaknesses in a prosecutor's case. For example, medical examiners botch autopsies or comically inept police officers neglect to analyze the fingerprints they found at a crime scene. When Rumpole points out this failure on cross-examination, the police inevitably find the real culprit and Rumpole's client goes free.

Rumpole's cases frequently provide the characters with insights into their personal lives. For example, Phyllida Erskine-Brown is the prosecutor in a case in which Rumpole's client is on trial for the attempted murder of his business partner. The alleged motive is that the defendant was in love with his partner's wife, and so wanted to get rid of him. In her opening speech, Ms. Erskine-Brown tells the jurors that "if you have a stable home and a happy marriage, it may be hard to understand the lengths that unhappy people will go to inflict pain and suffering on others." This trial takes place during the period when Rumpole and Hilda are living apart. Rumpole is wistful and sad as he listens to this speech, and it leads him to try to patch things up with Hilda as soon as the trial recesses.

While Rumpole may have little use for the housekeeping rules that Ballard tries to impose on 3 Equity Court, Rumpole always observes the rules of his profession. He is devoted to his generally powerless clients and defends them zealously against the prejudices of comically inept judges who assume that all defendants are guilty. In one episode Rumpole's pupil, Liz Probert, reveals the identity of a witness who had patronized a brothel to a television reporter. In doing so, "Ms. Liz" violated the judge's order that the witness's identity not be revealed. Rumpole opposes the order, but he comes down hard on his pupil: "You cannot break the rules even if you disagree with them. Change them if you can. But if you violate them, how can you help anyone else?"

At the end of the day, the Rumpole character works so well because Rumpole is both an Insider and an Outsider. Rumpole's status as a barrister gives him entry into the colorful world of low-level criminals and the criminal courts, while enabling him to interact with judges and other powerful members of society. Yet within this group of Insiders, Rumpole remains an Outsider who can tweak his colleagues both in and out of court precisely because he has no desire to be one of them.

In John Mortimer's last Rumpole book, *Rumpole Misbehaves*, Rumpole continued to be a junior barrister, not a QC (John Mortimer passed away in 2009). Partly to satisfy Hilda and partly to satisfy his client, who is charged with murdering a prostitute, Rumpole does formally apply for silk. He is turned down, however, because he implicates a government minister in the course of his successful defense. To Hilda's eternal shame, becoming a QC was never in the cards for poor Rumpole.

CHAPTER 16

Blind Justice

YSAIAH ROSS

Blind Justice

Aired:
- October 12–November 9, 1988, BBC

Cast:
- Jane Lapotaire (Katherine Hughes)
- Jack Shepherd (Frank Cartwright)
- Julian Wadham (James Bingham)

Awards:
- RTS Television Award, Best Drama Series (1989)

Introduction

Although *Blind Justice* consists of only five long episodes, it has had an everlasting effect. The series presents an inspiring picture of a politically committed group of lawyers who are willing to go all out to represent unpopular clients. It has been shown in numerous other countries, including Australia, and the issues it raised of police brutality, racism, class structure, and the role of secretive state bodies, such as MI5, remain highly relevant. The use of the Official Secrets Act and the role of the Special Branch in two of the programs are just as pertinent today under the present terrorism legislation as they were in 1988. The series highlights numerous difficult ethical issues, and I was able to use it as a teaching tool in my own courses on legal ethics in the 1990s.

The programs are based on the true-life experiences of Helena Kennedy, who created the series along with Peter Flannery. Kennedy, who was made a baroness in 1997 and is a member of the House of Lords, has been a prominent English barrister since the 1970s. She acted in numerous well-known political cases, including the Brighton Street bombing and the Guildford Four (immortalized in the film *In the Name of the Father*). Kennedy is

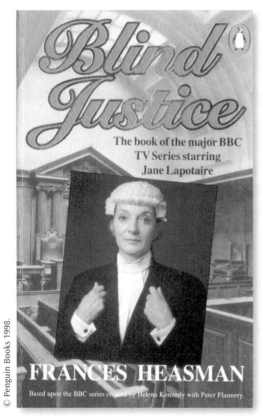

© Penguin Books 1998.

BLIND JUSTICE
Barrister Katherine Hughes (Jane Lapotaire) represents some highly unpopular clients.

one of the leading activists in England for the legal rights of women. In several books and articles, she has bemoaned the erosion of civil liberties in the wake of the September 11 terrorist attacks.

The series follows the experiences of a group of idealistic barristers who establish a leftist legal chambers, Fetter Court, in an old converted warehouse directly across from the Old Bailey (criminal courts) in London. The chambers are similar to the open-floor offices of Legal Aid and other poverty law programs that proliferated during the late 1960s and 1970s in the United States.

The main three characters are Katherine Hughes, an outspoken feminist who appears to be based on Ms. Kennedy; Frank Cartwright, a former member of the Communist Party and the most senior member of the chambers; and James Bingham, who is from the upper class. James is viewed with suspicion by the other members of Fetter Court and other leftist lawyers.

At first, Katherine refuses to join Fetter Court because she finds James to be too upper class and not a real representative of the people. She stays at a conservative chamber, where she is having a difficult time with colleagues and the senior clerk because of her views. By the second episode, Katherine has to face the fact that her chambers will not respect her views. For example, she refuses to accept rape cases in which the accused asserts the defense of consent. After turning down such a brief, she is forced into taking the case at the last moment, when a member of her chamber cannot appear and no one else is available. She does an excellent job and wins by destroying the credibility of the victim, but she is embarrassed when confronted by the woman who screams at her "How could you? Another woman!" After this episode Katherine knows she cannot stay, and decides to join Fetter Court.

The Episodes

The first few episodes focus on three cases, each of which raises important political and moral issues. The first case concerns the arrest of Cora, an older woman, who (while dressed as a nun) tries to import five kilos of heroin in her underwear. Customs receives a tip-off about the importation and is ready to arrest her when she is grabbed by two plainclothes policemen and pushed into their car. The woman is a courier for these corrupt police and for a larger criminal organization. An amusing incident ensues when the police undress the "nun" in the back of their car to obtain the heroin while a passing bus full of American tourists gaze down in horror. Katherine is briefed to defend her, but Cora refuses to give the names of the police, and pleads guilty because she fears her pregnant daughter will not receive the promised 30,000 pounds. Cora eventually is sentenced to three years in jail by a pompous and insensitive judge. At the end of the proceedings, Katherine is confronted by the customs officer, who forces her to look at explicit photos of young heroin addicts and asks her how she can represent these dealers.

The second case deals with an inquest into the death of a prominent black female activist doctor, Nola Marshall, which occurs while she is in jail. The police arrest Nola for disturbing the peace because she was drunkenly dancing and singing and attracted a large crowd. She dies during her overnight incarceration. The police allege she died from a fall before she was arrested; the black community believes the police killed her. Frank and James are briefed by the solicitor for the Black Alliance, which is paying Frank's fee. (James is representing the group pro bono.) The coroner, who supports the police, allows a large number of police who are witnesses to be present throughout the proceedings.

The third case deals with a neo-Nazi named Blinkho who knifes a young black man on a bus. The victim and several other youths had been terrorizing older people, and Blinkho acted in their defense. Katherine is briefed to defend him by a Jewish solicitor. Neither of them knows that

Blinkho is a neo-Nazi. When they find out, the solicitor continues to act, making a passionate argument that everyone is entitled to representation in order to maintain the rule of law. He says that what happened to the Jews in Nazi Germany was only possible when the rule of law disappeared. By contrast, Katherine returns the brief. As a result, Blinkho and his supporters threaten to report her to the Bar Association unless she represents him. James and other members of Fetter Court get into a heated argument with Katherine over her refusal to represent Blinkho. As a result, James is brought before the Black Alliance to defend himself. He makes an eloquent argument in favor of the "cab rank" rule, which would require him to represent someone like Blinkho. When James finishes, there is an ominous silence. The mother of Nola Marshall states that what he said is just "pretty words," and James is dismissed from representing the Alliance at the inquest.

In the third episode, Katherine represents Mr. Charnley, who is accused of killing a number of prostitutes, including his 13-year-old stepdaughter. He says he is guilty, but Katherine finds out that what he is guilty of is raping the stepdaughter since she was eight, which caused her to become a prostitute. However, he is not guilty of killing her and the others. Katherine finds Charnley repulsive and detestable. However, she agrees to represent him and convinces him to change his plea.

The final two episodes deal with the role of secrecy in the operation of government. Parliament had adopted draconian legislation to deal with IRA bombings, leaving potential IRA suspects with few rights. Frank and James discover this when defending a man charged under the legislation. They are convinced he is innocent, but they find it difficult to prove. It is not only the law they must overcome, but also the unethical and devious tactics of the Special Branch, which will do almost anything to get the accused convicted.

In the last episode of the series, a client, Bill, is an electrical subcontractor whose business mainly consists of defense contracts. He loses these contracts when he is mistaken for a leftist activist who happens to have the same name. As a result he loses everything—first his business, then his home and car. Frank and James investigate, find the radical clergyman with the identical name, and decide to sue the state for compensation.

A former government secret agent named Valentine is willing to serve as a witness for Bill. However, Valentine also wants to reveal the involvement of a secret state organization, the Safe Team, which deals with the purchase and shipment of illegal armaments. Valentine reveals his information to the press and is charged under the Official Secrets Act. Katherine and Frank are unable to obtain the evidence against him from the government, because the prosecutor claims that it is protected against disclosure under the Official Secrets legislation. Valentine holds a second press conference about the Safe Team, and the Attorney-General drops the charges against him to avoid the publicity of a trial. Valentine is then abducted by the State and disappears, so that Bill cannot prove his case against the government. A frustrated Katherine realizes the secret state has prevailed. In the final scene, she looks straight into the camera and states, "Here's what I believe—in England we've forgotten the meaning of liberty. That's why we don't care about justice." These are views that Helena Kennedy continues to assert down to the present day.

Ethical Issues

The main ethical focus of *Blind Justice* concerns the English "cab rank" rule. The rule requires barristers to accept a brief from a solicitor to appear before a court in a field in which the barrister practices. However, there are exceptions to this mandatory rule. The brief has to fall "within the barrister's capacity, skill and experience;" the barrister has to be available; the barrister has to be offered an acceptable fee; and, finally, the barrister can reject the brief if it will cause a conflict of interest or a breach of confidentiality. The New South Wales Bar had a rule that allowed a barrister to refuse to act if the barrister held a conscientious belief "which on reasonable grounds he consider[ed] would preclude him from fairly representing his client's case." England did not have such an exception, and it was removed in New South Wales in 1994. Thus, today a barrister is required to represent unpopular and repugnant clients. It is obvious from the exceptions to the rule that barristers can find some excuse if they are determined not to represent someone. The vast majority of barristers do not seek to evade their responsibilities under the "cab rank" rule, but many will not take a brief if the fee is inadequate. Katherine on numerous occasions is in breach of this rule, but she always manages to avoid discipline by the Bar. She feels the rule is hypocritical because it allows barristers to avoid taking briefs when the client is poor and cannot afford the fee. When the neo-Nazi Blinkho demands that she continue to represent him, she refuses. She avoids being reported to the Bar with the help of Frank, and is taken off the hook when the head of her former chambers agrees to take the brief.

In the United States, the "cab rank" rule has never existed. There have been calls to adopt such a rule, but in criminal cases, at least, it is not needed, because the government is required to appoint counsel for defendants. Generally, public defenders handle the representation, but those offices are often understaffed and cannot provide high-quality representation in many cases. In noncriminal cases, there is no provision for appointed counsel, and unpopular clients may find it very difficult to find lawyers to represent them.

Conclusion

Blind Justice highlights the manifest inequities that were present in the 1980s in the British legal system, and also the unethical practices of government bodies such as the police and the secret services. The acting is of a high standard, and since the stories are based on actual cases and true events, they are powerful and very credible. Sadly, the problems that existed in the 1980s are still present today.

CHAPTER 17

Kavanagh, QC

YSAIAH ROSS

Kavanagh, QC

Aired:
- January 3, 1995–April 25, 2001, Carlton Television

Cast:
- John Thaw
  (James Kavanagh, QC)
- Nicholas Jones
  (Jeremy Aldermarten, QC)
- Oliver Ford Davies
  (Peter Foxcott, QC)
- Cliff Parisi
  (Tom Buckley)
- Lisa Harrow
  (Lizzie Kavanagh)

Kavanagh, QC was among the best legal dramas shown on British television or overseas. Queen's Counsel (QC) is an honorary rank and denotes "recognition by the Sovereign of the professional eminence of the counsel upon whom it is conferred." The starring role is played by John Thaw, better known as the dour Oxford detective in *Inspector Morse*, which was shown on the British television network ITV from 1987 until 2000. Thaw portrayed Kavanagh with such ease that viewers can easily forget that he is an actor and not a real QC.

Three elements run throughout *Kavanagh, QC*. The main focus is on courtroom drama. The narratives provide a fairly accurate depiction of courtroom practice and the prison system. The other two elements are the office politics in Kavanagh's River Court Chambers and Kavanagh's home life, where due to work pressure he neglects his wife and two teenage children.

River Court Chambers

The head of River Court Chambers, Peter Foxcott, is a good organizer and leader. He is open to change, hiring women and lawyers from "red brick" universities (buildings made from red bricks in industrial cities) such as Liverpool and Manchester. Toward the end of the third season, Peter considers whether to leave his post for the bench. Kavanagh is reluctant to take over, although he does not want Jeremy Aldermarten to become the head of chambers because Jeremy is an upper-class snob. In the fifth season, Peter has a stroke and Kavanagh takes over. In the show's last episode, Kavanagh is offered an appointment to the bench (meaning he would probably be replaced by Jeremy), but the series ends with Kavanagh refusing the appointment.

Tom Buckley is the senior clerk of River Court Chambers. Senior clerks have tremendous power in the British system, because they allocate the work (the briefs). Tom inherited the clerkship from his father and is the fifth generation of his family to occupy the position. He is a likeable character, but has his prejudices. He dislikes Jeremy's upper-class snobbery and is uncomfortable with women in chambers. He also dislikes it when James takes on pro bono cases, because this reduces the Chambers' income.[1]

Kavanagh's Personal Life

Unlike many of his fellow barristers, Kavanagh comes from a lower-middle-class background, having grown up in Bolton in Northern England. He still sees his parents and other relatives, and is warm and gregarious. Kavanagh is a talented barrister, and is also funny, humanistic, and ethical. However, he does have his faults. He can be jealous and impatient, and is unable to understand his children.

Kavanagh's wife Lizzie comes from the upper class and is very wealthy. When Kavanagh was a young barrister in the Swinging Sixties, he represented Lizzie on a trespass charge resulting from her political activities. After their marriage, they became involved in demonstrations against nuclear weapons and the Vietnam War. Lizzie is a talented fundraiser and has trouble balancing her career with the demands of her family. We discover in the very first episode that she has had an affair with an upper-class barrister, but she and Kavanagh reconcile and work out their problems. Lizzie dies from cancer at the end of the third season, and James, devastated by her death, ages dramatically in the last two seasons. In the last episodes, Kavanagh finds a new love, but it is obvious that he is no longer the vigorous character of earlier days. In this way, the Kavanagh character reveals the true nature of actor John Thaw's own health problems and his forthcoming death.

The Episodes

A brief examination of some *Kavanagh, QC* episodes will help us understand the philosophical and ethical framework of the program, such as the moral ambiguity of criminal law practice, Britain's pervasive class structure, and the deep corruption of the government.

In the opening episode, "Nothing but the Truth," we find Kavanagh defending a young Cambridge University student named David who has been accused of rape by a middle-aged woman for whom he was working. He is charming, handsome, and intelligent, and comes from a wealthy family. Kavanagh believes that David is innocent. His trial strategy of using slow and deliberate questioning of the alleged victim is very effective and creates gripping drama. David is found not guilty. Later, a young student confronts Kavanagh with the fact that David had raped her. She had refused to come forward earlier out of fear that she would be destroyed because of the wealth of David's father. Kavanagh must live with the fact that his successful trial strategy allowed a serial rapist to go free.

In "The Family Affair," Kavanagh successfully prosecutes a woman accused of making obscene videos. However, he agrees with what she did and is thus upset when the conservative judge sentences her to one year in jail. In the same episode, a second case concerns the custody of a small boy and highlights the problems a barrister faces when his client is an excellent liar.

The second season begins with "True Commitment." Kavanagh defends a 17-year-old leftist named Mark, who knifes and kills a neo-Nazi during a demonstration. Although the boy has confessed to the crime, he later says he did it to protect his wealthy upper-class girlfriend, Miriam, who actually stabbed the Nazi. Mark's girlfriend testifies against him, but Kavanagh shows her to be an untruthful witness. Nevertheless, after a number of plot twists, Mark is found guilty.

In "Men of Substance," Kavanagh is prosecuting two men accused of smuggling heroin. He has a difficult time getting the full financial accounts of the main accused, a wealthy businessman. Kavanagh knows he is being blocked, but has no idea that a senior customs official is behind it. James comes up with key evidence near the end of the case—a recurring theme in the series, but not an event that commonly occurs in practice.

In "Burning Deck," Kavanagh defends a lieutenant before a military tribunal on charges of arson. The client refuses to reveal his homosexual affair with a mechanic, which would prove his innocence, and consequently is found guilty. After the trial, Kavanagh confronts the mechanic, who is the real guilty party. This episode is interesting because the viewer gets to see the workings of a military tribunal, which are quite different from those of the standard courtroom proceeding.

In the final episode of the second season, "Job Satisfaction," Kavanagh appeals the conviction of a brother and sister accused of killing their parents. Kavanagh wins, but knows in his heart that the brother did indeed kill his parents. When he is confronted by a half-brother of the defendant and accused of allowing a cold-blooded murderer back on the streets, he faces the usual questions: "How do you sleep? Doesn't the truth mean anything to you?"

The third year of the series starts to explore more worldly and philosophical issues. In "Ancient History," Kavanagh prosecutes a prominent doctor accused of performing experimental medical work on Jews in the Dachau concentration camp. The British government had passed retroactive war crimes legislation allowing such prosecutions. The vivid portrayal of what happened in the camps and the evidence of victims is persuasive evidence of the need for such legislation. "Diplomatic Baggage" concerns a murder case involving the daughter of a prominent British diplomat. The Foreign Office is more concerned with its image than with finding the truth, so it falsifies evidence to protect itself. In the last episode, "In God We Trust," Kavanagh works on a last-minute attempt to stop the execution of an innocent man in Florida. The episode confronts the political nature of the death penalty in the United States. Florida's governor is up for reelection, and refuses to stop the execution even though he is presented with strong evidence that the conviction was dubious and the trial lawyer incompetent.

In the fourth season, Kavanagh returns to work after taking time off because of Lizzie's death. In "Care of the Community," Kavanagh defends a young, poor, and uneducated couple accused of killing their two-year-old child. At first the couple maintains a united front, but eventually their evidence starts to differ. This is a sad story regarding the failure of the community to help young people coming from deprived backgrounds and desperate for some kind of love. In "Briefs Trooping Gaily," a wife is charged with murder for killing her husband, who had beaten her for 10 years. She still loves him and wants to be found guilty of killing him. Kavanagh is able to show how she was abused and is able to get her convicted of manslaughter instead of murder, resulting in a two-year suspended sentence.

In "Bearing Witness," a hospital seeks a court order allowing it to give a blood transfusion to a young boy who is a devout Jehovah's Witness. The court orders the transfusion but the boy flees the hospital. He later dies, and his father brings a private prosecution for manslaughter against his former wife, whom Kavanagh had represented against the hospital. Kavanagh is made to testify against his former client, and the court declares him a hostile witness.

"Dead Reckoning" is the most interesting episode of the fourth season. It involves charges of manslaughter against the owner of a fishing trawler that sank during a storm. Kavanagh is the prosecutor and has to prove that the owner was negligent in the maintenance of his ship. An interesting subplot emerges regarding the possibility that a foreign submarine might have collided with the trawler. It is revealed, away from the jury, that a Russian submarine was in the vicinity before the trawler went down, but the Defense Minister refuses to give the evidence in open court because of state security.

During the last season of *Kavanagh, QC,* the episodes raise fundamental issues of law and politics. In "End Games," Kavanagh represents Jimmy in a petition to overturn his murder conviction. Three robbers had been convicted, but only Kevin (who fired the fatal shots) had confessed. Kevin had falsely accused Jimmy because Jimmy had once had an affair with Kevin's wife. Kavanagh, who had been the junior counsel in the original case, knows that his then senior, Sir Ronald Tibbett, an arrogant and pompous QC, had negligently conducted the case. Sir Ronald later became a prominent judge but is now dead. Kevin commits suicide and leaves a note exonerating Jimmy. On a petition to reexamine the original decision because of fresh evidence (the suicide note), the judges of the appellate court decide to reopen the matter.

In preparing for the hearing, Kavanagh discovers that Sir Ronald had convinced the accused not to testify because he was in a hurry for the case to end so that he could go to the races. The appellate judges refuse to believe that Sir Ronald could have been negligent. They also refuse to accept the suicide note as establishing the innocence of Kavanagh's client. An injustice results, as they uphold the conviction, but since there is no capital punishment, at least the accused is still alive. At the same hearing, Jeremy represents another of the three accused robbers. Ironically, Jeremy's client, who is guilty, gets off because of the negligent handling of the case by the police.

The last episode of *Kavanagh, QC,* "The End of Law," is one of the best and most interesting of the whole series. Katia, a beautiful, intelligent blonde woman, is found dead in the hotel room of the accused, Harry Hatton. It is alleged that Katia was a prostitute and that Hatton had hired her and then killed her. Katia turns out to have been involved with the "longsiders," who are employed by the British government alongside its secret service. The longsiders are not on any government payroll and there are no records of their activities. Katia, an IT expert, had been hired to seduce Alan Rainer and obtain trade secrets. Rainer is the chief executive officer of a company that had created software that allowed users to hide their financial affairs from the British government. Rainer discovers Katia in the act of stealing the software and kills her. Rainer then moves Katia's body into Hatton's room. Hatton had pleaded not guilty at the original trial but stated that he was too drunk to remember what happened. Kavanagh is convinced of Hatton's innocence by Sarah, a junior barrister, and decides to take the appeal pro bono.

Kavanagh is offered and accepts an appointment to the bench. In order to remove Kavanagh from the appeal, the Lord Chancellor's office speeds up the appointment so that it will take place just before the appeal hearing. Kavanagh is warned that if he does not take up the appointment on that date, he will lose the position, but he refuses the appointment in order to conduct the case.

Jeremy is representing the Crown on the appeal, and it becomes apparent that Kavanagh will lose unless Rainer is called as a Crown witness. By a combination of Sarah's use of charm on Jeremy and the private investigator for the accused's use of pressure on the "longsider" who had hired Katia, the Crown calls Rainer as a witness. During the questioning of Rainer, it becomes obvious that he will reveal important government information during Kavanagh's cross-examination. The government instructs Jeremy not to oppose the appeal and the case comes to an abrupt end, which stops Kavanagh from cross-examining Rainer. Kavanagh's client goes free, but so does the murderer. The episode concludes in River Court Chambers with Jeremy congratulating Kavanagh on winning. Conflicted by the outcome, Kavanagh angrily responds with the final words of the series: "Balls, Jeremy! None of us won."

Ethical Issues

Kavanagh is an extremely ethical lawyer. He does not pressure clients into making guilty pleas when they are innocent. He never misleads the court or opposing counsel and never breaches Bar Rules. For example, in "The End of Law," the client's private investigator illegally hacks into a hotel's computer system and obtains valuable information. Kavanagh explains to the investigator, "I won't mislead the court or the Crown on how this evidence was obtained."

In the eyes of American lawyers, it might appear that the conflict of interest rules are constantly being violated in *Kavanagh, QC*. The members of River Court Chambers often oppose each other in court and are even shown discussing the matters over lunch or in chambers. They are careful never to disclose any strategy, yet the question remains: are the clients getting full and proper representation when opposing lawyers are in the same chambers? The conflicts rules are quite different in the United States, where lawyers from the same firm are never permitted to be on opposing sides of a case. Difficult issues arise when a lawyer who changes firms might have had access to information about an opposing client in his or her previous job. In some situations, this may disqualify the new firm entirely from working on the case, but at other times the problem can be dealt with by constructing an "ethical screen" that prevents any communication within the firm about the case.

The legal profession in Britain was, until recently, a rigidly divided profession. Even with the recent changes made by the Legal Services Act 2007, barristers must practice as sole practitioners. They group together in chambers to share overhead costs. Barristers are proud of their independence and their ability to represent any client in their field of expertise. As a result, the notion of the "appearance of conflict" is not strongly enforced against a barrister. The ethical rules reject the idea of "positional conflict," such as the disqualification of a lawyer who has worked for insurance companies from taking a case against one. Barristers frequently change sides and one can be either a plaintiff's or defendant's lawyer.

The "cab rank" rule prohibits barristers from rejecting any client that can pay. Therefore, they ordinarily must accept a brief in their field of expertise. Kavanagh considers himself to be a "criminal hack" and is very reluctant to take on civil work. Although the "cab rank" rule does not require him to accept civil clients, he often does so when the civil case has strong social implications.

Kavanagh, QC also features a number of other ethical problems. In one case, Jeremy becomes romantically involved with an attractive client whom he has successfully defended against a charge of theft. He argues that the case is now over, so there is nothing wrong with the affair. When she steals again, this time from Jeremy, he learns a hard lesson. The ethical rules concerning sex with clients or former clients are quite specific in a number of American jurisdictions. They include the misuse of the lawyer's authority and possible breach of the fiduciary relationship, as well as questions of competence, care, and objectivity. In other American jurisdictions, and in the United Kingdom and Australia, sexual relationships with clients fall under the broader topic of conflict of interest.

A final ethical problem raised in the *Kavanagh* series concerns confidentiality. In "Bearing Witness," the court forces Kavanagh to testify against a former client. He has important confidential information and thus refuses to cooperate, causing the court to declare him a hostile witness. This allows the plaintiff's barrister to cross-examine him vigorously. This episode presented a real-life ethics dilemma. Lawyers in similar circumstances who have refused to testify have consequently been found in contempt.

Conclusion

James Kavanagh is a noble and socially conscious lawyer. He is an excellent criminal lawyer who cares deeply for his clients and at times will work pro bono. Whether such barristers exist is debatable, but we would like to hope that they do. Of course, he is far from a perfect human being and his various faults crop up constantly.

Kavanagh believes in the English criminal justice system. In "The End of Law," Kavanagh tells the client's daughter, "I am sure we will get a fair hearing." The daughter replies, "I do not want a fair hearing. I want my father back." These comments vividly highlight the dichotomy between lawyers and clients. For lawyers like Kavanagh, if the procedural rules are followed, the system is working properly and fairly. However, the client is indifferent to procedural rules and cares only about the outcome.

I believe that *Kavanagh, QC* is one of the finest legal dramas that has ever appeared on television in any country. It resembles *Rumpole of the Bailey*, especially in its depiction of family life and political struggle in chambers, but the *Kavanagh* scripts probe more deeply into sensitive political issues. Like *Blind Justice*, *Kavanagh* exposes the injustices caused by the government and its secret services. Because of the inherent quality of its scripts and the superb acting and production values, *Kavanagh, QC* deserves a long life in reruns throughout the English-speaking world.

Endnote

1. Senior clerks receive their salary based on a percentage of the combined income of the chambers. However, senior clerks in some of the former British colonies have lost this power. The senior clerks working at the Bar in Sydney, Australia, for example, do not receive a percentage of the chambers' income.

CHAPTER 18

Judge John Deed: British TV Lawyers in the 21st Century

STEVE GREENFIELD, GUY OSBORN, AND PETER ROBSON

Judge John Deed

Aired:
- January 9, 2001–January 18, 2007, BBC One

Cast:
- Martin Shaw (Judge John Deed)
- Jenny Seagrove (Jo Mills)
- Barbara Thorn (Rita "Coop" Cooper)
- Simon Chandler (Sir Ian Rochester)

The Context

Although the bewigged lawyer is familiar beyond the shores of the United Kingdom in the form of Horace Rumpole and James Kavanagh, QC,[1] these are only two of the many televised incarnations that the British lawyer has enjoyed since 1958. As in the United States and to a lesser extent Europe, TV lawyer series have long been a staple of British television. The would-be successors to the late Leo McKern and John Thaw have not been slow in coming forward, and in the 21st century there have been no fewer than seven series featuring British law and lawyers.

As with the 30 shows and series that appeared between 1958 and 2000, these seven have included a whole range of styles. The current crop of fictional lawyer shows includes *The Brief*, featuring a fighter for justice who works alone (or with some technical assistance), as did *Perry Mason* in the 1950s and 1960s and *Matlock* in the 1980s.[2] They include the office format—*New Street Law*, *Outlaws*, *Trust*, and *Kingdom*—featuring subplots and insights into the individual lives and motivations of a range of major and minor characters in the mode popularized in the 1980s by *L.A. Law*.[3] One show—*The Courtroom*—has a pared-down, courtroom-only setting where we hear only the evidence in the case and never leave the courtroom, in the mold of shows like *You, the Jury* that pioneered in the 1950s. Finally, we have pseudo-reality shows in the style of *Judge Judy*,[4] where real disputes are aired in a brief and informal setting before a judge who has "character" and the ability to produce confrontational "car crash" television. The development of cheap technology means that unlike the deeds of most of their predecessors, who exist only in the memory of viewers, the 21st-century exploits of Jack Roper of *New Street Law* (John Hannah), Bruce Dunbar of *Outlaws* (Phil Daniels), Peter Kingdom of *Kingdom* (Steven Fry), and their like are permanently available on DVD to those who missed the original airings.

Law show producers have a marked preference for using well-established actors or even stars in the main roles so they can build on preexisting fan bases. Thus we see people with track records from previous series; for example, in *Trust* the main protagonist, Robson Green, had several successful series behind him, including *Soldier Soldier* and *Touching Evil*, as well as a career as a pop balladeer with three British number-one hits. Similarly, a stand-up comedian, Alan Davies, had experienced success with the murder mystery *Jonathan Creek* before he took on the role of a brilliant but wayward advocate in *The Brief* (whose title is taken from the slang for a lawyer). One of the stars of the cult film *Quadrophenia* (1979), Phil Daniels has gone a long way since he sent his scooter off Beachy Head. He went on to success in *Breaking Glass* (1980) and *Chicken Run* (2000) before he played cynical legal aid lawyer Bruce Dunbar in the first televised look at legal practice in the lower courts— the excellent *Outlaws*. *Kingdom* is the pet project of the ubiquitous film actor, comedian, quiz-show and award-ceremony presenter, and all-round British "national treasure," Steven Fry. *Kingdom* started filming a second series well before the end of the first run due to Fry's personal charisma rather than the show's critical success, and a third series followed in autumn 2008. Finally, screen actor John Hannah, from *Four Weddings and a Funeral* (1994) and *Sliding Doors* (1998), teamed up with comedian John Thompson to head up the radical political chambers in *New Street Law*. So we can see that while the formats varied, they all took on board the advice of the producer of the successful 1990s series *Kavanagh, QC*, Chris Kelly, who suggested that in developing the idea of a big-budget lawyer series, it was crucial to have a star name to secure backing for the project.

The British 21st-century fictional series have covered a range of issues, from the traditional serious crimes of murder and rape to corporate wrongdoing, planning, and environmental problems. However, the perspective has been constant. We are in the corner of the wronged person. Our lawyer protagonist is fighting impossible odds, prejudice, and a mountain of damning evidence to clear the name and secure the freedom of a victim.

This has been the standard default mode of TV lawyering over the years in Britain, just as it has been in the United States. What has varied has been the amount of insight we get into the lives of the characters. Some, like *Outlaws* and *New Street Law*, have been gritty in style and content, while others, like *Trust* and *Kingdom*, have been rather more escapist. Steven Fry identifies the latter as being akin to warm cocoa and relaxation on a Sunday evening: "*Kingdom* does promise viewers a glimpse of the locations I love, and an hour in front of the television that will wash them in colors, textures, landscapes, and characters that delight."

Here Comes the Judge

Into this familiar and comfortable world, with its self-righting mechanism for dealing with social problems through our dedicated lawyers, comes an altogether more unsettling prospect. *Judge John Deed* shares many of the characteristics of the other series mentioned. It has a well-established lead actor with a series pedigree in Martin Shaw, action hero Ray Doyle from the British version of *Starsky and Hutch* and *Miami Vice*, *The Professionals*. The new series has a familiar "heritage TV" setting with barristers in wigs and gowns and the main protagonist clad in an impressive red gown and wing collar.

This series comes from the pen of Gordon Newman, and is superficially the same as everything else, while at the same time radically different. It is novel in that it is told from the perspective of the trial judge rather than the defense counsel. This perspective had been tried once before on British television in a six-episode summer "filler" series, *Mr. Justice Duncannon*, in the 1960s. This was based on the light comic writings of Judge Henry Cecil, the author of *Brothers in Law*, but only the scripts remain. Modern audiences are more likely to be familiar with the judge as protagonist through *Judging Amy*[5] and the title character's travails with her mother, Maxine Gray. With *Judge John Deed*, though, we get rather more than a shift of view from below the bench to behind it. An understanding of the significance of the change of focus requires consideration in the context of the creator of the series and his earlier work.

Writer and producer Gordon Newman's reputation derives principally from his work on the British series *Law & Order*. This series of four interlinked episodes from the 1970s put the legal system under the microscope. It looked at a bank robbery and how it was processed through the system. It also looked at the crucial participants and entitled its four 90-minute episodes "A Villain's Tale," "A Policeman's Tale," "A Brief's Tale," and "A Prisoner's Tale." In each of these Chaucer-like stories, we have a take on law and life that is both downbeat and cynical. They are portrayed in a neo-documentary style. The lighting is subdued, the sound is naturalistic, and the acting style is muted.

Each version of the justice system leaves us in no doubt that the whole world is trying to work a scam. Nobody does their job honestly. People betray their colleagues and the ethos of their profession, whether they be police, lawyers, or thieves. The police fabricate evidence and invent confessions to secure convictions. This process was recently shown in the retro drama *Life on Mars* (which involved a modern-day police officer transported back to 1973, with its much more robust police tactics). Newman's *Law & Order* was credited with helping bring about major changes in the way in which the police conduct interviews, including the requirement that they be taped. All this found expression in the Police and Criminal Evidence Act 1984, which introduced an up-to-date equivalent of *Miranda* rights in Britain. It was, however, over 20 years before Gordon Newman returned to the theme of systemic corruption in the institutions of the legal system. In this instance, the series is "created, written, and produced" by Newman. The vehicle is improbable but at the same time astutely realized. Newman's political critique is enfolded in the life of a sympathetic, charismatic lawyer with an interesting private life and a commitment to his version of justice.

Judge John Deed

When we first encounter Deed he conforms to our standard expectations of the television lawyer. He resembles at first blush that other successful

Copyright ©BBC.

JUDGE JOHN DEED
The judge checks a precedent—or more likely the number of a cutie in his electronic "little black book."

TV lawyer of the 1990s, *Kavanagh, QC*. Prior to the untimely death of John Thaw, the actor who played James Kavanagh for five seasons, there was discussion of elevating his character to the Bench. In fact, the makers of *Judge John Deed* seem to have taken this possible life plan of Kavanagh and passed it on. Kavanagh, as we got to know him, was a brilliant lawyer. He was suspicious, and slightly disrespectful, of authority. He was a bit of a maverick. This upward judicial move made sense in standard career terms in a way that would have been inconceivable for Horace Rumpole. Alas, it never took place, and instead a brand-new character was unveiled to the public in January 2001.

John Deed is, of course, a brilliant lawyer, too. Like Kavanagh, he is suspicious, disrespectful of authority, and a bit of a maverick. So far, nothing unexpected. The question that emerges for anyone who has followed Gordon Newman's career was "What on earth was Newman doing getting involved in this most formulaic of dramatic vehicles, the television lawyer hero?" This is a milieu in which the system works and allows us to believe that modern-day capitalism can resolve the social problems it throws up—a view not really in tune with Newman's earlier bleak outlook. The answer lies in his perspective on the levers of power in *Judge John Deed*. Our eponymous hero is a fighter for justice. Unlike the others we mentioned, though, he is not an outsider. He is fighting from a relatively unpromising position within the system.

Unlike standard fighters for justice, he cannot choose his battles. Judges tend to sit in single areas covering a limited range of cases. This problem has been solved on the show by a careful selection of the kinds of issues that appear before the judge. It is one thing, however, to bring a series of distinctive and worthwhile issues of justice before a judge. The question is, how does one insert any drama around the judge's role in the judicial process? As we know from film, the role of the judge is limited. From *12 Angry Men* (1957) through *Kramer v Kramer* (1979) to *Philadelphia* (1993), the role of the judge is to allow others to speak. Occasionally questions may not be asked and lines of inquiry not pursued. The strategies to be adopted in court, however, are determined by prosecution and defense lawyers. The actual decisions as to guilt or innocence in the kinds of cases featured on our screens are made principally by juries. The role of the judge appears to consist of little more than directing the traffic. Deed is different.

The Judge Acts as Solomon

Like those of its British predecessors *Rumpole of the Bailey* and *Kavanagh, QC*, each episode of *Judge John Deed* is effectively freestanding but has some narrative continuity. Each contains three elements: case, office, and family life. There is a basic, central case in which Deed is involved, often combined with a minor case. There is also the ongoing equivalent of the office, with Deed under fire from the Lord Chancellor's Office and his fellow judges. He is supported by his personal assistant Coop as well as a police friend, but is routinely betrayed by other court functionaries. Finally, there are his relationships with his lawyer ex-wife, lawyer daughter, Appeal Court judge ex–father-in-law, Sir Joseph Channing, and a string of on-and-off lovers.

The legal issues that John Deed confronts are like a list of current social controversies. The cases encompass racism ("Exacting Justice," "Hard-Gating"); domestic violence ("Rough Justice"); corporate responsibility to workers ("Duty of Care," "Separation of Power"); the care of the elderly ("Hidden Agenda"); diplomatic immunity ("Political Expediency"); police powers ("Abuse of Power"); a Menendez-style murder charge ("Nobody's Fool"); patient consent to a medical procedure ("Everyone's Child," "Lost Youth"); personal injuries ("Health Hazard," "Separation of Power," "Silent Killer"); judicial corruption ("Judicial Review"); police corruption ("Lost and Found"); pedophilia ("In Defence of Others"); control of the media ("Popular Appeal"); direct political action ("Exacting Justice," "My Daughter Right or Wrong"); vaccine damage ("One Angry Man," "Heart of Darkness," "Evidence of Harm"); and war crimes ("War Crimes").

Newman has expressed surprise that his work is considered controversial. Given that *Judge John Deed* involves a shadowy world of hidden levers of power and words whispered in the "right ear" to secure the "right result" in the operation of justice, this sentiment seems disingenuous. Newman's approach allows Deed to dictate how the cases are presented. His most obvious trait is to be an additional counsel in the courtroom. He asks the questions he thinks the barristers should have asked. In "Exacting Justice," he even engineers a statement from a killer who is traumatized by the death of his daughter and beyond caring about whether he lives or dies. The statement causes the jury to rescind their original guilty verdict and find the accused not guilty of murder or even manslaughter. In "Duty of Care," he inquires about the level of training received by a worker killed on a demolition job. In the same episode, he suggests that the manslaughter charges that had been dropped by the Crown Prosecution Service should be reinstated, thus changing the case's whole complexion. He twists arms to discourage certain actions and has a much more active role than any trial judge of modern times in the British justice system.

The Judge Resists the State

The key to the *Judge John Deed* dynamic is the "real" forces that exist in British society. Beneath the obvious surface of a courtroom there are deeper forces at work—none of them mentioned in the syllabi of law schools. Some are broadly encapsulated in the British Establishment, which appears in the form of the Lord Chancellor's Office as well as the Foreign Office and the Prime Minister's office. The other forces at work below the surface include the Media, Fundamentalism, Big Money, and Foreign Influence. (Almost all the forces that Judge Deed has to resist come in capital letters.) It may be over a quarter of a century since Gordon Newman first pointed out the corruption in the institutions of the British state, but he has not mellowed in his stance.

The world of Newman and Deed consists of interconnecting levers and strings being pulled. Behind the formal relationships among the judiciary, the civil service, and the government, there is a set of interests whose exercise is subtle yet effective. At its simplest, the court clerks decide which judge gets particular cases—not on a random basis but on the discreet orders of their superiors. They are denizens of the Ministry of Justice (until recently called the Lord Chancellor's Department or LCD). Part of this stems from the strange and anomalous position of the head of the judiciary, the Lord Chancellor, who is first and foremost a politician and incidentally a judge. He is a political appointee, and in Deed's world is responsible for ensuring that the "national interest" is served in the courts.

In this loaded struggle for the "national interest," tricky cases must be dealt with by a "sound" judge who can be counted on to make the right decision. The List Manager at the court is under instruction to call the LCD when Deed does something out of the ordinary, such as snatching a case another judge was set to hear. A man at the LCD talks of having a word "up the road," meaning with his superiors, about developments. The judge's official chauffeur keeps an eye on the judge's movements and reports back to the LCD. Deed, though, is prepared to fight back and make sure such cases come to him. Accordingly, we find him in constant conflict with those who assign cases. Since the "national interest" does not have a formal existence, he is able to fight for the alternative principle of "Deed's justice" by seeking to retain cases or get them assigned to him.

This critique of the State might be hard to swallow were it not mixed in with the decisions of the Establishment to promote moral and personal feelings along with the broader "public good." The process is personalized. Hence, we have the Lord Chancellor's chief administrator, Sir Ian Rochester, suffering the embarrassment of Deed having an affair with his wife without making much effort to cover it up. The Establishment's motives to reduce Deed's role are not just political but also personal.

Deed, though, is no wide-eyed innocent. Just like those who would bring him down, he is prepared to use his own version of the "old-boy network." This involves reliance on his old university friend Row Colemore, who fortunately is now Assistant Police Commissioner in London. Colemore is close to power, too, and a source of vital information as to the real motives behind those seeking to prevent Deed from sitting on certain cases. His personal assistant (PA), Rita "Coop" Cooper, provides a counterintelligence service through her fellow justice-system clerical workers, as well as occasional subversion of the administration in the interests of "Deed justice." She ironically adopts the acronym she claims some of the Circuit judges use for them: POLEs, which stands for "people of low esteem." Deed is also happy to persuade his on-and-off lover Jo Mills to use her networks in the Crown Prosecution Service to get criminal charges resurrected that Deeds feels are more in tune with justice. With the Establishment unable to operate out in the open, the scene is set for the conflict between these two versions of justice to unfold.

The Judge Is Human

One thing that unites our judge with other modern fictional lawyers is that he is not a remote figure on a pedestal who arrives at his judgments through some kind of lofty intellectual process. We see him in conversation with his lovers, daughter, and PA discussing the issues involved in cases and how he should decide them. Coop provides Deed with an almost Greek chorus–like route into the minds and thoughts of ordinary people. Deed is also identifiably human and most definitely not an ascetic. He is divorced and has a lawyer daughter. In addition, when we first encounter him he is in a potentially sexual relationship with a senior barrister who appears in his court from time to time. This provides a constant source of tension. Deed sees himself as irresistible to women. The series finds him, indeed, enjoying great success at persuading women to sleep with him. This notion of judges having sex lives is a novel one in TV lawyer drama. It allows a new set of motivations and dramatic tensions to be played out when Deed's perceptions of various women are affected by his sexual relationships with them.

Charlie Deed, his daughter, lives in the shadow of her father. When we first encounter her, she is an environmental and animal-rights activist. She goes from law student to young assistant in the chambers of Deeds's occasional lover, widow Jo Mills. Her father is, if anything, an embarrassment to her with his colorful private life and tendency to rock the boat. His corporate lawyer ex-wife, Georgina, also finds his charm difficult to resist, but finds his serial infidelity intolerable. The daughter of an Appeal Court judge, she has provided Deed an entrée to the charmed circle of the bourgeoisie and been betrayed by him.

Deed is a product of his background and time. Coming from a working-class family and educated in the 1960s, his radical politics seem to have been bypassed by the second wave of feminism. His attitude toward women and his cavalier treatment of them may derive from his egocentricity. He is not a perfect human being. He is flawed in his own relationships—witness his failed marriage and problematic relationships with his daughter and occasional lovers. Deed seems to resemble Jed Ward in *Class Action* (1991). Jed also cared about "the people" as a class but not about individuals as such, including his daughter. That, to an extent, could sum up the approach of John Deed. It may be that the underlying thrust of his need to conquer all the women we see him involved with is a product of class envy. As a working-class lad made good, he is confronted by a wave of rich, available women on whom he can release his frustration at the unchanging nature of the system of power. Tellingly, Coop, the only attractive woman with whom he does not seek to have a sexual relationship, comes, like him, from modest beginnings.

Assessing the Judge

The audience for this mélange of intrigue, sex, and good old-fashioned legal conflict has been impressive. *Judge John Deed* was shown between January 2001 and January 2007 in five seasons running to 29 episodes of 90 minutes each. They were shown midweek on the advertisement-free BBC and attracted an impressive average audience of 6.4 million—in excess of 30 percent of viewing households. With the diversity of channels available in 21st-century Britain, audiences above 5 million are counted as excellent. Recent blockbuster series like *Big Brother* have in their heyday achieved audiences of between 4.6 and 5.8 million.

The series does not patronize its audience. It glosses over the public's lack of knowledge of the specifics of the law. People plead to a section 20 ("Rough Justice") or a section 33 ("Duty of Care") with no detailed indication of what these sections actually involve. Similarly, the show assumes that the audience understands how the LCD works. The screenwriters let the context explain these statutes and practices, rather than resorting to the clumsy device of the ingénue or relative to whom the law must be explained.

In terms of the portrayal of women, ethnic minorities, and sexuality, the series is a contrast to most 21st-century dramas with their "representative" mix of characters. The other judicial figures whom we see in the series are men. Women occupy crucial roles in the narrative but principally are minor satellites of the powerful men. The ethnic minority characters also are few and far between. When they do appear, they are shown as duplicitous and keen to serve their bosses.

Evidently, Newman is not content to just tick "political correctness" boxes. Given his history, his representation of a male-dominated, white, stridently heterosexual world is both ironic and a challenge to those dramas that would lead us to believe that major changes have occurred in the distribution of power. We are in a world linked to the dominant theme of a class-centered Establishment with its hands firmly on the levers of influence regarding the important matters of the day—a world that Herbert Marcuse would recognize. In *One Dimensional Man*, Marcuse critiqued the false notion of freedom supposedly enjoyed in the late–20th-century liberal capitalist society. Thus the ability of one individual, Deed, to exercise a modicum of autonomy sums up the process of repressive tolerance that is modern Western democracy. So head down to your local emporium (or visit the appropriate website) and get the DVDs as soon as they become available. They are a refreshing change and might even paint an accurate picture of how justice really operates in the British courts.

Endnotes

1. See the chapters in this book by Paul Bergman on *Rumpole of the Bailey* and Ysaiah Ross on *Kavanagh, QC*.

2. See the chapters by Francis M. Nevins, "*Perry Mason*," and by Steve Greenfield, Guy Osborn, and Peter Robson, "*Matlock*—America's Greatest Lawyer? A Transatlantic Perspective."

3. See Philip Meyer's chapter "Revisiting *L.A. Law*."

4. See the chapters by Nancy Marder, "Judging *Judge Judy*," and Taunya Banks, "Judging the Judges—Daytime Television's Integrated Reality Court Bench."

5. See David Papke's chapter "*Judging Amy*."

PART V

The Civil Justice System

This Part concerns television shows that focus on civil justice, meaning that the lawyers work on resolving disputes between private parties. These disputes range from family struggles over divorce and child custody, to employment discrimination, to major corporate misconduct. In real life, far more lawyers work on problems of civil law than on criminal cases. Of course, most private disputes are settled, rather than tried in court, and most of what lawyers do in working on them is stunningly undramatic. Nevertheless, the five U.S. and two foreign shows discussed in this Part all focus on the characterization of the lawyers who try these cases. Each show manages to find plenty of riveting dramatic material in civil disputes. The U.S. shows are presented in the order in which they premiered.

In the United States, the path-breaking *L.A. Law*, discussed in Part II, proved that shows built around civil disputes could be dramatic and pull a large audience as long as the scripts dwelt heavily on the personal life of interesting and empathetic lawyer characters.

Ally McBeal debuted in 1997 and achieved a large cult following. The show involved a small law firm consisting of some lovable but highly dysfunctional lawyers. It was mostly about the relationships and fantasies of its lawyer characters, particularly Ally herself. Since the show was set in a law office (though it probably could have been set in any kind of office), there had to be some semblance of legal business and trial practice. The lawyers on *Ally McBeal* worked mostly on civil disputes, often concerning different forms of employment discrimination or arising from issues of love and relationships. Strangely, these were the very concerns of the lawyers as well.

Judging Amy premiered in 1999 and enjoyed a successful six-year run. It revolved around the work of Judge Amy Gray, a family court judge who always tried to discover constructive ways to resolve the tragic cases that found their way into her courtroom. Judge Gray had plenty of family issues of her own to deal with, including her relationship with her social-worker mother, who had little use for the judicial system. In fact, one of the most interesting things about *Judging Amy* was the conflict of the legal and social work approaches to solving family problems.

girls club was an unsuccessful attempt to find marketable dramatic material in the cutthroat world of big-firm law practice. Three young female associates who are close friends and roommates must try to navigate this highly competitive milieu. Needless to say, the women confront serious issues of sexual harassment, lack of mentoring, and office politics. Unfortunately, the show was killed after only two episodes.

Vastly more successful was *Boston Legal*, which premiered in 2004 and has drawn consistently high ratings. It revolves around the close but rather implausible friendship between lawyers Alan Shore and Denny Crane, who are partners in a large firm that handles both criminal and civil cases. Shore is politically liberal and highly aggressive in his law practice. He gets away with vast numbers of ethical violations. Although he is edgy and often obnoxious, he is devoted to his clients and brings home the bacon for them. His closest friend is the much older Crane, who is extremely conservative. Once a great lawyer, Crane appears to be suffering from dementia (which he thinks is mad cow disease). The scripts often center on controversial social issues, about which Shore and Crane always disagree.

In 2007, *Damages* entered the fray. The show is a highly cynical (and rather melodramatic) look at the world of high-stakes civil litigation. Starring the great Glenn Close as bitchy litigator Patty Hewes, the first season of *Damages* serialized a class-action securities fraud case against a charming but unscrupulous businessman. The lawyers on all sides are vicious and unethical. The serialization technique (used 10 years earlier in *Murder One*) enabled the scripts to delve far more deeply into the intricacies of class-action litigation (and the impact of the case on the personal lives of the lawyers and witnesses) than was possible in the other civil litigation-based television shows, or even in a two-hour movie such as *Michael Clayton* (2007). The title *Damages* refers to more than the damages at stake in the lawsuit—a lot of people are damaged along the way. You won't like the lawyers in *Damages* much, but the show (presented on cable rather than network television) deserves a careful look from fans of legal television.

Finally, this Part turns to two extremely interesting foreign shows involving civil justice. The Spanish show *Anillos de oro* screened in 1983. It is well remembered in Spain as a critical event in the post-Franco transition to constitutional democracy. In 1981, Spain legalized divorce, a highly disturbing event for many conservative Spaniards. *Anillos de oro* involved a family law firm founded by two charismatic lawyers. It legitimized the divorce law by showing both the very human lawyers at work and the terrible family circumstances of the couples who were seeking divorces. The show illustrates the power of television drama to transform public attitudes about a vital issue of social policy.

In France, *Avocats et Associés* had a highly successful 11-year run. It involved a small firm of lawyers that handled both criminal and civil cases (including child custody and labor arbitration). This show, too, humanized the lawyers, delving deeply into their private lives, and dramatized what it means to practice law in France. It also showed the socialization of young lawyers into the ways of the French legal profession. One of the purposes of the show was to contrast French and American legal practice, given that French viewers have been heavily exposed to American shows. For example, lawyers in France do not conduct their own factual investigations, and they do not address judges as "your honor." Like *Anillos de oro*, therefore, *Avocats et Associés* played an important role in instructing the public about current realities of law and legal practice.

CHAPTER 19

Ally McBeal—Life and Love in the Law

CASSANDRA SHARP

Love did not come easy to Ally McBeal. As a 30-something, single Boston lawyer, she just couldn't seem to forget her childhood sweetheart Billy. Ally was self-absorbed, angst-ridden, and constantly in search of Mr. Right. This quirky and self-confessed romantic became extremely popular during the late 1990s as the title character in the award-winning legal series created by lawyer David E. Kelley. Once the flagship of the Fox network, *Ally McBeal* presented a familiar world of glam lawyering, yet there was something different about it.

Unlike many legal dramas before it, *Ally McBeal* used different production techniques to bring a "human" element to the law. The firm of Cage & Fish was constituted of a handful of young, successful, glamorous lawyers with well-appointed offices and high-fashion wardrobes. The show centered on the manic trials and tribulations of a young female lawyer, Ally McBeal. Although the lawyers on *Ally McBeal* maintained a successful law practice, this fantastical show revealed much more about the lawyers than their legal prowess. Using special effects, fantasy sequences, and music, the series uncovered the private lives of its lawyers and compelled the audience to recognize that these

Ally McBeal

Aired:
- September 8, 1997– May 20, 2002, Fox

Cast:
- Calista Flockhart (Ally McBeal)
- Greg Germann (Richard Fish)
- Jane Krakowski (Elaine Vassal)
- Peter MacNicol (John Cage)
- Lucy Liu (Ling Woo)
- Portia de Rossi (Nelle Porter)

Awards:
- Emmy for Outstanding Comedy Series (1999)
- Peter MacNicol, Emmy for Outstanding Supporting Actor in a Comedy (2001)
- Emmy for Outstanding Sound Mixing for a Comedy Series (1998, 1999, 2000)
- Emmy for Outstanding Casting for a Comedy Series (2001)
- Tracey Ullman, Emmy for Outstanding Guest Actress in a Comedy Series (1999)

Courtesy of Photofest.

ALLY McBEAL
Ally (Calista Flockhart) and her associates at Cage & Fish often blur the boundaries between professional and personal.

private lives have an impact on a lawyer's public performance. The series expertly exposed the lawyers as characters of complexity and multiple dimensions. The emphasis was on the personal or "human" response, which invited the audience to explore with the characters their motivations and desires. In *Ally McBeal*, there was no mistaking that the lawyers had flawed characters. They struggled between states of self-servitude and a zeal for justice; their personal lives always interfered with their employment; and they constantly revealed the state of their hearts to one another and to the audience.

Although controversial (and strongly criticized) at times, Ally's representation as a smart yet emotional "modern" woman was no doubt one of the main reasons for the success of the series. Ally was imperfection, both personified and glorified, and that was why so many loved her. The viewer was given intimate access to her imperfection via personal narration and fantasy sequences that showed Ally's inner thoughts as she related to the other characters. It was the presentation of the blurred boundaries between inner and outer realities that contributed to the show's unique appeal and audience identification. This technique of production had a winning effect on audiences, because it drew them into the complex and asymmetrical universe of lawyering within Cage & Fish and made them confront traditional ideas of normality.

The Characters

Part of the wide appeal of *Ally McBeal* was its daring spectacle of characterization. Ally was accompanied in her work by a host of inimitable characters, each of whom were at one time or another given cause (through the legal cases they were working on) to be introspective about their life and work. In particular, Ally and senior partners John Cage and Richard Fish were constantly reaching personal impasses that required self-reflection and rationalization in order to be resolved. Joined by other characters, including the supposedly conventional married couple Billy and Georgia, "ice queen" Nelle, and sexually promiscuous office manager Elaine, the cast portrayed a group of individuals who were nuanced and ambiguous. Together they challenged the notion that legal professionalism cannot tolerate emotion.

"I like being a mess. It's who I am."—Ally

Of course, the entangling of the personal and professional was most prominent in Ally herself, a neurotic who was strong, honest, and a capable lawyer, yet at the same time vulnerable to the ways in which law—as well as life—can diminish the pursuit of happiness and love. She threw tantrums, and while her arguments were sometimes intelligent and persuasive, at other times they were an incoherent babble. She often appeared as if she had no hold on reality; she hallucinated and imagined. Yet this was what endeared Ally to us as the audience. We lived inside her head—and as we saw and heard her every thought, we realized she was not so different from us. We knew exactly what she was thinking and feeling at every moment and with every encounter. As she negotiated her workplace and love life, we saw her as she saw herself: as an insecure little girl in a boardroom, or a strong, determined woman who could dance across the street and inspire others to follow suit. Knowing her every thought enabled the viewer to judge her actions based on some sort of intimate "inside knowledge," and in this way one could say that she represented the tension between desire and reality that is a part of our everyday life.

Ally was a character of ambiguity and complexity. Lasting happiness or contentment always seemed to elude her. She was prudish, conservative, sentimental, and extremely picky about the men she dated: "Men are like gum, anyway—after you chew, they lose their flavor." Too rotund, too Jewish, too much salad dressing on the face . . . these were just some of the excuses she used to rationalize her decisions to deny someone a second or third date. But the audience knew that most of the men were denied a relationship with her because they just weren't Billy. She even said to him once, "There's just so many ways he wasn't you . . . right! Wasn't right."

The Love Triangle: Ally—Billy—Georgia

Billy and Georgia were happily married, but Billy and Ally had an undeniably special connection. They had been childhood sweethearts, and then college lovers, who would keep an open phone connection at night to listen to each other's breathing. When Ally began at Cage & Fish, she quickly realized she would be working alongside Billy and his wife Georgia. Knowing that Billy and Ally still had a strong emotional attachment, the audience quickly became aware that Billy's legally binding and committed marriage relationship would be competing with the historic, unofficial relationship between Ally and Billy. As time passed, and certainly for the better part of the first two seasons, the audience was teased by the thought of an impossible reunion between Ally and Billy. Despite this, the audience still developed sympathy for Georgia, the wife who was so often on the outside. Although the connection between Ally and Billy was clear, as the series progressed we saw that Ally's desire for Mr. Perfect was less about reuniting with Billy and more about finding a true love that was based on her memories of the man Billy used to be. Despite her fastidiousness, Ally wound up working on the theory that "you have to kiss a lot of frogs before finding Prince Charming," and so she began to take more chances with men.

"That troubles me."—John "The Biscuit" Cage

Famous for his courtroom theatrics and tricks, "the Biscuit" pushed the boundaries of eccentricity. He was a partner in a successful law firm—and had a secret hideout behind one of the stalls in the unisex bathroom. He had a remote control to operate the toilet, because "I like a fresh bowl and remnants upset me." Often uncomfortable and awkward in normal social interactions, Cage was confident and in control in the courtroom. He was the lawyer most sought after to win the impossible cases, and he generally would succeed, using an impressive array of stunts and distraction tactics. Some of these included taking an eternity to pour a glass of water; using a clicker to make objections; squeaky shoes; a nasal whistle; stomach rumbles; whooshing blowtorches; humming the theme from *Mr. Ed*; and getting the jury to repeat key phrases and words (like "unacceptable") back to him. John was the "funny little man" who would regularly "take a moment" to quietly consider a new legal strategy, even if it interrupted a trial. He was an excellent advocate and quick on his feet, yet he would often be seen bolstering his self-confidence through a pretrial ritual of dancing to an inner Barry White tune.

Importantly, Ally and John became kindred spirits—they understood each other in a way that nobody else could, and they shared a vivid imagination and a constant quest to find true love. John saw profundity and significance in the apparently meaningless, and although he was often "deeply troubled" and engaged in "smile therapy" to handle difficult situations, for the most part he was optimistic and happy when times seemed hopeless. This is what endeared him to Ally, and the connection between them seemed to provide some measure of normalcy and humanity to both their eccentricities.

"Bygones."—Richard Fish

In contrast with the starkly emotional characters of Ally and John, Fish was the fast-talking, money-hungry, and chronically superficial senior partner that we loved to hate. We get this hint of his character in the very first episode:

> Let me tell you something. I didn't become a lawyer because I like the law; the law sucks. It's boring, but it can also be used as a weapon. You want to bankrupt somebody? Cost him everything he's worked for? Make his wife leave him, even make his kids cry? Yeah, we can do that.

Clients, colleagues, and audiences alike were treated to the cynical words of wisdom he liked to call "fishisms"; for example, "Helping others is never more rewarding than when it's in your own self-interest." He would say whatever was on his mind, no matter how outrageous, and excuse it with a word: "bygones." He was smarmy, self-seeking, and ethically dubious, with strange fetishes including finger licking and "wattles" (the flesh on a woman's neck). In essence, he was the lawyer joke personified, the conglomeration of all the world's negative expectations of lawyers.

The Blondes—Nelle and Elaine

Nicknamed "Subzero," Nelle was the ice queen of the office and oozed sex appeal. She faced mixed reactions on joining the law firm, because she was hated by the women and adored (or lusted after) by the men. She was thoroughly intimidating, a beauty with brains who was an excellent lawyer. Nelle came across as cold, but we soon discovered her to be a warm, sweet, and caring character who employed her cool demeanor as a defense to protect herself from the outside world.

Elaine was also disliked by many in the office, and she knew it. Self-described as the "office bitch," Elaine was the secretary who knew everybody's business. She was the chronic eavesdropper, who was often seen shamelessly listening to other people's telephone and private conversations and constantly haunting the unisex bathroom to seek out juicy office gossip. A desperate attention-seeker, Elaine used her sex appeal to be noticed, and prided herself on the number of people with whom she had had meaningless sex. She was efficient and organized, moody, funny, and witty. Like Ally, Elaine would say or do what most people would never do for fear of social rejection, and like Ally, Elaine was very lonely.

The Themes: The Reality of Life and Love in the Law

Hard to classify, *Ally McBeal* was often described as a legal "dramedy" because it spanned multiple genres and blended elements of soap opera, romantic comedy, and drama. Each episode explored the characters' relationships within a framework of fluctuating moral values and social issues, and they frequently seemed to be conducting cases that reflected the very issues that they were grappling with socially or personally. Ally herself was in a constant state of flux and constantly exposed to the audience her journey of self-exploration, defining herself through the cases she argued. One typical example of this was an episode where Ally represented a person who was suing his former employer for unfair dismissal because he claimed to see unicorns while he worked. As a child, Ally had experienced similar visions, and so her arguments on behalf of her client became a transformation of her own views on the matter. On occasions like this, when we were able to *hear* her thoughts and *see* her feelings, we were given a privileged and intimate view into how Ally viewed and constructed the intersection of her personal and private lives.

Love and Life in the Courtroom

That love and life were reflected in the law was never more prominent than in *Ally McBeal*'s courtroom scenes. The trial clearly was the anchor point for the thematic presentation that, in the law, there is a blurring of boundaries between the personal, professional, and legal. The cases that Cage & Fish took on were in one way or another concerned with love lost, the breakdown of relationships, or the loss of expectations. Funnily enough, these also happened to be the concerns of Ally's inner reality, and it often seemed that the law became personalized through Ally herself—that is, the legal dispute at hand was usually told through projections of her inner drama. For example, early in season one, Ally and Georgia represented an older woman who had been fired from her position as a TV news anchor on the basis that she looked too old. As two beautiful women who admit that they "trade on their looks," both Ally and Georgia get so wrapped up in their argument on the basis of ageism that it takes a comment from Elaine to make them realize that they are personalizing the case: "It can be disconcerting to realize that suddenly everything you think you are can disappear with a wrinkle."

Reality Seen through Fantasy

The "reality" of Ally's universe was made manifest to the audience through fantasy-based special effects. This sliding in and out of fantasy kept the audience apprised of her constantly changing feelings and secret desires. As a result, some criticism was leveled at the fantastical portrayal of these issues, and it was often said that the law and the characters were masked in absurdity. Still, this technique was one of the key aspects that helped to expertly and uniquely present the concerns and interests of the show. Although it might have appeared that the law was merely a backdrop in a show about relationships, there was much more to the series than that. The legal issues presented in the show actually gave the lawyers much fertile ground for discussing and reflecting on life's issues and the nature of love. It was through the law that life and love were explored and negotiated.

In this sense, the law was humanized. The audience was reminded that lawyers are capable of wishing and dreaming, of being vulnerable, of making mistakes, and of being afraid. Yes, the line between reality and fantasy was taken well beyond blurry in this show, but that was its appeal. That was what enabled the viewer to understand and empathize with the characters.

Take, for example, the occasions when we were transported from reality to see Ally swimming through a flooded office when she was overwhelmed, or to see her visualizing breathing fire at her colleagues when they angered her, or to watch her being haunted by visions of Barry Manilow singing sad love songs to her at work, in the street, and in the bedroom. It is these sequences of exaggerated circumstances and emotions that (as well as being entertaining) may have projected to the viewer the subtext that lawyers are human, too. These sequences revealed to the audience a woman who was struggling to navigate a professional life and a private social existence that were inextricably intertwined.

Writing as a woman who, when the show aired, was just entering the legal profession, I found this to be perhaps the most appealing aspect of the program. For me, and for many women, Ally's experiences, however dramatized and fantastical, somehow struck a chord with our more primal, secret desires and dreams. We either identified with her fears and hopes, or we completely rejected her attitude as unhelpful to the female cause. Either way, the fantasy sequences created, in female viewers at least, an immediate response as we either accepted or challenged her perspectives on life and love. Such a response was especially evident in the appearance of the "dancing baby."

The Dancing Baby

Arguably one of the more prominent Internet phenomena of the early 1990s, the computer-generated "dancing baby" video and its variations appeared in a broad array of mainstream media—including television—before making its way to *Ally McBeal*. We saw the dancing baby haunt Ally in recurring dreams, dancing around to the song *Hooked on a Feeling (Ooga Chaka)*, as recorded by Vonda Shephard. The baby then plagued her at the office, following her into elevators, appearing around corners, and even turning up in the unisex bathroom, when she least expected it. The baby served as a humorous reminder of a serious issue for Ally, her fear of childlessness and the remorseless ticking of her biological clock. With the baby personifying Ally's fears, we witnessed her literally wrestling with these issues as she either "kicked" the baby in anger or danced alongside the baby in the contented hope that motherhood was still a possibility.

The Music

Music was an integral part of *Ally McBeal*, with the theme song and background music providing another mechanism to expose the characters' desires. Far from the innocuous bouncy tunes that were the standard fare of previous television shows, the music in *Ally* was a clear reflection of exactly what was going in on the characters' lives. Consider the lyrics of the theme song *Searching My Soul*, written and performed by Vonda Shephard: "I've been down this road, Walking the line, Displaying my pride, And I have made mistakes in my life, That I just can't hide . . . I believe I am ready for what love has to bring." These words clearly reminded us from week to week that Ally was on a quest for love, and was, like everyone in the world, flawed and capable of making mistakes.

Like the theme song, the music used throughout each episode was not merely background music, but rather contributed to the show's plot and character development. The songs, performed by Vonda Shephard, were usually popular classics and were chosen because the lyrics reflected the theme in play at the time. This is made overt in several episodes from season two, in which Ally turns to therapist Tracy to help her with self-esteem issues. Tracy's major recommendation is to choose a personal "theme song" that will best boost her confidence. Of course, Tracy's audacious dancing to her own song, *Tracy*, is contrasted with Ally's struggle to settle on the right choice. When she does choose *I Know Something about Love*, we hear it playing at half-speed, and we know that for Ally the technique is not working. But slowly, over time, the song and Ally begin to find their feet together, and when she finally is able to dance across the street to the beat of the song, we find that it is infectious and that those crossing with her are enjoying the beat of their own inner tunes. It is one of the most memorable moments from the series—mostly because we, too, know the difference between feeling low and experiencing the rousing surge of confidence.

Music also played a major part in the other characters' depictions. For example, whenever Ling would appear, we would hear the "Wicked Witch of the West" refrain from *The Wizard of Oz*. Also, in one episode John explains to Fish his hearing of the bells as a way of preparing for the battle of the courtroom, but Fish cannot seem to make it work—all he hears is the clunking of bells.

Dancing to music was another major aspect of characterization, and interestingly, much of this happened in the unisex bathroom! An icon in *Ally McBeal*, the unisex bathroom was a unique variation on the classic office break room, where employees would congregate to chat, vent, and dance. Apart from some of the funniest scenes that took place in there, such as the time Ally got stuck in the toilet and required rescuing by the fire department, or the many times Cage failed to perform his "dismount" from the toilet, the unisex bathroom was the venue that enabled the characters to become familiar with each other through music. In one memorable scene, John is beginning his pretrial routine to the tune of a Barry White song, and Fish walks in on him. Surprisingly, Fish joins in, followed quickly by Elaine and then even hard-hearted Ling. The choreography is tight as they kick and turn in time and show that in the practice of law, a disparate group of individuals can still be unified.

Dancing also was an integral part of the bar the characters frequented at the end of the day. With the law office upstairs and the bar downstairs in the same building, we saw how these lawyers were able to effectively blend the professional and private aspects of their lives. The bar therefore provided an opportunity for reflection and consistent entertainment each evening for these hard-working lawyers. Office conflicts disappeared and legal disappointments were diffused through the party atmosphere of the bar. Just as Vonda Shephard would sing the day's worries away, we saw that when you stripped away the idiosyncrasies of these characters, they were just everyday people with normal life and love desires.

The Contribution of *Ally McBeal* to Public Perception

On one level, *Ally McBeal* entertains. It tells a story and engages the audience by displaying the neuroses as well as the expertise of its lawyers. On another level, whether it is intentional or unintentional, viewers come away from watching this show with an idea about how they think lawyers should behave and the type of characteristics they think are desirable in a lawyer. In its heyday, no legal series had spawned as many fan websites as *Ally McBeal*, and its popularity indicated that viewers were keen to tune in week after week to immerse themselves in Ally's universe.

Perhaps one of the main ways in which *Ally McBeal* contributed to the public image of lawyers was by appealing to a wide range of viewers. Using an unconventional approach that provoked thought and discussion about the actions and behavior of lawyers, it brought the law and its players to people who may have been quite unfamiliar with legal shows.

The unusual legal issues and the bizarre fantasy sequences on *Ally McBeal* were tools that allowed us entrance into the complicated world of the human spirit. The characters on this show, and most especially Ally, continually reflected the balancing game that we all play in our lives—our attempt to deal with the tension between the shifting borders of our inner and outer realities. The way Ally jumped in and out of conflicting planes of existence as she navigated her legal and personal obligations appealed to our desire to balance and organize our public and private personalities in a world of infinite modification.

Despite her being a lawyer, it was easy to relate to the character of Ally McBeal. We have all felt the sting of an arrow through the heart, experienced the cringe factor when we were belittled in front of others, or simply felt the pangs of loneliness. By allowing people to see and hear what was going on inside the heads of these lawyers, public perception may well have acknowledged that lawyers, like most individuals, indeed possess those human traits that have been denied them so long.

Conclusion

The lawyers on *Ally McBeal* displayed a mixture of skill, empathy, and determination. While they sometimes may have seemed to be oversexed and in serious need of therapy, what is clear about their collective legal identity is that they were a passionate, encouraging, and dedicated team that valued friendship within the firm. They showed that lawyers have a need for friends and confidantes, and sometimes benefit from friendly competition. As friends, these lawyers shared their lives with one another. They imparted and received advice and support on personal issues, they shared secrets, and they encouraged each other's professional and personal endeavors. They protected, guided, and rebuked one another, and at the end of the day, to the accompaniment of their favorite tunes, they gathered downstairs at the bar to sing, dance, and forget their troubles. On *Ally McBeal*, these lawyers struggled with ethical, personal, and social issues that were represented as parts of their lives—just as they would be in your life or mine. *Ally McBeal* revealed that lawyers are simply "human." As Ally herself once said, "Who wants to be balanced? Balance is overrated!"

CHAPTER 20

Judging Amy

DAVID RAY PAPKE

Judicial characters on commercial television have special potential to personify the vaunted American rule of law, but what type of approach to law does the television judge represent? Traditionally, television judges have been flat, one-dimensional figures who sit on high, rule on objections, and maintain order in their courtrooms. More recently, television judges have become more fully developed figures with active roles in their shows' plots, sometimes lecturing and denigrating those who stand before them.[1] Fortunately, Judge Amy Gray of the family drama *Judging Amy* offers another alternative. During her six-year run on prime time, Judge Gray struggled mightily—in her courtroom and in her own family—with difficult issues, but she always reaffirmed her commitment to the family as an institution. As a judge, Judge Gray represented an approach to law that combined intellect, passion, resourcefulness, and empathy. Her approach was one in which viewers could believe.

* * *

The original episodes of *Judging Amy* aired over six seasons, and as this lengthy run suggests, the series was popular with prime-time viewers.

Judging Amy

Aired:
- September 19, 1999–May 3, 2005, CBS

Cast:
- Amy Brenneman (Amy Gray)
- Tyne Daly (Maxine Gray)
- Richard T. Jones (Bruce Van Exel)
- Karle Warren (Lauren Cassidy)

Awards:
- Tyne Daly, Emmy for Outstanding Supporting Actress in a Drama Series (2003)
- Amy Brenneman, TV Guide Award for Actress of the Year in a Drama Series (2001)
- Amy Brenneman, TV Guide Award for Favorite Actress in a New Series (2000)
- ASCAP Award for Top TV Series (2000, 2003, 2004, 2006)

Courtesy of Photofest.

JUDGING AMY

Judge Amy Gray (Amy Brenneman) and her loyal bailiff Bruce Van Exel (Richard T. Jones) are ready to serve the public in Hartford's Family Court.

At the peak of its popularity, *Judging Amy* attracted 15.5 million weekly viewers, the majority of whom were women. Roughly half of the viewers were in the 35–54 age range, with the other half being 55 or older.

Amy Brenneman was not only the series' star, but also its chief creator. She drew inspiration from the experiences of her mother, Frederica Brenneman. The latter graduated from Harvard Law School in 1953 as a member of the first class that included female admittees. When she garnered a judicial appointment to Connecticut's juvenile court in 1967, Frederica Brenneman became only the second woman to serve on the Nutmeg State's bench. A decade later, when the state courts merged, Judge Brenneman joined the Superior Court bench, where she developed a strong reputation for thoughtfulness in child abuse and neglect cases. She also tried to convince her daughter Amy to follow in her footsteps in the legal profession. Every time Amy Brenneman returned to her family home, Frederica Brenneman asked her daughter the question, "When are you going to law school?"[2]

Amy Brenneman did not follow her mother's advice and become a lawyer, but rather chose acting as her career. She attracted attention for playing a troubled policewoman named Janice Licalsi in the earliest episodes of *NYPD Blue* and also appeared in films such as *Heat, Your Friends and Neighbors,* and *The Suburbans.* Then, in 1998, she successfully pitched to CBS a dramatic series starring herself as a Harvard Law School graduate who becomes a Connecticut juvenile court judge. The similarities between the fictional judge and her mother surely registered on Brenneman. When production began, her parents came to California and visited the set. "There I was with my robe on," Brenneman said, "and suddenly it all became too Freudian. I thought, I'm playacting, pretending to be my mother."[3]

The real-life Judge Frederica Brenneman subsequently worked as a consultant to the show. She reportedly provided her daughter with voluminous notes suggesting how the courtroom cases and the conduct of the fictional judge could be made more realistic. In the end, television production has imperatives other than faithfulness to real life, but the relationship of a juvenile court judge to a daughter playing a juvenile court judge on television was nevertheless unique.

In the series itself, a character named Amy Gray separates from her husband of 10 years, abandons a lucrative corporate law practice in New York City, and returns home to Hartford, Connecticut, with her six-year-old daughter Lauren in tow. Gray makes the fateful decision to move back in with her mother, a feisty social worker named Maxine Gray, played by actress Tyne Daly. Returning to the nest does not impede Amy Gray's resumption of a legal career, and in the blink of an eye, she obtains an appointment to the bench.

As is often the case with prime-time television series, it is probably best not to dwell at great length on the general plot setup. Suffice it to say, Judge Gray's first day as a judge is frightening. She dons her robe, looks in her bedroom mirror, and jumps back in bed, pulling the covers over her robe and her head. However, before long Judge Gray settles into her new role. Assisted by her bailiff Bruce Van Exel and loyal law clerk Donna Kozlowski, Judge Gray presides over at least one complicated family-related case weekly.

When Judge Gray returns home from a long day at the courthouse, a range of intriguing family members awaits. The matriarch, Maxine Gray, while well-intentioned, is bossy and stubborn. "What's anorexia?" her sweet granddaughter asks. "It's something women catch from magazines," Grandma fires back. When she interacts with her daughter rather than her granddaughter, Maxine Gray hardly defers. She is unimpressed that her daughter has become a judge and is even heard to comment about the apparent decline of the judiciary that her daughter's appointment suggests. Maxine Gray seems to mean it when she gives Judge Gray a three-part prescription for successful service on the bench: (1) Pee before you go on the bench. (2) Do not wear perfume. (3) Make sure there's no food in your mouth.

In addition to her busybody of a mother, Judge Gray also has two adult brothers and an adult cousin who require much support and assistance. Her brother Vincent, played by Dan Futterman, is an aspiring novelist who must support himself with various jobs, including being a dog-washer. Her brother Peter, played by Marcus Giamatti, is a frustrated insurance agent who dreams of playing in a rock 'n roll band. And her cousin Kyle McCarty, played by Kevin Rahm, is a young doctor whose first residency ends prematurely because of his drug addiction.

Then, too, there are Judge Gray's boyfriends and lovers, who average roughly one per year and range from Lauren's karate teacher to a fellow judge. Judge Gray becomes engaged at one point to Stuart Collins, a lawyer played by Reed Diamond, but she literally leaves him standing at the altar. Needless to say, romance can more easily be a regular feature of a dramatic series if the lead character remains single. Six months after breaking off with Collins, Judge Gray learns Collins has married a Polynesian woman he met on the trip that Judge Gray had envisioned as her honeymoon.

In the typical one-hour episode of *Judging Amy*, Judge Gray does her best to fashion useful rulings from the bench and also to attend to matters involving her relatives and boyfriends. With a few exceptions, each of the legal cases has its beginning, middle, and end within a single episode. The crises and controversies involving relatives and boyfriends, meanwhile, often extend across episodes. Overall, there was a great "busyness" about the series, a trait more intentional than accidental. "Unlike movies or plays," Brenneman observed, "you need an inexhaustible source for TV. One story ain't gonna do it."[4]

As late as its sixth year, *Judging Amy* maintained good ratings and a large, loyal viewership. Yet, in a familiar television industry decision, CBS executives decided to cancel the show in hopes that newer series would attract younger viewers. Reruns appeared for a while on TNT, but for the most part, the series has now disappeared from American television screens.[5] Perhaps in the unbroadcast afterlife of the series, Judge Gray continues to fight the good fight. In the final 2005 episode, titled "My Name Is Amy Gray," Judge Gray resigns from the bench and announces her plans to run for the U.S. Senate.

* * *

Many Americans consider family to be the most valuable sanctuary in their hectic lives. We began adding "family rooms" to our homes in large numbers in the late 1940s and early 1950s,[6] and the rooms became sites for children's play, hobby activities, and—perhaps more than anything else—television-watching. One of our favorite types of programs to watch on the family room television is a show about a fictional family. Shows of this sort, both comic and dramatic, took over large portions of daytime and prime-time schedules as network television developed.

Judging Amy fits within a group of prime-time dramatic series that self-consciously revolve around "family" and feature adult family members who continue to work out their relationships with one another. This group includes such shows as *Sisters* in the 1990s, *Brothers and Sisters* in the 2000s, and the millennial series to which *Judging Amy* is most frequently compared—*Providence*. Both *Judging Amy* and *Providence* begin with a female professional in her 30s stepping away from a demanding career: Amy Gray leaves her corporate practice in New York City, and in *Providence* Sydney Hansen backs off a practice as a plastic surgeon in Los Angeles. Both return to homes in which only one parent survives, and, coincidentally, both homes are in midsized New England cities. Apparently it was even possible to mistake the two series for one another. In the third-season episode "The Justice League of America," Judge Gray attends her 10th law school reunion, and her classmates have difficulty remembering that she is on the bench in Hartford. They think she calls Providence home, causing Judge Gray to forcefully tell a classmate, "It's Hartford, David. Providence is a whole other universe."

Similar rhythms in the various family-themed dramatic series notwithstanding, *Judging Amy* adopted and perfected one major, distinctive tack, to wit, the main character wrestled with family difficulties in both her professional life and in her home. Judge Gray's courtroom is in the public sphere, and her home is in the private sphere. But the stories from the two spheres resonate with one another.

The exact jurisdiction of Judge Gray's court is a bit obscure. Everyone refers to it as "Family Court." Cases involving divorce, separation, and civil commitment appear on the docket, but the majority of cases involve children and their actual or alleged misconduct. We know at least that it is not "Criminal Court." Judge Gray is transferred to that court at one point, where she watches the high-powered attorneys at work, notes the better furnishings, and is seriously tempted to abandon "Family Court" once and for all. Then she comes to her senses. "When you hear a criminal trial," Judge Gray says to the chief judge, "you make a big difference in the life of one person. In Family Court, I can have an impact on six people at once."

A full range of complicated and struggling families comes before Judge Gray. In an intriguing 2003 episode titled "Ruminspringa," Judge Gray struggles to understand the Amish custom of the same name, in which Amish teens temporarily leave their families and experience non-Amish society with reckless abandon. An Amish girl becomes pregnant during "Ruminspringa," and Judge Gray has to decide if she should receive custody and be able to keep the child in the Amish community, or if the non-Amish teenage father of the child should receive custody and be able to raise the child in his more worldly family. In a 2004 episode titled "Baggage Claim," Judge Gray has before her a disturbed single mother and her nine-year-old son. The boy had been conceived after the mother was raped. The rapist/father remains in prison, but his mother, a loving and well-intentioned person, seeks to alter the boy's family structure by obtaining custody of him as a grandparent.

Lest Judge Gray think she can leave the complexities of family life behind her when she goes home from work, her own family presents comparable complexities. The problems begin with her three-generation home environment. The matriarch, Maxine Gray, is hardly shy about criticizing the way Judge Gray is raising her daughter and failing in various romantic relationships. Meanwhile, Maxine Gray has child-rearing issues and tortured romantic relationships of her own. During one year of the series, Maxine Gray becomes engaged to a wealthy businessman, played by Richard Crenna, despite the strong objections of the businessman's adult sons. The couple set the wedding date, but the businessman dies suddenly two days before they are to take their vows. Later, Maxine falls for a Latin landscape designer played by Cheech Marin. She is then rudely surprised to learn he is married and has two children. Through all of this, Judge Gray criticizes, consoles, and advises Maxine Gray, rather than vice versa.

Some of the most pointed and poignant private-sphere dilemmas in *Judging Amy* involve Judge Gray's idiosyncratic siblings and relatives. Her brother Vincent, for example, marries a woman with breast cancer and moves with her to California. Later he returns, claiming his wife left him for her oncologist, but it turns out Vincent has deserted his wife because of the stress and strain of caring for her. Judge Gray's brother Peter and his wife Gillian adopt a child who, to their surprise, is half African American. Shortly after the adoption, Gillian gets pregnant. She and Peter then separate. Finally, Judge Gray's cousin Kyle overcomes his drug addiction, but an affair with a fellow doctor leads him to quit his new residency. Kevin then accompanies his new lover to Minneapolis, where she is entering a rehabilitation program.

If summarized briefly, the situations Judge Gray encounters in the courthouse and at home might seem the tired fare of many prime-time soap operas. However, the drama is earnestly intended to be representative of serious contemporary family problems. "Sure, there are lots of comfy kitchen scenes bathed in honey-gold New England light," says the series' executive producer, Barbara Hall, "but the show never resorts to the easy cliché or the cheap satisfaction of a sappy moment."[7]

The sensibility at the heart of things—presumably Amy Brenneman's more than anyone else's—is always sympathetic to human frailty and the value of family. Furthermore, the key to successful family life, we are reminded in each episode, is not proximity to the bourgeois nuclear family model, but instead is mutual support and respect among whomever might count as family members. In the 2004 episode titled "Lullaby," Judge Gray's cousin has decided to care for his illegitimate baby while the baby's mother completes rehabilitation. The Gray clan gathers with Kyle and the baby around the dining-room table, and Maxine Gray begins to sing a soft lullaby. The song moves the others, and one by one they join in. If its members take seriously their responsibilities to one another, a family can fill to the brim with love.

* * *

Judge Gray's commitment to and involvement with family is in itself enough to make the show engaging. But recall that *Judging Amy* offers an additional twist: it is a law show. For those prepared to reflect on it, Judge Gray is a personification of the law, and *Judging Amy* portrays what the rule of law might be like.

In general, Judge Gray eschews an unduly rigid and technical approach to law and, in that sense, differs from many of the lawyers and judges she encounters in her fictional Hartford courthouse. Judge Gray's approach to the law even occasionally collides with the dominant one. In an episode titled "The Long Goodbye," Judge Gray encounters difficulty during her short-lived assignment to the "Criminal Court." The chief judge summons her to his office after Judge Gray dismisses a murder case despite a guilty verdict from the jury. He castigates her for failing to follow the rules and suggests she obtain counseling. When she balks at the latter idea, he warns her there will not be much on her docket if she does not go along with his recommendation. This causes Judge Gray to realize she had best return to "Family Court," where she has more freedom to address human problems without being bound by formal rules.

And indeed, in her own court, Judge Gray rarely refers to rules and precedents and frequently grants a continuance in order to contemplate a seemingly intractable problem that has presented itself. This approach might seem flawed to some. One such critic is Professor Chris Jackson, who dismisses *Judging Amy* as "comfort food for tired, hungry professionals who feel adrift in the career world."[8] Jackson suggests better legal role models are available in *The Practice* or *Law & Order*, two immensely popular television series featuring lawyers who often excel in the courtroom.

But to deplore Judge Gray for her failure to be a more precise legalist is to overlook the ways she unites and reunites families by refusing to be rule-bound. In a 2004 episode titled "Conditional Surrender," Judge Gray has before her a mother with multiple sclerosis whose medical condition is making it impossible to care for her son and endangering his well-being. The situation appears to dictate a termination of parental rights, and many in the courthouse call for just that. Instead, Judge Gray creatively fashions a kinship care arrangement that uses the good services of the mother's sister-in-law and orders the mother to get treatment for her depression. In the previously mentioned 2003 episode titled "The Long Goodbye," Judge Gray presides over a proceeding against a teenage girl charged with smearing feces and animal guts on another girl, and discovers that the "victim" had previously terrorized the "perpetrator." Judge Gray's solution? She orders both girls to perform 500 hours of community service in a recycling program that had been created by one of the girls to bolster her college application. The girls learn their lesson about how to treat one another and, in the process, convert a sham operation into a genuine public-service undertaking.

Of course, this is all prime-time fiction, but if we abstract and distill Judge Gray's efforts on the bench, we see an appealing combination of intellect and passion, creativity and empathy. This is how the law could and should work. The name of the series, after all, has a double meaning. Judge Gray is on the bench, making decisions and judging things. She is "Judging Amy." In addition, we, as viewers, are judging Judge Gray as we watch her judging. We, too, are "judging Amy." On the latter score, most of us are inclined to like what we see. Judge Gray presents a humane and humanistic approach to law and personifies a rule of law that helps people live up to their potential for compassion and integrity.

Endnotes

1. For a review of the evolving image of the judge in popular culture, see David Ray Papke, *From Flat to Round: Changing Portrayals of the Judge in American Popular Culture*, 31 J. LEGAL PROF. 127 (2007).

2. Quoted in Yahlin Chang, *Here Comes the Judge*, NEWSWEEK, Nov. 22, 1999, 88.

3. Quoted in Julia Collins, *Brennemans on the Bench*, HARV. L. BULL., summer 2000, 17.

4. *Id.*

5. A DVD set with 138 episodes, constituting the full six-year *Judging Amy* run, became available in 2007.

6. *See* Michael Wentworth, "Family Rooms," *in* THE GUIDE TO UNITED STATES POPULAR CULTURE 272 (Ray B. Browne & Pat Browne eds. (2001)).

7. Quoted in Chang, *supra* note 2.

8. Chris Jackson, Judging "Judging Amy" (1999), PICTURING JUSTICE, THE ON-LINE J. OF L. AND POPULAR CULTURE, http://www.usfca.edu/pj/amy.htm.

CHAPTER 21

girls club Does Not Exist

JENNIFER L. SCHULZ

girls club

Aired:

- October 21, 2002–
  October 28, 2002, FOX

Cast:

- Gretchen Mol
  (Lynne Camden)

- Kathleen Robertson
  (Jeannie Falls)

- Chyler Leigh
  (Sarah Mickle)

- Giancarlo Esposito
  (Nicholas Hahn)

- Sam Jaeger
  (Kevin O'Neil)

Did you start reading this chapter thinking, "*girls club*? What show is that?" You have certainly heard of *L.A. Law* and you have undoubtedly watched *Law & Order* or one of its spin-offs, but *girls club* simply does not ring a bell. Do not worry. You have probably never heard of this show because only two episodes of it ever aired on television. *girls club*, spelled in lowercase letters, was another David E. Kelley television program in a one-hour drama format, but it had an unbelievably short run. *girls club* both debuted and ended on the FOX television network in October 2002.

I tuned in to *girls club* for personal reasons. At the time, I was in the midst of research for my doctoral dissertation on mediation metaphors in movies. I was examining how female dispute resolvers—such as negotiators and mediators—were depicted in film, especially in contrast to male lawyers. I was particularly interested in how the metaphors and images used to describe dispute resolvers differed from those used for lawyers. As such, depictions of women problem solvers were at the forefront of my mind. Therefore, a new television program about women lawyers, created by someone with a successful track record for legal television

243

Courtesy of Photofest.

girls club
Lynne (Gretchen Mol), Sarah (Chyler Leigh), and Jeannie (Kathleen Robertson) will take on the world, if their law firm doesn't crush them first.

programming, piqued my interest. I wanted to see what metaphors and images would be used and how young professional women, a group very rarely seen on prime-time television, would fare as protagonists in a legal drama.

As a young, female Canadian law professor, I also thought, "Hmm. . . finally a show specifically about the experience of junior female lawyers in big firms. This might be interesting." I am often asked by my students what they should expect when they join a law firm, because law school rarely prepares them for daily life in legal practice. Students also report that they turn to popular culture depictions of legal practice to glean information. Therefore, I was fascinated to see what picture of law firm life *girls club* would provide to its viewers. In particular, my curiosity was aroused because the advance promotional material for *girls club* noted that the pilot episode would address how one of the female protagonists, played by a Canadian actress with whom I was familiar, dealt with sexual harassment. Having worked in a very large corporate law firm myself and been exposed to sexual harassment, I was intrigued to see how this important topic would be handled.

Although the title of the show put me off, being a fully postmodern third-wave feminist with a sense of humor, I thought I could give the show a chance. Besides, based on the tag lines and promotional materials for the series (e.g., "You're In" and "If You're Not Part Of The Club, Make Your Own"), I correctly surmised that the title was a riff on the infamous "old boys club" that women are still unable to break into, and so I tuned in to the pilot episode on Monday, October 21, 2002, at 9 PM.

In the first episode of *girls club*, viewers meet the three young and ambitious women protagonists, who became best friends in law school and are now roommates. They work at the same prestigious, male-dominated law firm in San Francisco. (Winding up at the same firm is a relatively common occurrence, given that very large law firms hire dozens of new associates every year.) Because it is a TV program, the three lead characters are all attractive. In fact, in a *Charlie's Angels* sort of way, each of the three woman protagonists has a different hair color: there is a blonde, a brunette, and a redhead.

Lynne Camden is blonde and facing her first real criminal trial. Unrealistically, it is a death penalty case that she is defending by herself, which would, of course, never happen in a real law firm of this size. (Indeed, such a firm would probably never undertake non–white-collar criminal defense work). However, realism is not the point of *girls club*. In fact, most of the "law stuff" in the show is not realistic, and that is okay. Being overly concerned with the distortions perpetrated by law shows is the pastime of lawyers with positivistic bents. After all, where does one find an undistorted version of law? There is no one legal truth or reality. There are, however, real feelings. Where viewers find realism in *girls club* is in the feelings experienced by Lynne and other young lawyers like her. Lynne, who is just embarking upon her career, receives virtually no support from her law firm and yet is somehow expected to know what to do. While such lack of guidance would be unusual in most big firms, the arduous expectations placed on Lynne ring true. She is understandably terrified, receives no mentorship, and, not surprisingly, does not handle her case well. Later, when she is devastated, viewers can easily empathize with her.

Sarah Mickle, the brunette, is doing badly at the firm because she cannot navigate office politics, and none of the senior members of the firm has reached out to guide her. She is battling with another associate, Rhanda, because both are competing for the attention of Meredith, a cynical and unpleasant female partner who is called "the preying mantis" behind her back. Rhanda lies to Sarah and outmaneuvers her, so she receives the choice piece of legal work and Sarah is passed over. Sarah reacts very unprofessionally and calls Rhanda a "dyke" in front of many colleagues. Consequently, Sarah is required by firm management to spend 10 weekends taking anger management classes.

Jeannie Falls, the redhead, has been asked to conduct settlement negotiations on behalf of a senior partner's sister whose gynecologist fainted into her vulva during an exam. Although the partner's sister understandably suffered emotional distress, this highly sexualized plot is unrealistic, is designed to grab viewers' attention, and does not present a real legal claim, since it arose from an accident and not from negligence. (However, it must be stressed again that the point of *girls club* is not legal realism, but rather the feelings of the protagonists.) Interestingly, the pilot episode focuses on the negotiation that Jeannie conducts, and for that it bears closer analysis.

Very few legal television programs focus on negotiation. We see plea bargaining, a form of negotiation, on shows like *Law & Order*, and *L.A. Law* used to depict some boardroom negotiations, but other than that, the vast majority of legal programming on television is focused on the trial. As a result, viewers are bombarded with images of dramatic wins and losses in highly adversarial courtroom settings, as opposed to the potentially more collaborative and creative outcomes that might be obtained through negotiation. Given that over 90 percent of all civil and criminal cases are settled rather than litigated, I was pleased to see such prominent airtime given to settlement negotiations in this first episode. In this way, *girls club* valiantly tried to expand our understanding of legal practice to include nonadversarial problem solving and settlement negotiation, thereby more properly depicting the reality of legal practice.

Surprisingly, the pilot episode made it clear that Jeannie, a junior female lawyer, handled the negotiation "brilliantly" even in the presence of the senior male partner who was sexually harassing her. This is note-worthy because it is unusual to see young women depicted as competent in legal dramas. *Ally McBeal*, for example, often focused on the short-comings of lawyer Ally, and virtually all legally themed films starring female lawyers portray them as in some way incompetent.[1] Thus, the fact that Jeannie is shown to be brilliant is nothing short of remarkable.

The viewer is supposed to think Jeannie is brilliant because she is tough, hard-nosed, and uncompromising. Jeannie adopts a very com-petitive negotiation style because her firm has a lot invested in the case, given that the plaintiff is the senior partner's sister. In addition, Jeannie, as a "green lawyer" (opposing counsel's words), has a lot invested person-ally because she wants to impress her superiors. Thus, Jeannie handles the negotiation in a very adversarial fashion, correctly deducing that this approach will best please her supervising counsel. She appears brilliant because, in the face of senior opposition, she emerges victorious. Jeannie manages to settle the case by threatening to "litigate it to death," which would, of course, greatly embarrass the physician. Opposing counsel, who originally wanted to offer nothing, is persuaded to make a settle-ment offer of $71,000. Jeannie is thrilled, as is her supervising partner.

So on the plus side, for those of us who would advocate greater use and depiction of dispute resolution processes such as negotiation and mediation both in practice and on television, negotiation is not only highlighted in *girls club*, but made to look as interesting and exciting as courtroom work. On the negative side, Jeannie negotiates in a tough win/lose manner. In so doing, she mirrors the adversarial posturing we are used to seeing on legal TV shows, rather than employing the more creative, collaborative benefits of interest-based negotiation. Negotiation is supposed to be a principled dispute resolution process that achieves results through dialogue, not threats. Although dispute resolution schol-ars agree that collaborative, interest-based negotiation is to be preferred over competitive, positional bargaining,[2] *girls club* showed us the latter and called it "brilliant."

Despite her failure to implement negotiation theory in her practice, Jeannie, the lawyer-negotiator, is depicted as effective, fearless, and artic-ulate. If she were a man, the story would end here, with the male lawyer emerging heroic. However, in *girls club*, the story is not over. Rather, a sad reality of life in a large firm is played out in the next scene. Jeannie's super-vising senior male partner is "so impressed" with Jeannie's negotiation prowess that he sexually assaults her. The partner touches Jeannie on her breastbone and invites her out to dinner, promising her better legal work if she will date him. Jeannie's negotiation victory is tainted, and she leaves the room swallowing tears. This is a very depressing, well-captured, and realistic scene that is experienced far too frequently by junior women members of law firms.

By showcasing sexual harassment, girls club was unique. The pilot episode highlighted the legitimate concerns women have about reporting sexual harassment. Reporting rarely results in any real repercussions for the harasser, and it usually results in negative consequences for the victim. Jeannie, for example, is devastated, angry, confused, and concerned about job security should she tell anyone. When she is at home with her girlfriends she displays her anxiety and the insecurities she has as a junior lawyer in such a poisoned environment. Although this young woman lawyer-negotiator is effective, fearless, and articulate, she is not portrayed as heroic because she has insecurities and is the victim of sexual harassment. Female lawyers have fewer opportunities than male lawyers to emerge as heroes.[3] Unlike male television and film lawyers, female lawyers cannot have it all. The male lawyer who questions his motives and his commitment to the law is perceived as heroic for being willing to do so.[4] The same is certainly not true for female lawyers, who are characterized as inexcusably weak for questioning their own convictions or their commitment to law.

Sometimes lawyers emerge from the end of their workday victorious, and other times they go home depressed over their shortcomings. The three women protagonists in girls club are no different. They are still learning the skills of lawyering, and they are not afraid to share their worries with one another. This is remarkably different from popular images of male television lawyers, who seem to have no insecurities whatsoever. Most shows featuring male lawyers are too busy portraying them as heroes to show any lack of confidence. girls club, despite its unrealistic plot lines, was realistic in its portrayal of lawyerly doubts.

girls club showed viewers the difficulties faced by many female lawyers and highlighted the fact that young female lawyers are not treated well in law firms. Law firms are not fair workplaces, senior lawyers rarely right wrongs perpetrated against junior lawyers, and some, such as the sexual harasser in girls club, commit those wrongs themselves. Many lawyers simply do not support junior lawyers, preferring to encourage rivalries between them. Sadly, this appears to be true regardless of the gender of the senior lawyer. The only female partner we meet at the law firm in *girls club* is just as obnoxious as the male partners, and is called "the preying mantis" behind her back. This is unfortunate because it perpetuates the stereotype that strong, successful female lawyers in positions of power must be evil. The fact that the young female lawyer protagonists also call the female partner by this derogatory name further demonstrates the work women need to do to better support one another. In one poignant scene, the"preying mantis" makes Jeannie tell her what her nickname is. When Jeannie reveals the nickname, the partner responds that to survive at a large law firm like theirs, women *have* to be that way. How depressing. *girls club* underlines the sad reality that many women lawyers do their work at great personal cost in highly dysfunctional professional environments.

In the second episode of *girls club*, Jeannie continues to battle sexism and harassment at the law firm, but this time it is Lynne who talks about "the preying mantis." Lynne's male colleague notes that the preying mantis is "a little sexy in a bite-your-head-off kind of way." When I heard that I thought, "Why are women still enduring this?" (These types of comments continued even after *girls club* was cancelled. Internet commentary after the series went off the air included such comments as "Not enough lesbian sex—well, I was hoping to see some. Weren't you?"[5]) Despite the fact that over half of all first-year law students in Canada and the United States are women, we are still enduring extremely sexist commentary and behavior in law school and in practice. While it is true that men are also subjected to nicknames, theirs seem to lack the negative connotations of the nicknames ascribed to women. For example, in episode two, the three women protagonists refer to the powerful senior male partners in their firm as the "power dicks." This nickname, like "preying mantis," also sexualizes its recipient, but the nickname suggests the men are powerful in a positive way, whereas the sole female "preying mantis" is so power-hungry and evil that she might actually kill someone!

Episode two of *girls club* also highlighted another conundrum faced by junior female associates in large law firms: their appearance. Jeannie is counseled by Lynne that she should wear less makeup. When Jeannie asks why, Lynne says, "Because the men look for any opportunity to dismiss us." Thus, women receive mixed messages. Looking too good is taboo because it might result in men dismissing us, yet not looking good enough means we will not be hired in the first place. In big law firms, "looking good" is part of the job. Indeed, during the opening credits of *girls club*, one of the images is of stiletto heels under the negotiating table. The message is that powerful women negotiators and lawyers must have (hetero) sex appeal. What are junior female lawyers to make of these mixed messages? On the one hand, episode two of *girls club* tells women that they should be concerned about wearing too much makeup. (Even Jeannie's boyfriend accuses her of sending the "wrong signals.") On the other hand, the same episode depicts Sarah wearing an unbelievably low-cut blouse to work and experiencing only "positive" repercussions. Young female lawyers might be forgiven for feeling they cannot win.

Focusing on young professional women, highlighting negotiation, and depicting lawyers' real feelings made *girls club* unique. The show posed interesting questions for young women lawyers: Can we be in the "boys club"? Do we want to be in it? Can we change the club? Should we just form our own club? Alas, we did not receive answers to any of these questions, because after two episodes *girls club* was cancelled for lack of viewership.[6] Although there could be many reasons, *girls club* probably failed because it lacked central male protagonists. Viewers are accustomed to seeing middle-aged men as their television lawyers, and *girls club* challenged these expectations by presenting viewers with the perspectives of young women. *girls club* showed what it is like to be a young female associate in a male corporate world. That world involves sexual harassment, nonsupportive partners, mixed messages, and real anxiety. A television program about young women professionals and the feelings engendered by working in a sexist law firm was presumably too much for the ordinary viewer to take.

I believe that *girls club* might have been interesting had it not been canceled. *girls club* focused on young women lawyers trying to manage their careers in a big firm. It accurately depicted the insecurities and feelings of anxiety suffered by lawyers, and it highlighted the importance of negotiation and dispute resolution skills to legal practice. The show also examined the dark side of life in a big firm by tackling a serious problem like sexual harassment, thereby exposing problems with the way partners run law firms. *girls club* portrayed the tough, unpleasant reality of legal practice for women, and was canceled for doing so. The show was not on television long enough to determine whether it would ever attempt to mount any real feminist critique of legal practice. (Indeed, any attempt it might have made to challenge legal practice would more likely have reproduced legal hierarchies.) However, it was never given the chance. The cancelation of *girls club* after only two episodes speaks volumes about sexist sentiments in North America.

Endnotes

1. Among numerous discussions of female lawyers in pop culture, see Carole Shapiro, *Women Lawyers in Celluloid: Why Hollywood Skirts the Truth*, 25 U. Tol. L. Rev. 955 (1995).

2. Andrea Kupfer Schneider, *Shattering Negotiation Myths: Empirical Evidence on the Effectiveness of Negotiation Style*, 7 Harv. Negot. L. Rev. 143 (2002).

3. Judith Grant, *Lawyers as Superheroes: The Firm, The Client, and* The Pelican Brief, 30 U.S.F. L. Rev. 1111, 1114 (1996).

4. Christine A. Corcos, *We Don't Want Advantages: The Woman Lawyer Hero and Her Quest for Power in Popular Culture*, 53 Syracuse L. Rev. 1225, 1231 (2003).

5. http://www.imdb.com/title/tt0316984/board/thread/82021666 (last accessed September 2, 2008).

6. According to industry reports, *girls club* did badly in its debut, scoring only a 5.1 rating and a 7 share to come in fifth in its 9 PM time slot. Despite lavish promotion for the show, the ratings were 35 percent below those of its lead-in, *Boston Public*, another Kelley production, which scored a 7.9/11 in its season premiere. Moreover, the numbers were off 39 percent from its predecessor, *Ally McBeal*, and critics were harsh. For example, David Bianculli, writing in the Oct. 21, 2002, *New York Daily News*, stated, "What's really shocking about *girls club* is how unimpressive it is."

CHAPTER 22

Reality Bites: *Boston Legal*'s Creative License with the Law

CORINNE BRINKERHOFF

Boston Legal is an amped-up, reality-be-damned version of life and law, a place where trials begin and end in one day, a mute assault victim can testify via cello, and a lawyer can commit hundreds of ethical infractions without disbarment. We've sued a snack food company for causing diabetes and a "reparative therapy" center for failing to cure "same-sex attraction disorder."[1] We've represented a clown, a zoophile, and a homeless cannibal. Needless to say, it's a really fun show to write.

However, it does get some flak—especially from lawyers—for the degree of creative license it takes. To the lawyers who might criticize the show for being unrealistic, I say: picture what a typical day of work is like for you. Would you watch an hour of that on TV. . . for *fun*? Here's how I imagine a realistic legal show would be:

> INTERIOR LAW OFFICE—DAY. An ASSOCIATE sorts through a stack of documents. Turns to the computer. Clicks a few times. Looks mildly irritated by something on screen. Types. Turns back to the papers. Makes a notation on one.
>
> This goes on for 10 minutes or so.

Boston Legal

Aired:

- Oct. 3, 2004–Dec. 8, 2008, ABC

Cast:

- William Shatner (Denny Crane)
- James Spader (Alan Shore)
- Candice Bergen (Shirley Schmidt)
- Rene Auberjonois (Paul Lewiston)
- Christian Clemenson (Jerry Espenson)
- Tara Summers (Katie Lloyd)
- John Larroquette (Carl Sack)

Awards:

- Emmy, James Spader, Outstanding Lead Actor in a Drama Series (2008)
- Emmy nomination, William Shatner, Outstanding Supporting Actor in a Drama Series (2008)
- Emmy nomination, Candice Bergen, Outstanding Supporting Actress in a Drama Series (2008)
- Emmy nomination, David Kelley, Outstanding Drama Series (2008)

Then—music change—a PARTNER appears in the doorway.

PARTNER: We just got the plaintiff's initial disclosures by fax.

ASSOCIATE: Anything notable?

PARTNER: Not really.

The associate nods. The partner nods, moves off. The associate turns back to the paperwork. Takes a sip of coffee. And we: SMASH CUT TO BLACK. END OF ACT 1.

Riveting stuff. Meanwhile, on a typical day at Crane, Poole & Schmidt—

LEWISTON: We need to survive a 12(b)(6) on a pretty untenable claim. How would you feel about joining us for oral arguments?

SCHMIDT: What's the claim?

LEWISTON: We're suing the United States government for the genocide taking place in Sudan.

SCHMIDT: What's so untenable about that?

LEWISTON: This is why I love her. (To Shore) Alan. We're making a show of force on a high-profile matter, could we trouble you to join us for a motion this morning?

SHORE: I'd love to, but I have a client who hit his mother on the head with a skillet. We're trying to take her off life support and the police have brought some nuisance action to try and keep her breathing, buggers that they are.

International human rights atrocity *and* attempted murder by skillet—not quite the average day at work. For the record, we do have a very astute legal consultant whose job is to scrutinize each script and notify us of everything that is incorrect, improbable, or entirely impossible.[2] Each time he finds such an issue, a high-level writer–producer must decide to (1) tweak it, (2) lose it, or (3) forge ahead under the cover of creative license.

While it is always useful to know when we've landed in unrealistic territory, option 3 tends to win out the most often, and with good reason. Without bending reality a bit, we lose much of what makes the show the bold, provocative, comical, and cerebral gem that it is. (I realize I am incapable of objectivity here.)

Take the show's central relationship, for example. On one side we have the incredibly articulate, emotionally complex, far-left–leaning Alan Shore, known for his politically divisive cases and eloquent closing arguments. On the other side we have Denny Crane: a gun-slinging, staunchly conservative egomaniac with self-diagnosed mad cow disease whose idea of eloquent speech is repeating his own name ad nauseam. Reality would be unlikely to bring these two together. On the show, they have become complex, hilarious, beautifully crafted soul mates through the agency of creator David E. Kelley, whose propensity for creating memorable character-driven series is, I believe, well-documented.[3] Together Crane and Shore form the backbone of a show that bends the law to keep the entertainment and the substance in equal proportion. How do we depart from reality? Let me count the ways. . . .

First, a real-life lawyer might need to commit only *one* instance of bribery, extortion, or witness intimidation to get disbarred. Shore makes a sport of each of them—then bounds, often victoriously, on to the next episode. In the pilot, he helps out in the case of a mother fighting her spiteful ex-husband for the right to take their children out of state. When traditional methods don't work, Shore doesn't hesitate to play dirty, ambushing the ex-husband in his office with a folder of incriminating material.

SHORE: Photos—snapshots, really—some delightful little business between you and a hooker. Friend of mine, actually. I earn frequent-flyer miles. (Flips through the photos.) She's a lovely woman. I arranged for her to seek you out at the bar. I particularly like that one, don't you, gives your bottom a nice aura. Here's the deal. Sharon and the kids get to go to New York or I start printing copies. (Re: photo) Is that powdered sugar you're snorting off her magnificent porcelain breasts?

MATTHEW: You're a lawyer in a prestigious firm, for God's sake.

SHORE: I know. Awful. Hate to extort and run, but I'm afraid I'll need an answer on this.

When Shore is dealing with fellow lawyers, he will rein it in a bit, but he doesn't hesitate to push the limits, as exemplified in this scene with opposing counsel in "An Eye for an Eye:"

SHORE: One last proposal, and it's entirely possible I'm kidding, by the way, depending upon your reaction. Three hundred thousand, sealed, we kick back 50 to you under the table.

MASON: Mr. Shore, I guarantee you. . . I am not that kind of attorney.

Courtesy of Photofest.

BOSTON LEGAL
Lawyers Denny Crane (William Shatner) and Alan Shore (James Spader) are intimate friends with little in common beyond their mutual disregard for legal ethics.

SHORE:	Really. I am.
MASON:	I should report you directly to the bar, if not the district attorney.
SHORE:	Well, if that's how you feel, then I *was* kidding.

In "Change of Course," the CEO of a Fortune 500 company—CPS's biggest client—is arrested for shoplifting a scarf and makes it clear the firm will lose the company's business if she gets anything but a not-guilty verdict. Slight wrinkle: she is completely guilty. The one eyewitness becomes Shore's target, so he dispatches associate Sally Heep (Lake Bell) to work undercover.

SHORE:	Their entire case is the store clerk. I want to put a private investigator on him, follow him, we pick the opportunity for you to meet him. Lunch perhaps.
SALLY:	And then what?
SHORE:	Then you order appetizers [and] elicit some disparaging information, allowing him to believe you're anyone at all—other than the defendant's lawyer.

SALLY: Is that fair?

SHORE: I don't understand the question.

Once Sally has reported on her recon work, Shore confronts the eye-witness with the newfound, ill-gotten information.

SHORE: Since I know that you take beta blockers for your anxi-ety, some possible side effects being dizziness and confu-sion, I am duty-bound to raise it. Also, the idea that you invited a few friends down to the courthouse to hear you testify, it would be malpractice for me not to make a small snack of that. Of course, I'll have to get into your inferior-ity complex, stuff about if a girl smiles at you, she must be a hooker, that sort of thing. . . . You collect autographs, that must be fun, standing around on cold, drizzly nights, waiting for famous people to give you a cursory glance, a moment of their time perhaps, if they take pity on you. Do people often take pity on you, Miles? Wouldn't surprise me, I'm seeing a pattern here, pity, anxiety, inferiority, all those ity words.

MILES: This isn't fair—

SHORE: You're right. It's not. But you have a job to do and so do I. Yours is to sell socks and suspenders. Mine is to cross-exam-ine people like you and crush them.

Suffice it to say, the tactic works, and Miles recants his story. The district attorney lodges a complaint against Shore for witness tampering, intimidation, obstruction of justice, and extortion, but Shore, of course, lives to practice another day.

Another entertaining application of creative license is the probably-not-relevant-but-very-compelling witness, my favorite example being Reverend Al Sharpton, who appeared in the case of a department store Santa Claus fired for being a gay cross-dresser. Several episodes earlier, Reverend Sharpton, as a favor to his friend Denny Crane, had made a rousing courtroom statement in support of the plaintiff, a young African-American actress denied the chance to play Little Orphan Annie because she didn't look the part. This time Shore implores him to bring in his courtroom theatrics again.

SHORE: I want you to be Reverend Al Sharpton in all his massive glory. I want you to charge in there, say, "Give us a gay Santa Claus,"

> and button it with three "God Almighty's". . . (proffering a doc-
> ument). I've written it all out for you, just give it a look-see.

Technically, Reverend Sharpton has no personal knowledge of the case, and he has not been disclosed in response to an interrogatory or designated as an expert witness.[4] Nevertheless, just before the judge rules, he bursts in to offer this:

> REVEREND SHARPTON: Let the bells of tolerance ring out this Christmas,
> let people open their minds as they open their
> presents underneath the tree, we need your mind,
> Judge, today. Let the gay man be my brother, be
> your brother, be the schoolteacher, the construc-
> tion worker, give the world a gay Santa Claus. God
> Almighty! God Almighty! God Almighty! Leave the
> cookies and milk out on this Christmas Eve for a
> holly jolly homosexual! God Almighty!

> SHORE: And cut.

As the gallery applauds—

> REVEREND SHARPTON: I threw in one extra.

> SHORE: Thank you.

—and the gay Santa is reinstated, leaving Shore free to represent white supremacist twins, a topless protester, and homicidal secretary Catherine Piper (Betty White). But Shore isn't the only one with the novel cases. In "The Mighty Rogues," Carl Sack (John Larroquette) represents residents of Nantucket who want to go to court because they've been denied the right to make their own nuclear bomb. His colleagues can't fathom why he would possibly take the case.

> SACK: Well, first, their security concerns are legitimate. Second, nuclear
> bombs are becoming more and more viable, easier to build, the
> world landscape one day will be dotted with them, why not Nan-
> tucket? And third, most importantly, when an island full of million-
> aires asks us to represent them, we do not refer them to another
> firm. (then) I need you three to arm me with research and legal
> analysis as to why Nantucket should have a bomb.

Ultimately the effort fails, of course, but not before sparking an in-court discussion of arms control treaties and the global nuclear threat. Another long shot, but an entertaining case, is the above-mentioned suit holding the U.S. government responsible for the genocide in Sudan.

Associate Lori Colson (Monica Potter) conjures up a novel way to frame the case.

LORI: In tort law, you see a guy lying on the side of the street, you have no obligation to pull over and help. But if you do pull over, you incur a duty to complete the rescue. The theory being other would-be rescuers pass by, thinking help is already on the scene.

LEWISTON: And?

LORI: The United States has declared a war on terrorism. We've talked the talk when it comes to Sudan, we've even given financial aid. Our theory of law would be analogous. Other countries have stayed out, thinking America is stepping in when we're not.

Of course, opposing counsel balks at the idea:

JOYNER: They're seeking damages for acts committed by a foreign government against a foreign citizenry. There is no jurisdiction here, no standing, and even if there were, any such lawsuit would be barred by sovereign immunity, which prohibits the U.S. government or its officials from being sued for foreign policy decisions.

Just as the judge looks ready to dismiss the case, Shirley Schmidt (Candice Bergen) steps up.

SCHMIDT: We know this lawsuit is a bit of a stretch.

JUDGE O'KEEFE: You understate it.

SCHMIDT: But the truth is . . . our country puts it out there. We will root out terrorism wherever it thrives. We elect our presidents on that theme. We go to war over it. Wherever oppression abounds, we get involved; it's almost become a motto. No one here denies an ethnic genocide is taking place in Sudan. Arab militia are wiping out the black population in Darfur. . . . Am I boring you?

JUDGE O'KEEFE: Ms. Schmidt, the court recognizes the atrocity. Why should the United States be held liable?

SCHMIDT: Well, if we're not going to do anything about it, maybe we should just say so. Lord knows, the world will understand, we've certainly got our hands full. But when our leaders do their bipartisan puffing, saying the genocide

> must end ... other countries think *we're* going to do
> something, *they* then stay out of it and in the end noth-
> ing gets done. While millions of people are being per-
> secuted. Maybe as a compromise, we could just get the
> U.S. government to declare for the record, "Hey. Not our
> problem." That way the world would be on notice that
> somebody else should play hero. I could try to sell that
> to my client.

JUDGE O'KEEFE: Mr. Joyner?

JOYNER: The United States' response to an ethnic genocide is cer-
                tainly not going to be, "Hey. Not our problem."

SCHMIDT: See, this is how other countries get confused.

I love this storyline—partly for Schmidt's smart snarkiness, partly
for Lori's inventive way in, but mostly because it is an excellent example
of another reality-bending technique of *Boston Legal*. For all the deli-
cious bravado, ethical breaches, sex scandals, and debauchery, I think
Boston Legal shines the most when finding a clever way to examine a
serious topical issue—and often that means going up against the U.S.
government.

In "Witches of Mass Destruction," for example, Shore represents a
woman suing the U.S. government because her brother was killed in Iraq.
The motion to dismiss is granted—but only after Shore gets a chance to
scrutinize the Iraq war and its human costs. And in "Nuts," Crane learns
he is on the federal no-fly list, giving him (and Shore) a chance to take
on Homeland Security.

In "Stick It," Shore comes to the aid of his assistant, Melissa Hughes,
whose act of political protest—refusing to pay her taxes—has landed her
in court. In defending her, he forgoes a tedious review of the Internal
Revenue Code or the 16th Amendment in favor of an impassioned closing argument examining the infringement of civil liberties in the name
of national security:

SHORE: When the weapons-of-mass-destruction thing turned out not
       to be true, I expected the American people to rise up. They
       didn't. Then when the Abu-Graib-torture thing surfaced, and it
       was revealed that our government participated in rendition, a
       practice where we kidnap people and turn them over to regimes
       who *specialize* in torture, I was sure *then* the American people

would be heard from. We stood mute. *Then* came the news that we jailed thousands of so-called terrorist suspects, locked them up without the right to a trial or even the right to confront their accusers. *Certainly* we would *never* stand for *that*. We did. And now it's been discovered the executive branch has been conducting *massive illegal* domestic surveillance on its own citizens. You and me. And I at least consoled myself—that *finally, finally* the American people will have had enough. Evidently, we haven't. (a beat) In fact, if the people of this country *have* spoken . . . the message is, "we're okay with it all." Torture, warrantless search and seizures, illegal wiretapping, prison without a fair trial or *any trial*, a war on false pretenses . . . we as a citizenry are apparently not offended. There are no demonstrations on college campuses . . . in fact there's no clear indication that young people even seem to notice. Well, Melissa Hughes noticed. (then) Now you might think, instead of withholding her taxes, she could've protested the old-fashioned way, made a placard and demonstrated at a presidential or vice-presidential appearance. But we've lost the right to that as well. The Secret Service can now declare free speech zones to contain, control, and in effect, criminalize protest. Stop for a second and try to fathom that. At a presidential rally, parade, or appearance, if you have on a *supportive* T-shirt, you can be there. If you're wearing or carrying something in *protest*, you can be removed. This in the United States of America. *This in the United States of America.* Is Melissa Hughes the only one embarrassed?

And in "Guantanamo by the Bay," Shore takes on the U.S. government again on behalf of an Arab man who was apprehended by the United States while on a humanitarian mission in Afghanistan. When he is abruptly released after two years, he wants to sue the United States for the torture he endured during his imprisonment. Shore is on board; the judge is not.

JUDGE FOLGER: Thirty seconds as to why I should entertain this lawsuit.

SHORE: OK. I realize the jurisdictional barriers are prohibitive, but Your Honor, we don't let little things like the law stand in our way in this great country. The law, for example, recognizes the Geneva Convention, but we say the hell with it. The law has very strict regulations on domestic wiretapping; we say the hell with it. The law

> says if you shoot somebody with a shotgun, mistaking him for a quail, you really should call the police, but ... we're cowboys, Judge, we do what we want, whether it's starting wars, changing Daylight Savings Time, we play it fast and loose in this country, we like to make it up as we go along.

Shirley Schmidt gets in on the fun in "Do Tell," where she represents a decorated general being booted from the Army after admitting he's gay.

SCHMIDT: Thank God for America, holding out for real values while Canada, England, Australia, Israel all welcome gays into their military. In fact, every member of NATO, with the exception of Turkey, says it's OK to be gay and in uniform, but what do they know? If you're going to impose democracy across the world, you've got to take a stand against civil liberties.

When Judge Brown rebukes her—"I will not have you attacking the United States of America"—she responds as follows:

SCHMIDT: Why the hell not? On this issue, we've taken the decidedly low road, we are not only tolerating intolerance, we're codifying it into national policy, how can we all not be ashamed?. . . As a practical matter, we've thrown 10,000 good soldiers out because they admitted being gay. Do you know how desperately the Army could use those men? As a practical matter, the policy stinks. As a moral one, I repeat, how can every one of us not be ashamed, and why the hell aren't *you*?

But by "No Brains Left Behind," even Shirley has had enough of taking on the government and tells Alan he can't sue the National Guard for failing to protect a pizza parlor from a flood.

SHORE: Of course we can. Isn't it just grand, Shirley? We do these things that seem completely absurd and then, incredibly, we manage to make them not only watchable, but fun and informative. Aren't you just dying to see how we do it this time?

It *is* grand. The show's bending of reality has let us dissect topics like congressional redistricting, the morning-after pill, Alzheimer's, Asperger's, cockfighting, bullfighting, salmon farming, euthanasia, abstinence-only education, subprime loans, video game addiction, gun control, and global warming—all of that while Crane shoots men and chases women, Shore conceals murder evidence and counsels the occasional client to flee, and the two of them recap their exploits every night via a poignant and/or comedic exchange over scotch and cigars.

Cross-dressing lawyer Clarence may have best summed up the uniqueness of Crane, Poole & Schmidt in a scene from the fourth season premiere, in which the straight-laced Carl Sack says he plans to turn CPS "into something resembling a law firm." Clarence responds that CPS's atypicality is its chief allure.

> One lawyer likes to purr. And hop. Partners and associates have sex with each other sometimes. We've got two men who take five minutes out of every single day to celebrate their friendship on a balcony. Now how many people do you know who actually do that? I occasionally throw on a dress and I like to sing. I don't want to be one of those lawyers at other firms choking on modesty and reasonableness. I'm surprised that you do. If your mission here is to make this into a normal law firm, I really hope you fail. For everybody's sake.

Hear, hear.

Endnotes

1. "Same-sex attraction disorder" is not a creation of the writers' room, but of real-world "reparative therapists." *See* http://www.guardian.co.uk/lifeandstyle/2004/apr/03/weekend.deccaaitkenhead.

2. For the point of view of *Boston Legal's* technical consultant, see Charles Rosenberg's chapter "27 Years as a Television Legal Adviser and Counting."

3. *See Ally McBeal, The Practice, Boston Public, Chicago Hope, Picket Fences,* etc.

4. Special thanks to real-life lawyer Megan Winter for her input here and elsewhere.

CHAPTER 23

Damages: The Truth Is Out There

CHRISTINE A. CORCOS

Even though popular-culture women lawyers, like the protagonists in *Damages,* have been on small and large screens for decades, they still struggle to be taken seriously. Either they seem bitchy, arrogant, and unfeminine because they succeed in a male-dominated profession, like Rosalind Shays on the 1990s drama *L.A. Law,* Ling Woo on *Ally McBeal,*[1] and Karen Crowder in the film *Michael Clayton* (2007), or they are criticized because they are easily intimidated, overly feminine, or not quite smart enough, like Abby Perkins on *L.A. Law* and Reggie Love in *The Client.* Such women fail to maintain personal relationships, lose custody of their children, or sacrifice everything just to win in court, and in the process become objects of pity to their families and friends. In other formulations, they fail to maintain business relationships, lose valuable time in building their careers, lack understanding of the "rules of the game," and become objects of pity to their colleagues and a disappointment to their families and friends.[2] These images are the common stuff of legal TV and movie drama, and to some extent they have the ring of truth.[3]

In many legal dramas, the filmmaker or creator of the television series is interested in

Damages

Aired:
- July 24, 2007–present, FX

Cast:
- Glenn Close (Patty Hewes)
- Ted Danson (Arthur Frobisher)
- Zeljko Ivanek (Ray Fiske)
- Rose Byrne (Ellen Parsons)
- Anastasia Griffith (Katie Connor)
- Philip Bosco (Hollis Nye)

Awards:
- Glenn Close, Golden Globe Award for Best Performance by an Actress in a Television Series—Drama (2008)
- Glenn Close, Emmy for Outstanding Lead Actress in a Drama Series (2008)
- Ted Danson, Emmy nomination for Outstanding Supporting Actor in a Drama Series (2008)
- Zeljko Ivanek, Emmy for Outstanding Supporting Actor in a Drama Series (2008)

the impact of the legal system on the lawyer, on the client, or on society at large. Normally, she has two hours in a film or one hour in a television episode to examine that impact. In the television show *Damages*, the creators use an entire TV season—13 episodes—to measure this impact.[4] Further, they tell a related set of stories during that period.

Spoiler alert: Briefly, the first season of *Damages* revolves around a class action lawsuit brought by the clients of Hewes and Associates against Arthur Frobisher for fraud. The opening scenes of the series show Ellen Parsons, an associate with the firm, covered in blood, a scene that doesn't initially seem relevant to the lawsuit. Patty Hewes, a legal barracuda, hires newly graduated Ellen Parsons for her firm, not because she is a promising young attorney (although she is), but because she is engaged to a young physician whose sister Katie, a caterer, is a prospective witness in the lawsuit. Ellen's mentor, an older attorney named Hollis Nye, warns her not to take the position with Patty and offers Ellen a comparable position at his firm, but her ambition wins out and she accepts the Hewes offer. Obviously, she knows nothing about Patty's agenda.

Patty thinks Ellen can "deliver" Katie as a witness. However, Frobisher has already arranged to finance Katie's new restaurant, which makes her skittish about testifying. Meanwhile, another mysterious witness, Gregory Malina, with whom Katie has had a one-night stand, turns up to manipulate Katie further but is subsequently murdered. Eventually, Ellen's fiancé David is also murdered, and someone tries to kill Ellen in Patty's apartment. Now we can associate this event with the opening scenes of the series showing Ellen, covered in blood, staggering from the apartment she shares with David. She is eventually arrested for the crime. Along the way, we see Patty's legal antagonist and Frobisher's lead attorney, Ray Fiske, commit suicide, and one of the shareholders try to kill Frobisher. It's safe to say that *Damages* is not *Perry Mason*.

Damages could easily be a trivial, trite television show. Indeed, a good deal of the show's plot is ordinary: a ruthless CEO makes off fraudulently with billions, aided by flunkies that include a stereotypical Southern lawyer,[5] and an ambitious attorney is hired by defrauded shareholders. The subplot consists of the awakening of a naïve young woman attorney (Ellen Parsons) to the distasteful ways of the legal world. Some of the episodes feel padded, and the storytelling—which uses flashbacks to show the viewer various events, including the murder and other situ-

Courtesy of Photofest.

DAMAGES

Patty Hewes (Glenn Close) tells Ellen Parsons (Rose Byrne) she'll pay next time.

ations involving the run-up to the shareholder suit—can be confusing. Discussing the show is difficult, if not impossible, without explaining the plot, so if you haven't seen the show, and don't want to know what happens, stop reading now.

In addition, if one is looking for "real law," *Damages* is not the place to find it. The show does not, for example, emphasize accuracy in its discussion of the rules of discovery or the Federal Rules of Civil Procedure. What *Damages* does do is examine how one lawsuit affects the lives of everyone it touches—lawyers and nonlawyers alike—and how the legal system affects lawyers. How does knowledge of the way the legal system works affect a lawyer's moral compass? Does knowledge corrupt? Or does the corruption come first? Do corrupt people seek out the law in order to facilitate their own penchant for bad behavior? And what happens when yet another ambitious, bitchy, talented, and manipulative attorney persuades herself that nothing is as important as the good of her clients and the good of her family, and that somehow she is best placed to decide what those values are? What makes *Damages* interesting is that no side has a monopoly on morality. The defendant is a powerful and rather unattractive man who has apparently defrauded his workers and investors. They need a champion; however, their champion is someone who is herself morally unattractive. And the defendant does love his family. At the same time, the nasty lawyer for the plaintiffs has lost a baby in childbirth, a little girl whom she still mourns. The story, like life, is not simple.

The lawyers in *Damages* all suffer from some kind of emotional trauma brought on, suggests the show, by the practice of law and the effort of balancing the demands of the law against the demands of life. Further, because this show is not really about law, but is a thriller about morality and justice, Ellen is ultimately on a search for truth. Of course, most real-life attorneys will concur that the law is about settling disputes, not about finding truth. Patty tells Ellen, "the truth is out there," echoing Fox Mulder, another popular-culture character who sometimes wandered off in unreality on the *X-Files*. Like Fox Mulder, Patty is sometimes not believable. The truth may be "out there," but as the screenwriters portray her, so is Patty Hewes. If we, the viewers, want "truth," we must piece it together "out there"—outside the courtroom—because that is where we will find it.

One of Patty's other beliefs is "trust no one," another creed she shares with Fox Mulder, although Patty seems not to take it too literally. She trusts her subordinates to do her bidding, even when it puts her in ethical danger. One display of this is when she confides a dangerous file to Ellen's keeping after Ray Fiske's suicide, even though she has already fired Ellen for contacting a potential witness without permission.

Ellen Parsons originally comes to Hewes & Associates relatively undamaged, happy in her relationship with a young medical resident, and pleased with the deal she has negotiated with Patty. Her former boss and current mentor, Hollis Nye, warns her against accepting an offer from Patty, and, when she repeatedly contacts him for reassurance and then assistance, he tries not to remind her of her folly. He seems to be the only lawyer untouched by the emotional drama that disfigures the other characters in *Damages*, but as we discover in the first season's final episodes, he is working for the government in a sting operation in an attempt to catch Patty in some sort of crime. By the end of the first season, Ellen's most trusted friends are either dead (David) or not what they seem (Hollis Nye). As Patty has warned her, she can truly "trust no one."

Ellen herself ultimately becomes disenchanted with the law because she finally understands that it is not a good vehicle for determining truth. In a telling exchange with her father, she counsels him not to be forthright with opposing counsel during a deposition about the circumstances of a traffic accident in which he was at fault. This advice appalls him, even though it is good advice and by not heeding it, he will pay dearly.

The clients in the show are equally damaged. Katie Connor, Ellen's future sister-in-law, is a victim of a seemingly accidental relationship with Gregory Malina, who has a relationship with Patty's antagonist, Arthur Frobisher. The relationship destroys her life. Why should such things be? And what are the limits of the law? Ellen knows intellectually that the law does not provide a remedy for all wrongs, but it takes her personal dealings with Katie to finally understand what this concept means. Patty refuses to assist a frightened Katie unless Katie "deals" with her—that is, unless Katie gives Patty the information Patty wants about Arthur Frobisher. Patty senses that Katie is lying. Ellen is oblivious to that possibility; if she had been aware of it, Ellen could never have been as hard-nosed with Katie as Patty is. In making Patty so implacable, the show makes the character extremely unlikeable, even possibly unredeemable, in a way that a male lawyer would not be. Thus, when Katie leaves Patty's office in distress, perhaps facing violence at the hands of Arthur Frobisher's hit men, Patty seems even more unlikable. We expect women to be kind and understanding and certainly not to put others in harm's way. Consequently, when Patty smiles a feline smile as Ellen objects, we are even more discomfited.

While *Damages* amplifies and reaffirms the traditional stereotype of the nasty female lawyer, it also seems to create a successful female lawyer, albeit one who at the end of the first season seems ready to abandon the law. We see Ellen stumbling around the streets of Manhattan covered in blood in the first scenes of the first episodes, and we know something dreadful has happened. Very soon, we know that her fiancé is dead and that she is the chief suspect. Of course, she *cannot* be the guilty party—to make her the guilty party would be to shatter entirely too many conventions for television, since she is the heroine of the drama.[6] Ellen asserts herself and uses what she has learned as Patty's protégée. "Protégée" (French for "protected one") is an ironic term to apply to Ellen. Patty has never really protected Ellen, and very few other characters in *Damages* are willing or able to do so—not even Ellen's parents. Patty, the lioness, doesn't really believe that the cub Ellen is dangerous, but the cub quickly develops claws of her own.

Damages is also about a woman's use of power: Patty's use of legal power against Arthur, her use of power within her firm against her associates, and her use of power against other attorneys outside the firm. When a package containing an explosive device turns up at her office, the security detail hired to protect her asks Patty whether anyone in her past might want to harm her. She admits that there is someone, a defendant against whom she won an important case. "Taking power away from a man is a dangerous thing. Someone always pays."

Patty knows that Ellen's engagement party is set for a Friday evening, and informs a senior attorney in the firm (Tate Donovan) that she questions Ellen's priorities. In order to exert her power over Ellen, she tells Ellen that she wants the judge in the Frobisher case to "put a name to the face." She tells Ellen to hand in the opposition brief personally, knowing that the judge is holding a settlement conference in another case that day and is notorious for long conferences. Ellen stays at the courthouse for hours, missing her party. This ploy reasserts Patty's power over Ellen—Ellen will not have both a happy private life with her physician fiancé and a successful career as a young attorney if Patty decides to deny them to her. Clearly, Patty sees Ellen as a rival, and plans, for whatever reason, to test her, if not to destroy her outright. Hollis Nye's prediction to Ellen in the first episode—that Patty will be a danger to Ellen—is already being proven correct.

Consider also how Ellen tries to mimic Patty's use of power in her own relationship with her future husband. She tries unsuccessfully to get David to choose their wedding cake and to participate in social occasions at Hewes & Associates. Like many career women, Ellen wants to make David a part of her professional life as well as powerful in their personal life. David dislikes Patty and only reluctantly agrees to go to dinner with her, regardless of the fact that this might cost Ellen professionally. He complains about Patty's husband's lack of conversation. However, were the situation reversed, he might well expect Ellen to go to dinner with his supervisor and make no complaint. That David may be right to dislike Patty is not the issue. His intransigence, should the pair marry, might have forced the two to decide whose career should take precedence, and it might well have been his, as his earning power might have been higher and because he had already indicated that he did not like Ellen's dominant attitude. Ultimately, Ellen and David call off their wedding, partly because Ellen refuses to take a back seat to David's career, and partly because she discovers that he has had an affair during their engagement. Ellen's discovery that she is powerful in this way—that she can make the decision to leave such a relationship—gives her the confidence to make certain decisions once she is under arrest for David's murder.

Patty's attempt to strong-arm Ray Fiske so he will push his client into settling the Frobisher case backfires. She miscalculates the extent to which Fiske is committed both to the law and to his conscience. Believing in herself so fervently, Patty cannot believe that Fiske is anything but Frobisher's tool, but she is wrong. Rather than collapse under the weight of Patty's blackmail, Fiske kills himself in her office. The choice of her office, rather than some other locale, is symbolic—he clearly wants to implicate her emotionally in the deed.

Similarly, Patty's attempt to control her son Michael is only partly successful. Although he does not accept her offer to emancipate himself, as she correctly anticipates—the notion of supporting oneself at the age of 17 is a frightening one for any coddled teenager—he still harbors a great deal of resentment toward her. We can presume that only some of this resentment is the result of teenaged hostility. Some of it may be the result of well-deserved anger of a son toward his manipulative mother, which may never disappear.

The results of Patty's dissembling are everywhere, including in her marriage. As she tells Ellen, "A man should *want* to be in charge." She confides that she "dumped" her college boyfriend because, after he put her through law school, she found that his passive nature "disgusted" her. Whether this story is true or not is irrelevant. It reveals that Patty will manipulate anyone to get what she wants. But what *does* she want? In life, she wants to win for herself, and at law, she wants to win for her clients. In this particular case, her clients are the little people whom she believes Arthur Frobisher has defrauded. If she cannot win ethically, or at least legally, then she will win in any way she can, and she does not believe that the law should stand in her way. The ends always justify the means. If murdering Ellen, or anyone else, is the way to win the case, then she will murder in order to do justice—or at least, her version of justice.

Ultimately Patty is the kind of person from whom the laws are designed to protect us. It does not matter to her if she is technically on the side of the person she deems to be a threat. If she perceives that person as a risk, she acts. She may even like that person—she certainly likes Ellen—but she will still use the tools that she has to eliminate the problem she perceives. This moral and ethical flaw is the danger that Hollis Nye warns Ellen about in the first episode of the show. He tells Ellen to stay away from Patty, saying that she will not be strong enough to protect herself from the threat Patty represents. Few people could, and certainly not a young and inexperienced woman like Ellen. Ultimately, in order to free herself from suspicion that she murdered her fiancé, Ellen must turn to Patty. In order to discover who actually did kill him, she returns to Patty's firm and asks for her help. Patty believes that Ellen still does not know the depths of her betrayal. In the final episode of the first season, Ellen prepares to hide her own knowledge of that betrayal, and uses Patty's resources to search for the killer. The question now becomes whether Ellen herself can remain resolute or whether she is irreparably damaged, since she has lost her taste for the law. Does she now want justice, or revenge?

Damages presents us with serious moral questions about lawyers who are damaged and inflict damage themselves. But which came first? At the end of the first season of *Damages*, left standing are the morally bankrupt Patty Hewes, Hollis Nye (who seems to be opposing Ellen's interests by working with the government), and the now bereft but resolute Ellen Parsons. Ray Fiske, who finally found his ethical compass after having lost it due to years of zealous advocacy, comes to the conclusion that the only way to absolve himself for his past misdeeds is to commit suicide.

The story line of *Damages* is complex,[7] confusing, and emotional. It illustrates once again that power corrupts and that those with both knowledge and power will inevitably do damage, both to others and to themselves. They may not do so intentionally. In fact, like Ellen, they may set out with the best of motives and intend only to do good. But the whole purpose of the law is to protect us—both from those who would substitute their knowledge and power for law in an effort to do evil, and from those who would do so in an effort to do justice. This theme is the driving narrative of *Damages*.

Endnotes

1. See Phil Meyer's chapter "Revisiting *L.A. Law*" and Cassandra Sharp's chapter "*Ally McBeal*—Life and Love in the Law."

2. For more on the image of the "female lawyer" stereotype, see Christine A. Corcos, *We Don't Want Advantages: The Woman Lawyer Hero and Her Quest for Power in Popular Culture*, 53 SYRACUSE L. REV. 1225 (2003).

3. AMERICAN BAR ASSOCIATION COMMISSION ON WOMEN IN THE PROFESSION, THE UNFINISHED AGENDA (2001), *available at* http://www.abanet.org/ftp/pub/women/unfinishedagenda.pdf.

4. *Murder One* pioneered the technique of serializing a single legal case over an entire season. See Michael Asimow's chapter "*Murder One:* The Adversary System Meets Celebrity Justice."

5. Zeljko Ivanek's Southern attorney could be a twin of Charles Ludlam's Lamar Parmental in *The Big Easy* (1987).

6. The novel or film that uses the device of the "unreliable narrator" is interesting but frustrating for the audience. See, for example, AGATHA CHRISTIE, THE MURDER OF ROGER ACKROYD (1926).

7. In an attempt to explain what is going on, the show's creators provided a Hewes and Associates Web site at http://www.hewesassociates.com/full/ (last visited Jan. 18, 2009).

CHAPTER 24

French Television Lawyers in *Avocats et Associés*

BARBARA VILLEZ

French television audiences have been exposed to so many imported American legal dramas over the last 20-odd years that they know more about American lawyers and courtroom procedures than they do about their own. Delinquents expect the reading of their *Miranda* rights and everyone calls judges "Your Honor." Actually, there is no such obligatory warning in the French system, and judges must be called *Monsieur le president/Madame la présidente*, because most courts are presided over by a panel of judges.

It is clear that these ideas come from contact with the American legal system through cinema and (especially) through television. Most of the series in the *Law & Order* universe have been broadcast on French terrestrial channels, usually in the afternoon or late evening. *Ally McBeal*, *The Practice*, *Judging Amy*, *JAG*, and even *Matlock* have been seen on terrestrial channels, usually dubbed in French. Additionally, they occasionally appear on cable in English with French subtitles. The French had access to *L.A. Law* in the early 1990s as well as Lumet's *100 Centre Street*, which was called *Tribunal Central*, losing something in translation. Cable and pay

Avocats et Associés

Aired:
- October 23, 1998–present (scheduled to end in 2009), France 2

Cast:
- François-Eric Gendron (Robert Carvani)
- Victor Garrivier (Antoine Zelder)
- Micky Sébastien (Michelle Berg)
- Frédéric Gorny (Laurent Zelder)
- Muriel Combeau (Gladys Dupré)
- Julie Debazac (Caroline Varennes)

Awards:
- 1999 PROCIREP award for Best Producer of the Year
- 1999 Best 52-minute series, Festival of TV fiction, St. Tropez, for episode seven, "Groupes sanguins"
- 2004 Best series (Access Day Time category), Festival of TV fiction, St Tropez, episode "KpoT"
- 2006 Award for Best Producer of TV fiction for 2005 (jointly with Le Film Français), International Festival of Television Film, Luchon

television stations have brought recent shows like *Boston Legal* and *Damages* to the public with virtually no delay.

Very few French productions dealing with law and justice have given priority to entertainment over information. Consequently, the vast majority of French programs on aspects of the legal system have been documentaries. However, the French, like all audiences, seek entertainment from television, and the fictional law shows offered have been mostly American. There have been a few short-lived attempts to produce local fictional law shows in the last two years, including one using the *Law & Order* format. Yet, despite the familiarity of this structure to French audiences, the local show failed to get the ratings needed for its survival. In fact, the program was never feasible because the *Law & Order* format does not correspond to how French criminal procedure is organized.

French and American Legal Procedure

There are many differences between the common law system, especially in its American version, and the civil law (also called "Roman law") system that exists in France. One of the most obvious differences lies in the roles of judges and lawyers in court. French judges are not merely umpires during trials, as common law judges are. Instead, they are at the center of all debates and discussions. It is they who question witnesses and lawyers. All answers and testimonies are directed to them, not to jurors. In criminal trials at the *Cour d'Assises* (the tribunal for serious offences), the nine members of the jury sit on either side of a three-judge panel and they all arrive at a verdict together. There is no cross-examination as in American trials; instead, there are specific moments when lawyers may address the court. If lawyers want to ask a witness a question, they must obtain permission from the principal judge. In civil trials, witnesses do not even appear in court. If there are ambiguities or discrepancies in their depositions, the judges will call them in for an interview, but this does not take place in court. Outside of the *plaidoirie* (closing statements), a rhetorical exercise that is often seen more as a formality than as a determining moment in the proceedings, French lawyers are much less active than their common-law counterparts when defending their clients in court.

Another important difference is the organization of time in a case. The French system is inquisitorial and based on a written procedure. It is not adversarial, as it is in the United States where the testimony and oral arguments made in court determine the outcome of a trial. In the French system, the trial is not the most important moment of the process,[1] but is used to confirm the information contained in the *dossier* (file) before a final decision can be reached. It is the work of a special judge, *le juge d'instruction*, to gather information about the crime and the principal suspect. He or she must collect facts that can establish the suspect's guilt as well as innocence. If the former outweigh the latter, the *juge d'instruction* will give the dossier to the prosecutor, who will bring the case to court. The work of the *juge d'instruction* during this pretrial period takes much longer in France than do police investigations in the United States. This is because the American trial is where truth is sought, but in France, the dossier already contains the results of questioning witnesses, weighing the facts, and coming to conclusions. The *juge d'instruction* is an administrative officer and is considered a specialist in truth finding. Once the *dossier* is believed to be complete, the case can go to trial, which rarely lasts more than a few days. The requirements of this procedural system have a major impact on any attempts to create French courtroom fiction.

In France, trials are essentially administrative proceedings, and the real intrigue of the case occurs in the investigative pretrial period. It is logical, therefore, that nationally televised law dramas revolve around either the police and their fight against crime, or the work of the *juge d'instruction*. Very few series use the point of view of lawyers, and even fewer deal with litigation. It is also true that in France, lawyers are traditionally unpopular figures, while *juges d'instruction* have traditionally been seen (at least until recently) as the lone servants of justice, *les petits juges*, independent of the judicial and political machines.[2] They work alone to get at the heart of a violation against society, disclose corporate corruption, or battle hierarchical obstacles. Lawyers, on the other hand, have always been portrayed in French cinema and literature as slimy, greedy, and perhaps drunken villains, and this has carried over to their portrayal on television.

Avocats et Associés

Given all the police dramas and the strong position of the *juge d'instruction* in French popular culture, the 11-season series *Avocats et Associés* merits special attention because it centers on the work of lawyers in a firm.

The series uses their relations with other members of the profession as a frequent, although not unique, means of shedding light on their role in the legal system. However, the main characters are all lawyers. Television viewers see them in their professional roles as well as in their private lives, which helps the audience to know who these people really are. In addition, the series is one of the only shows, if not the only one, to deal with civil disputes, especially family law, as well as the usual, more easily dramatized criminal defense cases.

Two partners run the small firm of Zelder & Carvani in Paris. There are two other lawyers working for the firm as well as an office manager, a secretary, and a receptionist. The firm is located in a bourgeois building in a posh area of Paris and the office space is a large apartment, as is often the case with doctors' and lawyers' offices in France. Small firms cannot specialize in particular areas of the law and Zelder & Carvani is no exception, nor is there really a division in this firm between those practicing criminal law and those handling civil cases. Antoine Zelder, the older partner, is close to retirement. He is kind but demanding and is well respected in his profession. His partnership of 10 years with his good friend Robert Carvani, about 15 or 20 years Zelder's junior, is successful, although there are sometimes conflicting discourses. They often talk about problems like paying the bills and needing more "big" clients, yet there is clearly too much work for each lawyer and recruitment is a frequent topic. Carvani starts out in the series as a serious, although playful, professional who is much more reluctant than Zelder to let in other partners. Michelle Berg, 40-ish and a good lawyer, is single and impatient to become a partner. She leaves the firm briefly for a better offer elsewhere, but the questionable ethics at this new firm quickly bring her back to Zelder & Carvani, which is finally willing to give her partnership status. The fourth lawyer in the firm is Zelder's son, Laurent. He is about 30 and may be gay. The beginning of the series finds him not particularly enthusiastic about his career choice.

Caroline Varennes

The first episode opens on the first day at the firm for Caroline Varennes, a new lawyer, fresh out of law school, who has just been hired. She shares an office with Robert for a while and learns the ropes from him and from the serious mistakes she makes at the beginning

© photographer Aurélien FAIDY/EPP.

AVOCATS ET ASSOCIÉS
Robert Carvani (François-Eric Gendron) and the lawyers of Zelder & Carvani give audiences a view of what happens in French courtrooms.

of the show. She comes to Paris, and to the firm, full of ideals and fleeing some secrets. Caroline's first case is a custody suit between a boy's foster parents and his real mother, who has come back for him.[3] In another case, she is assigned to do legal aid in the prosecution of a minor drug dealer. The drug dealer begs Caroline to warn his wife, who is about to give birth, of his arrest. He pleads with her, but she tells him (and the television viewers) that a lawyer is not allowed to serve as an intermediary between a person in jail and the outside world. In France, a detained person does not have the American right to a phone call. If the detainee is allowed to contact someone, the police make the call. Caroline finally agrees to help him, knowing full well—and telling French audiences—that should this gesture be discovered, she risks being disbarred.[4]

The first season and the role of Caroline are very interesting because both display a concerted effort to rectify some of the public's confusion about the differences between French and American lawyers. After years of *Perry Mason*, *Matlock*, and *Boston Legal*, French television viewers (and potential clients) have come to believe that their lawyer should be a knight in shining armor, sacrificing his or her life and time to save the poor, the innocent, and the helpless. In the first episode of *Avocats et Associés*, Caroline goes to the residence of the natural mother in the custody case. She questions the *concierge* (a mixture of superintendent, security guard, and housekeeper) to find out about the mother's character and her visitors. At a morning meeting, reminiscent of those that start the characters' day in *L.A. Law* and *Ally McBeal*, she informs Zelder and Carvani of the progress of her case. Instead of the approval she expects to hear from her bosses, Zelder furiously informs her that investigation is not the role of a French lawyer. "What do you think you are? A social worker? You watch too many American television series. Stick to the facts in the *dossier* and from now on respect the deontology of the profession."[5] In a later episode, Caroline defends a married man accused of killing a young girl. Caroline suggests engaging a private detective to help find evidence that she could use to rebut that found by the *juge d'instruction* in charge of the case. Again, when she reports this idea to Zelder he starts screaming and slamming doors. "This is not Los Angeles. Get back to work!"[6]

Caroline is a very useful character because as she learns the ropes, the audience learns about the French legal system and especially about what is expected of a French lawyer. Information about the obligations and responsibilities of the job are often slipped into dialogue, especially during the first season of the series. When Zelder finds out that his son, who left town for a few days without telling anyone where he was going, neglected the deadline for filing a client's appeal, he screams that the client can sue them for malpractice. "We are liable. That is the law!" he yells, to which Carvani reassuringly shoots back, "The insurance will cover it."

Teaching the Audience What French Lawyers Do

The audience sees the lawyers in all the places where they intervene professionally. They plead in court, of course, but courtroom scenes take up less time than they would in an American series because there are many other formal situations in which robed lawyers represent their clients before judges. They accompany clients to the *juge d'instruction*'s office, where an American viewer would be surprised to see that only the lawyers appear in robes and not the judge. Scenes also show lawyers carrying out legal aid defenses or pleading before a panel of lay judges (also not robed) of the *Conseil Prud'hommes*, a labor arbitration court. Lawyers appear in ordinary dress when they meet with clients in the offices of the firm or at prison.

The requirements, behavior codes, and hierarchical conventions of the profession are a constant leitmotif: Lawyers call each other lawyers "My dear colleague" while screaming threats at them; judges and clients call lawyers "*Maître*," which would translate loosely as "counsel" but really means "master of a trade." There is a lot of smiling hypocrisy, as well as some courteous backbending and backstabbing. The polite distrust that is apparent between lawyers and judges is not just made for television. It comes in part from the fact that they do not belong to the same camp. There comes a point in the study of law where some students decide to stay at university and prepare for the Bar, while others choose to take a competitive exam to enter the *École Nationale de la Magistrature* (the Judicial Training School). These individuals will become either prosecutors or judges. "*Magistrats*" and lawyers are therefore not members of the same club.

The Firm of Zelder & Carvani

Private and professional spaces constantly overlap in *Avocats et Associés*. There is so little time for outside relations that the characters cultivate most of their romantic interests with their fellow associates or, occasionally, other members of the profession. The firm of Zelder & Carvani seems at times to be a big and rather dysfunctional family. The lawyers spend much of their time together, arrive early, leave late, and sometimes sleep in the office. What goes on in each one's private life is a subject of conversation and interest to everyone else. Teasing and the common French wisecracks, thrown nonchalantly around like hot potatoes, are frequent fare, no matter what one's position in the firm is. Nevertheless, there is kindness also. At times, the characters show approval as well as concern for others. Zelder, a widower at the end of season two, and Carvani, divorced by season three, spend their time together talking about cases, the firm's finances, and women, whom they never seem to understand. Office space is used for meetings, interviews, confrontations, and cocktail parties.

A regular parade of clients passes through the series, sometimes arriving at the firm in the middle of a row or an escapade behind closed doors. Clients range from moneyed litigants and old family friends to neighbors, ghetto delinquents, and members of the government. Carvani's cynicism grows toward clients he seems to have little esteem for, and Gladys Dupré, recruited at the end of season two, becomes a regular troublemaker, using unethical tactics that often turn simple cases into bloody battles. She, too, does some investigating but keeps quiet about it. As the program progresses, its representation of clients' attitudes toward lawyers becomes more critical and more in keeping with the traditional image lawyers bear in French culture. It should not go unnoticed that it is a foreigner, a British client seeking an amicable divorce after a long marriage, who strikes a heavily accented and brutal blow to the image of the lawyer: "You lawyers, you are so obsessed with making money that you forget the human side of things. You don't even know what that word means."[7]

With the exception of Laurent, during the first two seasons the lawyers of the firm show caring and concern for clients and their problems. Carvani tells Caroline that his humanitarian side makes him feel younger. It is perhaps also a way to make himself more appealing to Caroline, whose hand he will ultimately ask in marriage, but only after she has become engaged to someone else. Laurent's interest in and concern for his clients' stories develops as Robert's "social side" hardens. Laurent takes his profession more seriously and outwardly becomes closer to his father at the same time as he finally brings order to his personal life, coming out of the closet and falling in love with another lawyer.

The series asks questions about the role of the lawyer in modern French society. Concerns are expressed about what makes a good lawyer and how to win indefensible cases given the constraints of the profession. Between old-school Antoine Zelder's devotion to exemplary ethics and Gladys's efforts to deglamorize the job for intern Claire, there are bouts of worry and guilt ("It's not your fault"), determination ("I will defend this case!"), and self-preservation ("If we begin to care about our clients, we're doomed"[8]).

Correcting Misperceptions about French Law

The observation that French citizens have been quickly acquiring an American legal culture through television, as well as annoyance over people calling judges "Your Honor," led to concerted efforts by the French government to encourage production companies to do something to correct the situation. Several different measures have been taken. The production of documentaries has flourished. Some explain the roles of the different types of judges in the French system, or explain the legal profession, while others tell the stories of particular cases.

Historically, cameras had never been allowed in French courtrooms except at trials of crimes against humanity, such as that of Klaus Barbie. Journalists were only able to interview parties and their counsel outside the courtrooms, in the corridors, or on the famous stairway of the *Palais de Justice*. These were also the only places where photographs could be taken. A commission was set up under the authority of Judge Elisabeth Linden to determine the advantages and disadvantages of filming trials. The 2005 report did not come to a clear conclusion, but following publication of the study, permission was granted in some cases to allow cameras in the courtroom under specific circumstances and with the permission of the presiding judges. One of the findings of the commission concerned the "right to be forgotten," which is denied de facto to people whose trials appear on television. This is also true of someone whose story is the basis of a documentary, especially if it is repeatedly rebroadcast.

For a time, more attention was also given to law-themed fiction. The cast of *Avocats et Associés* was invited to a breakfast at the Ministry of Justice in Paris. Made-for-television movies about legal professionals became slightly more frequent. However, mistakes were deliberately inserted in the courtroom scenes; for example, jurors sat in jury boxes. It would seem that producers were too concerned with giving audiences what they might expect after watching so many American legal dramas. In 2006, a new series, *Engrenage* ("The Spiral"), was produced by Canal Plus (a private channel that often coproduces cinematic works). It focused on the different legal professions that interacted on one case. The show's gory forensic work was clearly an effort to emulate American series. The first season of *Engrenage* received good ratings and was even imported to the United Kingdom by the BBC.

In its first seasons, *Avocats et Associés*, which will end in 2009 after 115 episodes, was more efficient than other shows in correcting these misconceptions about French law and the legal professions. This was fortunate because the series consistently obtained relatively high ratings during those seasons. It may be coincidence that after the death of Victor

Garrivier, who played Antoine Zelder, ratings began to decline. A two-hour media event created by the cross-over of this program with a popular police series, *PJ* (*Police Judiciaire*), sent the ratings temporarily back up.

It is difficult to say whether *Avocats et Associés*, like *L.A. Law* and *Ally McBeal*, has had an effect on law school enrollment. Some French lawyers, however, have been noticeably influenced by American television lawyers. They are directing their closing arguments more clearly and dramatically at the lay members of judging panels in court. French lawyers may not yet be pulling white rabbits out of hats, as Denny Crane would advise, but they have begun to realize that their experiences could make the courtroom a livelier source of television storytelling.

Endnotes

1. The French word for this stage of procedure is *procès*. It comes from the word *"processus,"* meaning process, rather than from anything resembling "trial."

2. The recent Outreau cases did much to tarnish the image of the *juge d'instruction*. In December 2000, suspicions of sexual abuse of children in the town of Outreau were reported to the regional social services. Two months later, an investigation was opened and a recently recruited young *juge d'instruction*, Fabrice Burgaud, was put in charge of the case.

A Mr. and Mrs. Delay and several of their neighbors were placed under investigation. Mrs. Delay made a number of declarations to Judge Burgaud. They led to the identification of about 20 children who had been victims of sexual abuse and, by mid-November 2001, the detention of 13 people. Among them were a court officer and his wife, a taxi driver, and a priest. Several detainees were parents of identified victims. One suspect committed suicide in prison in June 2002.

Judge Burgaud was transferred to Paris in early 2002, but on the basis of the information in his dossier, 17 people were indicted. At the trial in the Cour d'Assises of Pas-de-Calais (a department of France), Mrs. Delay admitted committing the crimes and also confessed to having lied to Judge Burgaud. Her husband and another codefendant also pleaded guilty. They were sentenced to prison. Seven of the other defendants were acquitted but six were found guilty.

The seven acquitted persons demanded that the government recognize the grave error committed against them, and the Minister of Justice offered a formal apology along with damages for each. The six convicted of the crimes appealed in November 2005, and two of the children retracted their accusations against the priest. Mrs. Delay's lies to Judge Burgaud were exposed and he was accused of having been manipulated by her. The six defendants were acquitted in December

2005, and the president of France, Jacques Chirac, presented a public apology to all 13 defendants acquitted.

In January 2006, a special legislative commission was created to investigate what had gone wrong and what judicial reforms might be necessary. Exceptionally, the hearings were broadcast on national television. Judge Burgaud claimed to have carried out his role conscienciously and honestly, but the trials of Outreau remain in the public mind as a scandal that severely damaged the image of the *juge d'instruction.*

3. *"Premier dossier,"* first aired Oct. 23, 1998 (season one).

4. *"Radiée,"* first aired Nov. 6, 1998 (season one).

5. *"Premier dossier," supra* note 3.

6. *"L'affaire Cindy,"* first aired Nov. 12, 1999 (season two).

7. *"L'Ogresse,"* first aired Mar. 16, 2001 (season four).

8. *Id.*

CHAPTER 25

Divorce in Your Living Room: TV Lawyers in Spain's Transition to Democracy

ANJA LOUIS

When looking for heroic lawyers in Spain, an obvious point of reference is the transition from dictatorship to democracy. Given the reluctance of the old guard to cede power, the interim period—generally known as the "Spanish Transition"—between General Franco's death (1975) and the Socialist Party's (PSOE) election victory (1982) was a time of intense social tension. The process of democratization rested very much on the shoulders of a new generation. Young and innocent lawyers (and those not so young, but politically above suspicion) were called upon to participate in, and construct, democracy. What better way to celebrate heroic lawyers than with a television series set in one of the most challenging times of recent Spanish history, in which democracy was in the making and law was instrumental, both real and imagined, in major social changes of the time?

The Constitution of 1978 proclaimed democratic principles after almost 40 years of dictatorship. In 1981, the Divorce Law allowed full dissolution of marriage rather than judicial

Anillos de oro

Aired:

- October 7, 1983–
  December 30, 1983, RTVE

Cast:

- Ana Diosdado
  (Lola Martínez Luque)

- Imanol Arias
  (Ramón San Juan)

- Aurora Redondo
  (*doña* Trini)

- Xavier Elorriaga
  (Lola's husband Enrique)

- Nina Ferrer
  (Lola's daughter Sonia)

- Antonio Vico
  (Lola's son Dani)

- Helena Carbajosa
  (Lola's daughter Pepa)

Awards:

- Ana Diosdado, Fotogramas de Plata Award for Best TV Performer (1983)

- Ana Diosdado, Teleprograma de Oro Award for Best Actress (1984)

- Imanol Arias, Teleprograma de Oro Award for Best Actor (1984)

- Teleprograma de Oro Award for Best Spanish Series (1984)

- Teleprograma de Oro Award for Best Spanish Series (1984)

separation. This groundbreaking new law exacerbated tensions between the Catholic Church and the state, and hence became the issue of a wide-ranging public debate. The TV show *Anillos de oro* ("Wedding Rings") convincingly captures this *Zeitgeist* of change. It is the story of two heroic lawyers, Lola Martínez Luque and Ramón San Juan, who personify social progress by setting up a law firm to specialize in divorce cases. Each episode of *Anillos de oro* deals with a particular divorce case, and each narrative guides the viewer through the social reality and social change that the Divorce Law of 1981 brought about. It might seem odd that the 13 episodes of this highly acclaimed and award-winning TV show of the Spanish Transition should concentrate on one issue only—that of divorce—but this attests to the national anxiety about the supposed breakdown of marriage and its consequences for the family as the most basic structural unit of society. The Divorce Law of 1981 was one of the most controversial laws passed by the interim Christian-Democratic government, since it contradicted canon law regarding the sanctity of marriage. Divorce was a litmus test for the new democracy, and *Anillos de Oro* was particularly interesting because it made the private sphere public and allowed people to discuss issues they could relate to.

It should also be noted that the specter of Francoism still loomed very large. Hence, television was used to erode Francoist values. The pedagogical value of television programs, at a time when democracy needed to be imagined and democratic values taught through narratives of private lives, should not be underestimated. Although the Divorce Law had come into force, social mores and attitudes did not change overnight, and the debates in the show attest to that fact. If we consider television to be a primary mediator in the public sphere and one of the most influential agents of value construction, we can see how *Anillos de oro* was a powerful tool that guided its viewers through the moral climate of its time.[1]

Not only was the show emblematic of Spain's transition to democracy, but—for reasons that are not entirely clear—it captured the public imagination. The show made both protagonists famous almost overnight: the young and dazzling Imanol Arias became the heartthrob of his generation, while Ana Diosdado—already known as one of Spain's few female playwrights and television scriptwriters—was now given a recognizable public face. One element of the show's success might have been the long list of prestigious actors who guest starred on the show, such as Hector Alterio, José Bódalo, Alberto Closas, Juan Luis Galiardo, María Luisa Ponte, Mónica Randall, Amelia de la Torre, and Ana Torrent, to name but a few. Their stunning performances have become part of popular memory, and it is no coincidence that the best-scripted episodes star those actors.

One of the challenges in understanding the popularity of a TV show involves identifying how it represents both universal themes and contemporary issues in a way that strikes an emotional chord with viewers. Implicit in the huge success of *Anillos de oro* was the broader sociopolitical context that it evoked. The Spanish Transition witnessed one of the most infamous attacks on lawyers' lives in Spanish legal history: the assassination of the "lawyers of Atocha." On January 24, 1977, two right-wing extremists went into the Atocha Street office of a firm of labor lawyers in Madrid and opened fire, killing five and wounding four. As a direct attack on the figure of the lawyer who was instrumental in the application of democratic values, and hence the process of democratization itself, the massacre earned public indignation and is commemorated to this very day. The original viewers of *Anillos de oro* would have watched the show against this contemporary backdrop, and Ramón's hero status is reinforced by the fact that he is both a labor lawyer and a divorce lawyer, making him the epitome of heroic lawyers in post-Franco Spain.

As already mentioned, the topic of divorce was used as a litmus test for democracy, and the fictional discussions in *Anillos de oro* reflect with startling accuracy the range of opinions expressed in the national press. Law, however, is conspicuous by its absence. *Anillos de oro* is an interesting hybrid of a domestic sitcom, a workplace drama, and a lawyer show. Staple scenes take place in the lawyers' office, at the local bar, at Lola's family home, and at Ramón's bachelor pad. The personal and the professional do not separate easily: most of the lawyers' clients are friends or distant relatives and, not unlike many American legal dramas, the show also focuses very much on the private lives of the two lawyers. Lola's bourgeois family life and Ramón's bohemian lifestyle feature heavily in each episode, making their own private lives a case study and an integral part of the ongoing debate about divorce. The mix of narrative strands usually combines deep-level plot lines about the lawyers' private lives, which remain unresolved from episode to episode, with surface stories about divorce cases, which are concluded by the end of each episode. These patterns of repeated and unresolved storylines are etched in memory after only a few viewings, and give viewers a sense of connection and continuity. In every episode the viewer is dying to know what Ramón's latest flame looks like, how Lola copes with her rebellious adult children, and how *doña* Trini, the Francoist voice of the past, insults everybody who dares to set foot in the lawyers' office in search of a better life.

Since the legal topic is that of divorce, the entire show is implicitly or explicitly about gender. Many of the scenes revolve around the family setting of the divorce cases. Out of 13 episodes, only four end in divorce, and viewers witness only one divorce proceeding before a judge. The new Divorce Law is never actually explained to us: does there have to be a serious matrimonial offense (such as adultery or physical abuse), or does a spouse have the right to file for a divorce by mutual consent? In other words, is it a fault-based or a no-fault divorce? None of those legal details is ever explained to the viewer, and in a sense, there is little specific legal education to be had. Perhaps the self-conscious dramatization of social issues, combined with the absence of the nitty-gritty details of legal proceedings, are the strengths of this show. *Anillos de oro* is aimed at a generalist community. The fictionalized divorce debates are reenacted at different levels and offer more indirect than direct educational value in the sense that they look at real-life scenarios of marital melodrama.

As an exposé of a cross-section of society and a cross-section of divorce cases, the show is a potpourri that includes something for everybody. There is an aristocratic marriage as a cover for homosexuality; a medical doctor whose wife betrays him; an emotionally abused lower-middle-class woman who finally has enough and falls in love with an actor; a butcher with an emotionally abusive wife; a mother of two who wants to leave her marriage of convenience to lead a self-determined life; the young wife of a much older husband who falls in love with a man of her own age; and a man who has been living in sin for decades and has had children with his de facto wife, rather than with his de jure one, whom he can now divorce. This assortment of cases is a careful mix of injustices in which neither gender is blamed for its supposedly egotistical desires to file for divorce. In each episode, the viewer empathizes with the spouse who wishes to leave, and it is precisely this empathy through storytelling that gives us the indirect educational value. Personalized emotive accounts of petitioners lend themselves to melodramatic narratives of family life and law. At its simplest, then, divorce is where law meets melodrama. Maybe therein lies the success of the show.

Within the logic of the show, the stigma of divorce looms understandably large. The first hurdle for our hero lawyers—that of getting an office—is made more difficult by their admission that they will specialize in divorce cases. The landladies, two elderly women representing the voice of a Francoist past, are disgusted at their tenants' professional convictions. In a comical misunderstanding at the very beginning of the pilot episode, they assume that Lola is a prostitute and Ramón her pimp. While not delighted at the prospect of prostitution in their private home, the landladies would still have considered it for their own financial gain. At the end of the first episode, Ramón comments, while sitting in the local bar with his friends, "If we started a whorehouse, or a money-laundering or arms-trade business, they would have been delighted. But that divorce stuff, good God, none of that! That goes against their principles."

One of the landladies in question, *doña* Trini, becomes a recurrent commentator who reminds our hero lawyers of their "dirty business," of the good old days under Franco when everything was better and people were less egotistical, and of Lola's and Ramón's single-handed responsibility for the downfall of Spanish society. The voice of the past here is taken to such comical extremes that nobody takes her seriously, but it is nevertheless an important reminder of the conservative and (sometimes fascist) factions that were still very much part of the new, and now democratic, Spain. For many people law and order, and thus stability, were preferable to the perceived insecurity of a democratic system.

As early as episode three, Lola considers giving up her job because she is receiving threatening anonymous phone calls. While sewing a button on one of her husband's shirts, she explains to him:

> I think I'm going to give it up. I'm very vulnerable, these phone calls really frighten me. I'm not a natural rebel and I don't need to be given medals. I'm happily married, what do I care. . . . It's not gonna make a big difference anyway if I'm around or not. . . .

The anonymous phone calls were not a fictional exaggeration. Such calls were very much part of social reality at the time and reminiscent of the threats to which lawyers were subjected. The Atocha lawyers, to name but one example, were threatened through a series of anonymous phone calls before being killed.

Lola is forever anxiously justifying her existence as a divorce lawyer. Contrary to the default feminist representation in the 1980s (the more career-oriented the character, the more feminist she is), she is not a heroic lawyer desiring to become an icon of feminist progress, but instead is a woman who wrestles with her career. The extent to which Lola is struggling to have both a career and a family is never more obvious than the summarizing sections of the divorce narratives, which are set in her kitchen—the female private space *par excellence.* There, Lola comments and reflects on her current cases while cooking a meal and talking to her husband Enrique. This scene is a pertinent reminder that it seems natural to ask women to juggle professional and private duties. From her screen presence, you could be forgiven for thinking that she is primarily a housewife who happens to turn up at the office in the afternoons.

When some of Ramón's clients assume that she is his secretary, Lola puts them straight with a tone of voice that is a mixture of anger and satisfaction: "No, I'm one of the partners." Nevertheless, there is no overtly feminist motivation in her choice of profession, other than the liberal conviction that divorce is good for society and that women have a right to self-determination. Calista Flockhart once commented on her role as Ally McBeal, "Men are just characters. The moment a woman is on TV as a lead character, she is expected to be a role model."[2] If that holds true for Ally McBeal, it must be doubly true for Lola who, as a token personification of progress, comes as little surprise in a TV show depicting a new and democratic Spain.

In this sense, Lola in *Anillos de oro* can be considered a representative character through whom larger sociological questions about gender symbolism are communicated. During the Spanish Transition, women were fighting for both democracy *and* women's rights, the latter not necessarily being automatically subsumed in the former, even though de jure equality was proclaimed in the 1978 Constitution. Arguably, cultural narratives are written and resisted on the Lola character. She can be read as vacillating between a self-confident mother of three/divorce lawyer superwoman and a middle-aged back-to-work–type mom, constantly on the verge of a nervous breakdown, who desperately needs the support of her male colleague and husband. The viewer can find evidence for both constructions in the TV show.

We should also distinguish between feminist issues at the character/private level and feminist issues at the case level. Her female clients appreciate her views, and in one particular episode, when a client wants to leave her husband and children to lead a self-determined life, Lola's words of wisdom about the ultimate form of female selfishness (abandoning your children) are significant:

> The part of the self-sacrificing mother who would never leave her children I know all too well. And there are two types. [There are] those who decide to leave with their children and need to make ends meet from one day to another. To those, hats off! But I also know the other type, the sinister mother who uses her children as a bargaining point in the divorce settlement. And on top of it, they feel like saints. I don't have the slightest prejudice against a woman who, for whatever reason, decides to divorce her husband and give up her children because they are better off with their father. I have much more respect for that kind of mother, I consider her less egotistical and much braver.

These observations, spoken by Lola, whom we have come to love as the motherly career woman, have more impact than they would if they came from another character. It is, perhaps, in comparison to other characters in the show that her views, and their significance, become obvious. Despite constant family quarrels, Lola is happily married. Additionally, part of the narrative function of her character is the juxtaposition of her good marriage and happy family life with the bad marriages of the divorce cases. In episode eight, one of Lola's many marital fights is juxtaposed against the marital fight of the couple who are getting divorced. Both fights are of a symbolic nature, but while Lola's marital fight ends quickly in a kiss-and-make-up scene, the bitterness of the other couple's argument shows why a divorce would be liberating for both parties. For the considerate viewer, the beauty of the message lies in the subtle juxtaposition: a robust exchange of opposing views, ending in an affectionate truce, versus an emotional and bitter argument of melodramatic proportions. This is the sum total of the difference between good and bad marriages.

The strength of the show partly lies in its depiction of lawyers as human beings who have as many relationship problems as the next person. *Anillos de oro* does not depict the perfect world of powerful lawyers who carelessly decide upon the destiny of other people. Both Lola and Ramón constantly struggle with their own private lives. Due to her family situation, Lola can easily relate to complex narratives of family life (and law) and understands that people are entangled in webs of complicated relationships. While for Lola nothing is ever clear-cut, Ramón is a self-professed lawyer for the socially disadvantaged, and advocates divorce at almost any price. Lola is also the voice of reason and harmony whenever couples decide not to get divorced, whereas Ramón imagines justice in divorce and gets frustrated at the limited usefulness of legal change. Lola is a seemingly conservative family woman in her private life, and hence may be more suspicious of divorce, while Ramón is the antiestablishment hero lawyer, champion of people who attempt to get out of oppressive marriages.

Ramón is the show's most forceful voice for women's equality, and often disagrees fervently with his female colleague. It is he who strengthens the feminist message of the show. It is clear that Ramón's choice of profession was politically motivated: he is an illegitimate child of a working-class mother, and his family background gives him ample left-wing credentials as well as a hunger for social justice. He frequently blames Lola for not having the courage of her convictions, and calls her "Milady" (using the English term), alluding to her bourgeois background, age, and marital status. He teases her by calling her a "bastion of traditional values" and reminds her that her seemingly conservative life is out of sync with her profession as a divorce lawyer. She, in turn, calls him *El Progre* (the lefty), alluding to his anarchist views, which denounce legal marriages sanctioned by church or state.

Ramón advocates the complete revolution of intimate relationships and rejects not only marriage's legal framework but also its traditional link to monogamy and nuclear family primacy. This conviction is tested a few times, twice at a private level and once at the case level. In two separate episodes, when Ramón himself falls seriously in love, he immediately reverts to conservative rules of monogamous relationships in order not to lose the woman in question, only to find that she just wants an affair and will never leave her husband. At the case level, Ramón once conducts a case for an elderly gentleman who would like to divorce his wife in order to marry his long-standing extramarital partner. The final scene of that episode shows the happy newlyweds in the foreground while the camera zooms in on Ramón's face in the background. The anarchist lawyer is almost in tears of joy, proud to have been involved in somebody else's marital bliss.

As in all quality drama shows, continuing narrative threads are used to lend regular characters unexpected traits and thus render them "round." At the end of the day, Lola is not quite as bourgeois as Ramón would have it, nor is Ramón quite as anarchist as he would like to be. In an almost fairy-tale conclusion to the show, Lola and Ramón become a couple after Lola's husband dies. All's well that ends well, although I am sure that this ending really annoyed some educated viewers for being so cheesy, happy, and unrealistic. It also shows how conservatism and antiestablishment attitudes go hand in hand in *Anillos de oro*. Ramón relinquishes his strict bachelorhood to a woman 10 years his senior, which in 1980s Spain was certainly going against social conventions. They declare their love for one another in a fake, and deliberately unromantic, ceremony in a car. Ramón, ridiculing the wedding vows, asks:

> Do you take this complete wreck to be your partner . . . for better or worse, etc., etc.? [*Puts wedding ring on her finger*] Do you take this stupid cow who is going to spoil your life from this day forward? Yes, I do. Inside your ring it says "Ramón." As you can see, I'm very vulgar.

The conservative ending of the entire show, and the mostly conservative endings of each episode, remind us that *Anillos de oro* represented a careful mediation between the opposing factions of the old and the new Spain. However, *Anillos de oro* is also a good example of cultural texts that reveal an interpretative space that can work against the seemingly conservative textual surface. The point that needs stressing here is that it may be precisely this apparent conservatism that could conceivably convert *Anillos de oro* into a tool of social critique and change. At a macro level, the careful mediation of values might also explain why the Spanish Transition is considered one of the more successful governmental transitions in recent history.

Endnotes

1. At the time of writing, the Spanish Radio and Television Corporation (*Corporación Radio Televisión Española*, or RTVE) was in the process of making its archival material (TV shows and documentaries) available online. Interestingly, out of the six emblematic shows they deliberately made available first, two are lawyer shows: *Anillos de oro* and *Turno de Oficio* ("Public Defender").

2. ELLWOOD WATSON, SEARCHING THE SOUL OF ALLY McBEAL 23 (2006).

PART VI

Daytime Television Judges

One of the most important trends in contemporary television is the rise of reality shows. Something about seeing supposedly unscripted drama involving the personal lives and true adventures of ordinary people is very attractive to viewers. The world of law on television is no exception. In this arena, law and entertainment have truly merged. Although Judge Joseph Wapner invented the reality court show with the original *People's Court* back in 1981, *Judge Judy* now is the highest-rated show on daytime television. Numerous *Judge Judy* clones have followed in her footsteps, so that in big cities, you can watch judge shows nonstop from 9 AM to 5 PM. Right now, millions of people are watching someone who looks like a judge decide small-claims cases (many of which relate to sex in some way or other) on a set that looks like a courtroom. The impact of reality judge shows on viewers should not be underestimated, because they are wildly misleading about the real world of courtrooms and litigation.

What is the attraction of the daytime judge shows? Why would people who are stuck at home during the daytime watch these shows rather than, say, soap operas, which have much better actors as well as better plots and production values? Is it that people want to learn some law? Do they like seeing thorny disputes definitively resolved at the end of a few minutes of simulated trial? Do they want to take a peek into the personal lives and bedrooms of people like themselves? Do they take secret pleasure in seeing how others have messed up their lives? Do they enjoy hearing people scream at each other? Or is it that people enjoy watching the judges articulate their own values by berating the litigants and calling them irresponsible creeps?

This Part takes a critical look at the *Judge Judy* phenomenon. Nancy Marder bemoans Judge Judy's terrible judicial behavior and the way she decides legal issues off the cuff, but likes the way the judge encourages women to take responsibility for their lives. Taunya Banks studies the peculiar demographics of the judge shows. Why is it that the judges on these shows are mostly female? Why are most of them black or Hispanic? These demographics are wildly different from those of real judges. And what is the consequence of this gender and ethnic mismatch? Will it teach ordinary people that women and minorities are overrepresented on the bench? (This is contrary to reality.) Will it reinforce stereotypes about black women?

Reality judge shows are an international phenomenon. This Part turns to two extremely interesting examples of foreign reality judge shows that differ, in important ways, from their American counterparts. In Germany, according to Stefan Machura, a number of judge shows have done very well on daytime television. They were led by *Richterin Barbara Salesch*, who closely resembles Judge Judy in appearance and judicial demeanor. However, the American model of televising real antagonists in small-claims cases did not work in Germany, so the program turned instead to staged criminal cases (typically with lay actors but also with real lawyers). Later, *Das Jugendgericht* presented Judge Ruth Herz, who resolved fictitious juvenile court cases in a way that educated the public about youth problems and juvenile justice.

Vicente Riccio tells us about *Ratinho*, an extremely successful Brazilian daytime television phenomenon that aired for over 10 years. Like the American shows (and unlike the later German shows), *Ratinho* was about the true-life disputes of ordinary Brazilians. Ratinho felt free to berate the party whom he thought was at fault, cheered on by the studio audience. However, Ratinho also engaged in a lot of criminal law discourse and demanded the punishment (and even execution) of various criminals who had made the lives of ordinary people miserable. Finally, Ratinho functioned as an ombudsman, demanding that local government provide a range of social services and social justice for the Brazilian downtrodden.

CHAPTER 26

Judging *Judge Judy*

NANCY S. MARDER

Judge Judy

Aired:
- September 16, 1996–present, CBS

Cast:
- Judith Sheindlin (Judge)
- Petri Hawkins-Byrd (Bailiff)

Awards:
- Daytime Emmy Award nomination for Outstanding Legal Program (2008)
- Daytime Emmy Award nomination for Outstanding Special Class Series (1999, 2000, 2001, 2002, 2003, 2004, 2005, 2006, 2007)
- TV Guide Award nomination for Favorite Daytime Talk Show (2000)

Judge Judy is a long-running[1] daytime television program that reaches millions of viewers and enjoys top ratings.[2] Judge Judy hears real small-claims cases presented by real litigants, yet she is no longer a real judge and the setting is not a real courtroom. Nonetheless, in each case Judge Judy renders a verdict that resolves the dispute between the parties. She does this without reference to law and without pause for reflection. Her approach seems to be entirely intuitive. Along the way, she yells at litigants, interrupts them, and insults them. Her brash persona is far from the judicial ideal.

The program teaches several harmful lessons about judges and courts. One harmful lesson is that a judge is someone who is quick to form a judgment and who belittles those who appear before her. Judge Judy conveys her disapproval of parties and witnesses through harsh words and body language. In these and other ways, Judge Judy's behavior is antithetical to how a judge should act. Another harmful effect of the program is that it blurs the line between entertainment and judging. This courtroom seems to have many of the attributes of an actual courtroom: a judge, a bailiff, two parties, and public spectators. And yet this courtroom

Courtesy of Photofest.

JUDGE JUDY

Judge Judy (Judith Sheindlin) admonishes the party to tell the truth and to take responsibility for her actions.

is merely a stage for Judge Judy, whose main purpose is to entertain. The problem is that viewers who are unfamiliar with actual courts and judges might think that they are watching the judicial system at work, rather than a television program intended merely to entertain them.

In the midst of negative lessons about judges and courts, does Judge Judy offer any positive lessons to her viewers? Surprisingly, she does. Although Judge Judy is everything a judge should not be, she manages to impart life lessons that go beyond the cases, particularly when the litigants are women. Judge Judy uses her role to teach the parties, and by extension the viewers, that women should not always do what a man asks them to do, that they should think for themselves, and that the men in their lives need to take responsibility for their actions.

Teaching Harmful Lessons about Judges

Judge Judy's behavior is entirely inappropriate for a judge. Like other daytime judge shows, such as *Judge David Young* and *Judge Mathis*, the program is all about the judge. Even the title, *Judge Judy*, reflects this focus. Yet television judges need to distinguish themselves from the competition, and they usually do so by their persona and approach to judging. Judge Judy's character is outspoken and often rude. She says what is on her mind and she says it whenever she feels like it. She interrupts the parties, but if they try to explain she tells them to "shush." Her style is no-nonsense and her approach to decision making is commonsensical.

Judge Judy makes snap judgments and uses hyperbole to express her assessments. Thus, in one episode in which the parties are two teenage girls who got into a fight, leading to 50 stitches for one of them and a claim of assault against the other, Judge Judy questioned why the injured girl had agreed to go to the park with her new boyfriend, knowing that the ex-girlfriend and her friends would be there. Judge Judy described this decision as "really stupid" and the boyfriend who suggested the plan as an "idiot," a "moron," and (sarcastically) as a "genius" and "Prince Charming."[3]

If Judge Judy does not like the behavior of a party or witness, her words become harsher and her tone more strident than usual. When a group of high school students missed their prom because the defendants, two limo service owners, failed to send a limo on time and failed to instruct the driver properly, Judge Judy told the two limo owners, "On your best day, you're not as smart as I am on my worst day." In another case, where a young woman was stopped for speeding by a police officer and tried to avoid the ticket by having her father, a retired police officer, speak by cell phone to the officer issuing the ticket, Judge Judy yelled at her for being "a big baby" and "a spoiled brat who was driving a little too fast," and for looking to her father to get her out of trouble. Judge Judy then delivered the ultimate insult: "You've been living in L.A. too long."

Judge Judy's body language reinforces her strong words. She rolls her eyes when she disbelieves one of the parties. She often exchanges a look with her bailiff, who plays the straight man to her stand-up comic role. Judge Judy dresses like a judge, wearing a robe and even a collar like the ones worn by Supreme Court Justice Ginsburg and former Justice O'Connor, but her eye rolling, grimaces, and dramatic pauses are hardly judge-like, and reveal her views as much as her words do.

Judge Judy reaches instant verdicts without recourse to law and without much explanation to the parties or viewers. For example, in the case of the limo owners who failed to get the high school students to their prom on time, Judge Judy predictably decided in favor of the plaintiff students. The only explanation she gave to the defendant limo owners was that the limo had arrived late and the driver should have known the address, even though the plaintiffs had given the driver the wrong name—the Yorba Linda Equestrian Center instead of the Yorba Linda Community Center—as the destination. One can only surmise that Judge Judy, as a mother, empathized with the students' plight of having missed their prom, or that Judge Judy, as a consumer, had experienced her fair share of car services that failed to send cars on time.

Although the fast pace of these decisions and the over-the-top personality of Judge Judy might keep viewers focused on the television program day after day, her portrayal of a judge does a great disservice to actual judges and the way they perform their job. Foremost, a judge is supposed to be impartial and to maintain the appearance of impartiality. One way for a judge to appear impartial is to speak carefully and to choose words that do not reveal his or her opinion one way or the other. Another way is to refrain from body language that shows support for one party or the other. In contrast to this ideal, Judge Judy reaches her judgments quickly and reveals them even more quickly in her word choice and body language. It goes without saying that real judges usually do not insult those who appear before them, use harsh language, make instant credibility findings, make jokes at the parties' expense, or look for laughs from the public spectators, and if they do, they may be removed from the case.[4] Although Judge Judy might don the robe (and even collar) of a judge, her behavior on the bench is far from judicious. Moreover, Judge Judy fails to perform other basic responsibilities of a judge, including following the law and giving reasons for her decision. Admittedly, there might not be much law in many of these cases, but at the very least, Judge Judy could give reasons for her decisions and make sure the parties understand them. Instead, her decisions are merely pronouncements. Judge Judy's explanation to the young lady who had tried to avoid a speeding ticket by using her father's influence was merely "You were wrong."

Blurring the Line Between Judging and Entertaining

Judge Judy teaches harmful lessons about appropriate behavior for a judge, and these lessons are particularly harmful to viewers who have never been inside a courtroom and who believe the show teaches them about what judges actually do. This show blurs the line between judging and entertaining and may lead viewers to conflate the two. Whereas a television viewer knows that a television sitcom does not portray actual family life, because the viewer can draw from his or her own experience with family life and compare it to the television show, a viewer might not have similar knowledge of the courtroom and thus fail to realize that the show is for entertainment, just like a sitcom or a soap opera.

Judge Judy is an unusual blend of the real and the fake, and this can contribute to viewer confusion. Judge Judy is played by Judith Sheindlin, who was once a family court judge. Although she now plays a judge on her television show, she is no longer a real judge. The parties who appear before her are real parties who have real small-claims cases that need to be resolved. Instead of turning to a real judge, however, they have agreed to appear on television before Judge Judy to give their version of the case, and sometimes to present actual witnesses in support of their case. The parties receive some financial benefit for appearing on *Judge Judy*, although this arrangement is never explained to the television audience.[5] The others present in the courtroom include a bailiff, played by an actor, and an audience. Thus, the show includes a mix of actors and nonprofessionals, led by Judge Judy, who plays a brasher version of her old role as an actual judge.

There are other features that further blur the line between judging and entertainment for the television viewer. The set looks like a real courtroom. The judge wears a robe and sits at a raised bench with flags (one American and one created for the show) behind her. There are times when Judge Judy also seems to act like an actual judge. For example, when one party fails to listen to her, she sends the bailiff over to eject the belligerent man from the courtroom unless he behaves properly. When she decides a case for the plaintiff, she orders the defendant to pay. After the case has been decided and the parties are outside the courtroom, they are interviewed about the decision, much like the press often interviews parties or jurors after a trial.

Of course, there are other times when Judge Judy's over-the-top behavior is that of an entertainer rather than a judge. When she insults parties, yells at them, and rolls her eyes, she is doing this for dramatic effect. The difficulty is that a television viewer might not know this. Given the mix of actors and nonprofessionals and the television program's goal of resolving actual disputes, the behavior of Judge Judy might not be understood by a television viewer as entirely inappropriate for a judge. The viewer might think that this is how judges are supposed to act. One empirical study found that potential jurors who often watched television judge shows like *Judge Judy* tended to believe that judges should ask a lot of questions, hold opinions, and express these opinions in the courtroom.[6] A study by the National Center for State Courts found that 61.4 percent of those polled relied on prime-time television drama as an important source of information about courts, and 40.5 percent of those polled said they relied on shows like *Judge Judy* to learn about courts.[7]

Admittedly, the opening image of justice, in which Judge Judy is shown peeking out from the blindfold that usually depicts the figure of justice as impartial, and the opening words delivered by Judge Judy, which present a moral about the case, should serve as cues to the viewer that what follows will be more entertaining than educational, but not all viewers will recognize these cues. The show is troubling, then, because it conveys bad judge behavior as acceptable and gives the impression that this is how actual judges behave since this is how Judge Judy behaves. Because this is a program involving actual parties and actual disputes, viewers may think that Judge Judy is an actual judge and this is how actual judges are supposed to act. Members of the public who submit complaints about Judge Judy to the California Commission on Judicial Performance certainly make that mistake.[8] The program blurs the line between judging and entertainment, and in the process, does a disservice to judging. So, is there anything positive that can be said about this program?

Empowering Women

Judge Judy uses her position as a television judge to impart some important lessons to women who appear before her as parties and to the women who constitute the majority of her television viewers.[9] Although her style is brash, and may be intimidating to some who appear before her, she tries to teach life lessons that go beyond the cases. In particular, she tries to teach women to think for themselves and not just to do what the men in their lives tell them to do. She also wants them to insist that the men in their lives act responsibly.

In a number of the cases that Judge Judy hears, the parties before her are two women, but the dispute was caused by a man who is not a party. In such cases, Judge Judy asks where the man is, makes him stand if he is in court, identifies his responsibility, and makes sure that the women understand this point.[10] For example, in the case of the two young women (the new girlfriend and the ex-girlfriend) who got into a fight at the park, Judge Judy makes the young man stand up, even though he is not a party or a witness. She points out to the new girlfriend that she should not have listened to this young man when he suggested that they go to the park where the ex-girlfriend and her friends had gathered. Judge Judy tells the new girlfriend that she "shouldn't be an idiot" and do what the boyfriend suggested, and she refers to him as a "moron" because his plan had been so ill-conceived. Her underlying lesson to the young woman is that just because her boyfriend is an idiot does not mean she has to be one; rather, she has to think for herself. If she does not think for herself, then she may end up again with 50 stitches in her head, as she did this time. Although Judge Judy's word choice is poor and her manner is insulting, her message to the young woman is a positive one: think for yourself.

In another case in which two young women are the parties, a man is again at the root of the dispute, though this time he is not present in the courtroom. The plaintiff's car had been damaged by the defendant after the plaintiff and Joey, the absentee provoker, had sex in the car. The defendant had a two-year old child with Joey and was pregnant again by him. She thought that they were working on their relationship when she discovered Joey was having sex with another woman, the plaintiff. Judge Judy refers to Joey as "a moron" and chastises the defendant for not having used birth control. She renders judgment in favor of the plaintiff and requires the defendant to pay the bill for repairing the dents she had made to the plaintiff's car. Her lesson to both women is that they need to take control of their lives and not to engage in impulsive behavior— whether it is having unprotected sex or denting a car—because of a man like Joey. Both women seemed to have learned this lesson. The plaintiff was no longer seeing Joey and the defendant had learned, "Don't fight over a guy. They're not worth it."

Judge Judy's lesson to the young woman trying to get out of a parking ticket is that she needs to take responsibility for her mistakes rather than relying on someone else to bail her out. A police officer had stopped her for driving over the speed limit. The young woman wanted the officer to speak to her father, a retired police officer, by cell phone; however, the officer refused. The young woman charged the officer with improper behavior and wrote a letter, with the assistance of her parents, complaining of his conduct and requesting that the letter be placed in his file. A tape had also been made of the entire exchange between the young woman and the police officer and was played for Judge Judy.

She found that the officer had acted properly and she lambasted the young woman for evading her responsibilities—from trying to get out of the ticket to using her father's influence to trying to mar the officer's record. Judge Judy criticized the woman for being "a spoiled brat," for calling her father to get her out of trouble, for being a "big baby," and for having been "wrong." Although Judge Judy's criticisms are inappropriate for a judge, they are appropriate for a parent who is trying to get a child to take responsibility for her actions. Once again, Judge Judy uses cases such as this one as a vehicle to reach women and to urge them to take responsibility. While one can take issue with her approach,[11] her message is an important one, and one that resonates not just with the parties but also with the viewers, as her show's long run proves.

More Harm Than Good?

It is unfortunate that the important lessons Judge Judy teaches about women taking charge of their lives get made in a courtroom by a judge who does not act like a judge. One possibility is that Judge Judy needs to act in this manner in order to get her audience's attention and to make her message stick.[12] If she just delivered her message in terms that were fitting for a judge, no one would listen. When she name-calls, she grabs everyone's attention. Or maybe the loudness and brashness are expected, given other television shows that are competing for Judge Judy's viewers. Even if that is the case, I am waiting for the television program in which a judge can behave civilly and treat parties respectfully and still encourage women to take responsibility for their lives. Such a show might not win the ratings contest, but at least it would contribute positively to the image of justice and the empowerment of women, without requiring that one be sacrificed for the sake of the other, as happens in *Judge Judy*.

Endnotes

1. *Judge Judy* began in 1996. *See* Kimberlianne Podlas, *Should We Blame Judge Judy? The Messages TV Courtrooms Send Viewers*, JUDICATURE, July–Aug. 2002, at 38, 39. CBS has renewed the show through 2012.

2. *See* Paige Albiniak, *Who'll Win in Court?*, BROADCASTING & CABLE, May 22, 2008, at 11 (describing the show as "sitting pretty on the top of the ratings heap").

3. Material quoted from *Judge Judy* episodes are taken from the DVD entitled "Justice Served" (2007).

4. For example, Judge J. P. Mauffray, who called the Jena 6 criminal defendants "troublemakers" and "a violent bunch," was removed due to "an appearance of impropriety." *Judge Ousted for Remarks*, Chi. Trib., Aug. 2, 2008, at 4.

5. *See* Samantha Slipock, Judge Judy and The People's Court: The Phenomenon of the 'Real Court' Television Genre 7 note 13 (1998) (unpublished paper on file with author).

6. *See* Podlas, *supra* note 1, at 38.

7. David Ray Papke, *From Flat to Round: Changing Portrayals of the Judge in American Popular Culture*, 31 J. Legal Prof. 127, 151 (2007) (citing study).

8. Podlas, *supra* note 1, 38, 39 ("Apparently, many viewers do not 'understand that Judge Judy and most of her cohorts are not present members of any judiciary.'") (citation omitted).

9. *See, e.g.*, Steven A. Kohm, *The People's Law versus Judge Judy Justice: Two Models of Law in American Reality-Based Courtroom TV*, 40 Law & Soc'y Rev. 693, 696, 698 (2006); Papke, *supra* note 7, at 147.

10. For a character in a novel who takes the same approach to judging as Judge Judy in that she insists that the man should be present and take responsibility, see Cristina Garcia, Dreaming in Cuban 111–16 (1992) (describing Celia's service as a judge in a People's Court in Cuba).

11. *Compare* Kohm, *supra* note 9, at 712 (describing Judge Judy's approach as authoritative with an emphasis on individual responsibility) *with* Christina R. Foust, *A Return to Feminine Public Virtue: Judge Judy and the Myth of the Tough Mother*, 27 Women's Stud. Comm. 269, 286 (2004) (characterizing Judge Judy's approach as the "Tough Mother" who combines an aggressive style with promotion of neoconservative virtues).

12. *See* Curt Anderson, *Miami Judges a Popular Draw for TV Court Shows*, http://www.law.com (last visited May 30, 2008) ("'To bring the educational aspects of the show, we have to avail ourselves of the entertainment aspects. . . . You can't divorce one from the other.'") (quoting Cristina Pereyra, host of *Final Verdict*).

CHAPTER 27

Judging the Judges—Daytime Television's Integrated Reality Court Bench

TAUNYA LOVELL BANKS

Critics of reality daytime television court shows remain divided over whether the possible educational benefits of these shows outweigh their distorted images of judicial proceedings. However, few pay much attention to the shifting demographics of the reality court judges since 2001, when they first beat out soap operas in the daytime ratings. That television viewing season, seven of the 10 judges were male, but, surprisingly, six of the judges—two females and four males—were black. Only four judges were white. In 2008, female television judges outnumber their male counterparts. Additionally, four judges are Latina/o and another four are black. Only Judy Sheindlin of *Judge Judy*, the best-known and most popular reality court judge, and David Young of *Judge David Young*, an openly gay man, are white. There are no Asian-American judges on reality court shows, although Asian Americans occasionally appear as judges on nighttime lawyer shows.

In the real world, women comprise only 18.6 percent of federal judges and about 20 percent of state judges. Black Americans of both genders comprise only 6–8 percent (8.6 percent federal, 5.9 percent state), Latina/os 3–6 percent (5.4 percent federal, 2.8 percent state) and Asian Americans approximately 1 percent (0.8 percent federal, 1.1 percent state) of all judges.[1] Thus, the judicial world of daytime reality television court shows is far more diverse in terms of gender and race than real courts.

The increased presence of nonwhites on television over the past decade is no doubt a by-product of political action initiated by civil rights organizations like the NAACP to boost ethnic diversity on television as well as a response to the demographic composition of the viewing audience.[2] Social scientist Steven Kohm writes: "The preponderance of female judges—and to a lesser extent African-American male judges—. . . is strong evidence of a presumed female and indeed racialized audience."[3] The more recent addition of Latina/o judges on daytime reality television reflects the continued push of political organizations for wider diversity, as well as a conscious targeting by networks and syndicators of the daytime viewing audience.[4] (Although Hispanics, including Latina/os, can be of any racial group, they are treated as nonwhite and marketed as a racialized group.)

More than five years ago I worried that the overrepresentation of women and nonwhite male judges on daytime reality court shows might mislead the viewing public into thinking that most real-life judges are nonwhite and female, a misperception that could have harmful consequences.[5] After almost a decade, the popularity of television reality court shows continues and the judges are even more diverse. This essay looks at the reasons for the persistent overrepresentation of female and nonwhite male judges on these shows and possible implications for the American legal system.

The Integration of the Reality Courtroom

In the 1980s, when retired Los Angeles County judge Joseph Wapner of *The People's Court* was America's most famous jurist, his bailiff Rusty Burrell was a white male. Wapner retired from the show and it went into syndication before being cancelled in 1994. When the show was revived in 1997 with former New York City Mayor Ed Koch as the judge, a white female news reporter was added. A year later, when Jerry Sheindlin, the real-life husband of Judge Judy, replaced Koch, both the bailiff and the reporter/legal commentator were white males. Ratings lagged. In 2001 Jerry Sheindlin was replaced by Marilyn Milian and the bailiff became a black male, while the reporter/legal expert remained a white male. Ratings improved significantly.

Today the integration of women and nonwhite males on all the reality daytime television court shows extends beyond the judiciary. Every aspect of the television courtroom is integrated as well. The courtroom audience is sexually and racially diverse, and as the chart here indicates, even the race and/or gender of the fake court bailiff and news reporter or legal advisor are different from that of the judge. Since all the shows share this feature, clearly race and gender are factors considered by networks or syndicators in the creation of these shows. Perhaps producers realize that race- and gender-integrated courtrooms appeal to a larger daytime television audience.

Court Show	Judge Race/ Gender	Bailiff Race/ Gender	Reporter/Advisor
Judge Alex	L/M	B/F	None
Judge Joe Brown	B/M	W/F	W/F
Christina's Court	L/F	B/M	None
Divorce Court	B/F	W/M	None
Judge Hatchett	B/F	W/M	None
Judge Judy	W/F	B/M	None
Judge Maria Lopez	L/F	L/M	None
Judge Mathis	B/M	W/M	None
Judge David Young	W/M	B/F	None
The People's Court	L/F	B/M	W/M

Marketing the Judges

Unlike real judges, reality court judges are mediators *and* entertainers. According to Kohm, there are two types of reality court shows—judge-focused shows like *Judge Judy,* and court-focused shows like *The People's Court* or *Judge Joe Brown*. On court-focused shows, the personality of the presiding judge is not the driving force. Instead these shows rely on a third party, usually billed as a news reporter or legal advisor. The constant presence of the advisor or reporter to provide commentary adds to the theatrical aspect of the show. This relieves the judge of the entertainment burden, so that the judge on court-focused shows functions more as a conventional legal decision maker.

Most reality court shows follow the *Judge Judy* (judge-centered) model, and it is the judicial behavior on these shows that is most troubling. The reason is that TV judges, mindful of the connection between ratings and advertising revenues, may modify their behavior to satisfy the viewing audience. By doing this, they distort public notions about the legal system and legal actors.

Kohm warns,

> As a consequence of their orientation toward female and marginalized viewers, these programs speak not so much to the American population as a whole but to a segment of the population that has traditionally been denied a powerful role in civic and legal affairs.. . . . [M]essages contained in these programs about the role of the law in the lives of women and other marginalized groups are becoming less and less about participation and democracy. Instead, we are witnessing an evolution in the way daytime reality courtroom television addresses its presumed audience: an evolution that places little emphasis on formal legal intervention by the state and instead stresses personal responsibility in the management of one's own disputes and legal affairs.[6]

What follows are a few examples of how these judges are marketed to the viewing public and my concerns about their marketing claims.

Unconventional Judges, Unconventional Justice

Unlike Judge Judy, who is marketed as a real judge deciding real disputes involving real people, other judges, especially nonwhite judges, market themselves as meting out unconventional justice. Glenda Hatchett, a former Atlanta juvenile court judge, who appeared on *Judge Hatchett* from 2000–2008, consciously adopted a therapeutic rather than legalistic approach to decision making, touting her "unconventional brand of justice" and saying that she "will do whatever it takes to make a difference." Hatchett told one news reporter that "It won't be enough to hit the gavel and make a judgment. It's more important that they understand the life lessons after the judgment ends."[7] When this approach did not translate into high ratings, she modified her behavior, alternating her therapeutic demeanor with that of a tough-talking, berating judge, but her ratings never made her competitive, and now the show is in reruns.

In contrast, Greg Mathis of *Judge Mathis* promises unconventional justice because of the perspective he brings to the bench as a former gang member, school dropout, and jail inmate who turned his life around on his mother's deathbed. Following his mother's death, Mathis completed his education and was elected a superior court judge in Michigan. He assures viewers that he made the law work for him, thus implying that, because of his background, he can make the law work for the viewer/litigant as well.

Mathis strongly believes in self-empowerment and conducts workshops on the subject; his inspirational life seems to reaffirm the notion that hard work can translate into success despite poverty and racial discrimination. This message makes his otherwise conventional show attractive to many daytime television viewers, and very popular with black audiences, who comprise a substantial portion of his viewer demographic. Consequently, Mathis survives despite consistently poor overall ratings.

Other judges send viewers somewhat mixed messages. Maria Lopez of *Judge Maria Lopez* was marketed using her personal biography as a hard-working immigrant who, like Mathis and Hatchett, promised unconventional justice. Lopez is billed as "passionate," "strong," "experienced," "fair," "tough," and a "pioneer"—a Cuban refugee who came to America as a child. During the show's introduction, she speaks a few words in untranslated Spanish ending with: "You talk about the American dream, I *am* the American dream." The Hispanic Press describes Lopez as a hard-working Cuban immigrant whose first language was Spanish, and who was educated at Smith College and Boston University Law School before being appointed Massachusetts' first Latina judge. She is touted as willing "to keep an open mind regardless of the situation," having "empathy for the oppressed," and rendering "unconventional, creative sentencing."[8]

Unfortunately for Lopez, the television public has not been sufficiently entertained by her spicy demeanor; *Judge Maria Lopez* currently is

Courtesy of Photofest.

DIVORCE COURT
Judge Mablean Ephriam combined personal responsibility and judicial clowning.

the lowest-rated reality court show.[9] Perhaps her lack of ratings success is tied to these two potentially conflicting narratives. Nativists may feel uncomfortable with a foreign-born judge promising "unconventional" justice, because that might translate in their minds to foreign or "un-American" justice. Ironically, nothing on the show suggests Lopez renders unconventional justice. Nevertheless, the fear of potential viewers that the promised justice would not provide helpful information about how the legal system works may explain why they have decided not to tune in.

Finally, there is Mablean Ephriam, a formerly well-regarded black woman lawyer who presided over *Divorce Court* from 1999–2007, and one of the few reality court judges without any real-life judicial experience. Personal responsibility was a hallmark of her rulings. In one episode Ephriam lectures an outraged wife on why she had to financially support her estranged husband: "we are all equal now," and as a result wives, like husbands, have an equal obligation to support their estranged or former spouses. She continues to lecture the woman about the difficulty of moving on with one's life when you still love someone, a bit of moralizing clearly aimed at the audience.

Nevertheless, Ephriam's demeanor raised a few eyebrows, as she was quite expressive on the bench and prone to make inappropriate wisecracks. For example, when a white man complained that his Hispanic wife's family called him a "cracker," she remarked, "Don't y'all know that crackers and beans go together?" In another case, where a wife accused her spouse of infidelities based on hickies she spotted on his neck, Ephriam responded, "Let me see the hickies on your neck. Come up here so I can put another one up there. Not from kissing you, trust me." In yet another cases she shouted at a former husband accused of infidelities, "You were a cheater and a liar." Later in the same case, she said: "This is cockamamie bull and it's just an excuse for him to go play around." While this behavior may have endeared Ephriam to her viewing audience, real lawyers and judges worry that her conduct created "grossly false impressions of what transpires in courtrooms."[10]

Repeated use of this type of humor by real judges would subject them to disciplinary proceedings. Yet Ephriam's combination of preaching personal responsibility and judicial clowning made her competitive, as *Divorce Court* consistently ranked third among the court shows. When she was replaced at the end of 2007 with another black woman judge, the show's rating dropped significantly. Now *Divorce Court* ranks in the lower half of the 10 judge shows.

Christina Perez of *Christina's Court* illustrates most clearly the tendency of reality court shows to favor entertainment over legal decision making. Perez, an American born to immigrants from Colombia, hosts *La Corte de Familia* (Family Court) on Telemundo Television Network/ NBC.[11] She is promoted as passionate about the law—triggering in the minds of those susceptible to racial and ethnic stereotypes the image of the Latin spitfire—but Perez shows little passion in court. Her demeanor, although appropriately judicial, collides with her tendency to interview parties about unrelated issues before handing down unexplained legal rulings. When a former Miss India sued another person for failing to repay a personal loan, Perez questioned her at length about her experiences as a beauty queen and even showed photographs and video clips of the plaintiff at various events—all unrelated to the legal claim. Perhaps because there is so little focus on the law, *Christina's Court* has not been a ratings success.

Conventional Justice Equals Ratings Popularity

Ironically it is a white woman and former New York City Family Court judge, Judy Sheindlin, who is largely responsible for the rebirth of reality court television shows. Her show, *Judge Judy*, consistently ranks among the top daytime television shows, lately even beating out *Oprah*. Billed as "a no-nonsense mother with little patience for squabbling litigants,"[12] Sheindlin, perhaps a variation on the stereotypical Jewish mother, demands accountability from legal rule breakers.

The show's website describes her as "smart, savvy, and opinionated," with a reputation for being "tough but fair." There are no claims about unconventional justice, and the trials portrayed on *Judge Judy* look very much like those in small claims courts around the country.

Similarly, the two next most popular shows, *Judge Joe Brown*, with black former Memphis judge Joe Brown and *The People's Court*, with Cuban-American Marilyn Milian, are law-focused courtroom shows. This might explain why among the Latina/o television judges, only Milian has been successful in this venue. Her show, *The People's Court*, currently ranks third among the daytime court shows. *Judge Alex*, with Alex Ferrer, the lone male Latina/o judge, ranks just above *Judge Hatchett*, which in the June 2008 sweeps of syndicated TV reality court shows beat out *Christina's Court* and *Judge Maria Lopez* as well as *Judge David Young*, which features the first openly gay reality court judge.[13] Milian's success may have more to do with her show's law-focused approach than her brand of justice or personality. If so, her success may suggest that the current crop of Latina/o TV judges, all light-skinned with no accent, might fare better ratings-wise on law-focused rather than personality-focused shows, because law-focused shows rely less on stereotypical behavior to drive the show than do their judge-focused counterparts. On the other hand, the lack of ratings success for most Latina/o judges may be more easily explained as a result of the individual personalities of Perez, Lopez, and Ferrer than as a function of show format or audience receptiveness. Interestingly, none of the Latina/o judges are Mexican Americans, although this ethnic group constitutes the largest Latina/o population in the United States. Undoubtedly, the television producers and syndicators will continue to explore whether there is a large enough market for more than one Latina/o judge.

The Good and Bad of Judicial Diversity on Daytime TV Reality Court Shows

The presence of female and nonwhite male judges in integrated settings reassures viewers that justice in the United States is meted out impartially. While there are positive aspects to this portrayal of the courts, there are negative aspects as well. Arguably, the overrepresentation of women and nonwhite men on daytime reality court shows creates a "'synthetic experience,' a substitute for reality that feels real." Leonard

Steinhorn and Barbara Diggs-Brown call this phenomenon *virtual integration*, "creating the impression that the world is more integrated than it truly is."[14]

When virtual integration occurs in the minds of television viewers, it is easy for them to doubt claims that women and nonwhite men are underrepresented in the real-life judiciary and that American society needs to take meaningful steps to address this problem. Resulting misperceptions about the extent of judicial diversity may actually undermine popular support for increased racial and gender diversity on the bench by suggesting that our nation's benches are already diverse. Even worse, some members of the public may fear that women and nonwhite men have taken over the courts.[15]

This is not a farfetched concern. Political scientist Keith Reeves found that the least affluent and educated Americans have the greatest misperceptions about the socioeconomic status of blacks in America, believing them more successful than statistics suggest.[16] Television is an especially prominent presence in the daily lives of this segment of American society, and these viewers tend to rely disproportionately on television as a primary source of information about the legal system.[17] Distorted information about the prevalence and behavior of female and nonwhite male judges suggested by reality court shows can be powerful, because real-life courts remain largely hidden from public view. Further, since most reality TV judges are former real-life judges, even more sophisticated television viewers, who should know better, may unconsciously be influenced by the virtual integration phenomenon into believing that the real-life bench is more diverse than statistics suggest.

The Bottom Line

There are some distinctive differences between female and male reality television judges. Female judges are more likely to scream at and berate litigants, whereas male judges are more likely to use sarcasm. The behavior of black female television judges, who are just as likely to scream and berate litigants as the other female judges, may be judged more harshly by viewers because of preexisting negative stereotypes about "angry" black women.

There also are some lessons to be learned when comparing the popularity of these shows. A judge's television style may have a greater influence on a show's popularity than the judge's race and/or gender.

Shows where the judge's style seems too nontraditional are less popular than shows where the judge acts like viewers expect judges to behave. Georgia State Supreme Court Justice Sears reminds us, "Courtrooms must be places of order and decorum, places where justice is meted out. Judges must preserve this environment, lest the public comes to see the courts as uncaring and ineffectual circus, not to mention entertainment bonanza."[18] This observation seems to apply to daytime television reality court shows as well.

For almost a decade, *Judge Judy* has reigned over daytime syndicated courtrooms. The success of Judge Judy, and highly rated black reality judges, may reflect the extent to which their on-screen behavior comports with conventional entertainment stereotypes ascribed to various groups based on race, religion, or sexuality. The fate of two white male former reality court judges suggests that the merger of law and entertainment on these shows results in a spectacle that perhaps demands a judge who is not a dull white male. *Judge Mills Lane*, starring the former Washoe County, Nevada, judge who gained national notoriety as a boxing referee when he disqualified Mike Tyson for biting off part of Evander Holyfield's ear in 1997, lasted only three seasons, never garnering respectable ratings. Likewise, *Texas Justice*, with Larry Moe Doherty, a Texas lawyer, ran for four and a half seasons before being cancelled in 2005, also due to low ratings.

If the spectacle of reality court shows disfavors white male judges, then the overrepresentation of women and nonwhite men among these shows reflects not only the demographics of the viewing audience, but also the commodification of nonwhites, particularly blacks, as sources of entertainment. Accordingly, who plays whom on daytime television today may have more to do with who is watching and what generates more money for corporate media owners than with any conscious effort to shape viewers' choices or influence viewers' perceptions about race and gender in American courtrooms.

Endnotes

1. Native Americans comprise less than 0.10 percent of all judges. *See* Federal Judicial Center, Judges of the United States Courts, http://www.fjc.gov/public/home.nsf/hisj (searchable database providing statistics of sitting federal

judges confirmed through Sept. 7, 2007); ABA National Database on Judicial Diversity in the State Courts, http://www.abanet.org/judind/diversity/national .html (last visited Mar. 25, 2008); Lynn Hecht Schafran, *The Amazing Rise of Women in the American Judiciary*, 36 U. Tol. L. Rev. 953, 955 (2005).

2. NAACP, *Out of Focus Out of Sync Take 3: A Report on the Film and Television Industry* 7–8 (Nov. 2003), *available at* http://www.naacpimageawards.net/PDFs/ focusreport1_master.pdf (last visited May 25, 2008); Report: *TV Networks Crawl Toward Ethnic Diversity*, USA Today, Nov. 19, 2004, *available at* http://www.usatoday .com/life/television/news/2004-11-19-ethnic-diversity_x.htm.

3. Steven A. Kohm, *The People's Law versus Judge Judy Justice: Two Models of Law in American Reality-Based Courtroom TV*, 40 L. & Soc'y Rev. 693, 694–96 (2006).

4. *Law and Disorder Are Hot: English-language Telenovelas, Court Shows Are on the Rise as Syndicators Reach for Hispanics*, Advertising Age, Mar. 27, 2006, at S13.

5. Taunya Lovell Banks, "Will the Real Judge Stand Up: Virtual Integration on TV Reality Court Shows," Picturing Justice: The On-Line J. of L. & Popular Culture (Jan. 2003), http://www.usfca.edu/pj/realjudge_banks.htm.

6. Kohm, *supra* note 3, at 696–97 (footnotes omitted).

7. *On Sept. 11, Here Comes the Judge: Hatchett*, N. Y. Amsterdam News, Sept. 13, 2000, at 22.

8. Hispanic PRWire, *TV's Judge Maria Lopez Hopes to Inspire Others, available at* http://www.hispanicprwire.com/print.php?=in&id=9486.

9. Roger Catlin, TV Eye: *Back in the Court*, Sept. 18, 2006, *available at* http:// blogs.courant.com/roger_catlin_tv_eye/2006/09/back_in_court.html.

10. Roger M. Grace, *Mablean Ephriam: Well-Regarded Lawyer Portrays Crass Judge on Television*, Metropolitan News-Enterprise, Oct. 15, 2003 at 7, *available at* http://www.metnews.com/articles/perspectives101503.htm.

11. CristinasCourt.com, About the Show, http://cristinascourt.com/inside .asp?category_id=27 (last visited June 30, 2008).

12. Smillie, *Legal Eagles Fly High Through TV Airwaves*, Christian Science Monitor, Oct. 2, 1997, at 12.

13. Paige Albiniak, *Syndication Ratings: Judge Judy Strong in Courtroom, Resilient in Ratings*, Broadcasting & Cable, Mar. 11, 2008, *available at* http://www .broadcastingcable.com/index.asp?layout=articlePrint&articleID=CA6540146.

14. Leonard Steinhorn & Barbara Diggs-Brown, By the Color of Our Skin: The Illusion of Integration and the Reality of Race 144–5 (1999).

15. Sherrilyn A. Ifill, *Racial Diversity on the Bench: Beyond Role Models and Public Confidence*, 57 Wash. & Lee L. Rev. 405, 480 n. 362 (2000).

16. Richard Morin, *Misperceptions Cloud Whites' View of Blacks*, Wash. Post, July 11, 2001 at A1 (quoting Keith Reeves of Swarthmore College).

17. Valerie Karno, *Remote Justice: Tuning in to Small Claims, Race, and the Reinvigoration of Civic Judgment*, in PUNISHMENT, POLITICS, AND CULTURE 261, 264 (Austin Sarat & Patricia Ewick., eds., 2004).

18. Leah Ward Sears, *Those Low-Brow TV Court Shows*, CHRISTIAN SCIENCE MONITOR, July 10, 2001, *available at* http://csmonitor.com/durable/2001/07/10/p11s1.htm.

CHAPTER 28

German Judge Shows: Migrating from the Courtroom to the TV Studio

STEFAN MACHURA

The History of German Judge Shows

The work of a judge in a German court can be very tedious, with judges at the bottom of Germany's criminal court hierarchy plowing through more than 1,000 cases per year. As a release from this daily grind, judges often resort to writing articles, working as mediators, joining political causes, or engaging in various other side activities. Thus, it is no wonder that judges lined up when a TV company announced a casting call for the German version of *Judge Judy* in 1999.

This positive response was a bit startling, since applying to become a television personality ran contrary to a longstanding ethos in the German judiciary: a judge does not seek the limelight and does not risk his or her prestige or that of the profession by entering the entertainment industry. As a rule (subject to a few exceptions), cameras are not allowed in German courtrooms. The judge has traditionally been viewed as a servant of the state, because German judges are not elected, but instead must pass rigorous exams and complete long apprenticeships.

Despite these institutional hurdles, TV producers have more than once found talented judges to appear on the screen. In October of 1999, Barbara Salesch was given the chance to appear on the SAT.1 channel as the German equivalent of *Judge Judy*. Her appearance is strikingly similar to that of Judge Judy Sheindlin: she is about the same age, with the same hair color and a similar disposition. In other words, SAT.1 took no risks. Two years and an overhaul of the concept later, Barbara Salesch was proclaimed the "quota-queen of SAT.1" by Germany's leading TV listings publication,[1] and nine short years later, the show passed the 1,500-episode mark.

However, the real pioneer was the German public broadcaster ZDF, which, a few months before Salesch's show debuted, premiered an adaptation of *The People's Court* called *Streit um Drei*. "Streit" means "dispute" and "Drei" alludes to the timing of the show at 3 PM. Just as *The People's Court* was tamer than the later *Judge Judy*, *Streit um Drei*, in the tradition of public broadcasting, emphasized educating the public and kept things more reasonable and peaceful than *Richterin Barbara Salesch*. The latter featured more aggressive behavior, both by the parties and Salesch, as well as commentary on the moral qualities of the parties, although Salesch never was as offensive as Judge Judy was toward many of her "guests." Guido Neumann, the judge of *Streit um Drei*, was very similar to Judge Joseph A. Wapner of the original *The People's Court* in that he was always calm and respectful toward the litigants.[2] Like the American *People's Court*, the show incorporated a moderator who accompanied the viewer to the courtroom and interviewed the "parties," as well as a legal expert who gave general legal advice to the audience. But the concept of *Streit um Drei* significantly differed from that of the American judge shows: Although real cases inspired some of the scripts, the cases on the show were not real and the parties were played by professional actors.

While Guido Neumann had some success competing with loud and offensive psycho-talk shows in the early afternoon, Barbara Salesch found the early evening to be a much less favorable time slot. After the broadcaster threatened to end the show, the makers of *Richterin Barbara Salesch* abandoned the premise of real antagonists with small-claims cases in favor of showing staged criminal cases featuring verbal fighting among lay actors. Scheduled earlier in the afternoon, the new criminal court of Barbara Salesch also worked extremely well.

The production firm Filmpool, headed by the former leftist journalist Gisela Marx, soon sold the same concept to yet another private channel. Since Barbara Salesch dealt with adult criminal cases on SAT.1, Marx invented a TV juvenile court for rival RTL, aptly called *Das Jugendgericht* (juvenile court), which also involved fictitious cases. However, she still needed a judge. One day, a friend introduced her to Dr. Ruth Herz, a judge–scholar who had been honored by the state for her extraordinary achievements in initiating victim–offender mediation at juvenile courts. When Marx saw Herz, she touched Herz's black wavy hair, declaring "yes. . .this would work,"[3] and offered Herz a new job that paid much better than a judgeship. The marketing strategy for *Das Jugendgericht* stressed the personality of Ruth Herz. The advertisement shown in Figure 1 announces the new show's setting (a juvenile court) and asks in big letters, "Guilty or not guilty?" Judge Herz is equipped with a fountain pen, a commentary on the criminal code, and a file, and wears a black robe. Oversized letters looming in the background add another element of uncertainty, while Judge Herz's facial expression seems to indicate a moment of enlightened decision.

SAT.1 did not wait long to counter and contracted with Constantin Entertainment to produce another TV judge show. *Richter Alexander Hold* came with a younger male judge who was tall, sporty, and elegant, and possessed broad intellectual interests. He, like the other judges, tried criminal cases. Compared to Salesch, Hold played a judge who was a bit friendlier and more sympathetic to the parties. RTL responded with yet another judge show. This time, Ulrich Wetzel presided quite authoritatively over adult criminal court cases, hence the title *Das Strafgericht*. As if this were not enough, RTL now also offered a family court show called *Das Familiengericht*. In addition, there were short-lived appearances of

Foto: RTL Television.

Figure 1   Advertisement announcing the start of *Das Jugendgericht.*

additional judge shows with other areas of jurisdiction. On weekdays between 2 and 5 PM, RTL broadcast three hours of court shows, while SAT.1 showed two hours of the same. On occasion, there were "specials" of *Richter Alexander Hold* during prime time. Reruns were shown late at night as well as on weekends. As competition became fiercer, the style of argumentation in court plummeted. Strong language was used more and more, cases often involved sexual behavior, and strange personalities clashed unchecked in the courtroom. As concerns arose that these shows presented a danger to youth, RTL and SAT.1 curbed the more egregious aspects in order to protect their revenues. Meanwhile, the public broadcaster ZDF withdrew from the genre after four years. In 2007, RTL partially followed ZDF's lead, looking for new formats to outperform SAT.1, but still retained *Das Strafgericht.*

Undoubtedly, while the shows were heavily dependent on the personalities of the judges, economic factors were the driving force behind the development of German TV judge shows. The shows were the result of the broadcasters' search for cheap productions that would attract mass audiences. On commercial TV, producers insisted that parties and witnesses behave aggressively, and only curbed excesses when public criticism endangered the business. Further demonstration of the monetary interests behind the shows was the conveyor-belt fashion in which they were made, with sometimes three or four episodes being filmed in one day. Commenting on this production system, Judge Herz remarked, "I never worked that hard in my life."

The Superior Figure of the Judge

The personal archive of former TV judge Ruth Herz contains boxes of evidence of her popularity. It is filled with newspaper clippings from Germany and neighboring countries such as Austria. In the tradition of media self-reflectivity, an article in the Israeli *Haaretz* on December 14, 2001, depicted German newspaper coverage of Herz. The headlines, read clockwise, say "Like in real life," "In the name of the people—End talk shows," "RTL takes juveniles to the TV court," "New RTL woman judge: Her name is Herz [which translates as "Heart" in English] and she has lots of reason," and "The juvenile court is in session on RTL." These clippings show the great attention and free advertising that these judge shows were able to receive. Judge Herz received volumes of fan mail, some with marriage proposals. Drawings and various other artworks were submitted by viewers. An entire cellblock of a women's prison wrote to Herz that they watched every episode, as did the wardens. The female prisoners explained that they learned a lot about law and liked her way of presiding over the court. They noted that, in their trials, they had not dared to behave in such a rude manner as many of the TV defendants.

Showing the wide range of her audience appeal, Herz also received a complimentary letter from a young girl (Figure 2). It translates (with writing errors) as follows:

> Dear Mrs. Dr. Ruth Herz!
>
> My name is [name] and I am 7 years old. We always watch you on TV at the juvenile court. My mama works at the adult court. I very much like watching you because you look so Beautiful. Please give me a photo of you. Your [name].

The remainder of the page is a drawing that shows Judge Herz, the two lay judges ("Schöffen") at her sides, the bench of the defense lawyer ("Verteidiger"), and the bench of the public prosecutor, "Staatsanwalt Küchmeister." The red book in front of the judge is the code of criminal law.

Figure 2 A girl's letter to Judge Ruth Herz.

Why Are German TV Judge Shows So Popular?

Arguably, what makes the TV judge a prominent figure is the social function of the genre. Before judge shows emerged, it had become increasingly common for afternoon TV talk shows to pit people with extreme views against one another. These confrontational shows often left the viewer unsatisfied, as no solution was ever presented. The social problems debated in these talk shows—real or invented—gave viewers the impression that their society had lost its bearings. People crave orientation about what is and is not acceptable, and it is this feature that sets judge shows apart from their talk-show competitors. In the judge shows, the judge gives a legal and moral evaluation. Since the TV judges have previously served in German courts, the audience ascribes a certain authenticity to their remarks. This, along with the use of legal symbols like law books, robes, and court furniture, lends credibility. Further, the judges explain their judgment at the end of a TV case with legal reasoning and common sense, so while the dispute between the parties might have put the boundaries of acceptable behavior into question, the TV judge sets things right—in the name of the law and in the name of society. It is therefore truly "the people's court" and the judge is the audience's trustee.[4]

Part of the reason that mass audiences cling to judge shows is the opportunity to watch real judges at work. In Germany, the same opportunity exists regarding the lawyers who play the parts of public prosecutor and defense attorney. Newspapers and TV listings have increased the credibility of these shows by announcing that these actors are all lawyers who have their own offices and only act on television part time. They act "as if" they were prosecutors or "as if" the TV litigants were their clients. However, their acting creates a distorted image of German court procedure.

Generally, in German television the line between educational–informational formats and entertainment formats has become increasingly blurred. TV court shows are a prime example of this: they are entertaining, but at the same time are meant to educate the public about law and about rules for living together peacefully. The TV judge always provides legal reasons for the verdict, thus connecting the evaluation of evidence with the letter of the law. For example, Ruth Herz made it clear that her initial motivation for becoming a TV judge was to educate the public about youth problems and youth justice. While many viewers say that they find judge shows ridiculous, many others say that they indeed learn a lot. Of these, many are ready to discount the most spectacular and disgusting performances as the price they must pay for the aspects that seem more authentic and informative. Regular viewers of TV judge shows should not be misunderstood as ignorant of the "real" law. Besides the aforementioned female inmates who were regular viewers, there are others to whom legal issues are of special importance. In one interview of an avid viewer, the interviewee said that she was a trained lawyer but had never actually practiced law. She saw the judge shows as an opportunity to "stay in touch with legal topics."

In many episodes, colorful, stereotyped characters are involved in violence, recklessness, heinous intrigues, sexual transgressions or irregularities, and various other human dramas. Of course, these are the stories that popular media has been dramatizing for centuries. These are sure-fire recipes for selling newspapers, books, cinema tickets, and, of course, TV judge shows. Also, behaviors like these are what societies often define as criminal.

The TV shows seek to cast colorful characters to further entice the audience. (In some cases they employ professional actors to play difficult roles.) The producers compel the lay actors to perform in an outlandish manner—for example, by requiring women to wear seductive dresses. Nevertheless, thousands flock to the casting calls, wishing to have their day on TV in the hopes of impressing their classmates and friends.

Extraordinarily emotional behavior is typical for the defendants, plaintiffs, victims, and witnesses on TV judge shows. Witnesses break down in tears and confess to a crime, defendants and witnesses explode in front of the camera and can hardly be kept from a brawl, and people swear until their temper has to be curbed by the judge. One reason for the exaggerated emotions is that they are an attempt to intensify the conflicts. Another reason is the amount of time judge shows have to tell their story. Whereas a typical Hollywood courtroom drama has enough time for the exposition of the story, judge shows must help viewers to immediately understand the case and the characters involved.

While this has caused much contempt for judge shows among lawyers, since the average court case is quite boring, there are bizarre trials in German courts. I have witnessed many outlandish cases at the lower criminal court, such as a young mother breaking out in tears after being accused of stealing shampoo, an unemployed drunkard with no driver's license insisting that an East German-made scooter was really just a bicycle, and a taxi owner suggesting at the outset of his trial that he earned less than a welfare recipient. Judges in divorce cases have even been stabbed by furious husbands. No TV judge has been hurt (yet).

The Adversary System in German Judge Shows

"Good" versus "evil" is the main pattern in legal dramas. Two parties, their lawyers, and their divergent stories clash in front of the court. No wonder that the adversarial system of trial lends itself nicely to such confrontations. Hollywood courtroom dramas have had worldwide success, and often audiences believe this is the pattern of all trials, even if their country employs a different kind of procedure. This certainly is the case in Germany. In German criminal procedure, the judge investigates the case, interrogates witnesses, and grants the lawyers opportunities to join in. The judge knows the file, has worked out hypotheses, and tests these during the hearing. The public prosecutor must take into account the aspects that favor the defendant. The defense lawyer is defined as "an organ of justice." Both roles are designed to be much less partisan than in the United States. The ideal is that the court "establishes the truth" and the lawyers and judge work together to achieve this. Conversely, in the U.S. adversarial system each side zealously represents a client and presents its version of the "truth" to the judge and jury.

Because of its innate dramatic qualities, the adversarial system was adopted by German TV judge shows even though it does not actually exist in German courts. On television, the trials take the form of a duel. Here, the lawyers, not the judges, often interrogate witnesses. This was especially true in *Das Jugendgericht*, where Judge Ruth Herz appeared relatively passive while allowing the lawyers to do their job. This model gave rise to new stars: the lawyers who appeared on TV judge shows. Some of them became quite popular. One even got his own show, called *Lenßen und Partner* on which the lawyer essentially does detective work.

Ordinary court cases are quite foreseeable. The German prosecutor checks every case for its merits before it goes to court in order to conserve valuable resources. (Notably, the police serve as a primary filter for the legal system.) When the file reaches the judge's desk, it is again checked to see if there is enough substance to start a trial. Only in rare cases does a defendant go to court against dubious evidence. Consequently, most cases that do proceed this far end with a conviction or with the defendant paying a fine to avoid having a criminal record. That is also why it pays for a defense lawyer to be "cooperative." The aim is not to obtain an (unlikely) acquittal, but to reduce the client's penalty. This business is quite boring for everyone involved, except possibly the defendant. TV justice is different. Surprising developments and sweeping changes, such as a witness revealing the real culprit, produce suspense. Viewers of TV judge shows can always count on surprise events occurring. Because the outcome of a trial is open, viewers are invited to guess about who committed the alleged crime, whether the crime even happened, the perpetrator's background, and the forthcoming legal response by the judge.

The entertaining fights between the parties and their lawyers are not the only conflicts on judge shows. The shows also present clashes of values and interests. TV judge shows often revolve around the social roles of men and women, children and parents, workers and bosses. The shows delve into neighborly relations, the intermingling of vastly different classes of society, and even animal experiments. Of course, the shows have an appetite for the extreme. But in many cases, they deal with real social problems.

TV judge shows also provide a chance to peer into unfamiliar social spheres. TV producers have always exploited the curiosity people have about the lives of others, particularly social outsiders. In judge shows, rockers, prostitutes, career offenders, the super-rich, and members of countless other stigmatized or strange groups regularly appear as defendants and witnesses. Through their physical appearance and behavior in front of the judge, as well as the stories they tell, the audience is made to believe that they are getting a glimpse into the lives of these intriguing people. That this occurs on judge shows should not be a surprise, as these are the same traits that attract viewers to courtrooms in sensational real cases.

The public's understanding of law is complex. Law defines acceptable behavior and thus allows for a diverse society to live together. All viewers have a stake in the application of law, which explains its appearance in fictional and nonfictional stories in print, theatre, radio, and on the big screen. Criminal law possesses an especially symbolic value for any society, as the French sociologist Emile Durkheim has pointed out.[5] In their shows, TV judges reinforce and define the rules of the society.

Procedural fairness in the exercise of power also forms a key interest for all members of society. In addition to being admired for reaching reasonable conclusions, German TV judges are also held in high esteem for their procedural fairness: they give parties sufficient opportunity to state their case, they treat people in court with respect, they are unbiased, and they respect everyone's status as a citizen with equal rights.[6] At first glance, this seems at odds with the public's desire to punish rulebreakers. However, studies of German lay judges (called *Schöffen*) have shown that the norms for fairness in court extend to defendants, who are expected to be treated fairly.[7] It is standard practice that Hollywood courtroom dramas often position the viewer as a kind of juror. TV judge shows are based on the same premise. Indeed, one of the shows even invited its viewers to its web page by telling them they should be *"online-Schöffen."*

The Public's Lesson

Consumers of pop culture media are always affected by what they watch or read, and research suggests that audiences learn lessons from TV judge shows. In an international comparison of first-year law students, respondents at the Ruhr-Universität Bochum in West Germany watched TV judge shows less often, and indicated that they watched lawyer movies more often, than their counterparts in other countries. Combined, these metrics correlated with German students' belief that lawyers have high prestige.[8]

Two other studies addressed broader groups of students. Students in Munich did not learn about crime from TV judge shows. Instead, they were instilled with the belief that trials at court involve insults and abuses among witnesses and defendants and that witnesses are often revealed as the real culprits. Further, they felt that judges should give a moral judgment, as opposed to following the law objectively. Trials were seen as emotional, turbulent, and entertaining.[9]

Students at the Ruhr-Universität Bochum also showed a positive correlation between consumption of TV judge shows and belief in the high prestige of German courts. Finally, frequent viewers of Barbara Salesch and her judge colleagues were more likely to say that German citizens are fairly treated at court.[10]

But the subjects of all these studies were students, sometimes even law students. What does the wider audience think? From April to June

2005, a telephone survey was conducted in the area of Bochum. It involved 1,015 residents above the age of 14.[11] The survey revealed that TV judge shows "cultivate" the stereotypes that trials involve aggression, contingency, and emotion. The results led to three main points:

- These stereotypes may encourage viewers to mobilize the law in case of conflict. They are more likely to go to a lawyer or to court if they suffer damage. Viewers feel the need to avail themselves of legal remedies to solve problems.

- Consequently, those who share these stereotypes also expect to be exposed to aggressive behavior (be ridiculed, subjected to awkward attacks, etc.) once they find themselves in court.

- The same stereotypes cause viewers to believe in the lawyer characters. Court trials are seen as dangerous and viewers seem to project their wishes on the figure of the zealous lawyer, a guardian angel.

This all sounds good for the legal profession. Yet, the more respondents believed they would suffer as parties in court, the less they actually trusted courts. Thus, TV judge shows may actually have a detrimental long-term effect. Should that happen, an ironic twist may occur. The hard and tedious life of German judges—the reality that drove many judges to the TV court in the first place—might become even more difficult.

Endnotes

1. In 2001, her show commanded a 26 percent share of the viewing audience. HÖRZU, Aug. 17, 2001, at 47.

2. For a discussion of *The People's Court*, see HELLE PORSDAM, LEGALLY SPEAKING: CONTEMPORARY AMERICAN CULTURE AND THE LAW 89–106 (1999).

3. Author's interview with Dr. Ruth Herz, 2006.

4. Similarly, see Porsdam's analysis of *The People's Court, supra* note 2 at 102–05.

5. EMILE DURKHEIM, REGELN DER SOZIOLOGISCHEN METHODE 181 (René König ed.) (4th ed. 1976).

6. For fairness criteria, see Tom R. Tyler & E. Allan Lind, *A Relational Model of Authority in Groups*, in 25 ADVANCES IN EXPERIMENTAL SOCIAL PSYCHOLOGY 115–91 (Mark Zanna ed., 1992).

7. STEFAN MACHURA, FAIRNESS UND LEGITIMITÄT (2001).

8. Michael Asimow, Steve Greenfield, Guillermo Jorge, Stefan Machura, Guy Osborn, Peter Robson, Cassandra Sharp, and Robert Sockloskie, *Perceptions of Lawyers—A Transnational Study of Student Views on the Image of Law and Lawyers*, 15 Int'l J. Legal Prof. 407, 426–28 (2005).

9. Barbara Thym, Kultivierung durch Gerichtsshows. Eine Studie unter Berücksichtigung von wahrgenommener Realitätsnähe, Nutzungsmotiven und persönlichen Erfahrungen (2003) (MA dissertation, Ludwig-Maximilians-University, Munich).

10. Stefan Machura, *Fernsehgerichtsshows: Spektakel des Rechts*, 15 Paragrana 185 (No. 1, 2006).

11. Stefan Machura, *Ansehensverlust der Justiz? Licht und Schatten des Gerichtsshowkonsums*, in Im Namen des Fernsehvolkes. Neue Formate für Orientierung und Bewertung 83–101 (Katrin Döveling, Lother Mikos, and Jörg-Uwe Nieland eds., 2007).

CHAPTER 29

Between the Lawyer and the Judge: Ratinho and the Virtual Delivery of Justice in Brazilian Reality Television

VICENTE RICCIO*

Ratinho Livre and
Programa do Ratinho

Aired:
▪ 1997–98, 1999–2006

Cast:
▪ Carlos Roberto Massa
(Ratinho)

Introduction

Since the beginning of the 1990s, television stations all over the world have been showing a specific type of program that reports the daily experiences of common, anonymous persons. These are "reality shows," an entertainment formula emphasizing the public disclosure of real facts. This format emerged in the United States in the 1990s. Unlike other television genres, this type of programming establishes a nebulous zone between information and entertainment, drawing on the following elements: exaggeration, drama, the grotesque, and popular humor.

Reality shows have various formats and are structured in relation to different themes, such as personal and family drama, social problems, adventure, competitions among participants, and police cases. Although they take various forms on the television screen, they share two common themes: the public exhibition of

*Translated by Dr. Eoin O'Neill, Dept. of History, UFF, Brazil.

333

Veja/Editora Abril.

RATINHO
Ratinho (Carlos Roberto Massa) speaks up for poor Brazilians and demands that government punish criminals and serve social needs. On the stage he is a mix of lawyer, judge, and entertainer.

individual experiences and the opening of bandwidth to ordinary people. In their different modalities, reality shows open the television screen to the world of intimacy, publicly exposing personal questions involving violence, alcoholism, homosexuality, legal disputes, and other subjects with great popular appeal.

In Brazil, a television program that was part of this reality show tradition became an audience phenomenon for the nearly 10 years that it was broadcast. Presented daily from Monday to Friday, it was commanded by the presenter Carlos Roberto Massa, better known by his nickname of "Ratinho." In 1997 and 1998, the show was called *Ratinho Livre*. From 1998 to 2006, after moving to another television channel, the name changed to *Programa do Ratinho*. Both shows adopted a formula that combined entertainment with the provision of social services and placed them against a background of questions of justice.

The most striking aspect of the program was the exhibition of personal problems, which were always shown from an individual viewpoint. The cases covered a disparate range of questions, such as infidelity, DNA exams to check paternity, fights between neighbors, cases involving the police, and the state's failure to provide services. There was plenty of time for accusations, which could include unresolved heinous crimes, public sphere corruption, or personal damage resulting from medical negligence or omission. Irrespective of the issue of the day, the role of Ratinho was the same. Whether one viewed him as the "people's lawyer" or as the judge in an informal court, Ratinho was there to judge and to either absolve or condemn. No matter whether the drama exposed in the studio related to a family feud, a shocking crime, or a dispute over state actions, he did not hesitate to say what was right or wrong, just or unjust, moral or immoral. In this role, Ratinho reinforced the media's role as social control, an important characteristic of reality television shows. In this essay, I identify three types of discourse that Ratinho brought to the television screen: penal law, civil rights, and social rights.

The Penal Law Model

The *Ratinho Livre* program debuted in 1997 on the Record channel. The following year, it achieved something unprecedented in Brazilian television: at prime time, between 8:30 and 9:30 PM, *Ratinho Livre* allowed Record repeatedly to beat the audience figures for Rede Globo, a channel that is practically hegemonic in the country and is actually the fourth biggest television channel in the world. Success led Ratinho to appearances on interview programs with national followings, to the cover of *Veja*, the biggest news magazine in Brazil, and to the first page of *Le Monde*, the renowned French daily newspaper.

Ratinho's formula for success, as previously noted, was a combination of entertainment and questions of public interest. Supported by an enthusiastic and vibrant audience, who booed, applauded, and shouted his name, Ratinho moved through a series of subjects with wide popular appeal. During this trajectory, he would rant against the state and criminals, threaten those on the fringes of society, criticize politics, and take on the role of spokesperson for the oppressed. While doing this, he would sometimes hit the table with a club, even breaking the fax machine in the studio. This theatricality of gesture, however, suggests much more an appeal to comedy than a real intention to express the magnitude of his indignation.

During the show, Ratinho presented situations and arguments in which the idea of justice was constructed based on the model of penal law. In these situations, the ideas of coercion and punishment are the essence of the discourse, which reveals a concern with the preservation of security. A good example of this type of discourse is the classification of criminals (*bandidos* in Portuguese), who are presented not as citizen-perpetrators but as people who have broken ties with the community. Therefore, when an individual was classified as a rapist, for example, Ratinho presented him as someone stripped of all rights and deserving the worst punishment. For these cases, he generally called for the death penalty, which is nonexistent in Brazilian law. In this way, he was simultaneously the judge, who instantly applied the penalty, and the people's lawyer, who prosecuted criminals on behalf of law-abiding citizens.

Other situations observed on the show also demonstrate this practice. On August 24, 1998, Ratinho brought a couple onto the show to denounce the stealing of a child from a hospital in Jandaia do Sul, a town in Paraná state in the south of Brazil. Accompanied by a lawyer, the parents discussed the problem with Ratinho. He then threatened the person who had taken the boy, stating on air, "You bastard, return this kid to his mother, you pervert!" A man called Sílvio who was suspected of having taken the child was vehemently threatened by the presenter: "Sílvio, either you phone here now and say where the boy is, or when they catch you I will beat you to a pulp!"

Another situation evidencing this penal law discourse was the episode originally shown on August 29, 1998. The report accused a doctor, a typical married middle-class man, of paying for sex with two girls, aged 16 and 11. The image of the accused, who is 39 years old and in prison, was displayed on air. Ratinho became indignant and shouted out, "Does the Commission of Human Rights not see that child prostitution is alarming?" Shortly afterwards he continued his attacks against the accused: "Look, this bastard of a doctor has to go to jail." Ratinho also suggested that in prison the accused deserved to be raped by the other convicts. He thus presented jail not as a venue for resocialization, but rather as a place for the punishment and the expiation of the criminal. The barbarity of the crime makes the sexual violation of the perpetrator acceptable. This practice, it is emphasized, is a reality in Brazilian prisons. This discursive model is typical of repressive law in which the distinction between justice and morality appears in a diffuse manner and punishment is seen as something immediate, with the authority of the state the principal value to be protected. Here Ratinho instantly enforces the law as the judge.

The Civil Law Model

The second group of issues found on the program are ones that would normally be dealt with by civil law. These topics were generally manifested in questions related to family, neighbors, formal and informal contracts, and consumer relations. In these situations, people look to the program for help in obtaining, for example, a DNA exam in order to resolve doubts about the paternity of a child. Ratinho adjusted his discourse to fit the dynamics of the situation and the interaction between the litigants in the studio. The studio audience participated in the construction of this scenario by constantly giving its opinions about the development of the questions being raised.

Normal civil procedure consists of letting both sides speak before an impartial judge makes the decision. However, Ratinho established his own rules during the interactions, leaving the ideas of impartiality and procedure aside in order to have a more interesting show.

In the program dated February 25, 1999, Ratinho presents the case of Rosângela. She comes into the studio with her face covered with a mask. The public is told that she had a relationship with a man called Fernando, resulting in the birth of four children, whom she is now raising with great difficulty. The union did not prosper and Fernando left Rosângela to live with another woman. He comes into the studio, without a mask, together with his new companion. Rosângela accuses her former partner of having maintained sexual relations with her after their separation, which resulted in another child whom he does not want to acknowledge. Fernando responds, saying that the child is not his. His current wife says she is there to support her husband. The audience, as is usual, shouts effusively.

Fernando's current partner complains that Rosângela has threatened her and asks Ratinho for a DNA exam. The public interferes, calling her a *pistoleira* (a gangster or gunman), and a caption appears on the screen with the following message: "Husband does not want to acknowledge the child of his ex-wife." Rosângela, in turn, challenges the two to prove that she goes out with other men. The discussion and the insults become even more heated and end up in a fight. The music from the Batman television series plays and one of the characters from the program, Bola, appears raising a placard reading: "1st Round."

Things calm down a bit and Ratinho asks Fernando if he pays his wife alimony. His current wife answers, confirming the payment. Rosângela replies that she is only given food vouchers and once again says that she has no lovers. Ratinho intervenes and asks Rosângela if she still likes Fernando. She says she does, and the audience sighs in satisfaction. To resolve the problem, Ratinho proposes that a DNA exam be carried out, to which both sides promptly agree. Playing in the background is a well-known romantic *sertanejo* song called *É o amor* (It's love). Although they have come to a small point of agreement, the litigants leave the stage arguing. Ratinho considers the problem to be resolved and moves on to the next attraction. The role of Ratinho in this case varies from lawyer, presenting the demands of one of the parties, to that of judge, who later makes a decision.

The Social Rights Model

The third type of discourse in Ratinho's shows, the one dealing with social questions, was perhaps the most striking aspect of the program. The situations revolved around the failure of public authorities to carry out their duties toward citizens, particularly those in the less-favored sectors of society. In Brazil, and indeed in much of the world, social programs that can reduce inequalities are constantly demanded but are seldom adequate to meet the public's needs. Here Ratinho seemed to link justice with responsive law in that he adapted the law to the demands of social reality.

When presenting cases of people who have no access to basic social rights, such as health, justice, education, and security, Ratinho resorts to lectures about inequality and the incompetence of the state. In these cases, he is the people's lawyer, because the resolution of these demands depends on public authorities. Exhibiting the image of a sick child in need of medical treatment is justified by the social nature of the action—looking for help—which overrides the idea that minors should not be subjected to embarrassing publicity.

The role of the people's lawyer can be seen in the program broadcast on July 6, 1998, in which the case of a woman, shown in a previous program, is once again raised. The woman, Roseneide, had tattooed her back and buttocks when she was younger and now, 26 years old and with a child, cannot find a job due to the images on her body. Because she is poor, Roseneide cannot afford plastic surgery to remove the tattoos. Ratinho says that he will do whatever is possible to help her and criticizes the lack of medical assistance in the country. In other words, although it is not a real public health problem, he immediately condemns the state, without making any detailed analysis of the facts.

Another interesting case, televised on August 23, 1998, shows the court-ordered forcible removal of squatters from a watershed area on behalf of the city government of São Bernardo do Campo. Men, women, and children greeted the police by throwing stones at them. The riot squad was called in by the city government and the ensuing battle went on for more than 11 hours. Ratinho, after showing the images of the conflict, says in a serious tone of voice: "I only want to know the following: I only want to know who are the criminals in this story, because the people are workers! I want to know who is guilty. The city government of São Bernardo, I don't know. . . I want to know who the real squatters (*grileiros*) are, the people are not guilty!" The audience applauds his declarations. Ratinho says that the scene looked like Bosnia or Vietnam. The poor people who lost their homes are shown on the screen. Ratinho declares that these people do not use pencils or pens to write, but that the *doutores* (lawyers and government officials) do not know how to read, since they do not understand the word "solidarity." Then he protests in an indignant tone, "Will the *doutores* look for those who sold the land to these people?"

In the studio, where the families who lost everything are gathered, the camera focuses on people crying. Ratinho then calls the Government Secretary of São Bernardo do Campo, the representative of the Environmental Council, and the Secretary of Works to discuss the question with the inhabitants. In the background romantic-sounding music is played. Before allowing the other people to speak, Ratinho makes some declarations. "What this program actually wants is to clarify—because these scenes do not stay just in Brazil! This is what Brazilians have to understand. They are shown in France, in the United States, and in South Africa, and it is Brazil that catches fire!" The audience applauds enthusiastically.

The city government representative explains that the origins of the episode predated the administration of then-mayor Maurício Soares. In 1996 the Prosecution Service had been made aware of the squatters and brought an action asking for the area to be cleared and prohibiting the lots of land from being sold. Later the lower courts ordered the clearance of the land and the demolition of the houses. Resorting to the idea that justice is not equal for everyone, Ratinho says that he does not understand why the Prosecution Service "does not arrest the *grileiros* but fucks the workers." He is told that the evicted families are still paying for the lots and that the president of the Residents' Association is currently in jail. One of the state representatives also says that the arrest of the *grileiros* had been ordered in April 1992. From the studio, one of the evicted persons interrupts, saying that the legal action against them was not just and that they have nowhere else to go. The city government representative responds, saying that the case was actually being handled by the Prosecution Service. Ratinho says that it is easier for the city to knock houses down than to solve the problem of proper housing for poor people.

From the audience another woman, also a resident of the area in question, interrupts, saying that the representative is conspiring with the mayor. Ratinho abruptly interferes in the discussion and passes the microphone to the representative from the Environmental Council (*Conselho do Meio Ambiente*). Very calmly, this person says that the conflict is not good, but that the area has to be protected, since it produces water. (It is in a watershed.) Constantly interrupted by the residents, the representative attributes responsibility for the problem to the government at the federal, state, and municipal levels. The residents do not let him speak any more. In the end, Ratinho says that he will end the debate and, at the order of the president of *Rede Record*, he will resolve the question. "We will return the money to the people!" he vehemently promises.

Conclusion

Through the situations described above, it is possible to draw some conclusions about the role played by Ratinho as judge and lawyer, which varies according to the three types of discourse about legality that are dramatized on his show: penal, civil, and social. In the first type he approximates the role of a judge who instantly applies a penalty and presents a model of justice based on coercion and the stigmatization of the criminal. This characteristic is already significantly present in Brazilian television and radio crime shows, in which the punishment stipulated in law is considered to be too lenient.

In the second type of discourse, about civil law, Ratinho assumes the role of a zealous lawyer, especially for the poorest people. At the same time that Ratinho mediates among the different interests presented in the studio, he arbitrates a decision between the parties. Thus, his role of lawyer and judge is reaffirmed in this situation.

The third type of discourse, the social, articulates the economic wants common to the poor majority of the country and the deficiencies of the state in meeting these needs. In this mode, Ratinho assumes the role of the people's lawyer—one who defends the interests of the poorest. Due to the nature of the problems presented in this type of discourse, he does not assume the role of judge because the problems are outside of his virtual jurisdiction.

During the period in which it was broadcast, the *Programa do Ratinho* mobilized different opinions in Brazilian society. Some people saw the program as opportunistic, but others viewed it as an escape valve from the weight of bureaucracy in the country. Its broadcast allowed for a discussion of the role of justice and government during a time marked by the consolidation of Brazilian democratic institutions and the beginning of the reorganization of Brazilian economic life after 20 years of constant crises. Thus, the paradoxical role played by Ratinho is an important instrument for understanding the roles of lawyers and judges in contemporary Brazilian society.

PART VII

Lawyers on Non-Law TV Shows

While the preceding parts of this book concentrated on shows about civil and criminal law, as well as reality judge shows, this part looks at lawyers on non-legal TV shows. Lawyers present tempting targets for satire, and TV show creators have not overlooked that opportunity. *Green Acres* and *Seinfeld* were not, and *The Simpsons* is not, primarily about lawyers, but they got a lot of mileage out of making fun of them. Moreover, the addition of lawyer characters and legal subplots intensified the narrative on noncomedic dramatic shows such as *The West Wing* and *Picket Fences*. As in our society generally, many of the social and political issues that both comedic and dramatic non-legal shows use as narrative material end up being resolved in court.

We first look way back to *Green Acres*, a show from the late 1960s that involved a burned-out Wall Street lawyer who moved to the country to become a farmer, accompanied by his very cosmopolitan wife. The resulting culture clashes provided a great opportunity to poke bucolic fun at know-it-all lawyers.

Seinfeld teemed with lawyers, most significantly Jackie Chiles, who was modeled on the bombastic Johnny Cochran. Chiles often represented Kramer in personal injury cases (such as a takeoff on the famous McDonald's hot coffee case), but he was always undercut by his client, who snatched defeat from the jaws of victory. Often the *Seinfeld* characters acted like (or even pretended to be) lawyers, and they even lived by a code of laws of their own design, such as the "regifting rule," which allows a giver to repossess a gift if the recipient gives it to somebody else.

The Simpsons frequently and hilariously spoofs the legal profession, along with just about everything else in American culture. The classic sleazeball lawyer Lionel Hutz was often the subject of the writers' barbs. Hutz was the kind of greedy "law-talkin' guy" that everybody loves to hate. He chased ambulances, engaged in false advertising, and was stunningly incompetent. At one point, Hutz assured his client: "Don't you worry. I watched *Matlock* in a bar last night. The sound wasn't on, but I think I got the gist of it."

Picket Fences was an innovative dramatic show created and produced by David E. Kelley, perhaps the most prolific creator of legal television shows (including *Ally McBeal*, *The Practice*, and *Boston Legal*). *Picket Fences* concerned the small town of Rome, Wisconsin, and it centered on major social and political issues such as euthanasia, polygamy, transsexuality, and animal rights. In this respect, *Picket Fences* was a 1990s embodiment of *The Defenders.* Many, but far from all, of the stories involved issues of law enforcement or legal cases. Two key characters—the no-nonsense Judge Henry Bone and the rather unpopular lawyer Douglas Wambaugh—appear in many *Picket Fences* episodes, and the great issues of the day are often fought out in Judge Bone's courtroom.

The memorable television drama *The West Wing* was all about policy and government, but many of its story lines revolved around the legal problems confronting President Josiah Bartlet and the people who worked in his administration. Our essay focuses on the work of four lawyers who worked as or for White House counsel during the Bartlet administration. Although Oliver Babish was the most important of these characters (and was centrally involved in much of the drama of the later seasons of *The West Wing*), perhaps the most unforgettable was White House Associate Counsel Ainsley Hayes. Ainsley was a conservative southern Republican who was invited by the president to work for the White House after she skewered one of his staffers on television. Putting aside her disagreement with the liberal politics of the president and his staff, Ainsley took the job, asking her boss, the White House counsel, "Is it so hard to believe, in this day and age, that someone would roll up their sleeves, set aside partisanship, and say 'What can I do?'" (He answered, "Yes.") Ainsley did a great job, despite being given a grim basement office and suffering considerable hazing, and was also much funnier and far more charming than Babish.

CHAPTER 30

Greener Acres

ANTHONY CHASE

"Or would you rather be a pig?" Bing Crosby asks in the Burke/Van Heusen tune, "Swinging on a Star." Perhaps you *would* prefer a pig's life— if you were Arnold the Pig, that is, from the TV show *Green Acres*—considering that Arnold lives indoors, watches television, and is a big John Wayne fan. But it is a farmer that Oliver Wendell Douglas, the central character in *Green Acres*, would rather be, and he is willing to quit his prestigious big-city profession of corporate law in order to return to the land whence, at least in his imagination, all good things come. If *Green Acres* counts as a lawyer TV show, it is only because the theme of "lawyer burned out in practice wanting to do something else" has a certain currency.

Oliver W. Douglas may, in fact, have been one of Jean Stefancic and Richard Delgado's original lost lawyers whose wires got crossed, whose Gail Sheehy–style passages were not as predictable as promised. For example, in their book, *How Lawyers Lose Their Way*, Stefancic and Delgado suggest that lawyers who wallow in high-paid misery "need more room to experiment, grow, and breathe." The inability to breathe deeply in the big city, at least without developing contact tuberculosis, is one of

Green Acres

Aired:

- September 15, 1965–
  April 27, 1971, CBS

Cast:

- Eddie Albert
  (Oliver Wendell Douglas)

- Eva Gabor
  (Lisa Douglas)

- Tom Lester
  (Eb Dawson)

- Frank Cady
  (Sam Drucker)

Awards:

- TV Land Award nomination for Theme Song "You Just Cannot Get Out of Your Head" (2005)

- Eddie Albert & Eva Gabor, TV Land Award nomination for Favorite "Fish Out of Water" (2004)

- TV Land Award nomination for Favorite Pet–Human Relationship (2003)

347

the main complaints Douglas lodges against Manhattan. As he drives endlessly back and forth to work through a collage of honking and heavy traffic, he sees his legal life as sandwiched between layers of smog and pollution. Stefancic and Delgado employ similar metaphors when describing the "suffocating" corporate workplace. All the time, however, Oliver has a dream in the back of his mind, a vision of a better world and a better life.

Young Oliver Wendell Douglas has carried that dream around with him for a long time. As a youth, he loses himself in agricultural reveries while, at the same time, carefully laying out the rows and furrows to shape his farming future. But when his father asks him what he wants to be and Oliver replies, with enthusiasm, "I want to be a—," his father interjects "lawyer" before Oliver can finish. His school, Harvard, has already been picked out as well. Oliver acquiesces and soon finds himself behind a desk in a dreary seven-name law firm office high above Gotham. The portrait photo of Oliver's namesake, O.W. Holmes, does not follow him from his father's study, however, and Douglas can hardly wait until lunchtime, when he is able to turn from "briefs, complaints, answers, demurrers, and writs of replevin," to his passion, Department of Agriculture brochures and farm bulletins.

Curiously, *Green Acres* signals lunchtime over Wall Street with an image of a factory whistle at full blast, followed by a cut to Oliver's black metal lunch bucket. Maybe the show's creators couldn't think of how lunchtime would be announced in a New York law office. Or maybe they had tapped into some of the same material that C. Wright Mills used to describe the fate of the modern corporate lawyer, increasingly a salaried clerk to big business, in his groundbreaking sociological study, *White Collar*. If you compare a large-firm lawyer to an assembly-line worker or a mechanic in a big auto-repair shop, as Mills did, then maybe the factory whistle and lunchbox are not entirely out of line. Similarly, Stefancic and Delgado warn novice lawyers of the regimentation, stress, speed-up, and pressure to produce billable hours that usually await them on Wall Street.

Oliver's farm fetish (and desk drawer full of mushrooms) gets him fired and he soon finds himself in the unemployment line, which is quickly followed by the induction line as he gets drafted by the U.S. Air Force. Dropping bombs over what looks a little like Korea but a lot more like the barren rocky territory between southern California and Arizona, Oliver worries he may injure young tomato plants. Back in New York, Douglas has a chic new wife, a Park Avenue penthouse apartment decorated with sitcom versions of paintings by Still, Mondrian, and Pissarro, and another Wall Street law job; in short, "everything a man could want." Except pruning planters on a posh apartment porch does not a farm make, so Oliver again yearns for the fresh air and wide open spaces of the country. And we all know, as a character in Hitchcock's *The Thirty-Nine Steps* puts it, "*God* made the country."

Although they make no appearance in this CBS spin-off from *Petticoat Junction*, sunflower-seed-and-granola-crunching back-to-the-land hippies, living through the same Sixties that backlight *Green Acres*, shared Douglas's faith in the family farm—or at least shared his belief in the possibility of an arcadian paradise where the hard-working and early-rising could recapture a certain lost American innocence. And it was all waiting just around the rural bend. A bend of mind, at any rate, as Roger Waters' grim reflection on life in the woods, "Go Fishing," makes clear: the leaves all fell down, their crops all turned brown, and it was over. "Life at Total Loss Farm," as Tom Fels acknowledges in his book *Farm Friends*, a mellifluous memento of these golden harvest years, was entirely allegorical. "Everything had a name and a significance," recalls Fels, "even if it were sometimes only whimsical, in an attempt to imaginatively possess the object, experience, or person, or to free it from the grip of the system."[1] Much earlier, even de Crevecoeur's letters from an American farmer had let slip the flip side of Oliver's story.

Soul brother to these reclusive rural radicals was the most important lawyer to hit bottom and quit in the Sixties, Charles Reich. Reich's *The Greening of America* was published in 1970, during the first run of *Green Acres* on the small screen. Like O.W. Douglas fleeing the urban nightmare, Tom Fels's farm friends finding peace in the valley, and Huck Finn, Reich lit out for the West—via Arnold & Porter, Yale, Berkeley, and Bolinas Reef. Reich captures an image of himself as a corporate lawyer, circa 1950s, in a floor-length mirror in the austere lobby of his Washington apartment. "A young lawyer in a Brooks Brothers suit, shined shoes, and a short haircut. A young man already old, already encased in that suit: stiff, taut, inflexible. . ." Except maybe for the suit, who wouldn't quit? What Reich found in Berkeley, facing the San Francisco Bay, lying on the grass or reading all afternoon perched on a fire escape, was just what he was looking for; their "profiles showed the blue jeans, the long hair, the figures of youth."[2]

Of course, Oliver already had the white-puffed-fur Lisa, that Hungarian honey-cake of a wife, back on Park Avenue, so he was looking for something else in the not-so-fertile soil surrounding his Hooterville homestead. To be sure, a decade or so later, Oliver would probably have been sent by his law firm's consulting therapist to an employment counselor who would have steered him toward Uchtmann, Looney, Krausz, and Hannah's *Agricultural Law: Principles and Cases*. Today, the frustrated painter who finds herself trapped in law school need only pursue a career in Art Law. But there was no middle ground for O.W. Douglas, so he grabbed Lisa, packed a suitcase, and headed for higher ground down on the farm.

Perhaps fully half of six years' worth of *Green Acres* is taken up with the purposefully inane repartee between Oliver and Lisa, which derives from her mispronunciation of common English words, her lack of familiarity with anything related to housework, and her desire to catch the very next Hooterville Express back to the Big Apple. But the most interesting interactions in the show take place between the big-city lawyer, his sleeves rolled up and pitchfork in hand, and his new neighbors. In the catalogue for the Washington University Gallery of Art's exhibition, "Green Acres: Neo-Colonialism in the U.S.," Jimmie Durham is quoted as saying that the "United States is a kind of prototype; it was the first permanent colony to establish itself *against* and through the denial of local inhabitants."[3] Even this high-culture critique is grist for Oliver Douglas's mill.

It is his interactions with "the local inhabitants" of his and Lisa's newfound farm community that make *Green Acres* so much fun. In one episode, for example, Oliver attempts to establish himself as a real agricultural expert *against* (and through denial of) the local inhabitants' traditional farming methods. While they rely upon Doris's lumbago or Emily's cranky spells to diagnose likely relations between long-term weather trends and which crop they should plant, Douglas openly rejects their silly superstitions in favor of the reports filed by an army of agriculturalists, agronomists, chemists, bacteriologists, and meteorologists in the Department of Agriculture. Just as he relied upon his broker in New York

GREEN ACRES
Oliver Wendell Douglas (Eddie Albert) is a burned out lawyer seeking to exchange a gothic metropolis for prettier pastures.

Courtesy of Photofest.

to predict the stock market for him, and relies upon a numerical electrical chart to prevent Lisa from blowing another "fooz" in the farmhouse kitchen, Oliver depends on the radio report of ups and downs at the Chicago commodities exchange in order to determine what seed to buy and which crops to plant.

Historian Robert H. Wiebe, recounting the influence of scientific agriculture (and the American Farm Bureau) in rural America, says that "firm business values, the new vocabulary of marketing and chemistry, and the exaggerated repudiation of the Populist heritage" marked what he calls "an official declaration of these farmers as agricultural businessmen. . ."[4] While this is the kind of scientific revolution Oliver seeks to foster among his farm friends, resistance, even from the fellow representing the local farm bureau, remains stiff. This kind of confrontation, repeated throughout the series, is the heart and soul of *Green Acres*. They say you can take the boy out of the country but you can't take the country out of the boy. It would seem you can take Oliver out of the legal profession and out of the city, but it is very hard to take the commercial values of corporate practice out of O.W. Douglas.

Endnotes

1. TOM FELS, FARM FRIENDS 34 (2008).
2. CHARLES REICH, THE SORCERER OF BOLINAS REEF 118 (1976).
3. *Green Acres: Neo-Colonialism in the U.S.* 11 (Richard Bolton et al. eds., Washington Univ. Gallery of Art, 1992).
4. ROBERT H. WIEBE, THE SEARCH FOR ORDER 1877–1920 127 (1967).

CHAPTER 31

Seinfeld

ROBERT M. JARVIS

Seinfeld

Aired:

■ July 5, 1989–May 14, 1998, NBC

Cast:

■ Jerry Seinfeld (as himself)

■ Jason Alexander (George Costanza)

■ Michael Richards (Cosmo Kramer)

■ Julia Louis-Dreyfus (Elaine Benes)

Awards:

■ Emmy for Outstanding Comedy Series (1993)

■ Golden Globe for Best TV Series—Comedy or Musical (1994)

■ People's Choice Award for Favorite TV Comedy Series (1996, 1997, 1998, 1999 (tie))

Throughout its long run, *Seinfeld*, NBC's hit 1990s comedy, often described itself as a show about nothing. But as George finally admitted in "The Ticket," even a show about nothing has to be about something if it wants to be on television. And a good case can be made that *Seinfeld* was, at least in part, a show about lawyers.

The fact that the series featured enough lawyers to start a small law firm is not surprising, given that nearly all of its 180 episodes were set in New York, a city teeming with lawyers, and like most sitcoms, its stories featured recurring characters who each week found themselves in ever more elaborate jams.

Although numerous works have examined the show over the years,[1] its use of lawyers has been overlooked. And as Jerry would say, "that's a shame."

Lawyer Characters

It is not known how many of the show's characters were lawyers, for more than once a character's occupation was left unspecified; Wyck Thayer, the chairman of The Susan Ross Foundation, was almost certainly a lawyer, yet

Courtesy of Photofest.

SEINFELD
Although they were not lawyers, Kramer (Michael Richards), George (Jason Alexander), Elaine (Julia Louis-Dreyfus), and Jerry (Jerry Seinfeld) often found themselves immersed in legal matters.

he was never identified as such. But in a number of instances, the script made it clear that a particular individual was a lawyer.

Work

For the most part, the lawyers on *Seinfeld* performed the traditional tasks of advisor and advocate. Thus, in "The Comeback," a lawyer named Shell-bach (Ben Stein, in a role recalling his performance in the movie *Ferris Bueller's Day Off*) prepared a living will for Kramer that made Elaine his medical surrogate. Likewise, in "The Diplomat's Club," Mr. Pitt had his estate lawyer, Lenore Walker, update his will to include Elaine (a decision Walker soon managed to get reversed). And in "The Pen," Evelyn, a neighbor of Jerry's parents, suggested that they hire her nephew Jack when the condo board accused Morty of embezzling funds.

In "The Chinese Woman," George's father Frank was observed talking to a "man in a cape" (series co-creator Larry David), who turned out to be his divorce lawyer. In a later episode ("The Conversion"), Frank threatened to call his lawyer after George announced he was converting to Latvian Orthodox, although whether Frank was referring to the man in the cape or a different lawyer was unclear.

In "The Sniffing Accountant," Jerry spoke to a lawyer about a bankruptcy matter, although we neither saw this lawyer nor learned his name. In "The Cartoon," Jerry had a lawyer send a cease-and-desist letter to fellow comic Sally Weaver, but viewers again were given no information about this lawyer.

In "The Little Jerry," Elaine's boyfriend Kurt was jailed for hitting a cop. When she asked how long he would be incarcerated, he replied, "Well, my lawyer says 14 months, but with good behavior, maybe . . . 10?" Upon hearing this, Elaine decided it was best to move on.

The series' best-known lawyer, of course, was Jackie Chiles. Modeled after real-life lawyer Johnnie Cochran,[2] Chiles defended Jerry, George, Elaine, and Kramer when they were put on trial in Latham, Massachusetts, for violating that town's "Good Samaritan" law ("The Finale, Parts 1 and 2").[3] Notwithstanding Chiles's spirited defense, Judge Vandelay sentenced the foursome to a year in jail after the district attorney presented dozens of adverse character witnesses. Throughout the trial, commentary on the proceedings was provided by real-life lawyer Geraldo Rivera.

Chiles's first appearance on the show had come three years earlier, when he was hired by Kramer to sue the Starbucks-like Java World for selling coffee that was too hot ("The Maestro"). Despite being undermined by Kramer, who dropped the suit in exchange for a lifetime supply of café lattes, Chiles subsequently agreed to handle two more personal injury cases for Kramer. In the first, he went after Sue Ellen Mischke, the heiress to the *Oh Henry!* candy bar fortune ("The Caddy"), while in the second he sued the Philip Morris tobacco company ("The Abstinence"). Once again, Kramer took matters into his own hands and managed to snatch defeat from the jaws of victory. Having temporarily learned his lesson, Chiles later refused to represent Kramer's ex-girlfriend Connie when she was accused of trying to kill him ("The Friars' Club").

Play

Just as in real life, the lawyers on *Seinfeld* also had lives outside the office. In "The Comeback," for example, Kramer, having decided he did not want a living will, went to Shellbach's office, only to learn he was out playing tennis. Likewise, in "The Yada Yada," Elaine described a date she had with a lawyer. Although they ended up sleeping together, the most memorable part of the evening for Elaine turned out to be the lobster bisque.

In another episode, Elaine revealed that she had a crush on John F. Kennedy, Jr. She eventually met him when they both signed up for the same aerobics class, but then missed their first date. As a result, the dashing prosecutor went home with Jerry's ex-girlfriend Marla ("The Contest").

In "The Stakeout," Jerry wanted to date a particular lawyer but did not know her name (Vanessa). However, at a birthday party for another lawyer (Elaine's friend Pamela), he learned that she worked at the law firm of Sagman, Bennet, Robbins, Oppenheim & Taft. This led him to hang around its building in an attempt to meet her, a strategy he later admitted was "fairly ridiculous."

In "The Visa," George fell for Cheryl, a lawyer he met while waiting for Jerry and Elaine at Monk's Café (the gang's favorite coffee shop). Cheryl turned out to be more interested in Jerry, but broke up with him after catching him in a lie.

In an earlier episode ("The Virgin"), Elaine's jaywalking had caused a delivery boy named Ping to have an accident. Being Ping's cousin, Cheryl sued Elaine, but had second thoughts after learning that Elaine and Jerry were friends. This came as a great relief to Elaine, who had been shocked to find out how much lawyers cost.

> ELAINE: Oh listen, guess what? Cheryl convinced Ping to drop the case against me.
>
> JERRY: Drop the case? Well, congratulations, that'll save you some money.
>
> ELAINE: Yeah, no kidding. That lawyer was gonna charge me a fortune.

To get back at Jerry for lying, Cheryl reinstated the suit, leading Ping to warn Elaine.

> You think she nice girl? Wait till you see her in court. She's a shark! They call her the Terminator. She never lose a case. Now you make her mad. She double the damages. Hasta la vista, baby.[4]

Nonlawyer Characters

Most of the characters on *Seinfeld* were not lawyers, although in "The Seinfeld Chronicles" Kramer, after explaining he could be very persuasive, cryptically told Jerry, "I was almost a lawyer." Likewise, in "The Frogger," Elaine, during a particularly bad day at work, wondered, "Is it too late for me to go to law school?" And in "The Stand-In," Mickey Abbott, one of Kramer's friends, fretted that if he lost his current acting job, "I'm gonna be out on my ass doing that paralegal crap."

Despite their lack of legal training, the show's main characters often ended up acting like lawyers. In "The Implant," for example, Jerry "cross-examined" Elaine after she claimed that Sidra, his new girlfriend, had undergone plastic surgery:

ELAINE: You know, uh. . . they're fake.

JERRY: What? Don't say that!

ELAINE: Nah! They're fake!

JERRY: How do you know?

ELAINE: I can tell. . .

JERRY: Have you ever seen her naked in the locker room?

ELAINE: No.

JERRY: Oh, well, then I can't accept your testimony.

As matters turned out, Jerry was right to doubt Elaine, for in "The Finale, Part 2," Jackie Chiles slept with Sidra while the jury was deliberating and later advised Jerry, "They're real, and they're spectacular."

In "The Pie," Elaine was mortified to discover that a mannequin that looked just like her was being posed in a sexually suggestive manner in the window of a high-end clothing store. When she complained to the shop's snooty saleswoman, she haughtily replied, "It's our store and our mannequin, we can do whatever we want with it." Elaine then grabbed a befuddled Jerry and claimed he was her lawyer.

SALESWOMAN: Yeah? What law am I breaking?

JERRY: Well, I believe there's some legal precedent—*Winchell vs. Mahoney.*

ELAINE: (*agreeing vigorously*) Uh-huh.

JERRY: The Charlie McCarthy hearings.

ELAINE: (*agreeing even more vigorously*) Uh-huh. Are you taking this down?

SALESWOMAN: I'm getting the manager. (*walks away*)

ELAINE: Jerry, get the car.

JERRY: What are you doing?

ELAINE: Just get the car!

JERRY: Elaine, as your legal counsel, I must advise against this! (*Jerry and Elaine are seen running out of the store with the mannequin.*)

The show's legal lunacy also got a boost from George. In "The Sponge," for example, he told Susan, his fiancée, that Jerry altered the labels on his pants to make people think he was thinner than he was. After revealing this information, however, he immediately had regrets.

GEORGE: I can't believe I just told you that.

SUSAN: (*laughing*) Why not?

GEORGE: Well, Jerry doesn't want anyone to know.

SUSAN: Well, it's all right, I'm your fiancée. Everyone assumes you'll tell me everything.

GEORGE: Where did you get that from?

SUSAN: Well, we're a couple. It's understood.

GEORGE: I never heard of that.

SUSAN: Well, you've never been a couple.

GEORGE: I've coupled! I've coupled!

SUSAN: Keeping secrets! This is just like your secret bank code.

GEORGE: This is totally different! That was my secret, this is Jerry's secret! There's. . . there's attorney-client privileges here!

In "The Cadillac, Part 1," George got a chance to go on a date with the actress Marisa Tomei. Enthralled by the prospect, he rented her legal comedy *My Cousin Vinny*.[5] When Susan caught him watching it and became suspicious, George tried to throw her off the track by pointing at the screen and yelling, "Ahh. . .Oh, oh, the judge! I hate this guy!"

After Susan died licking wedding invitation envelopes (the culprit being cheap glue), George dated a woman named Maura ("The Strongbox"). Although recognizing that their relationship had no future, he cringed at the thought of telling her. "She's like a district attorney. If it's not the truth, I'll break under the cross."

In "The Statue," however, George turned the tables. Believing that Ray, Jerry's new housekeeper, had stolen a figurine, George got Jerry to ask Ray about it. When Ray insisted he was innocent, George confronted him.

GEORGE: That's it! That's it! I can't take it. I can't take it any more! (*gets up, turns around, and confronts Ray*) You stole the statue! You're a thief! You're a liar!

JERRY: (*pleading*) George.

RAY: (*to Jerry*) Who is this?

GEORGE: I'm the judge and the jury, pal. And the verdict is. . . guilty!

RAY: What's going on here?

GEORGE: Guilty!

In another bit of uncharacteristic boldness, George went up to Corbin Bernsen and pitched a script idea to him ("The Trip, Part 1"). Although George reported to Jerry that the encounter had been a huge success, he quickly learned otherwise.

ANNOUNCER: It's *The Tonight Show* with Jay Leno. Tonight Jay welcomes Corbin Bernsen, George Wendt, and comedian Jerry Seinfeld. (*Camera cuts to Bernsen, who is in mid-sentence.*)

BERNSEN: Oh yeah, yeah, people are always coming up to me trying to give me a great case for *L.A. Law*. Just a few seconds ago, right here, right outside in the hallway, this nut, some sick nut comes up to me and says he's supposed to watch this girl's cat while she's away out of town. Anyway, he forgets to feed the cat, the cat dies, starves to death, he kills the cat, refuses to get her a new one, won't give her any money, won't pay her, and he wants Arnie Becker to represent him. Nice guy. Yeah, that'd make a *great* case for *L.A. Law*. Thanks a lot. (*Camera cuts to the audience, where everyone, except George, is seen laughing.*)

The show's most memorable legal moments, however, were provided by Newman, Jerry's archenemy. In "The Ticket," for example, Newman, representing himself, tried to talk his way out of a speeding ticket but failed to convince a skeptical judge. Likewise, in "The Scofflaw," a different judge ordered Newman to keep his car in a garage after he "piled up more parking tickets than anyone in New York City."

One of Newman's finest performances came in "The Seven." After successfully treating her aching neck in return for a bicycle, Kramer forgot to tell Elaine that she would need to sleep on a wooden board for at least a week to make the cure permanent. As a result, Elaine refused to pay up. To settle matters, the pair turned to Newman.

NEWMAN: Well, you've both presented very convincing arguments. On the one hand, Elaine, your promise was given in haste. But was it not still a promise? Hmm? And Kramer, you did provide a service in exchange for compensation. But does the fee, once paid, not entitle the buyer to some assurance of reliability? Hmm? Huh? Ahh. These were not easy questions to answer. Not for any man. . . . But I have made a decision—we will cut the bike down the middle and give half to each of you.

ELAINE: *(shouting)* What?! This is your solution?! To ruin the bike?! Alright, fine. Fine. Go ahead. *(standing)* Cut the stupid thing in half.

KRAMER: No, no, no. Give it to her. I'd rather it belonged to another than see it destroyed. Newman, give it to her, I beg you.

ELAINE: Yeah, yeah, y-yeah.

NEWMAN: Not so fast, Elaine! Only the bike's true owner would rather give it away than see it come to harm. Kramer, the bike is yours!

ELAINE: What?!

KRAMER: Sweet justice. Newman, you are wise. *(Kramer picks up the bike and gets on it.)*

ELAINE: But this isn't fair! Lookit, my neck is still hurting me, and now you have the bike?!

KRAMER: Well, tell it to the judge, honey. I'm going for a ride.

Conclusion

There is so much more one could talk about, including Michael, the lawyer who turned Kramer in for stealing lobsters ("The Hamptons"); Rudy Giuliani, the real-life lawyer who found himself with a sudden cholesterol problem ("The Non-Fat Yogurt"); Claire, Jerry's ex-girlfriend, whose lawsuit put Play Now Sporting Goods out of business ("The Voice"); and *Jerry*, the legally themed show-within-a-show ("The Pilot, Parts 1 and 2"). But of course, there really is no need to go on, for as George's ex-girlfriend Marcy would say, "yada yada yada." The evidence is clear: lawyers were a fixture on *Seinfeld*, even if we did not always notice them.

Endnotes

1.   *See, e.g.*, Tim Delaney, Seinology: The Sociology of *Seinfeld* (2006); *Seinfeld* and Philosophy: A Book about Everything and Nothing (William Irwin ed., 2000); *Seinfeld*, Master of its Domain: Revisiting Television's Greatest Sitcom (David Lavery & Sara Lewis Dunne eds., 2006); Nicholas Mirzoeff, *Seinfeld* (2008); Jerry Oppenheimer, *Seinfeld*: The Making of an American Icon (2002).

2.   According to one source, Cochran initially found the homage flattering but later asked Phil Morris (the actor who played Chiles) to stop using the character, a request Morris turned down. *See* Wikipedia: The Free Encyclopedia, *Jackie Chiles*, http://en.wikipedia.org/wiki/Jackie_Chiles (last visited June 15, 2008). At the University of Utah College of Law, students reportedly have established a Jackie Chiles Law Society. *Id.*

3.   Although panned by most critics, the storyline ended up sparking a national discussion about whether the legal system should require passersby to help strangers. *See, e.g.*, Shaya Rochester, Note, *What Would Seinfeld Have Done Had He Lived in a Jewish State? Comparing the Halakhic and Statutory Duties to Aid*, 79 Wash U. L. Q. 1185 (2001), and Marcia M. Ziegler, Comment, *Nonfeasance and the Duty to Assist: The American* Seinfeld *Syndrome*, 104 Dick. L. Rev. 525 (2000). *See also* Thomas J. Vesper, Seinfeld *Syndrome: The Indifference of Otherwise Nice Jurors*, Trial, Oct. 1998, at 39. The finale should not be confused with episode 37, entitled "The Good Samaritan," in which Jerry refused to turn in a hit-and-run driver because, after a long chase, he discovered she was a beautiful woman and wanted to date her.

4.   To punish Jerry further, Cheryl also reneged on her promise to help Jerry's neighbor, Babu Bhatt, avoid deportation to Pakistan. As a result, Babu vowed to get even with Jerry, which he did in the show's final episode.

5.   George often rented movies, and in "The Junior Mint" he could be seen carrying a recording of *Pretty Woman*. Of course, in that film Jason Alexander played an evil lawyer named Philip Stuckey, a far cry from his George role.

CHAPTER 32

The Funny Thing about Lawyers on *The Simpsons*

KIMBERLIANNE PODLAS

The Simpsons

Creator:
- Matt Groening

Aired:
- December 17, 1989– Present, FOX

Cast:
- Dan Castellaneta (Homer Simpson)
- Julie Kavner (Marge Simpson)
- Nancy Cartwright (Bart Simpson)
- Yeardley Smith (Lisa Simpson)
- Harry Shearer (Ned Flanders)
- Hank Azaria (Chief Wiggum)
- Phil Hartman (Lionel Hutz)

Awards:
- ASCAP award for Top TV Series (1995, 1996, 2001, 2002, 2003, 2004)
- Emmy for Outstanding Animated Program (1990, 1991, 1995, 1997, 1998, 2000, 2001, 2003, 2006)

Taking *The Simpsons* Seriously

The Simpsons is not your average cartoon. Through its exquisitely crafted humor and multilayered satire, *The Simpsons* has transcended the boundaries of the television sitcom to become an established feature of our cultural landscape. As a testament to its depth and intelligence, scholars have used it as a springboard for exploring everything from Nietzsche to environmentalism. The show is also rife with jokes and references to both our legal system and its practitioners. Inasmuch as its humor springs from our culture's lawyer jokes and stereotypes, *The Simpsons* is a fertile ground for considering popular perceptions and attitudes about lawyers.

The Simpsons

In 1989, *The Simpsons* debuted on FOX as a half-hour comedy. Despite being primetime's first animated series in two decades, *The Simpsons* quickly parlayed cult success into mainstream popularity and critical acclaim. As it enters its 20th season, *The Simpsons* is not merely the most successful cartoon in television history, but the longest-running scripted series. This global hit is broadcast in 60 countries and, since its 1994 syndication, is seen in most domestic markets six days a week. Indeed, it is difficult to imagine contemporary culture without *The Simpsons* or its vernacular ("Mmm. . . donut;" "D'oh!;" "Don't have a cow, man.") To put it in perspective, this year's college freshmen have never lived in a world without *The Simpsons*.

As popular as *The Simpsons* remains with audiences, it is revered by critics and the industry alike. *Time* named it "The Best Television Series of the 20th Century," *TV Guide* ranked it among the "Ten Greatest Shows of All Time," and *Entertainment Weekly* called it the "The Best TV Show of the Last 25 Years." It has earned 20 Emmys, a Writers Guild of America Selvin Award (for the script that "best embodies the spirit of constitutional and civil rights and liberties"), and a Peabody (for "stinging social satire"). The genius of *The Simpsons* is that on its face, it is the most traditional of television forms, the family sitcom, but in its heart, it is a parody of that form. This façade enables the show to take on not only the platitudes and easy answers common to the sitcom form, but also the ideologies and hypocrisies on which that form is premised. As *Entertainment Weekly* put it, *The Simpsons* is "America at its most complicated, drawn as simple cartoons."

The combination of humor and animation in *The Simpsons* provides a veil of innocence that dilutes some of the program's more biting jabs. As Homer once told Marge, "Cartoons don't have any deep meaning. They're just stupid drawings that give you a cheap laugh." Indeed, as implicit in the reproach "this is no laughing matter," humor is often dismissed as a means of serious commentary. Because its method of communication is not serious, its content is presumed not to be serious. Yet humor's mask of the inane endows it with communicative powers that serious commentary lacks. In this way, humor is a covert, insulated form of expression. Labeling a comment as "just a joke" makes it more palatable and obliges some level of acceptance. Or, as creator of *The Simpsons* Matt Groening has said, "You can get away with all sorts of unusual ideas if you present them with a smile on your face."

Indeed, subject matter reflected through comedy can more easily connect with audiences. Whereas heavy drama may cause viewers to change the channel, laughs and jokes can draw them in. Nonetheless, a sitcom's jokes tell us what society deems acceptable to laugh about as well as what parts of society deserve to be laughed at. *The Simpsons* understands this. It does not sacrifice serious commentary on the altar of humor, but uses humor to expose society's hypocrisies and incoherencies, to challenge "family values," and to question our cultural institutions.

Animation, long demeaned as a "children's medium," augments this ability because it can depict—and exaggerate—virtually anything, but carries no burden of authenticity. Thus, *The Simpsons* can take issues to illogically absurd extremes. (When Springfield destroys its ecosystem, it simply moves the town five miles down the road.) Also, the inherent artificiality of animation creates a distance that makes harsh depictions easier to take: A yellow cartoon dad choking a cartoon son until his eyes are popping out of his head is quite different than a real man choking a real boy on a live-action program.

Law-Talkin' Guys on *The Simpsons*

In depicting the law, *The Simpsons* differentiates the legal system from the individuals involved with it. Specifically, the program satirizes situations prompting legal action, but portrays them in a way that does not undermine the authority of law. Instead, it illustrates that the law is a rational mechanism on which the average person can rely to obtain justice. When the system fails, it is usually not due to the institution's breakdown, but rather to individuals who succumb to greed, dishonesty, arrogance, or vengeance. As *The Simpsons* reminds us, lawyers are just as susceptible to these human frailties as anyone else.

The status of lawyers in society is schizophrenic. On the one hand, they are revered as intelligent individuals who fight for our rights and protect us from wrongs. On the other hand, they are vilified as "hired guns" or "shysters" who are just interested in money and file unnecessary lawsuits. This variation is also evident on *The Simpsons* and is seen in the way that lawyers are portrayed as well as in the way that humor is employed. On *The Simpsons,* not all lawyer-related humor is alike and not all lawyers are alike.

The Springfield Bar

The Springfield Bar comprises approximately one dozen lawyers. The most noteworthy lawyers are Lionel Hutz, sole practitioner; Blue-Haired Lawyer, adversary du jour; and the "high-priced lawyers" retained by

Mr. Burns. As in real life, the group includes sole practitioners, corporate counsel, defense lawyers, prosecutors, and civil litigators. As detailed below, the principles and professionalism of these lawyers also cover a wide range, but Lionel Hutz anchors the lowest end of this spectrum.

Lionel Hutz

Lionel Hutz is Springfield's most visible lawyer, or as he calls himself, "law-talkin' guy." Though he claims to have attended Harvard, Yale, MIT, Oxford, the Sorbonne, and the Louvre, Hutz received his law degree from "The Knight School of Law," a diploma mill. (In fact, Hutz does not have a juris doctorate, but a "Doctor of Lawology.") His office, "I Can't Believe It's A Law Firm™," is conveniently located in the Springfield Shopping Mall, but he also conducts business in a nearby telephone booth. As anyone who has tried to use that phone can attest, Hutz is known to yell, "Hey, you! Get out of my office!"

Courtesy of Photofest.

THE SIMPSONS
Lionel Hutz (Phil Hartman) is a law-talkin' guy who's a bit ethically challenged.

Hutz's legal practice is wide-ranging, including criminal law, consumer claims, personal injuries, and wills. (Video wills are his favorite, because he "earn[s his] fee simply by pressing the 'play' button.") This does not seem to imply that he is a jack of all trades (or even a master of none), but instead underscores the economic realities of making a living as a sole practitioner: "Bread and butter" lawyers like Hutz must—and do—take whatever cases come their way.

His criminal cases run the gamut from minor to serious. For example, he represented Marge for shoplifting bourbon from the Kwikie Mart; Bart in the murder case of Principal Skinner; Krusty for a robbery; and a waiter who claimed to have been assaulted by Mayor Quimby's nephew over the "chowder" incident (dubbed "Waitergate" by the media). Personal injury claims, however, constitute the bulk of Hutz's practice. While this area showcases Hutz's legal skills, this does not inure to his benefit.

AMBULANCE CHASING

When it comes to pursuing personal injury claims and soliciting clients, Lionel Hutz embodies every negative stereotype of the personal injury lawyer. He is an ambulance chaser, not just figuratively but literally—we have seen Hutz chasing ambulances down the road, following them on a moped, and even running after hospital gurneys.

In Springfield, as in the rest of America, most people who are injured do not sue. Consequently, most potential cases never make it to a lawyer's office. But not to worry: where there is an injury, no matter how slight, Hutz will materialize to transform it into a viable legal claim. He doesn't merely evoke "litigation lottery" rhetoric, he invokes it. One of his ads says, "Why wait? Sue 'em today!! Calling us could be like winning the STATE LOTTERY!" His business card—which turns into a sponge when wet—proudly declares, "Clogging our courts since 1974." In this respect, Hutz's behavior conforms to the negative stereotype that lawyers encourage frivolous lawsuits, extract unwarranted settlements, and are driven by pecuniary interests.

Though some claims are legitimate, they are always motivated more by Hutz's self-interest than by that of his clients. To Hutz, a good case is an opportunity to revive his whiskey-sodden career. Hutz once introduced himself as "Lionel Hutz, court-appointed attorney. I'll be defending you on the charge of . . . Murder One! Wow! Even if I lose, I'll be famous!" His interest was also evident upon learning that Marge was sexually harassed. Marge wanted an apology, but Hutz had bigger plans.

HUTZ: Mrs. Simpson, you're in luck. Your sexual harassment suit is exactly what I need to help rebuild my shattered practice. Care to join me in a belt of scotch?

MARGE: It's 9:30 in the morning.

HUTZ: Yeah, but I haven't slept in days.

Hutz's personal interest, as expressed in dollars and cents, is even more apparent. Because litigation translates into profit, Hutz actively encourages it. His slogan is "We put the 'fortune' in your misfortune," and he even runs "$$$$ Lionel Hutz's COLLEGE OF LITIGATION $$$$," which trains individuals to become plaintiffs. According to its ad, the "college" teaches how to "LIE convincingly! WRITHE in agony! And MOAN with discomfort!" and offers advanced seminars in "The Art of the Limp" and "How to Slip and Fall on Cue." As Barney Gumble, a satisfied customer/student, gushes, "I've made thousands thanks to Lionel Hutz's malpractice training! If he did it for me, he can do it for you!"

This pecuniary interest creates an incentive to overstate claims, manufacture injuries, and produce fake expert witnesses. Indeed, this strategy seems to be the foundation on which many of Hutz's cases are built. Although this trickery might net higher verdicts, it can backfire. Notably, while *The Simpsons* regularly highlights the value of litigation, it consistently criticizes its illegitimate use. This is poignantly depicted in the $1 million personal injury lawsuit against Mr. Burns.

Mr. Burns, while driving his "luxury car of death," runs over Bart. Bart ends up in the hospital with some bumps and bruises and, of course, medical bills. Homer asks Mr. Burns to pay these expenses, but Burns responds to this reasonable request with insults and an offer of $100. (Indicative of Burns' cavalier attitude, he later testifies, "I should be able to run over as many kids as I want!") Homer then recalls Hutz visiting Bart's hospital bed.

> HUTZ: Hutz is the name, Mr. Simpson. Lionel Hutz, attorney at law. Here's my card. It turns into a sponge when you put it in water. . . .
>
> HOMER: [But] the doctor says it's just a bump on the head and a broken toe; nothing serious.
>
> HUTZ: Pfft. Doctors. Doctors are idiots!

Blinded by greed and anger, Homer hires Hutz, who then coaches Bart to lie on the witness stand and suborns false testimony about his injuries. Ultimately, however, as in most *Simpsons* "cheat" plots, the scheme is unsuccessful (thwarted by Marge's testimony), and Homer is left with nothing, not even the nickel that Burns had thrown at Bart. Although this episode indicts Hutz as masterminding an unethical scheme, it also holds Homer culpable for conspiring in the fraud. The message is clear: a sleazy lawyer may try to abuse the justice system, but he needs a willing and dishonest client-in-crime to pull it off.

LITIGATION

Corresponding with the public's belief that most lawyers spend a majority of their time trying cases, Lionel Hutz is frequently in court. He once boasted, "I've argued in front of every judge in this state. Often as a lawyer." He has been counsel in several noteworthy cases, though his efforts have met with varying results. Sometimes Hutz wins, but these victories are unrelated to, or in spite of, his lawyering.

Among his successes, Hutz represented Homer in his lawsuit against The Frying Dutchman restaurant. Enticed by their advertisement of an "all-you-can-eat buffet," Homer and Marge dined at The Frying Dutchman. Unfortunately, after Homer ate all of the restaurant's food, but not all that he could, it ejected him. Hutz called this "the most blatant case of fraudulent advertising since [his] suit against the film, 'The Never-Ending Story.'" At trial, he elicited from Marge key testimony about the lengths that she and Homer had to go through to satiate his appetite: they drove around looking for another All-You-Can-Eat fish restaurant until 3 AM, when they finally went fishing. Hutz's rhetorical question, "Do these seem like the actions of a man who had had *all he could eat?*" prompted "noes" from the jury as well as an amicable settlement from the restaurant. Hutz also successfully represented the artist who created Itchy (as well as cartoon violence) in a copyright infringement suit against Itchy & Scratchy Studios, resulting in an $800 million verdict. Hutz's contribution to this outcome, however, was debatable, as it was Bart rather than Hutz who found an old drawing that won the artist's case after the film showing the origin and creation of the Itchy character was destroyed.

Lionel Hutz even represented Homer in a breach of contract action against Satan, but absconded midtrial. After selling his soul for a donut, Homer was sent to the Ironic Punishments Division of Hell and force-fed an infinite number of donuts. To Satan's chagrin, the ironic punishment did not work, because Homer can happily eat an infinite number of donuts. Satan then sought to sentence Homer to eternal damnation, but acknowledged the necessity of a trial, remarking, "You Americans with your due process and fair trials. This is always much easier in Mexico." Desperate for a lawyer, Marge flipped through the phone book until she noticed the following ad: "Lionel Hutz. Cases won in 30 minutes or your pizza's free."

When Hutz arrived, he assured Marge, "Don't you worry. I watched *Matlock* in a bar last night. The sound wasn't on, but I think I got the gist of it." Hutz's hastily crafted opening statement underscored the strength of Satan's position while highlighting the weakness of Homer's position. Recognizing his mistake, Hutz called for a bathroom break and jumped out of the window. Nevertheless, Homer prevailed when Marge showed that *she* was the rightful owner of Homer's soul. (Homer had written on their wedding portrait, "All I can give you is my soul.") Therefore, Homer won in spite of, not because of, Hutz.

In the courtroom, Hutz is usually out of his depth and tends to throw around legal terms without understanding what they mean. He can't even spell "guilty." He once told a jury, "Ladies and gentlemen, I'm going to prove to you not only that Freddy Quimby is guilty, but that he is also innocent of not being guilty." Then, after eliciting helpful testimony from a witness, Hutz had this emblematic sequence:

HUTZ: I rest my case.

JUDGE: You rest your case?

HUTZ: What? Oh no, I thought that was just a figure of speech. CASE CLOSED.

On another occasion, Hutz delivered a closing argument unaware that he was half naked.

JUDGE: Mr. Hutz, do you know that you're not wearing any pants?

HUTZ: DAAAA!! I move for a bad court thingy.

JUDGE: You mean a mistrial?

HUTZ: Right!! That's why you're the judge and I'm the . . . [pause] law-talking guy.

These gaffes, so common to Hutz, are never committed by other Springfield lawyers. Thus, Hutz appears to be the one bad apple in the bunch, underscoring that most real lawyers are not like the stereotype that Hutz represents.

PROFESSIONALISM AND ETHICS

Recently, the Bar has voiced concerns that the once-noble profession of law is becoming just another business where aggressive advertising is the norm and professionalism and ethics are subservient to profit.

Paralleling this perceived "consumer-ization" of law, Hutz treats legal services like any other commodity for sale. His office is in a strip mall and he uses "gift with purchase" promotions, similar to those of cosmetics companies, to entice potential clients. For example, Hutz told Marge, "By hiring me as your lawyer, you also get this smoking monkey." In seeking Homer's case, he said, "You'll be getting more than just a lawyer, Mr. Simpson. You'll also be getting this exquisite faux pearl necklace, a $99 value, as our gift to you." Moreover, his yellow pages advertisement promises "Cases won in 30 minutes or your pizza's free!" and another print ad offers "FREE smoking monkey to first-time enrollers!"

Hutz advertises frequently, but just as frequently violates the profession's ethical rules. The ABA's Model Rules of Professional Conduct provide that "A lawyer shall not make a false or misleading communication about the lawyer or the lawyer's services." A communication is false or misleading if it contains a material misrepresentation of fact, omits information necessary to place the statement in context, or could create unjustified expectations about the outcome. This includes assertions about counsel's credentials and the ultimate cost to the client and ads for free consultations.

In complete disregard of this rule, Hutz promises outcomes, lies about his credentials (the *Louvre!*), and misleads clients about fees. He tells one prospective client, "The state bar forbids me from promising you a big cash settlement. But, just between you and me, I promise you a big cash settlement." To inflate his perceived expertise, Hutz has his secretary Della (referencing Perry Mason's secretary) enter a meeting with a fake message: "The Supreme Court called again. They need your help on some freedom thing." Finally, his ads range from misleading to untrue. In a particularly blatant example, Bart visits Hutz because his ad promised "works on contingency basis." Yet, once Bart is in the office, the fee structure changes.

> HUTZ: I'll take your case. But I'm going to have to ask for a $1,000 retainer.
>
> BART: A thousand dollars? But your ad says "No money down."
>
> HUTZ: Oh! They got this all screwed up.
>
> [taking the ad and "correcting" its grammar to read: *"Works on contingency basis? No. Money down!"*]

BART: So you don't work on a contingency basis?

HUTZ: No. Money down! Oops, it shouldn't have this Bar Association logo here either.

HUTZ'S RETIREMENT

Hutz was voiced by Emmy-nominated actor Phil Hartman, whom Matt Groening praised as able to produce "the maximum amount of humor out of any line given." Groening explained that "if a script ever dragged, we could throw in a Lionel Hutz scene and everything will perk right up." As a result, the program used his character frequently. In 1998, when Hartman was murdered, the writers retired the character. Consequently, later seasons provide some comparison to the Hutz years. Despite Hutz's numerous shortcomings, he was an average person's means of access to the law and its remedies, and enabled the Simpsons to have their issues heard. In his absence, they have had difficulty obtaining counsel. For instance, when Marge attempted to retain a lawyer for her class-action suit against the sugar industry, she could only muster Gil. Gil, who cannot hold a job, proved incompetent. He begged Marge for her case, but backed out when he realized that he would have to take depositions, thus leaving Marge to fend for herself.

Other Lawyers

Although Hutz is the most prominently featured lawyer on *The Simpsons*, the Blue-Haired Lawyer appears most frequently. Known for his pasty face, nasal New York accent, and blue hair, Blue-Haired Lawyer has been involved with virtually every legal issue depicted. To some extent, this is a function of our adversary system: Where there are two opposing sides, there must be two opposing lawyers. Blue-Haired Lawyer is that *other* lawyer.

He began as opposing counsel to Hutz, but expanded his practice to appear whenever another lawyer was needed. Consequently, the clients or legal interests Blue represents are often antagonistic to the Simpsons. For instance, Blue-Haired Lawyer defended The Frying Dutchman restaurant and Itchy & Scratchy Studios. He has also accompanied Mr. Burns when he signed various legal documents, and served as Springfield District Attorney, prosecuting members of the Simpson family.

This has resulted in a seemingly infinite practice area and limitless expertise. In this way, Blue-Haired Lawyer exemplifies the positive stereotype of a lawyer who is clever, knows the answer to every question, and is the penultimate professional. Blue's lawyerly skill has also produced some comical results: In one case, he was both the prosecutor and the defense lawyer.

Blue-Haired Lawyer is juxtaposed against Hutz not only as opposing counsel, but also because he is highly competent and ethical. Admittedly, some of the settlements he has negotiated have been a bit lopsided. For instance, when health violations at the nuclear power plant rendered Homer impotent, Blue-Haired Lawyer appeared at Homer's doorstep offering an immediate $2,000 settlement. Although this settlement seems low, it reflects a lawyer's ethical obligation to vigorously represent the interests of his client.

The other lawyers in Springfield (i.e., the "10 high-priced lawyers" retained by Mr. Burns and those periodically appearing as corporate counsel) share many of Blue's attributes. They are competent, ethical, loyal to their clients, and, most importantly, nothing like Lionel Hutz. As typified by Mr. Burns' "10 high-priced lawyers," these lawyers are anonymous. (Even Blue-Haired Lawyer has no name.) Though varying in gender and ethnicity, they are otherwise indistinguishable, dressed in identical gray suits, white shirts, and red ties, and carrying matching briefcases. They are not independent of one another, but operate as a single entity. Additionally, these lawyers are extraordinarily loyal and exhibit no interest other than that of their client. (Of course, they really have no choice, since Mr. Burns keeps them behind a wall panel in his office, releasing them only when he needs legal advice.) Moreover, despite working for the most amoral, malevolent man in Springfield, these lawyers do not appear to engage in illegal or unethical behavior, but represent Burns within the bounds of the law. Notwithstanding this, they are still unfairly condemned and scapegoated. This point was humorously made when Mr. Burns ironically harangued them, "I want your legal advice. I even pay for it. But to me you're all vipers! You live on personal injuries, you live on divorces, you live on pain and misery!. . . It's so hard for me to listen to you, I hate you all so much!"

Getting the Joke

When it comes to competency, client representation, and ethics, *The Simpsons* lawyers fall into one of two groups: Lionel Hutz and everyone else. Tellingly, but for Hutz, Springfield lawyers do not manufacture claims, cheat the system, or put their interests above those of their clients. Therefore, by treating Hutz as an exception, *The Simpsons* does not indict the entire legal profession, but only unethical, money-hungry, ambulance-chasing lawyers—like Hutz. This is further evidenced by the comedy itself. *The Simpsons'* lawyer jokes rest on the mythologies and stereotypes (both positive and negative) about lawyers. With regard to Hutz, the show ridicules every negative stereotype manifested by him, designating that he is to be laughed *at*. With regard to other lawyers, however, jokes are usually not at their expense. Instead, the humor tends to make fun of their clients, the circumstances of legal practice, or their positive qualities, such as courtroom prowess and adroitness. (In fact, some of these jokes are probably understood only by lawyers.) The humor does not target these competent lawyers, who, after all, are the majority of the legal profession, but instead laughs *with* them.

CHAPTER 33

All Roads Lead to Rome, Wisconsin: Judge Henry Bone, Douglas Wambaugh, and the Strange World of *Picket Fences*

LANCE MCMILLIAN

The Tin Man is dead. And not by natural causes. In the words of one sheriff's deputy, "Murder has come to Rome, Wisconsin." As a result, the local production of *The Wizard of Oz* has come to a premature end. The Tin Man's widow knew that trouble was in the air: "I told him not to be the Tin Man. The man has a bypass, [and] plays a character who needs a heart. I told him he was mocking God. He should have been the Lion." The widow should know. She and the town pharmacist conspired to kill her husband. Their motive is not too hard to understand. The Tin Man was sleeping with the pharmacist's 16-year-old daughter.

So begins the first episode of one of the great dramas of the 1990s: *Picket Fences*. Unlike creator David E. Kelley's other legally themed shows (*L.A. Law*, *Ally McBeal*, *The Practice*, and *Boston Legal*), *Picket Fences* is not a show about lawyers. Rather, it is a show about how the application of law reverberates throughout a community and the individual citizens who live in it.

Picket Fences

Aired:
- September 18, 1992– June 26, 1996, CBS

Cast:
- Kathy Baker (Dr. Jill Brock)
- Tom Skerritt (Sheriff Jimmy Brock)
- Ray Walston (Judge Henry Bone)
- Fyvush Finkel (Douglas Wambaugh)

Awards:
- Emmy for Outstanding Drama Series (1993, 1994)
- Kathy Baker, Emmy for Outstanding Lead Actress in a Drama Series (1993, 1995, 1996)
- Ray Walston, Emmy for Outstanding Supporting Actor in a Drama Series (1995, 1996)
- Tom Skerritt, Emmy for Outstanding Lead Actor in a Drama Series (1993)
- Fyvush Finkel, Emmy for Outstanding Supporting Actor in a Drama Series (1994)
- Leigh Taylor-Young, Emmy for Outstanding Supporting Actress in a Drama Series (1994)

Courtesy of Photofest.

PICKET FENCES
Judge Henry Bone (Ray Walston) takes no nonsense but dispenses rough justice in Rome, Wisconsin.

Lawyers, though, are not irrelevant to the story. The denouement of many episodes occurs in the Hogan County Courthouse before Judge Henry Bone (played by veteran character actor Ray Walston, who also starred in *My Favorite Martian* and *Fast Times at Ridgemont High*). Part mediator, part lecturer, part conscience of the community, Judge Bone is an irascible, no-nonsense jurist who follows his instincts as often as he follows the law. Indicative of his general demeanor, the phrases "Shut up!" and "Get out!" frequently emanate from his lips. When really riled up, he delivers his orders while standing for greater emphasis.

Judge Bone's thorn in the flesh is lawyer Douglas Wambaugh (played by Fyvush Finkel, who starred as Tevya in *Fiddler on the Roof* and later played Harvey Lipschultz in David Kelley's *Boston Public*). Throughout the four years that *Picket Fences* was on the air, district attorneys came and went, but Bone and Wambaugh remained. The two characters could not be more different. Unlike many lawyers, Wambaugh actually seems to enjoy his work, especially his role as the titular town villain. He is bombastic, sarcastic, theatrical, and irritating. He is the type of person who dresses up as Dracula for a costume party and serenades the crowd with renditions of "The Wambaugh Mash" and "I Left My Heart in San Francisco."

Wambaugh is particularly adept at pushing the buttons of everyone around him, but without ever going that one step too far. Paradoxically, he usually performs all of these antics with a smile. Still, his style wins him few fans. A pastor refers to Wambaugh as "a moral sinkhole," the sheriff thinks him "a reptile who disgraces his profession just by being alive," and his own rabbi chastises him, "With Jews like you, who needs anti-Semitism?" The town doctor wonders, "I don't know what's worse—being wrong or having it pointed out to me by Douglas Wambaugh." Finally, even Wambaugh's wife admits to him, "In 40 years of marriage a day hasn't gone by [when] I didn't think about killing you." On the surface, Wambaugh seems to take it in stride. Instead of being defensive about the negative perception many have about lawyers, Wambaugh embraces such disdain. Accordingly, when he comes to the defense of the Frog Man, he explains without missing a beat, "I represent reptiles for free; professional courtesy."

Yet the dislike toward Wambaugh transcends the typical distaste the public feels toward the legal profession. Wambaugh is unique in his ability to strike a nerve. He will unabashedly say anything—no matter how outrageous—to advance the cause of his client. For all his faults, Wambaugh is exactly the type of lawyer that people hate when he is on the other side, but love when he represents them. He is also creative with his craft. Take the case of the woman who ran over her husband with a steamroller. Three eyewitnesses saw the flattening. The wife even confessed! Lesser lawyers would have sought a plea deal in the face of such odds. Not Wambaugh. His innovative defense: temporary insanity by reason of menopause. Wambaugh's dedication to the case becomes apparent when we see him in bed, cigar in mouth, reading the book *Menopause: The Golden Lochness* in preparation for an important cross-examination the following day. This little scene highlights how every case totally consumes the life of the trial lawyer. This work does not go unrewarded. Amazingly, the defense succeeds with the jury. Then again, this is television.

Judge Bone and Wambaugh often tangle over the great questions of the day. Even though a small town, Rome is a mecca for social controversy of lasting legal significance. The issues that arrive at the courthouse include euthanasia, polygamy, transsexualism, gay adoption, separation of church and state, racial bussing, animal abuse, the rights of dentists with the HIV virus, the presence of sex offenders in the community, and all manner of bizarre fetishes (to name one, sexual arousal through bath toys). In this cutting-edge legal world, a simple matter of constitutional criminal procedure appears almost pedestrian. But when a police officer is shot, the basic constitutional requirement of probable cause poses a difficult professional challenge to both Judge Bone and Wambaugh.

This is the saga of the Frog Man—a burglar whose calling card is to leave frogs at the scene of his heists. When a jewelry store robbery goes bad, a deputy lies on the ground fighting for his life. An arrest is made, a search is conducted, and evidence is obtained. Confronted with the evidence, the suspected Frog Man confesses. Under clever questioning by Wambaugh, however, the arresting officer concedes that she did not get a warrant before conducting the arrest and search, despite having had the opportunity to do so. The significance of her testimony becomes plain when Wambaugh, who often refers to himself in the third person, helpfully points out, "Douglas Wambaugh has trapped you." All the evidence following the arrest must be thrown out, leaving the prosecution with no case other than the defendant's vast collection of frogs. Despite the unpopularity of his ruling, Judge Bone has no choice but to set the Frog Man free. Even Wambaugh seems chagrined as he reflects on the fact that his efforts led to the freedom of the man alleged to have shot an officer whom Wambaugh knows and respects. This is a constant tension in many small-town legal communities, where a lawyer or a judge sometimes has to take positions that seem incomprehensible to friends and acquaintances within a tight-knit community.

The variety of cases arriving on Rome's doorstep invariably come with interesting offers of proof. For Judge Bone, though, the prospect of hearing testimony about a person's sex change from a man into a woman induces a serious bout of squeamishness. He knows his weaknesses and warns Wambaugh not to bring the matter to his courtroom. "Now you listen to me. I can put up with elephants, exploding cow udders, and serial bathers, and killing nuns, but I've got no stomach for a transsexual. It could make me faint." Compounding matters, the transsexual is an elementary school teacher. Another wrinkle: the transsexual is slated to play the Virgin Mary in the town's Christmas pageant. To understate the obvious by a factor of at least one million, this state of affairs has many in the religious community of Rome concerned, and the teacher is fired. Judge Bone's worst fears are realized when the case comes to his courtroom. A few grimaces notwithstanding, Bone survives the trial and issues a ruling: the dismissal was illegal.

A sociological observer of Rome's judicial process would conclude that litigation is simultaneously the chief economic engine and main entertainment activity of the town. Even when not directly affected by a case, the townsfolk congregate in court like other people meet around a water cooler. This is especially true for Rome's civic leaders. Frankly, it is amazing that anything ever gets accomplished, given the inordinate time these officials spend observing the wheels of justice in motion. The courtroom's role as town commons affects the tenor of proceedings: lawyers perform, witnesses give speeches instead of testimony, and observers in the crowd rise up to offer their thoughts. One lawyer from the big city of Madison, Wisconsin, becomes aghast at the spectacle until Judge Bone puts him in his place. Yet, the big city lawyer has a point: Bone's attempt to instill decorum aside, his courtroom oftentimes has a circus feel. Indeed, when circus dwarf Mr. Dreeb comes to town riding on a stolen elephant, the circus feel of the courtroom becomes literal. Wambaugh, adding to the chaos, announces his presence thusly, "Douglas Wambaugh, appearing for the midget, Your Honor." You can imagine the rest.

Things become more bizarre—and dangerous—when an Indian tribe declares war on Rome and barricades itself in the courthouse. Angered by Judge Bone's ruling that the city has a legal right to build a golf course over an Indian burial ground, the proud tribe strikes back. Bone displays some anger of his own as he exhorts the sheriff to do something to retake the courthouse. But things are not that easy. In face-to-face negotiations, the tribal chief flatly tells the judge that his people prefer suicide over genocide. Bone helplessly watches the armed standoff play out, recognizing that some things are best left to the police. Cases such as this begin to tax Bone's stamina. Reflecting on the ever-increasing litany of strange and perplexing legal issues that come before him, Bone laments, "I'm supposed to be a folksy country judge spending my golden years settling pig disputes between farmers. That's why I came to this town." He fancies himself a simple man in search of simple things.

But Judge Bone is more clever than he lets on. In an episode that would foreshadow the societal fissures caused by the Terri Schiavo controversy, Bone must decide the heartrending case of Cindy, a woman who is both brain-dead and three months pregnant. The husband seeks to keep her connected to breathing machines in order to have their child. Cindy's mother, however, recoils in horror at the indignity of keeping her medically dead daughter "alive" in such circumstances. And the mother has a Minnesota court order to back her up. The husband evades the reach of that order by moving to Rome and caring for his wife at home. With his secret discovered, the matter again plays out in the justice system. Wambaugh represents the husband and in typical Wambaugh style explains to a deputy, "Don't waste my time. If you charge him with kidnapping, I'll argue that she's dead. The medical records will back me up. If you charge him with stealing a corpse, I'll argue that she's alive. The church will back me up." This brilliant bit of dexterity carries the day.

Even though no criminal charges are forthcoming, the issue of whether Cindy's breathing machine should be turned off remains. In a case like this, with no villains and no unsympathetic parties, there are no easy answers. Nor is negotiation possible. This is a literally life-or-death case of absolutes. Judge Bone recognizes the stakes and finds himself "shocked and terrified" by the power that comes from being a judge. Legally, the issue centers on the intent of Cindy—not the desires of her husband or mother. On this point, the answer would seem clear, because she executed a living will expressing her wish to not be kept alive in such circumstances. In reviewing the file, though, Judge Bone discovers an interesting piece of evidence, the significance of which eludes even Wambaugh's discerning antenna. Among Cindy's papers is an organ donor card that allows her organs to be used after her death for the benefit of other people. This discovery leads Bone to a profound insight: a person who wanted to use her organs to preserve the life of others would not object to her body being used to deliver the life of her own child. The husband, therefore, wins the case. Judge Bone displays the wisdom of Solomon as he explains to Cindy's devastated mother that when she holds her grandchild in her arms, "Today's pain will be displaced by tomorrow's joy." Bone knows that love conquers all.

Bone's humility is what we should want from our judges. Like politicians, those who seek to become judges effectively say to the rest of us: "I ought to rule *you*." This is both a very dangerous and a powerfully seductive attitude. In theory, the solution to such a mindset would be that the only people deemed fit to be leaders and decision makers would be those who do not want the job. Practically speaking, of course, this is impossible. The next best thing, then, is for those in positions of power to recognize the awesome responsibility that comes from the privilege to rule, and to be ever mindful of their own limitations. Bone combines these attributes in his approach to judging. His approach also adds a third characteristic—compassion. A gut-wrenching scene occurs when

Bone explains to adoptive mother-to-be Deputy Maxine Stewart that she must return the baby girl to whom she has grown attached to the birth mother. It is the right ruling, but painful nonetheless. Later that night, Judge Bone visits Stewart at home to ensure that she is all right. His words of encouragement and insights into how the baby girl enriched Stewart's life help to salve her wounds. Because of his position, Bone's words carry not just legal, but moral, weight.

This type of personal touch is only possible in smaller communities where everyone is a neighbor to everyone else. In the vast majority of real courtrooms, the administration of justice is more akin to an assembly line where jurists quickly pass judgment on the strangers brought before them. This reality is not necessarily good or bad; it just is. But Judge Bone's relationship to the community—and the accountability that flows from this connection—strikes an idealistic chord. This closeness helps to check any cavalier impulses that might otherwise tempt a judge to ignore the seriousness of the judicial role. It is hard to be nonchalant when the effects of one's decisions will readily be witnessed in the lives of the neighbors who live down the street. Proximity breeds greater deliberation.

Still, there are limits. There are strong values behind the concept that justice should be blind. In this vein, Judge Bone is more "in" the community than "of" it. The visit to Stewart's house is a marked departure for him. Unlike Wambaugh, who is ubiquitous about town, Bone is rarely seen away from the courthouse. Like most judges, much of Bone's life remains a mystery to his neighbors. This is not unusual. Presidents are readily identifiable. Supreme Court justices are not. This dichotomy reflects our dual conception of what makes a good judge. We want a judge to be one of us and understand our concerns; at the same time, we also want him or her to be above the fray.

In the end, though, ours is a nation of laws, not men. While Bone is willing to be creative and innovative within the bounds of the law, he refuses to wholly ignore that which the law commands. Bone's ultimate fidelity to the law comes through in the difficult case of Bone's friend Bill McGrath. McGrath, who has Parkinson's disease, needs a fetal tissue transplant to battle his worsening condition. However, the surgery is too experimental and the hospital refuses to permit it. Can the hospital be ordered to allow the procedure? Bone searches fervently for a legal way to make it so. Alas, he cannot. He then does his duty and rules against

McGrath, possibly causing his friend to lose his life. The lasting lesson: doing the right thing is not always pain-free.

Wambaugh, for his part, is at his moral best in the case of the Potato Man (no relation to the Frog Man). There is a serial bather on the loose in Rome who breaks into the homes of teenage girls, takes baths in their tubs, and uses bath toys to satisfy his erotic fantasies. Frank, a poor recluse who lives alone in the woods and walks around town carrying a sack of potatoes, is the chief suspect. The evidence against the Potato Man is nonexistent, but fear and loathing of a man so different from everyone else lead to an arrest anyway. Wambaugh takes the case for free, and bail is set at $1,000. Given Frank's indigence, the number might as well as have been $1,000,000.

Wambaugh pays the bail himself, putting the Potato Man back on the street. At the time, Wambaugh is in the midst of a heated campaign to become mayor. Posting bond for such a reviled figure as Frank is politically stupid. No matter. When challenged by a police officer for letting Frank loose, Wambaugh becomes deadly serious: "My parents were murdered during the Holocaust. I know bigotry when I see it. I know oppression." With these solemn words, Wambaugh's zealousness begins to take on a new light. Yes, he might be prone to outrageousness and exaggeration, but this excess is borne out of a passion to defend the defenseless. As for Frank, he is not the serial bather. The culprit is the clean-cut, good-looking, well-regarded, and trusted district attorney. The world, as it turns out, was not as it seemed to the citizens of Rome. For Frank, however, the truth comes too late. The sting of accusation will long follow him. He will always be an outcast, subject to judgment and stares. His desire to live peaceably and to keep to himself shattered, the Potato Man leaves town on foot in search of another home.

While Wambaugh's tendencies are decidedly liberal, his worldview breaks down when it comes to his own home. After discovering his wife of over 40 years in bed with another man, Wambaugh seeks to invoke the power of the state to have his wife arrested for adultery. The relevant statute is exactly the sort of archaic and non-enforced law that Wambaugh the lawyer would have attacked with great gusto. However, in his personal pain and humiliation, he seeks the type of legalized vengeance he typically denounces. As he and his wife discuss the situation, Wambaugh begins to understand the deep isolation she feels as a result of being married to him. Wambaugh's clients receive his best; his wife does not. She wants companionship and romance from her husband. Wambaugh's hard stance begins to soften. He promises to be more attentive and to supply the intimacy his wife needs—provided she gives him two days notice! (This happens, after all, in the days before Viagra.)

The effort by Wambaugh to become mayor is another matter altogether. His is not a traditional campaign. He enters the small debate hall accompanied by a marching band and cheerleaders singing, "There's a brand new day with Wambaugh." In another unique electoral technique, Wambaugh happily sings about the issues of the day in a bar. All is not good feelings and sunshine, however. He shows a streak of opportunism and meanness when he attacks the current mayor for being overweight. He pretends to be shot by an assailant with a BB gun in a cheap and morally dubious ploy to garner sympathy. He even electioneers outside a polling place, in flagrant disregard of the law. Through it all, though, he maintains a sense of optimism, confidently predicting that win or lose, "Douglas Wambaugh will come out ahead!" His actions, however, reveal his words to be a lie. When the results are announced and Wambaugh realizes he has lost, he is devastated. He slowly walks out of the election hall, dejected and alone. The election really meant something to him, and losing the race damages his considerable ego.

But why? Why would Wambaugh embark on the quixotic quest to be the mayor of Rome? Pressed for the reason by his physician Jill Brock, Wambaugh reveals his vulnerable side. Even though he is a successful lawyer who wins over 80 percent of his trials, he still hears the laughs and snickers of those who refuse to take him seriously. Being mayor would silence his critics. When Brock reasonably points out that he invites derision by frequently playing the buffoon, Wambaugh refuses to concede fault. "I play my hand. That's all. I play my hand." Still, there is a touch of sadness in his recognition of how "playing his hand" has damaged his standing in the community.

He wins his cases, but at what cost? Despite the bluster and bravado, Douglas Wambaugh just wants to be loved.

CHAPTER 34

Is There a Lawyer in the (White) House? Portraying Lawyers on *The West Wing*

KEITH A. ROWLEY

At its creative and popular peak one of the best-written and most successful dramas in network television history, NBC's *The West Wing* ushered viewers into the inner sanctum of fictional President Jed Bartlet, offering unlimited access to the work and lives of the men and women who stood behind and helped the President formulate and implement his policy agenda. As with any real-life administration of recent memory, a number of President Bartlet's closest advisors during the show's halcyon seasons— notably Chief of Staff Leo McGarry, Deputy Chief of Staff Josh Lyman, Communications Director Toby Ziegler, and Deputy Communications Director Sam Seaborn—were lawyers by training. Of the four, however, we only saw Sam acting as a lawyer (for example, accompanying Josh to a Freedom of Information Act deposition, researching whether Josh could sue the Ku Klux Klan for money damages for the injuries he suffered during an assassination attempt, evaluating presidential pardon recommendations, and advising Josh's assistant, Donna Moss, before her deposition by congressional

The West Wing

Creator:
- Aaron Sorkin

Aired:
- September 22, 1999–May 14, 2006, NBC

Cast:
- Martin Sheen (President Josiah "Jed" Bartlet)
- John Spencer (Leo McGarry)
- Allison Janney (Claudia Jean "C. J." Cregg)
- Bradley Whitford (Josh Lyman)
- Richard Schiff (Toby Ziegler)
- Rob Lowe (Sam Seaborn)
- Janel Moloney (Donna Moss)
- Dulé Hill (Charlie Young)
- Stockard Channing (Abigail "Abbey" Bartlet)
- Tim Matheson (Vice President John Hoynes)
- Oliver Platt (Oliver Babish)
- Emily Procter (Ainsley Hayes)
- Matthew Perry (Joe Quincy)
- John Larroquette (Lionel Tribbey)

Awards:

- Peabody Award (1999, 2000)
- Emmy for Outstanding Drama Series (2000, 2001, 2002, 2003)
- Golden Globe for Best TV Series—Drama (2001)
- Martin Sheen: Golden Globe for Best Performance by an Actor in a TV Series—Drama (2001); Screen Actors Guild Award for Outstanding Performance by a Male Actor in a Drama Series (2001, 2002)
- Allison Janney: Emmy for Outstanding Lead Actress in a Drama Series (2002, 2004); Emmy for Outstanding Supporting Actress in a Drama Series (2000, 2001); Screen Actors Guild Award for Outstanding Performance by a Female Actor in a Drama Series (2001, 2002)
- Stockard Channing: Emmy for Outstanding Supporting Actress in a Drama Series (2002)
- Richard Schiff: Emmy for Outstanding Supporting Actor in a Drama Series (2000)
- John Spencer: Emmy for Outstanding Supporting Actor in a Drama Series (2002)
- Bradley Whitford: Emmy for Outstanding Supporting Actor in a Drama Series (2001)

counsel). Characters beyond President Bartlet's inner circle handled most of the interesting lawyering. This essay focuses on four of them: Lionel Tribbey, Ainsley Hayes, Joe Quincy, and Oliver Babish.

Trials and Tribbey-lations

Less than two years into President Bartlet's first term, he was on his fourth White House Counsel. Our first glimpse of Lionel Tribbey, in the sole episode in which he appeared, came as he burst into Leo's office bellowing.

TRIBBEY: Has anybody in this building heard of "contempt of Congress"?. . . Congress *will* hold the White House in contempt, Leo, which is nothing compared to the contempt in which *I* will hold the White House if this keeps happening.

LEO: What'd we do?

TRIBBEY: Steve Joyce and Mark Brookline testified at Governmental Affairs that the White House . . . didn't have the Rockland memo.

LEO: Do we?

TRIBBEY: Holding it in my hand, Leo!. . . When your guys go to the Hill, they can't drop their testimony on my desk at 9:15 and testify at 9:30! I was ready to take a vacation, Leo!. . . I had this thing closed. Now I've got to go back up there, hat in hand, because the circus is in town!

Tribbey's attention then shifted to Ainsley Hayes (more on her momentarily), whom Leo introduced. Tribbey recognized her name.

TRIBBEY: [T]he girl who's been writing the columns. . . . You're an idiot.

Courtesy of Photofest.

THE WEST WING
President Jed Bartlet (Martin Sheen), Press Secretary C.J. Cregg (Allison Janney), Communications Director Toby Ziegler (Richard Schiff), and Chief of Staff Leo McGarry (John Spencer).

LEO: She's not an idiot, Lionel. She clerked for Dreifort.

TRIBBEY: Well, Dreifort's an idiot.

LEO: Dreifort's a Supreme Court Justice, Lionel, so let's speak of him with respect and practice some tolerance for those who disagree with us.

TRIBBEY: I believe, as long as Justice Dreifort is intolerant toward gays, lesbians, blacks, unions, women, poor people, and the First, Fourth, Fifth, and Ninth Amendments, I will remain intolerant toward him. . . .[1]

Having watched Ainsley Hayes skewer Sam Seaborn on the fictional political talk show *Capital Beat*, President Bartlet had instructed Leo to hire Ainsley to work for Tribbey.[2] Tribbey's initial reaction was less than enthusiastic.[3] Later, he confronted Ainsley about her motives.

TRIBBEY: These people here are trying to do something. I'll have their backs while they're trying. What are *you* doing here?

AINSLEY: Serving my country. . . .

TRIBBEY: Why?

AINSLEY: I feel a sense of duty. . . .

TRIBBEY: What, did you just walk out of *The Pirates of Penzance*?. . .

AINSLEY: Is it so hard to believe, in this day and age, that someone would roll up their sleeves, set aside partisanship, and say, "What can I do?"

Despite replying "Yes," Tribbey entrusted Ainsley with cleaning up Joyce and Brookline's mess.

TRIBBEY: I want you to go up to the Hill this afternoon and I want you to talk to the Associate Majority Counsel at Governmental Affairs.

AINSLEY: You're sending me to the Associate Counsel 'cause I speak Republican?. . .

TRIBBEY: Yes. Read about it, then fix it.[4]

By the end of the day, after Ainsley had dutifully smoothed feathers on Capitol Hill, returned to the White House to offer Joyce and Brookline some friendly advice, held her temper while they berated her, and later returned to her office to find dead flowers and an obscene note awaiting her, Tribbey backed Sam's decision to fire Joyce and Brookline—and, by extension, backed Ainsley.

Tribbey occasionally loomed off-camera for a few more months before Oliver Babish replaced him. Ainsley, meanwhile, appeared in several episodes bridging the last few months of Tribbey's tenure and the first year of Babish's.

The Model of a Modern (Associate) White House Counsel

Unlike the blustery Tribbey, Ainsley Hayes seemed to have taken to heart the maxim that one can catch more flies with honey than with vinegar. After meeting with the House Governmental Affairs Committee's associate majority counsel, Ainsley advised Joyce and Brookline—her clients—to make a simple conciliatory gesture.

AINSLEY: [Y]our attitude during your testimony is being taken by some of the Republican committee members as a sign of disrespect.

JOYCE: Oh, please.

AINSLEY: No, hang on a second. This is so easy to fix we are gonna pick up yardage. Write a short note, have it delivered by messenger to the majority counsel, and copy the chairman and the Speaker.

JOYCE: Your first act on the job is asking us to apologize to the Republicans on the Governmental Affairs Committee . . . because they didn't like our attitude?

AINSLEY: Yeah, I know this doesn't look good. But the fact is, it's the smart thing to do, and if you don't do it at my suggestion, I know Lionel Tribbey is going to come down here and you're gonna have to do it at his.[5]

Instead of heeding Ainsley's advice, Joyce and Brookline retaliated, which cost them their jobs and fostered sympathy for Ainsley among the senior staff.

That is not to say that Ainsley didn't have some vinegar in her. Sometimes staking out positions contrary to those of more senior staffers, Ainsley demonstrated that "sweet" and "soft" are not synonymous. For example, when Sam asked her to summarize his 22-page recommendation regarding an amendment to a commerce bill, Ainsley reversed Sam's recommendation and then convinced him that she was right. Sam took it to Leo, who agreed to pass along Ainsley's recommendation to the President.[6] Similarly, Ainsley convinced Josh that a bill defining "marriage," for purposes of programs receiving federal funding, as being between a man and woman was not unconstitutional and, therefore, the President should not veto it.[7] Ainsley also stood firm against the need for an Equal Rights Amendment,[8] despite Sam's adamant support for one.

Ainsley became a valuable and valued member of the team—sometimes serving as a liaison between the White House and the Republican-controlled Congress,[9] or as a public face of an administration that had few female, Southern, or Republican faces,[10] and sometimes pulling back a senior staffer from the legal brink, as she did when Sam wanted to disclose privileged information after an oil tanker he helped purchase ran aground and spilled 700,000 gallons of oil.

AINSLEY: I know how you feel about these things. Trust me, Kensington's going to pay [for] it through the nose.

SAM: No, they're not. . . .

AINSLEY: You think their liability shield is that strong?

SAM:	I do. . . . I bought the *Indio* for them when I was at Gage Whitney.
AINSLEY:	Wow. Talk about your chickens coming home to roost.
SAM:	Yeah. . . . I know this is going to sound crazy; but I was thinking, if I could be deposed for the plaintiffs. . . .
AINSLEY:	Why?
SAM:	. . . Look, I was very proud of myself for making such a great deal . . . and it really didn't bother me that the boat was cheap for a reason. But then, at the 11th hour, I had a change of heart . . . and I told them the boat wasn't good enough, particularly with regards to the steering and navigation systems . . . and I suggested they spend more money, and they said. . . .
AINSLEY:	Stop talking right now!. . . You *know* better. Neither you nor your clients abdicated attorney-client privilege when you left Gage. If you gave that deposition, you'd be disbarred. And even if you were willing to be disbarred, there's no judge in the country who'd allow privileged testimony.[11]

Ainsley lived out her dream of serving the president of the United States and came to realize that the Bartlet White House was full of people earnestly striving to do what they thought was right for the country, even if their ideals often did not jibe with hers.

Mighty Joe Quincy

Emily Procter's departure for CBS's *CSI: Miami* prompted Ainsley Hayes's departure from the White House Counsel's office.[12] Into the breach stepped Joe Quincy, a former Supreme Court clerk who had lost his job when a new Solicitor General wanted his own staff. Joe was in the doghouse with his fellow Republicans for arguing in favor of limiting soft-money campaign contributions, and hoped that the opening in the White House Counsel's office would save him from having to accept a lucrative offer from Debevoise & Plimpton.[13]

Joe's first day on the job was a memorable one. C. J. Cregg referred to Joe what she thought would be a laughable assignment: following up on a blind tip the *Washington Post*'s science editor had received that the White House had suppressed a NASA commission report containing evidence of fossilized water on Mars. When Joe stopped by Josh

Lyman's office later to ask whether he should report his findings directly to Leo, Donna was telling Josh that the press office had asked about another anonymous tip to the *Washington Post*—that the White House had pressured the Justice Department to settle an antitrust investigation. It became clear to Josh that there was a leak. Joe also learned that Vice President John Hoynes, who headed the NASA commission whose report was allegedly suppressed, also knew the details of the antitrust settlement; that the *Washington Post*'s new gossip columnist was reporting that D.C. socialite Helen Baldwin had signed a lucrative "tell-all" book deal; and that White House phone logs showed that Vice President Hoynes had placed 47 calls to Helen Baldwin—all of which pointed to Hoynes as the source of the leak. When confronted, Hoynes admitted that he had had an extramarital affair with Baldwin while he was vice president. That revelation, together with the classified nature of some of the information Hoynes had disclosed, led him to resign the vice presidency.[14]

In Joe's only other on-screen appearance, Toby Ziegler asked him to convince Chief Justice Roy Ashland, for whom Joe had clerked, to meet with President Bartlet to discuss resigning so that President Bartlet could choose Ashland's successor. Despite Joe's extreme reluctance, he arranged the meeting.[15] While the meeting did not lead directly to Ashland's retirement, it laid a foundation, so that the untimely death of a young, conservative justice four months later created an opportunity for President Bartlet to appoint a worthy, ideologically liberal successor to Ashland (Judge Evelyn Baker Lang), as well as an ideologically conservative successor to the late Justice Owen Brady (Judge Christopher Mulready) to mollify the Republicans on the Senate Judiciary Committee, who otherwise would never confirm Lang to replace Brady.[16] By that time, Matthew Perry had returned to *Friends*, so Joe was not around to admire what he helped facilitate (or regret what he started).

Zen and the Art of Being White House Counsel

The most compelling character in the White House Counsel's office during *The West Wing*'s seven-year run was Oliver Babish, who succeeded Lionel Tribbey late in season two. Whereas Tribbey tended to bluster, Babish was—or at least appeared, like the above-water part of the proverbial duck—more calm and matter-of-fact.

When we first met Oliver, three months into his tenure, President Bartlet and Leo McGarry came to tell Oliver that the President had been diagnosed years earlier with multiple sclerosis—something neither he nor his campaign had disclosed when he was running for president—and to ask about the legal ramifications. The President began, "I'm going to tell you a story and then I need you to tell me whether or not I've engaged 16 people in a massive criminal conspiracy to defraud the public in order to win a presidential election."[17] Oliver, perched on the edge of his desk, reached over, grabbed a large gavel Justice Brandeis had given his grandfather, smashed a Dictaphone he had previously complained was stuck on "record,"[18] then turned back to the President and Leo and said, matter-of-factly, "OK." Throughout the conversations that followed with President Bartlet, Leo, C. J., and First Lady Abigail Bartlet, Oliver displayed a laudable mix of personal loyalty, professional detachment, patience, insistence, meticulousness, circumspection, and candor.

When he asked President Bartlet whether the latter's condition might affect his cognitive functions without anyone else knowing it (perhaps at a time that could compromise national security) and the President answered "Yes," Oliver immediately advised the President that attorney-client privilege would not protect anything he told Oliver. "So you want to be very careful about what you say in this room right now, Mr. President, because, if subpoenaed to give a deposition, I'm not going to lie under oath."[19] President Bartlet insisted he had no reason to be careful about what he told Oliver and did not want a personal lawyer, after which Oliver continued questioning him for some time. The President insisted that he had never lied about his condition under oath or otherwise under the penalty of perjury in any proceeding or in any document. When the President stepped out, Leo asked Oliver what he thought.

LEO: [I]n the two and a half hours we've been sitting here, have you discovered one thing that he's done wrong?

OLIVER: No.

LEO: So, what's your problem?

OLIVER: *That's* my problem, Leo. Are you out of your mind? He did everything right. He did everything you do if your intent is to perpetrate a fraud.[20]

President Bartlet, C. J., and the First Lady each displayed some petulance toward Babish's questioning. Oliver countered with patience, shrugging off the President's implication that he had better things to do than answer Oliver's questions,[21] allowing C. J. some time to vent, and deflecting Abbey's suggestion that he might benefit from the publicity of defending the President in prime time.[22] That said, his patience was not unbounded. After several surly responses from C. J., Oliver cut to the chase.

> OLIVER: I'm going to have to ask you some questions, and the less you can be pissed at the world for no particular reason the better I think. . . .
>
> C. J.: I was told to report to you. I don't know you. [W]hy should I trust you?
>
> OLIVER: Well, you can do that if you want, C. J. I've been through it a couple of times with Josh and Toby, but sooner or later you're going to have to answer questions.
>
> C. J.: Either to you or . . . ?
>
> OLIVER: A grand jury.
>
> C. J.: Compelled by . . . ?
>
> OLIVER: A Justice Department subpoena.
>
> C. J.: Well, I have to tell you it'll be the first time I've been asked out in quite awhile, so. . . .
>
> OLIVER: It's entirely possible that the President has committed multiple counts of a federal crime to which you were an accomplice.
>
> C. J.: That much has sunk in in the last six hours.
>
> OLIVER: Has it?
>
> C. J.: Yes.
>
> OLIVER: So why don't you knock off the cutie-pie crap and answer the damn question?. . . Have you ever lied about the President's health?
>
> C. J.: Many, many times.[23]

Oliver questioned meticulously and urged those he questioned to answer with equal meticulousness. For example, he discouraged C. J.'s tendency to volunteer more information than the questioner requested.

OLIVER: Do you know what time it is?

C. J.:   It's five past noon.

OLIVER: I'd like you to get out of the habit of doing that.

C. J.:   Doing what?

OLIVER: Answering more than was asked. Do you know what time it is?

C. J.:   Yes.[24]

By contrast, Oliver's primary concerns about First Lady Abbey Bartlet were her air of intellectual superiority and her tendency to give inconsistent responses.

OLIVER: [W]ould you mind if I asked you a few questions? . . .

ABBEY: About Zoey's health form.

OLIVER: Yep. . .. Was anyone else in the room when you signed it?

ABBEY: Oh, it was over a year ago. I really don't remember. . . .

OLIVER: I understand. . . . But a lawyer half my size, while cross-examining you during deposition, will say . . . "Mrs. Bartlet, do you have an M.D. from Harvard?"

ABBEY: Yes.

OLIVER: "Are you board certified in Internal Medicine?"

ABBEY: Yes.

OLIVER: "Are you board certified in Thoracic Surgery?"

ABBEY: Yes.

OLIVER: "Are you an Adjunct Professor of Thoracic Surgery at Harvard Medical School?"

ABBEY: Yes.

OLIVER: "Are you on the staff of Boston Mercy Hospital and Columbia Presbyterian?"

ABBEY: Yes.

OLIVER: "Have you been practicing medicine for 26 years?"

ABBEY: Yes.

OLIVER: "Are you not able to recognize a standard medical history form when it is put in front of your face?"

ABBEY: I didn't read it! I didn't think it was important. . . . Oliver, I am not an expert in the diseases of the central nervous system, but I can tell you that MS is not hereditary. The President's condition has absolutely no relevance to Zoey's health status.

OLIVER: Well, now you're changing your story. . . . Did you sign it because you were absent-minded or did you sign it because you knew best?

ABBEY: . . . I just signed it. . . . It was a form. . . . And I think making a big thing out of it is what makes it into a big thing!

OLIVER: Really?. . . [I]t's not a big thing because I say so, ma'am; it's a big thing. You're gonna get all the questions I just asked you, and quite a few more. And then they're gonna ask the President if he was in the room when you signed it. And that's when he's gonna give everyone's favorite answer from a President who has just announced that he has MS: "*I don't remember.*"[25]

Oliver was not one to jump to quick conclusions or make rash decisions. After questioning the President for quite a while, Leo asked his impressions. Oliver replied, "I am nowhere close to being able to answer that question."[26] Later, President Bartlet, realizing that Oliver might have felt ambushed by this crisis so soon after taking the White House Counsel's job, offered him the opportunity to resign—which Oliver declined. Instead, Oliver clearly demonstrated his ability to "speak truth to power"[27] and his unwillingness to compromise his professionalism or his ability to represent the Office of the President, notwithstanding the enormous political power and influence some of those to whom he was speaking wielded.

OLIVER: If I stay, will you do exactly what I tell you to do?

BARTLET: I guess it depends.

OLIVER: No, I'm afraid it can't depend, sir. . . .[O]rder the Attorney General to appoint a Special Prosecutor. Not just any Special Prosecutor—the most blood-spitting, Bartlet-hating Republican in the Bar. He's gonna have an unlimited budget and a staff like an army. The new slogan around here is gonna be "bring it on." He's gonna have access to every piece of paper you ever touched. If you invoke executive privilege one time, I'm gone. An assistant DA in Ducksworth wants to take your deposition, you're on the next plane. A freshman Congressman wants your testimony . . . what do we say?

BARTLET: Bring it on.[28]

Just as Oliver was able to tell the President, in essence, "It's my way or the highway," he had the confidence to tell the First Lady that her decisions to change the President's drug regimen, to write prescriptions in her own name, have them shipped across state lines, then administer them to her husband, and to not keep proper medical records appeared to make her the President's biggest liability in the proceedings that would follow his multiple sclerosis disclosure.[29]

It's About Duty

Lionel Tribbey left a lucrative private practice in Chicago to serve as Counsel to a president he considered too moderate on a number of key issues. Republicans Ainsley Hayes and Joe Quincy each served as Associate Counsel in a Democratic administration. Oliver Babish, about whose personal politics we know little (other than that he was integral to President Bartlet's electoral success in the Midwest), also left a lucrative practice in Chicago to serve as White House Counsel and stayed on the job through President Bartlet's multiple sclerosis disclosure and the grand jury proceedings and congressional hearings that followed, the decision to assassinate a member of a Middle Eastern royal family,[30] Vice President John Hoynes's resignation,[31] President Bartlet's decision to invoke the 25th Amendment after his youngest daughter was kidnapped on the night of her college graduation,[32] Leo's heart attack and C. J.'s appointment as new Chief of Staff,[33] and Toby Ziegler's dismissal[34] and indictment[35] for leaking classified information about a secret military space shuttle—despite never becoming part of the President's inner circle on issues not directly within the Counsel's purview. Why? The rare opportunity to serve and the duty that accompanied it were recurrent themes throughout *The West Wing*. The denizens of the White House Counsel's office we met appeared to embrace both and to value them more than perks, pay, or partisanship. We can only hope that truth mirrors fiction.

Endnotes

1. *See* "And It's Surely to Their Credit." *See* http://www.westwingepguide .com for episode synopses and the dates on which episodes first aired.

2. *See* "In This White House."

3. *See* "And It's Surely to Their Credit." ("Mr. President . . . when you have a few moments, I would like to discuss the hiring of blonde and leggy fascists . . . for positions in the White House Counsel's office."). So, for that matter, was Ainsley's. *See* "In This White House." (Leo: "Don't you want to work in the White

House?" .... Ainsley: "Oh, only since I was two.... It has to be *this* White House?")

4. *See* "And It's Surely to Their Credit."

5. *Id.*

6. *See* "The Lame Duck Congress."

7. *See* "The Portland Trip."

8. *See* "17 People" (".... It's humiliating! A new amendment that we vote on, declaring that I am equal under the law to a man. I am mortified to discover there's reason to believe I wasn't before. I am a citizen of this country.... The same 14th Amendment that protects you protects me. And I went to law school just to make sure.").

9. *See* "And It's Surely to Their Credit"; "The Lame Duck Congress."

10. *See* "Bartlet's Third State of the Union"; "Ways and Means"; "The U.S. Poet Laureate."

11. *See* "Bad Moon Rising."

12. Ainsley Hayes resurfaced late in season seven to pursue the White House Counsel's job in the newly elected Santos administration. *See* "Requiem." By this time, NBC had decided not to renew *The West Wing* (thus creating no conflict with Emily Procter's commitment to *CSI: Miami*).

13. *See* "Evidence of Things Not Seen." (Josh: "Is this your fallback?" Joe: "They're my fallback." Josh: "Why do you want to work here?" Joe: "I like public service. I want to serve. And you guys are the only ones left.")

14. *See* "Life on Mars."

15. *See* "Separation of Powers."

16. *See* "The Supremes."

17. *See* "Bad Moon Rising."

18. *Id.* ("It won't stop recording things; so, it's just what you want lying around the White House Counsel's Office, because there's never been a problem with that before.")

19. *Id.* By contrast, while interviewing C. J. Cregg in "The Fall's Gonna Kill You," Oliver insisted that he was her lawyer—so, presumably, the privilege would have attached. (C. J.: "Should I have my lawyer here?" Oliver: "I *am* your lawyer." C. J.: "You're the President's lawyer." Oliver: "I'm the White House Counsel, C. J.")

20. *See* "Bad Moon Rising."

21. *Id.* (Oliver: "Mr. President, I have some more questions. Is there time now?" Bartlet: "Well, the Mexican economy crashed, an oil tanker busted up about 120 miles from here, and 13 percent of Americans are living in poverty. So, yeah, I can hang out with you and answer insulting questions for a while." Oliver: "Good.")

22. *See* "The Fall's Gonna Kill You." (Abbey: "I think making a big thing out of it is what makes it into a big thing! ... And I'm not 100 percent sure that that's not what you're going for." Oliver: "Why would I want to make it a big thing?" Abbey: "Because defending the President in prime time looks good on a résumé." Oliver: "Well, I've got a pretty good-looking résumé already, Mrs. Bartlet.")

23. *Id.*

24. *Id.*

25. *Id.*

26. *See* "Bad Moon Rising."

27. Henry Kissinger and others interviewed in an Emmy-winning special episode, "The *West Wing* Documentary Special," asserted that the ability to speak truth to power is essential to one's ability to advise a president.

28. *See* "Bad Moon Rising."

29. *See* "Gone Quiet"; *see also* "18th and Potomac."

30. *See* "Commencement" (referring to events depicted in "Posse Comitatus").

31. *See* "Life on Mars."

32. *See* "Twenty-Five."

33. *See* "Third Day Story."

34. *See* "Here Today."

35. *See* "Undecideds."

ABOUT THE AUTHORS

Michael Asimow (asimow@law.ucla.edu) is Professor of Law Emeritus at UCLA Law School. He teaches contracts, administrative law, and law and popular culture, and is the past chair of the ABA Section on Administrative Law & Regulatory Practice. Michael is the coauthor, with Paul Bergman, of *Reel Justice: The Courtroom Goes to the Movies* (2d ed. 2006) and, with Shannon Mader, of *Law and Popular Culture: A Course Book* (2004). He has also written numerous articles about lawyers in popular culture.

Taunya Lovell Banks (TBanks@law.umaryland.edu) is the Jacob A. France Professor of Equality Jurisprudence in the School of Law at the University of Maryland, where she teaches and writes about law and popular culture, social justice, and constitutional law. She also is a contributing coeditor of *Screening Justice—The Cinema of Law: Films of Law, Order and Social Justice* (2006).

Paul Bergman (bergman@law.ucla.edu) is Professor of Law Emeritus at UCLA Law School. He received his J.D. from UC Berkeley (Boalt Hall). Among the books that Paul has written or coauthored are *Reel Justice: The Courtroom Goes to the Movies* (2d ed. 2006); *Evidence Law and Practice* (3d ed. 2007); *Trial Advocacy in a Nutshell* (4th ed. 2007); *Lawyers as Counselors: A Client Centered Approach* (2nd ed. 2004); and three books educating nonlawyers about the civil justice process, criminal laws and processes, and depositions. Paul's articles related to law in film include "Emergency! Send a TV Show to Rescue Paramedic Services" and "The Movie Lawyers' Guide to Redemptive Law Practice."

Corinne Brinkerhoff (corinnebrinkerhoff@gmail.com) is Executive Story Editor at *Boston Legal*, where she began her TV writing career in 2005. She graduated magna cum laude and Phi Beta Kappa from Truman State University in 2002 with a B.A. in English and earned an M.S. in Television Production from Boston University in 2004.

ANTHONY CHASE (chaset@nsu.law.nova.edu) is a professor of law at Nova Southeastern University Law Center in Fort Lauderdale, Florida. His short story "One Hundred Four," recently appeared in the *UMKC Law Review* and he participated in the 2008 Key West Writers seminar, "New Voices." His book, *Movies on Trial*, is published by the New Press.

CYNTHIA R. COHEN, PH.D. (ccohen@verdictsuccess.com) helps lawyers win major complex cases through jury research and effective storytelling. Cynthia, a leader in psychology and law as the American Society of Trial Consultants President (2009–2010) and in the ABA Section of Litigation (Task Force on the Image of the Profession, Trial Practice Committee Vice Chair, and Products Liability Committee), studies media effects in popular culture. She blends experience and education with psychology degrees from UCLA and USC. Cynthia is a frequent author, speaker, and media commentator on jury behavior.

CHRISTINE A. CORCOS (christine.corcos@law.lsu.edu) is Associate Professor of Law at Louisiana State University Law Center and Associate Professor of Women's and Gender Studies at Louisiana State University A&M, Baton Rouge, Louisiana. She teaches media law, entertainment law, advanced torts, and gender and the law. She publishes widely in the areas of law and popular culture, legal history, and media law, is a coauthor of *Law and Popular Culture: Text, Notes and Questions* (Lexis-Nexis 2007), and is an editor of the *International Journal for the Semiotics of Law*. Among her forthcoming publications is *Law and Magic: A Collection of Essays* (Carolina Academic Press). She would like to thank her colleague Darlene Goring for her valuable comments on an earlier version of this essay and Suzanna Johnson for research assistance.

DAVID R. GINSBURG (ginsburg@law.ucla.edu) is the Executive Director of the Entertainment and Media Law and Policy Program at the UCLA School of Law, where he teaches entertainment law. He served as the President of Artisan Pictures, the Alliance Atlantis Motion Picture Group, and Citadel Entertainment, and he was a partner of Sidley Austin LLP. He has produced over 50 films, which were awarded several Emmys, Golden Globes, and the Humanitas Prize. David is an active member of the Motion Picture and Television Academies, the British Academy of

Film and Television Arts/LA, and the Producers Guild of America. He is a graduate of both UCLA and its School of Law, where he was the Editor-in-Chief of the *UCLA Law Review*, and he was a Danforth Foundation Fellow at the Massachusetts Institute of Technology.

JILL GOLDSMITH is a writer and producer for television, with credits on Emmy-winning series including *NYPD Blue, The Practice, Ally McBeal, Law & Order*, and *Boston Legal*, and was a finalist for the 2008 Humanitas Prize. She has also been a featured speaker at numerous law schools, conferences, and writing programs, and has appeared as a panelist on *C-Span Close Up* and *CBS News*. She received her J.D. from Washington University School of Law, and served an internship with U.S. Senator Paul Simon on the Senate Judiciary Committee. Prior to writing for television, Jill spent seven years as a Public Defender in the Juvenile and Felony Trial Divisions of the Cook County Public Defender's Office in Chicago, Illinois.

STEVE GREENFIELD (greenfs@wmin.ac.uk) is a Senior Academic in Law at the University of Westminster, United Kingdom. He has written on many aspects of law and film as well as other areas of popular culture including music, sports, and leisure. Steve is one of the founding editors of the *Entertainment and Sports Law Journal* (http://www2.warwick .ac.uk/fac/soc/law/elj/eslj). His book *Film and the Law*, written with Guy Osborn and Peter Robson, is due to be published by Hart Publishing in early 2009. Steve is also co-editor of the Routledge book series "Studies in Law, Society and Popular Culture."

ROBERT M. JARVIS (jarvisb@nsu.law.nova.edu) is a professor of law at Nova Southeastern University in Fort Lauderdale, Florida, and the co-editor of *Prime Time Law: Fictional Television as Legal Narrative* (Carolina Academic Press, 1998). He received his B.A. from Northwestern University, his J.D. from the University of Pennsylvania, and his LL.M. from New York University.

ANJA LOUIS (a.louis@sheffield.ac.uk) is associate professor in Hispanic Studies at the University of Sheffield, UK, and specializes in the interdisciplinary field of law and culture in the Hispanic world. Her book

Women and the Law: Carmen de Burgos, an Early Feminist analyzes the representation of law in the work of the Spanish feminist Carmen de Burgos (1867–1932). Anja's research interests lie in the field of Hispanic cultural studies, in particular the interface of law and culture, gender studies, and popular culture. Her current research project examines the representation of lawyers in Spanish film and television.

STEFAN MACHURA (sos409@bangor.ac.uk) is Lecturer at the School of Social Sciences, Bangor University, Wales. He teaches classes on "Crime and Law in Film." He has also taught this subject at the Ruhr-Universität Bochum (Germany) since 1995. Recent publications include *Law and Film* (2001, edited with Peter Robson); *Recht im Film* (2002, edited with Stefan Ulbricht); and *Kreig im Film* (2005, edited with Rudiger Voigt).

SHANNON MADER (smader@gibsondunn.com) is a litigation associate at the law firm of Gibson, Dunn & Crutcher LLP, where he practices in the areas of antitrust law, copyright law, and legal malpractice, and is the co-author (with Michael Asimow) of *Law and Popular Culture: A Course Book* (Peter Lang 2004). He earned his J.D. from the UCLA School of Law. Prior to law school, he earned an M.A. and Ph.D. in Cinema–Television from the University of Southern California and taught film at Loyola Marymount University. Following law school, Shannon served as a law clerk to the Honorable Stephen V. Wilson of the United States District Court for the Central District of California.

NANCY S. MARDER (nmarder@kentlaw.edu) is a Professor of Law at Chicago–Kent College of Law in Chicago, Illinois. She clerked for Justice John Paul Stevens of the U.S. Supreme Court, Judge William A. Norris of the U.S. Court of Appeals for the Ninth Circuit, and Judge Leonard B. Sand of the Southern District of New York. Nancy has written numerous articles on the American jury system. She also has written about law and film and law and literature, and is the symposium editor for a law review symposium on the 50th anniversary of *12 Angry Men*. Nancy regularly teaches a law school course entitled "Law, Literature & Feminism." She would like to thank Lucy Moss for her assistance in providing research and David Townsend, Alton Jackson, and Sue Jadin for their assistance in collecting television judge programs.

Lance McMillian (lmcmillian@johnmarshall.edu) is a professor at Atlanta's John Marshall Law School. He teaches torts and constitutional law. Prior to going into teaching, Lance litigated a vast array of complex business cases. Based on his expertise, numerous federal and state courts appointed him as lead plaintiffs' counsel in class actions arising under the Telephone Consumer Protection Act and the Fair Labor Standards Act. Lance is married to fellow attorney Carla, who finished two spots ahead of him in their law school class. They have two children—James and Emily.

Carrie Menkel-Meadow (meadow@law.georgetown.edu and cmeadow@law.uci.edu) is A.B. Chettle, Jr. Professor of Law, Dispute Resolution, and Civil Procedure at Georgetown Law Center and Professor of Law at University of California, Irvine Law School. She is the coauthor of *Law and Popular Culture: Text, Notes and Questions* (Lexis-Nexis 2007) and many articles on lawyers and culture. She is an internationally recognized scholar and practitioner of dispute resolution (including negotiation, mediation, and arbitration), legal ethics, legal procedure, socio-legal studies, legal education, and feminist theory, and is the author of 10 books and over 100 articles in these scholarly fields. Carrie serves as the co–editor-in-chief of the *Journal of Legal Education* and the *International Journal of Law in Context*. While she was a law professor at UCLA (1979–1996) she occasionally served as an ethics consultant to writers of TV shows about lawyers.

Philip N. Meyer (pmeyer@vermontlaw.edu) is a Professor of Law at Vermont Law School where he teaches torts, criminal law, and law and popular culture. He has published several books and many articles on topics including law and popular culture, law and literature, criminal law, the death penalty, closing arguments, and clinical legal education. He also received an M.F.A. from the Writer's Workshop at the University of Iowa, published fiction, and was awarded The Mary Roberts Rinehart Foundation Grant in Fiction. Philip is a long-time film and television junkie and has written several screenplays.

Francis M. Nevins (nevinsfm@slu.edu) is Professor Emeritus at St. Louis University School of Law, where he taught from 1971 until his recent retirement. Much of his academic writing has been in the fields of estates and copyright, and he is considered one of the leading authorities on the legal issues incident to the divorce and death of authors. He has also written extensively on the intersection of law, literature, and film. His seminar "Law, Lawyers and Justice in Popular Fiction and Film," created in 1979, has been adapted in many other law schools in the United States and abroad. He is the award-winning author of six novels, around 40 short stories, and several nonfiction books. Among his recent works of fiction are *Beneficiaries' Requiem* (2000), *Night of Silken Snow and Other Stories* (2001), and *Leap Day and Other Stories* (2003).

Guy Osborn (G.Osborn@westminster.ac.uk) is Professor of Law at the University of Westminster, United Kingdom, and Professor II in the Department of Sociology and Political Science at NTNU in Trondheim, Norway. Guy is one of the founding editors of the *Entertainment and Sports Law Journal* and has written widely in the area of law and popular culture. His book *Film and the Law*, written with Steve Greenfield and Peter Robson, is due to be published by Hart Publishing in early 2009. Guy is a co-editor of the book series "Studies in Law, Society and Popular Culture" and is Chair of the Law and Popular Culture Working Group for the Research Committee for the Sociology of Law.

David Ray Papke (david.papke@marquette.edu) is Professor of Law at Marquette University in Milwaukee, Wisconsin, where he teaches property, family law, jurisprudence, and a range of courses and seminars relating to law and the humanities. He has a special scholarly interest in law in the context of American history and culture and is the author of five books, including the award-winning *Heretics in the Temple: Americans Who Reject the Nation's Legal Faith* (1997). He is presently at work on a book concerning law's role in the creation and perpetuation of an American underclass.

Kimberlianne Podlas (k_podlas@uncg.edu) is an Assistant Professor of Media Law at UNC Greensboro (Department of Broadcasting and Cinema). Her research considers the impact of television shows—such as *CSI*, *The People's Court*, *Law & Order*, and *The Simpsons*—on the public's understanding of law. She was a winner of the Broadcast

Education Association's National Paper Competition in both 2006 and 2007. Prior to entering academia, Kimberlianne was Associate Appellate Counsel with the Criminal Appeals Bureau (NYC). During that time, she argued more than 100 cases, including several in New York's high court.

NANCY B. RAPOPORT (nancy.rapoport@unlv.edu) is the Gordon Silver Professor of Law at the University of Nevada, Las Vegas William S. Boyd School of Law. She received her B.A., *summa cum laude*, from Rice University and her J.D. from Stanford Law School. Her specialties are bankruptcy ethics, ethics in governance, and the depiction of lawyers in popular culture. Among her published works is *Enron and Other Corporate Fiascos: The Corporate Scandal Reader*, 2d (co-published with Jeffrey D. Van Niel and Bala G. Dharan; Foundation Presss 2009). Nancy appeared as herself in the Academy Award–nominated movie *Enron: The Smartest Guys in the Room* (Magnolia Pictures 2005). For this particular essay, she wishes to thank one of her research assistants, Nicole Cannizzaro, and four of her favorite editors: Walter Effross, Keith Rowley, Morris Rapoport, and Jeff Van Niel.

ELAYNE RAPPING (erapping@gmail.com) is Professor of American Studies at SUNY Buffalo, specializing in media and cultural studies. Her books include *Law and Justice as Seen on TV* and *Media-tions: Forays into the Culture and Gender Wars*. She has written extensively on cultural topics of many kinds—from the 12-step Recovery Movement to the coming of local "Eye Witless News." Her articles on media and popular culture have appeared in such publications as *The Nation, The Village Voice, Cineaste*, and *Newsday*. Elayne is currently at work on a book about music as a communal experience expressing shared values in contexts ranging from tribal cultures to Woodstock to hip-hop.

VICENTE RICCIO (Vicente.Riccio@fgv.br) is Professor at the Brazilian School for Public and Business Administration at Fundação Getulio Vargas in Rio de Janeiro. Vicente earned his Ph.D. in sociology from Instituto Universitário de Pesquisas do Rio de Janeiro (IUPERJ) and has published papers in English, French, and Portuguese in academic journals and books. His main interests are law and social process, media and justice, and public policies for crime control. He also works as a consultant for different public agencies in Brazil.

PETER ROBSON (peter.robson@strath.ac.uk) is Professor of Social Welfare Law in the University of Strathclyde, Scotland. He is chair of Weslo Housing (a Scottish housing charity) and a part-time Judge in the Appeals Service, where he hears disability and incapacity appeals. Peter's major interests are law and popular culture, housing law, social security law, and clinical law. He is the author of numerous books, book chapters, and articles about the images of law in popular culture, including *Film and the Law* (2nd ed. 2009) and *TV Lawyers Today* (2010) with Steve Greenfield and Guy Osborn.

CHARLES B. ROSENBERG (lalawyercb@aol.com) is a graduate of Antioch College and Harvard Law School, where he was a member of the Law Review. He is currently a partner with Rosenberg Mendlin & Rosen LLP in Santa Monica, where he concentrates his practice on intellectual property and entertainment litigation. Chuck's media-related activities have included serving as technical legal adviser for *Paper Chase, L.A. Law, The Practice,* and *Boston Legal.* He was an on-air legal correspondent for E! Television's coverage of the O. J. Simpson criminal and civil trials. He has taught law and popular culture, copyright, and entertainment law at Loyola and Pepperdine Law Schools, contracts and civil procedure in Loyola's LLM program in Bologna, Italy, and legal strategy for business leaders at UCLA's Anderson Graduate School of Management.

NORMAN ROSENBERG (nrosenbe@uci.edu or rosenbergn@macalester .edu), DeWitt Wallace Professor of History and Legal Studies at Macalester College, is the author of numerous articles in the area of "legal reelism" and of other articles and books, including *Protecting the Best Men: An Interpretive History of the Law of Libel* (1990).

YSAIAH ROSS (ysaiah@operamail.com) is a barrister in New South Wales and a lawyer in California. He is based in Sydney, Australia, and taught for over 20 years at the University of New South Wales. He has also taught at universities in the United States, Africa, England, Papua–New Guinea, and New Zealand, and did research in France. Ysaiah is the author and coauthor of numerous books on legal ethics, income tax, law, and politics. He also wrote a book on lawyer jokes. He is currently writing the fifth edition of his book *Ethics in Law: Lawyers' Responsibility & Accountability in Australia* for LexisNexus Butterworths.

KEITH A. ROWLEY (keith.rowley@unlv.edu) is a William S. Boyd Professor of Law at UNLV's William S. Boyd School of Law, where he teaches ontracts, commercial law, and economic analysis of the law and founded and hosts the Law & Popular Culture Film Series. A graduate of Baylor University, Harvard University's Kennedy School of Government, and the University of Texas School of Law, and former clerk to Judge Thomas M. Reavley of the U.S. Court of Appeals for the Fifth Circuit, Keith has a lifelong love of literature, movies, music, sports, and television, a vast and eclectic collection of albums, books, CDs, DVDs, and videotapes, and an abiding interest in the many intersections between law and popular culture. His current writing projects include legal insights on and lessons from the 1919 Chicago "Black Sox" scandal, popular culture portrayals of law students, a lengthier exploration of lawyers and legal issues in *The West Wing*, and contract issues in Elizabethan and Victorian literature.

JENNIFER L. SCHULZ (j_schulz@umanitoba.ca) is a law professor at the University of Manitoba, Canada. She has studied law at the Universities of Toronto and Cambridge (UK) and Harvard University, with a particular emphasis on culture and dispute resolution. Jennifer has won a teaching award, is the recipient of federal research grants, and is the author of many refereed articles and chapters on dispute resolution and law and film subjects. She presents across North America on mediation in the movies, and she is a practicing mediator.

CASSANDRA SHARP (sharp@uow.edu.au) began teaching in the Faculty of Law at the University of Wollongong, Australia, in 1999. She has been heavily involved in teaching within the first-year program, with a particular focus on Foundations of Law and Contracts. Cassandra has a combined bachelor's degree in Arts (English Literature) and Law (Honors) from the University of Wollongong; and a Ph.D. from the University of Wollongong. Her primary research interest lies within the broad field of law and popular culture. In particular, her Ph.D. explored the transformation process of first-year law, and the use of popular stories by students in constructing identity. Of further interest to Cassandra is the way in which understandings of ethics are challenged or maintained through popular stories of law. Her postdoctoral research is now focused on understanding the concept of "justice" from both a public and a juridical point of view.

JUSTIN T. SMITH (justin.thomas.smith@gmail.com) is a Class of 2010 J.D. Candidate at UCLA School of Law. Prior to law school, Justin was the 2007 Outstanding Graduate in History at California State Polytechnic University, Pomona. He is the 2008–2009 Managing Editor for the *Journal of Islamic and Near Eastern Law* and the Business Manager for the International Law Society. He is also an active volunteer for the Los Angeles Legal Aid Foundation Landlord–Tenant clinic. During the summer of 2008, Justin was a Research Assistant for Professors Michael Asimow, Daniel Bussel, and William Warren where he assisted in editing this work, among other projects.

JEFFREY E. THOMAS (thomasje@umkc.edu) is Associate Dean for International Programs and Professor of Law at the University of Missouri—Kansas City. He received his B.A., *magna cum laude*, from Loyola Marymount University, and earned his J.D. from University of California, Berkeley (Boalt Hall). Jeffrey writes in the areas of Insurance Law and Law and Culture. He is currently editor-in-chief of the *New Appleman on Insurance* project for Lexis/Matthew Bender, which recently released the three-volume *New Appleman Insurance Law Practice Guide*. His current popular culture project is a book entitled *Harry Potter and the* Law, which he is coediting with Franklin Snyder at Texas Wesleyan School of Law. That book is expected to be published in 2009 by Carolina Academic Press.

BARBARA VILLEZ (Barbara.villez@gmail.com), a native New Yorker, came to France to study and ended up staying. She is full Professor of Legal Language and Cultures at the Université (Vincennes–St Denis) Paris 8 where she directs the research group Justices, Images, Langues, Cultures (JILC). She teaches Common Law and legal translation as well as courses on television representations of law and justice and comparative legal practices seen through images. Barbara has written a number of articles on American television legal series, as well as a comparison of these series to French televised representations of law in *Séries télévisions de la justice* (2005), soon to be translated into English.

SAM WATERSTON is one of the most familiar and successful American actors currently working in stage, film, and television. He may be best known for his portrayal of Jack McCoy on *Law & Order*, but he has also appeared in 47 movies, numerous other television shows and commercials, and many plays. He has often played Abraham Lincoln on stage and screen. Waterston was nominated for an Academy Award for his 1985 role in *The Killing Fields*. He received one Emmy and was nominated for seven more. He is a graduate of Yale University and is active in various humanitarian causes such as Oceana and Refugees International.

JAMES WOODS is an acclaimed actor, is the winner of multiple Emmys and the Golden Globe, and was twice nominated for an Academy Award. He attended the Massachusetts Institute of Technology before pursuing his career in acting. Among his many memorable roles, he has portrayed a notorious criminal defendant (in *The Onion Field*), a maverick defense attorney (in *True Believer*), and an unconventional prosecutor (in *Shark*). He is also a gifted poker player and chef.

INDEX